WILHELM REICH
VS. THE U.S.A.

Jerome Greenfield

WILHELM REICH
VS.
THE U.S.A.

W · W · Norton & Company · Inc ·
New York

R
154
R35
G73

Copyright © 1974 by Jerome Greenfield
FIRST EDITION

Library of Congress Cataloging in Publication Data
Greenfield, Jerome.
  Wilhelm Reich vs. the U.S.A.

  Includes bibliographical references.
  1. Reich, Wilhelm, 1897–1957. 2. United States,
Food and Drug Administration. I. Title.
R154.R35G73   615′.85 [B]   74–4175
ISBN 0–393–07484–6

All Rights Reserved
Published simultaneously in Canada
by George J. McLeod Limited, Toronto

This book was designed by Margaret F. Plympton.
Typefaces used are Times Roman and Perpetua.
Manufacturing was done by Vail-Ballou Press, Inc.

PRINTED IN THE UNITED STATES OF AMERICA
1 2 3 4 5 6 7 8 9 0

To the memory of my brothers

CONTENTS

Photographs appear between pages 192 and 193

WILHELM REICH
VS. THE U.S.A.

INTRODUCTION

This book would have been impossible to write ten years ago. On the one hand, no publisher in the early sixties would have been willing to sponsor a book on Reich and, on the other, the FDA would not have permitted access to its file on the Reich case. It became possible only in the early seventies, for within the widespread social and ideological upheavals of the intervening decade a new and rapidly growing interest in the work and writings of Reich developed, and at the same time the Freedom of Information Act was passed. It was the coincidence of these two events that made this book possible.

The first of these—the rediscovery of Reich and the expanding interest in his work, his writings, his ideas—merits some discussion. After Reich's death in 1957 there was diminishing interest in his work and a cessation of work in orgonomy among his followers. Reich's *Character Analysis* was reissued in the early sixties as well as a volume of *Selected Writings*. Neither of these attracted much attention or was widely reviewed, except that *Character Analysis* was still being used as a text in schools of psychoanalytic training. Though a handful of orgone therapists still continued in their practice, it was largely on an individual basis, for there was no longer any formal, centralizing organization among them. *Orgonomic Medicine,* a journal begun in 1955, was discontinued. Thus it seemed for a while that the basic purpose of the FDA—to disrupt what in the fifties was the growing work and interest in orgonomy and its ramifications—had indeed succeeded.

And yet some sparks of the fire Reich had lit remained unquenched. By the middle sixties the burgeoning wave of discontent among students led to the beginning of a rediscovery of Reich among them. Dr. Elsworth Baker—a close co-worker of Reich's during his years in the United States—had trained a second generation of orgone therapists. Dr. Alexander Lowen—also a former co-worker of Reich's—had published his book, *The Physical Dynamics of Character Structure* (more recently reissued as *The Language of the Body*), which launched an allied system of therapy that he called bioenergetics, and which drew many adherents. So, by the later sixties, the social climate was propitious not only for a reissuance of several of Reich's books but also for the appearance of books about Reich and about biopsychiatric orgone therapy, as well as a new journal dealing with Reich's work. Thus, Dr. Baker came out with the first elaborated and detailed account of biopsychiatric orgone therapy, entitled *Man in the Trap,* in 1967. In that same year, under Dr. Baker's editorship, a new publication was begun, *The Journal of Orgonomy,* which dealt with all aspects of Reich's many-faceted work. In 1969, Reich's third wife, Ilse Ollendorff, issued the first attempt at a biography—really a memoir—of Reich, entitled: *Wilhelm Reich: A Personal Biography*. And in 1970, Dr. Ola Raknes, one of Reich's co-workers in Norway, published a slender yet comprehensive volume entitled *Wilhelm Reich and Orgonomy*. Following in rapid succession, other books on Reich and his work appeared, some favorable and some not. Notable among these is Orson Bean's *Me and the Orgone* and Charles Rycroft's evaluative *Wilhelm Reich*. (In the latter book Reich's formulations concerning orgone energy are treated as psychological symptoms.) As of this writing, a very personal and moving book by Reich's son, Peter, entitled *A Book of Dreams,* has just appeared. There is, in addition, the recent interest of the New Left in the politically oriented writings of Reich in his early years. This interest is most clearly expressed in Herbert Marcuse's treatment of Reich in *The Freudian Left* and in the fact that in 1972 Reich's early, tendentious political writings were published as *Sex-Pol: Essays, 1929–1934* (edited by Lee Baxandall). Both books, in effect, explain why it was that Reich's name became so important in the abortive student uprising in France in 1968. (It should, however, be noted that Reich wrote in 1945: "I would have to protest at once, publicly, if anyone wished to exploit my name or my work for the support of socialistic, communistic, par-

liamentarian or any other kind of *power politics."* [1] [Italics in original.] In addition to these publications there is also the movie on
Reich, entitled *W.R.—The Mysteries of the Organism,* which won
a citation at the Cannes Film Festival in 1971 and for which its
Yugoslavian director, Dusan Makavejev is, at the time of this
writing, facing arrest in his country. In the course of the research,
I learned of some four or five other books being written on Reich
or his work. Notable among these are works-in-progress by Colin
Wilson—who sees in Reich's life an exemplification of his view of
the Outsider; a book by Kenneth Tynan, British theater critic; and,
above all, a biography of Reich and an analysis of the development
of his work by Dr. Myron Sharaf. The latter will undoubtedly be
the definitive critical study of Reich for some time to come.

My own book is not essentially a biography or an analysis of
Reich's work, though it involves elements of both. It is an attempt
to relate the ten-year process, in its legal and human aspects, that
began in 1947 and ended in 1957 with Reich's imprisonment and
death in the Lewisburg Federal Penitentiary.

The highlights of the legal aspects of this process can be briefly
stated. In 1947, the FDA began an investigation of Reich and his
work, deriving its jurisdiction from the fact that this work involved
the shipment of orgone energy accumulators in interstate commerce. This investigation ended in 1948. It was resumed in 1951,
when the FDA decided to seek legal action. This latter investigation led to a Complaint being issued in 1954 against Reich, the
Wilhelm Reich Foundation, and Ilse Ollendorff. Reich decided
not to appear in court to answer the Complaint; as a result a default injunction was issued, prohibiting not only the interstate shipment of orgone accumulators but also the distribution of the publications of the Orgone Institute Press. Fifteen medical orgonomists
sought to intervene in the case as persons affected by the injunction.
Their effort to have the injunction rescinded failed at the District
Court level and in the subsequent appeals to the Appellate and
Supreme Courts. In the meantime, Reich had refused to abide by
the terms of the injunction, and a suit against him, on the ground
of criminal contempt, was initiated by the government. The trial

1. Wilhelm Reich, *People in Trouble* (Rangeley, Maine: Orgone Institute
Press, 1953), p. xviii (published in a limited edition).

took place in May of 1956, at which time a verdict of guilty was rendered. Subsequent appeals to the Appellate and Supreme Courts left the original verdict intact, and in 1957 Reich and Dr. Michael Silvert—a medical orgonomist working with him at the time—were incarcerated. Reich died in prison some eight months after his arrest.

This book attempts to fill in the details between and within these highlights, to elucidate the issues and influences, both personal and circumstantial, to determine how it was possible that a person of Reich's stature—in the thirties he was considered a possible candidate for the Nobel Peace Prize—was, in the fifties, prosecuted by the American government and imprisoned as a criminal.

I have tried to write this book with the highest possible fidelity to the facts available to me, knowing, however, that there were other facts that I did not have access to. Some people who were involved on either side of the Reich case still felt so strongly that they refused to speak to me about it. One FDA official's only response was: "They were bad people, a bunch of maniacs, coming to court with guns." And Mr. William Moise—who was closely involved with Reich in the latter years of the case—refused to let me come to interview him, writing me that "I consider the trial of the *U.S.* v. *Wilhelm Reich* to have been nothing but a farce; therefore to treat it seriously would lend it an air of respectability and rationality it does not deserve." Others who had been in some way allied with Reich during the last year of litigation did not actually refuse to speak to me, but they seemed to have inordinate difficulty recalling things, and sometimes exhibited impatience and irritation when pressed. Peter Reich writes that Makavejev had a similar experience when he interviewed Reich people for his movie. Makavejev commented to him that many of these people seemed stunned—which may be an apt description. However, I venture to add that what continues through the years to stun and confuse them is not only the outcome of the litigation but also Reich's behavior and thinking regarding this litigation. The complex matter of Reich's apparently aberrant behavior and thinking will be discussed in its proper place.

Besides the difficulty I have encountered in getting information from certain key people involved in both sides of the litigation, there was another source of information that was closed to me: the Reich archives. The trustee of Reich's estate would not permit me access to any material in these archives and refused even to explain why. However, in this case, it was not a matter of strong feeling about the Reich case, for Reich's daughter wrote me that she herself was not permitted access to any part of the archival material. The reason for this policy on the part of the trustee, I suspect, is a conviction that the time is not yet ripe or the circumstances propitious for exposure of this material—the contents of which have not yet been listed.

Thus, though there was enough material available and enough information forthcoming from some people to enable me to reconstruct the main lines and issues in the process that ended with Reich's imprisonment, it is possible that future information will necessitate refinements or even revisions of some of my interpretation. But, to repeat, I have made every effort to deal faithfully with the facts that were available to me which, with the accessibility of the FDA material, were, at least from the governmental aspect of the case, more or less complete.

I have no illusion that my treatment of the subject will please all the people who were involved in it. The matter is still too highly charged and at its depth too intertwined with basic issues of freedom and jurisprudence. I know that there will be FDA people no less than Reichians who will take strong exception to my account. I would hope, however, that at least some of these exceptions lead to efforts of constructive refutation. Indeed, I do not regard this book as the last word, but only the first, in the study of the ten-year period of Reich's trouble in America. As an event in American legal history, this case may well come to take its place alongside the Scopes "monkey" trial or the Sacco and Vanzetti case; like the latter, it may well become a legal event in which the socio-psychological influences, values, and assumptions of a whole era converge and come to their clearest focus.

In any writing about Reich, a key problem becomes the writer's attitude toward Reich's formulations concerning orgone energy—which Reich saw as a cosmic life energy. This is particularly so in the present study, where the orgone energy accumulator occupies such a central place. I have attempted consistently to avoid the two extremes: the common one of regarding these formulations as nothing more than, at best, a fantasy, and, at worst, a psycho-pathic symptom; and the one of orthodox Reichians who regard these formulations as holy writ. An unbiased reading of Reich's writings on the discovery of orgone energy and all the ramifications of this discovery leaves no doubt that he was a brilliant and highly original thinker seeking new approaches to some of the most persistent of nature's secrets regarding man and his environment. The scientific community as a whole has to date failed to accept the challenge of his scientific formulations. No honest, comprehensive attempt—despite the assertion of the FDA to the contrary—has been made to confront and test the experimental work upon which these formulations are based. I have, therefore, attempted to deal with the matter of orgone energy as an open question.

The attitude I have tried to maintain in this matter is eloquently expressed by Lev Shestov, a Russian-born philosopher. He describes an experiment in which a glass partition was inserted into a fish bowl so that a pike was separated from the smaller fish it usually fed upon. The pike repeatedly bruised its nose in trying to get at its prey and eventually gave up the effort. Subsequently, when the glass partition was removed, the pike made no further effort to get at the small fish—even though they swam all around him. Shestov then asks: "Does not the same happen with us? Perhaps indeed a partition does exist, and makes vain all attempts to cross over. . . . But perhaps there comes a moment when the partition is removed. In our minds, however, the conviction is firmly rooted that it is impossible to pass certain limits, and painful to try. . . ." [2] My attitude, in other words, is that, until proven otherwise, Reich's formulations concerning orgone energy and all its far-reaching ramifications may be the removal of such a partition that, Shestov writes further, has separated man from what he has come, through conditioning, to think of as being unknowable.

I come now to the most gratifying part of this introduction: the acknowledgments. I cannot begin to list the names of all the people who have directly or indirectly, knowingly or otherwise, assisted me in the research and writing of this book. However, there were some who were available for factual assistance, consultation and,

2. Quoted in *Great 20th Century Jewish Philosophers,* ed. Bernard Martin (New York: Macmillan Co., 1970), pp. 7–8.

when necessary, encouragement during my whole engagement in this project and they deserve special mention. First and foremost among these is Nathan Cabot Hale, artist, sculptor, and author. He was the first to recognize the need for a study of the Reich case and, though he never began to write his own book, made available to me not only material he had gathered in his preliminary research, his thinking and ideas, but also gave me generous encouragement in the uncertain early stages of my work. I met him originally as a source of information to be interviewed, and over the ensuing months came to regard him as a friend. Myron Sharaf, who had been working for some time on his biography of Reich when I began my project, was also most generous in making available to me his knowledge of the extensive bibliography on Reich as well as his memories of his personal association with Reich and Reich's work. To Bernard T. ("Bud") Loftus, Deputy Director of the Office of Compliance of the Bureau of Drugs of the FDA, I am most grateful for cooperation extended to me during my research through the FDA file on the Reich case and for his readiness to take time then and in many telephone conversations thereafter to explain the workings of the FDA and FDA law. His honesty and open-mindedness, in combination with his dedication to the constructive and necessary ends for which the FDA was first formed, are to me the best proof of what he often told me: that the FDA of today is a different, more mature and sophisticated agency than it was during the period of the Reich case. I can't help feeling that if there had been more people like him in FDA decision-making positions in the fifties there would have been no need for this book to be written. Herbert Ruhm, a former English department colleague, was most helpful to me in the writing of this book. His preliminary editing of the manuscript has helped to make this book—whatever its virtues or faults—better than it would otherwise have been. James S. Turner, lawyer and author of *The Chemical Feast*—a Nader study-group report on the FDA—was very helpful in clarifying the manifold intricacies of the legal process. And, finally, I wish to express my gratitude to certain second-floor department colleagues whose friendship has, during the past year, helped make the milieu in which I teach so conducive to the research and writing of this book.

Needless to say, all judgments, evaluations, and interpretations made in the following pages are ultimately my own, and for them I bear sole responsibility.

October 1973
New Paltz, New York

1

REICH IN VIENNA
AND BERLIN

Before his trouble with the FDA began, Reich had already experienced opposition from professional groups and governments in Europe. The main difference was that the prosecution he was subjected to in the United States represented the first time that a governmental agency moved against him on legal grounds. It was the shipment of Reich's orgone energy accumulators in interstate commerce that made this procedure possible. Such shipment, in other words, enabled the deep and widespread opposition to his ideas and his work on the part of governments, political groups, and professional organizations to take, at last, duly constituted, legal form. A look at Reich's life—and, later, at the whole corpus of his work—is essential so that this extended opposition can be understood.

Reich was born on March 24, 1897, the older of two brothers, in a part of Galicia that was included in the Austrian Empire.* His parents were well off and shortly after Wilhelm's birth bought

* Much of the biographical information in this section is obtained from *Wilhelm Reich: A Personal Biography* (New York: St. Martin's Press, 1969) by Reich's third wife, Ilse Ollendorff.

a large cattle ranch in the Ukrainian section of Austria-Hungary. Though Jewish by birth, his parents—especially his father—were bent on assimilating. As part of this effort, young Reich was not allowed to play with the Jewish children in the area. (Reich, unlike Freud, never identified with the Jewish experience. In 1952, when he was interviewed for his reminiscences of Freud,* he was to say that Freud had been trapped by the Jewish family ethos in a marriage that had gone sour, and that he, Reich, had never been a part of this ethos.) Since he was also not permitted to play with the Ukrainian peasant children in the area, his was a somewhat lonely childhood. But he was an active, lively, curious youngster and he was later to attribute his naturalistic attitude toward sex in part to his early exposure to the sight of animal copulation on his father's farm.

He underwent in his early teens what must surely be one of the most traumatic experiences a young person can undergo. His mother had been having an affair with one of the tutors that used to come to the farm to instruct young Reich. Although the circumstances are unclear, it appears that Reich revealed this fact to his father, and shortly thereafter his mother committed suicide— presumably as a result of this exposure. Her suicide devastated Reich's father, who died a few years later as a result of tuberculosis incurred through deliberate self-neglect—actually, through indirect suicide. The effects of this experience on Reich's later development remain yet to be adequately evaluated.

Reich was seventeen at the time of his father's death. He was forced to leave the *gymnasium* he was attending and return home to run the farm. However, he continued studying on his own and passed the final examination with distinction. In the following year, 1916, he joined the Austrian army as an officer and saw action on the Italian front. ("There are a few photographs in the archives showing him as a dashing young officer. He wore a small mustache, and was a very handsome young man. I think, on the whole, he enjoyed his military life. He was not a pacifist by nature." [1]

* Published in *Reich Speaks of Freud,* ed. Mary Higgins and Chester M. Raphael, M.D. (New York: Farrar, Strauss & Giroux, Inc., 1967).
1. Ilse Ollendorff, *Wilhelm Reich: A Personal Biography* (New York: St. Martin's Press, 1969), p. 5.

This early military experience may have some bearing on the fact that during the last three years of his life, when Reich had become entangled in litigation with the FDA and was being harassed by its agents, he began increasingly to regard the situation as a war, with himself the commanding officer of an army made up of a handful of co-workers, all of whom were required to be armed.

After the war Reich began attending the University of Vienna's Faculty of Law. However, he quit during the first semester. ("[He was] dissatisfied with the dryness of his studies, their remoteness from human affairs." [2]) But here again, brief as this experience was, there might well be some connection with the fact that during the same critical final years of his life, Reich spent much time studying law books in the preparation of his various legal briefs.

Leaving the study of law, Reich turned to medicine—a course of studies that, due to special arrangements made for veterans, he was able to complete in four years instead of the usual six. It was during the early part of these studies—with Reich supporting himself by tutoring other students—that, quite by accident, he attended a seminar on sexology initiated by students who felt that this subject was being neglected in the regular university courses. In this first exposure to Freudian concepts Reich was not very impressed. ("The manner in which . . . sexuality was discussed . . . struck me as peculiar, unnatural." [3]) Though in later meetings an experienced psychoanalyst came to give talks on sexuality, Reich was still not impressed. ("He spoke well and interestingly, but I instinctively disliked his way of dealing with sexuality." [4])

He was an outstanding student, brilliant in his ability to grasp new concepts and correlate them with previous ones, omniverous in his reading, powerfully driven by curiosity—in short, well equipped to make the most of the intense cultural ferment that characterized Viennese intellectual life at that time. Though he became enthusiastic about Freud after his first exposure to Freud's writings, he did not become an immediate convert. ("I absorbed his discoveries . . . gradually and along with the thoughts and

2. *Ibid.,* p. 6.
3. Wilhelm Reich, *The Discovery of the Orgone,* translated by Theodore P. Wolfe, Vol. I, *The Function of the Orgasm,* (New York: Noonday Press, 1970), p. 4.
4. *Ibid.,* p. 4.

discoveries of other great men." [5]) He read much in natural science and natural philosophy. He was much impressed by Bergson ("For some time I was taken for a 'crazy Bergsonian'. . . ." [6]), read Lange's *History of Philosophy* with enthusiasm, sat in on lectures by Kammerer, who believed in the existence of a specific biological energy, and absorbed all of Darwin. ("The many-sidedness of my sympathies later led me to the principle that 'everyone is right in some way'; it is only a matter of finding out in what way." [7]) He studied Planck and Einstein and Heisenberg and Bohr. But his interest in Marx—which was to preoccupy him for a large part of this period—came later.

His brilliance and enthusiasm brought him the leadership of the sexology seminar in that same year, 1919; and it was in that capacity—in order to obtain some literature for the group—that he had occasion to visit some of the luminaries of the Viennese intelligentsia. Of these, he was most lastingly impressed by Freud. ("[He was] simple and straightforward in his attitude. Each one of the others [Steckel, Adler, Kammerer, Steinach] expressed in his attitude some role. . . . Freud spoke to me like an ordinary human being. He had piercingly intelligent eyes. . . . He asked about our work in the seminar and thought it was sensible. . . . His manner of speaking was quick, to the point and lively. The movements of his hands were natural. . . . I had come there in a state of trepidation and left with a feeling of pleasure and friendliness." [8])

This meeting marked the beginning of Reich's identification with psychoanalysis and the feeling of deep respect for Freud that he retained throughout his life, despite the fact that Freud later sided with Reich's opponents in the psychoanalytic movement and acceded to Reich's eventual expulsion. "I am happy to have been his pupil for such a long time [fourteen years] without premature criticism and with full devotion to his cause," [9] Reich was to write later: and then he added significantly: "Unlimited devotion to a cause is the best prerequisite for intellectual independence." [10]

Several important events occurred in Reich's life before his

5. *Ibid.*, p. 15.
6. *Ibid.*, p. 6.
7. *Ibid.*, p. 7.
8. *Ibid.*, p. 17.
9. *Ibid.*, pp. 17–18.
10. *Ibid.*, p. 10.

graduation in 1922. He married a student named Annie Pink, winning her against much competition at the university. He read a paper entitled "The Libido Conflict and Delusion of Peer Gynt" at the Vienna Psychoanalytic Society as a guest and was subsequently accepted into the Society as a full member. (This was a highly unusual honor since the Society did not ordinarily grant membership to undergraduate students.) And he began, shortly thereafter, at the age of twenty-three or twenty-four, to accept patients in analysis. After his graduation, Reich, while continuing to analyse, went into analysis himself, became active in the Psychoanalytic Society, and contributed regularly to its journal. As early as 1923 he published a paper entitled "On the Energetics of Drives" and in this established the direction he was to follow in the subsequent decades and which brought him to his formulations of the ubiquitous life energy he called orgone.

It was not until 1924, when Reich became first clinical assistant in the Psychoanalytic Polyclinic in Vienna—a job that brought him into touch with working-class people—that Reich became interested in the social etiology of neurosis. This led him to immerse himself, with his customary enthusiasm and energy, in the study of Marx and involvement in the large socialist movement of Vienna. During this involvement he wrote papers and articles seeking to reconcile Marx with Freud—an effort that, together with his attempt to bring psychoanalytic knowledge into the sphere of radical politics, eventually got him expelled from both the radical and psychoanalytic movements, as will be described in a later chapter.

Reich's own analysis was, for obscure reasons, never completed. After leaving his first analyst he hoped to be accepted as a patient by Freud. For a while Freud considered making an exception to his rule of not treating any of his co-workers—since he regarded Reich as one of the most promising younger analysts—but in the end he decided not to break this rule. There is some speculation that Reich experienced this as a rejection. If he did, it did not seem to affect his professional development, for in the meantime he became, in 1928, the vice director of the Psychoanalytic Polyclinic in Vienna and was lecturing to other analysts on his as yet embryonic orgasm theory.

In the meantime Reich's wife became a practicing analyst and they had two daughters—Eva and Lore. Both became estranged from their father after the breakup of the marriage in 1933, but Eva, the older one, eventually returned to Reich, became a doctor, and was one of her father's strongest supporters in the crucial last years of his life. Among FDA people she was reputed to be a "fire brand" in her devotion to her father's work. Reich's brother died of tuberculosis in 1926, and Reich himself developed some tubercular symptoms and spent several months in a Swiss sanitarium. It is at this juncture that, for the first time, the matter of Reich's "insanity" arose.

Annie Reich, as well as other of the Vienna psychoanalysts around Freud, was to claim in later years, when Reich's work took him into vegeto-therapy and orgone biophysics (both to be explained in a subsequent chapter), that mental deterioration began in him on his return from the sanitarium. One analyst in particular, Otto Fenischel, was to propagate this rumor from the middle thirties, both in Europe and America, with particular insistence. Ilse Ollendorff, after interviewing Annie, rejected her interpretation, writing: "I met Reich in 1939 and until 1951 our life together . . . did not make me feel that a 'deteriorating process' was going on in him." [11] She regarded Annie's view as "a rationalization of her personal difficulties in living with Reich because he was an unusual person with unusual energy. Reich had a driving force that made it very hard for anyone to follow him or live with him." [12]

However, there was something else involved in the readiness of so many of the other psychoanalysts then and in later years, down to our own time, to believe that Reich had gone off the deep end. This was the mechanism that Reich himself was later to deplore in a different context and which he termed "psychologizing." Thus, if a person engaged in radical politics, it was not that he was fighting against the reality of intolerable living and working conditions, but that he was symbolically rebelling against the introjection of paternal authority into his own psyche. The essence of this mechanism is a reductive fallacy: the denial of objective validity to any effort, activity, or formulation that goes beyond commonly accepted limits. Though it became a convenient means for psychoanalysts to avoid having to face the challenge of Reich's discoveries

11. Ollendorff, p. 15.
12. *Ibid.*, p. 15.

of such things as armor and the orgasm reflex, at the same time it marked the beginning of the process by which psychoanalysis achieved respectability at the cost of the radical thrust of Freud's early writings. In other words, opposition to Reich's approach to sexuality and character formation went together with the gradual drift of psychoanalysis from Freud's early emphasis on the role of sex in the formation of neuroses; and eventually, with the development of the Freudian idea that the pleasure principle has to give way to the reality principle, psychoanalysis began to see social adjustment as a basic criterion of emotional health. Anna Freud herself, in her book *Psychoanalysis for Teachers,* urged the restriction of the motor activity of children at an early age in order that they be capable of adjustment to "reality."

On returning to Vienna from the sanitarium, Reich became more active in the political work of the socialist party. He participated in marches and demonstrations that often involved him in personal danger from the violent countermeasures of the police. On the basis of the close contact he had with the life of working-class people in these activities—he later called it "practical sociology"—Reich became aware of their need for sex hygiene clinics. Accordingly, he and several colleagues set up such clinics in 1929. Their purpose was to make available to people information and counseling on sex in general and on birth control in particular. Parents were able to obtain help with problems pertaining to their children, which included counseling concerning the sexuality of children; at the same time, adolescents were also given counseling for their sexual problems and information on birth control. Besides these services, the clinics also provided frequent lectures and discussions on related matters. Though these centers were sponsored by the socialists, their services were open to the public at large.

Reich's rationale for these centers was twofold: on the one hand, since he saw all neuroses as being caused by sexual dysfunction, such clinics would help in the resolution of neuroses in the populace; on the other hand, the populace in turn would, through such services as these centers provided, naturally gravitate toward the party sponsoring them—whether socialist or communist—and support that party in its effort to effect a social order that would be nonauthoritarian and nonrepressive. Such a social order would remove the conditions behind the formation of neuroses. Thus, Reich saw the work of these clinics as simultaneously curative and preventive.

However, Reich's work in these clinics soon incurred the opposition of the socialist party, which began to be disturbed by the radicalism of his sociological ideas. Finally, when he read a paper critical of the sex reform movement before the Congress of the World League for Sex Reform, he was accused by the socialists of using "the sex hygiene clinics as a shop for communist propaganda," and the disaffection between him and the socialist party became final.

In 1930, Reich decided to move to Berlin in order to begin analysis with Dr. Sandor Rado. But first he arranged for a trip to Russia and there became particularly interested in studying the experimental nurseries and child-care centers. He was well received in Russia, gave several lectures, and met Vera Schmidt, a psychoanalyst who was, in effect, Russia's A. S. Neill. Though he was impressed by her and by the progressive legislation in matters of divorce and abortion, he felt that in general there was a lack of basic understanding in the way Russian doctors and educators approached and handled the matter of sexuality in children and adolescents. ("When I asked the Commissariat for Public Health how masturbation in adolescents was being treated, I was told by 'diversion, of course'." [13])

On his return from Russia, Reich settled in Berlin with his wife and two daughters and entered treatment with Rado. This analysis, however, was short lived. After six months Rado left for the United States; Reich had no further analytical treatment thereafter.

In the meantime, however, he had become intensely involved with the radical politics of the German communist party. His first significant action was to present the central committee of the party with a plan to start a sex-political mass movement on a communist basis. As a result, the German Association for Proletarian Sexual Politics was formed and quickly grew to a membership of more than 40,000 people. Sex hygiene clinics were established in the large industrial cities of western Germany. The platform of this organization called for better housing for the populace, abolition

13. Wilhelm Reich, *The Sexual Revolution*, translated by Theodore P. Wolfe (New York: Noonday Press, 1970), p. 186.

of all laws against abortion, homosexuality, and birth regulation; reform of marriage laws; free birth control counseling and information (including the free distribution of contraceptives); provision for sex education on a mass scale; nurseries and sex-counseling facilities at all large factories and businesses; abolition of laws restricting sex education; and home leave for prisoners.

In addition to his work with the sex clinics, Reich gave lectures on sexual politics and political psychology and wrote propaganda pamphlets that were so politically biased that he himself later repudiated them. And, again, he courageously participated in marches and demonstrations—often attired as a mountain climber, but with his knapsack full of medical supplies. His devotion to the communist cause was so extreme that he insisted on sending his two daughters to a communist children's center. Though Annie Reich protested, Reich threatened separation and she eventually—although reluctantly—acquiesced. "Already in those days only the absolutes were possible for Reich," Ilse Ollendorff writes. "Something was either black or white . . . and those close to him had to follow him or get out. . . . He overlooked the fact that few of those around him were equipped, emotionally or otherwise, to follow him or to understand his theories. They would follow, if they did, out of admiration, out of love, out of blind loyalty, or sometimes out of fear of being kicked out of his orbit. The power of his personality was enormous and . . . difficult to withstand." [14]

This situation of people following Reich, whether out of loyalty or fear, was to reach an extreme point at the time of his deepening legal trouble with the FDA. As will be seen, the few associates and co-workers who remained close to him during his desperate last years were only those who were willing to identify with and accept his often misconceived view of the nature of this trouble.

In the meantime, in Berlin, opposition to his work developed among the communist party leadership. Increasingly, German communist party officials took exception to his sex theories and to the emphasis of his work on sex, fearing that such emphasis would divert people's attention from the class struggle. The party eventually ordered Reich's writings withdrawn from its bookstores. Reich himself was branded a counterrevolutionary: first, because he was a psychoanalyst, and psychoanalysis was nothing more than a "phe-

14. Ollendorff, p. 24.

nomenon of bourgeoise decay" and altogether "un-Marxist"; and second, because his assertion that orgasmic disturbance was widely present in *all* classes "denied the existence of class differences." Moreover, for his efforts in behalf of sexual health and his belief that a sexually healthy population would strive more rationally and purposefully for the new order of civilized existence that Marxism promised, Reich was accused of "turning our gyms into brothels." The German communist party doggedly maintained that sexual problems would solve themselves once the property relations of society were radically altered.

Strangely enough, in this criticism the German communist party was joined by the Nazi press. Ignoring the communists' official disavowal of Reich's book, *The Sexual Struggle of Youth,* which came out at this time (1932), the Nazi paper *Völkischer Beobachter* referred to the book as "the Communists' call to German youth to revolt against all moral regulations."

It was during this same time that Reich was subjected to increasing criticism by members of the Psychoanalytic Association. There were, to be sure, personality differences and organizational politics involved in this criticism, but the main reason for it was Reich's increasing emphasis on sexuality in his theoretical formulations and his conviction that psychoanalysis should be committed to preventive work no less than to curative.

A case in point was Reich's criticism of Freud's rather tentative theory of the death instinct. In the way this theory was taken up by other psychoanalysts as a clinically proven fact Reich saw a desire to evade the social responsibility of psychoanalysis. That is, as long as the formation of neurosis could be attributed to an internal mechanism of the psyche, psychoanalysis did not have to look at, be concerned about, or deal with the social context within which this neurosis-prone psyche was formed.

The extremity of Reich's commitment to sexual-political work led to the breakup of his family life. Annie could not follow him in this work and sided with the opposition to him that was growing in the Psychoanalytic Association. In 1933, shortly after the Nazis took power, Reich and his family left Germany and returned to Vienna, and there his first marriage was dissolved.

2

REICH IN EXILE

Reich had left a ten-room house, a car, many personal possessions, and a lucrative practice in Berlin. When he returned to Vienna in 1933 he was almost penniless. His manuscript of *Character Analysis* was ready for publication, but the director of the International Psychoanalytic Press was afraid, because of the political situation and Reich's reputation as a radical, to fulfill the contract for the book's publication. So Reich had to borrow money and have it published at his own expense. "By a supreme irony," Boadella writes of this circumstance, "the very book on which Reich's principal claim to 'orthodoxy' rests, which contains his central psychiatric achievements . . . had to be printed privately . . . at a time when the analytic world no longer wanted to be linked with his name." [1]

Because of the generally unfriendly attitude of the Viennese psychoanalysts toward his work, and in response to urging from Danish psychoanalysts and trainees, Reich moved again, this time to Denmark. The IPA (International Psychoanalytic Association), in a further effort to dissociate itself from Reich's name, refused to grant its recognition to the psychoanalytic training and teaching Reich wanted to do in Denmark. Even Freud, for the same reason,

1. David Boadella, *Wilhelm Reich, the Evolution of His Work* (London: Vision Press, 1973), p. 89.

refused to write a letter in support of Reich's application for a Danish work permit.

Reich arrived in Denmark on May 1, 1933, and there Elsa Lindenberg—a dancer with the Berlin State Opera who, in Berlin, had been a member of the same communist cell as Reich (which, incidentally, had also included Arthur Koestler)—joined him. Though never legally married, she was in effect Reich's second wife in a relationship that lasted some six years—until the time Reich left for the United States in 1939. (The similarity of her first name to that of Reich's third wife, Ilse, was later to confuse matters hopelessly in the FDA files on Reich, where the distinction between the two women is never maintained.) In Denmark the students and psychoanalysts who had had previous contact with Reich eagerly awaited him, and within a few days after his arrival Reich was working busily at teaching, training, therapy, and also in preparing the manuscript of one of his most widely acclaimed books, *The Mass Psychology of Fascism,* for publication. He even found time to participate in the Red Help organization that had been set up to aid German communist exiles in Denmark.

Mass Psychology came out in August 1933. Shortly afterward, Reich was officially expelled from the Danish communist party. The fact that he had never been a registered member of the party was not important; the expulsion was in effect a gesture signaling the official disavowal and condemnation of Reich by the whole communist movement. Though there were other reasons for this move—primarily communist opposition to what was regarded as Reich's psychologizing of politics—it was the appearance of *Mass Psychology* that brought this growing opposition to a head. What is perhaps most significant in this circumstance from the standpoint of Reich's later trouble in the United States is that the official attitude toward this book was established at this time. Later, in 1946, when the English translation of the book came out, this attitude was to reappear in the *New Republic,* the leftist-oriented magazine that played a central role in arousing the FDA against Reich. The reason for the original communist condemnation of *Mass Psychology* as counterrevolutionary was that it analyzed the mass-psychological reasons for the defeat of communism in Germany at a time when the communist party itself had not yet realized it was defeated and persisted in regarding the victory of Nazism as nothing more than a temporary setback. Reich, in recognizing the defeat, maintained that it was due primarily to the unwillingness of "vulgar Marxists" to recognize that in any struggle for freedom the armored human character structure and the conservative ideology anchored in this structure have to be considered on the same level of importance as purely political and economic factors.

To Reich the expulsion—even as a gesture—was painful. He continued to identify himself with communist politics for several years afterward in spite of the growing disagreements between him and official communist dogma and in spite of his recognition, as early as 1934, that things in Russia had taken a reactionary turn. "The party was like a second home," he was to write in 1937. "So it becomes for everyone who gives up bourgeois security in favor of the battle for a better future. For many it becomes the only home." [2]

This sense of homelessness must, no doubt, have been intensified in Reich by the fact that a very short while later, due to the continued unwillingness of the IPA to endorse his work, his Danish visa was not renewed after its initial expiration. Undecided as to where to move next, Reich went on a tour of Europe and England. In London he met IPA president Ernest Jones and the anthropologist Bronislaw Malinowski. There had been an intense intellectual polemic between these two men over the issue of the Oedipal conflict. Jones maintained, in line with Freud's thinking, that this conflict was biologically given; Malinowski adduced anthropological evidence—as developed in his *Sex and Repression in Primitive Society*—to prove that this conflict was not biological but sociological in origin. Reich had read Malinowski's writings in this matter and found in them confirmation of his own views on the social responsibility of psychoanalysis; that is, if the Oedipal conflict was sociological in origin then psychoanalysis must address itself to the problem of altering the social conditions that produced that conflict.

The meeting with Jones was cordial ("Jones was, as always, amiable and very much a gentleman. . . ." [3]), but he politely opposed Reich's views in the matter of the social responsibility of science. Though he expressed opposition to Reich's expulsion from the IPA

2. Wilhelm Reich, *People in Trouble* (Rangeley, Maine: Orgone Institute Press, 1953), p. 157.
3. *Ibid.,* p. 162.

—there was, at this time, talk of that possibility—Reich later learned that his expulsion had already been decided upon before his meeting with Jones.

For a while Reich considered moving to London. Jones did not support this idea, and besides, as Reich was later to write, "London would have required a great deal of adaptation on my part. London was puritanical and I lived with my partner without a marriage certificate. Neither of us wanted to marry. We were very happy without that. We knew that a marriage license . . . confers the right to exploit and suppress." [4] Besides these considerations, Reich felt close to his Danish students. They understood and sympathized with his work and, in fact it was they who suggested that he move to Malmö in Sweden since this would place him close enough to Copenhagen so that contact could be maintained.

Reich finally decided on Malmö, writing: "I preferred quiet exile to a new career in a distant capital city. I was not to regret it although, once again, according to the usual way of thinking, it appeared to be a 'crazy' decision." [5] Whether at the time of his trouble in the United States Reich came to regret this decision there is no way of knowing. However A. S. Neill—who met Reich during this period of exile, went into therapy with him, and remained thereafter one of his staunchest friends—was later to say that had Reich gone to England he would never have been subjected to the prosecution, harassment, and eventual imprisonment he underwent in the United States.

Reich settled in Malmö in September 1933. Elsa remained in Copenhagen, where she continued her work as a dance teacher and choreographer, applying some of Reich's findings concerning muscular armor to her work. She came to Malmö regularly to be with Reich for three-day weekends—an arrangement that seemed to be very satisfactory. ("Four days of every week I was alone. I had sufficient leisure for scientific work." [6]) They had, in effect, what has since come to be called an open marriage.

Reich's expulsion from the IPA occurred in August of 1934, a year after his expulsion from the communist party. The underlying reason was the growing distance between his developing sex-

4. *Ibid.*, pp. 166–67.
5. *Ibid.*, p. 167.
6. *Ibid.*, p. 168.

economic views and the more conventional orientation of the Freudians. The immediate reason was that the IPA still hoped to avert the hostility of the Nazis by dissociating itself from the idea of commitment to radical social action that had become attached to Reich's name. He received a letter before the Lucerne congress convened on August 25, 1934, that his name would be omitted from the list of German members. "I would be glad," wrote the secretary of the German association, "if you could appreciate the situation and, setting the interest of the psychoanalytic cause in Germany above any possible personal feelings, would give your consent to this measure. Your standing in the international psychoanalytic world as a scientist and author is so well known that this omission of your name could not possibly do you the slightest harm." [7] But at the congress itself it turned out that beyond the omission of Reich's name from the list of German members, Reich himself was to be excluded in person. He was permitted to speak, but only as a guest. Jones was very concerned about this concession, fearing that Reich would use the occasion to throw him out bodily. "I confess," Reich wrote, "that later I was sorry I had not done it." [8]

The newly formed Scandinavian group of psychoanalysts, among whom Reich had been working, was threatened by exclusion from the IPA because of its support of Reich at the Lucerne congress. They would be admitted only if they did not insist on bringing Reich in with them. There was much politicking about this issue, but the Norwegian analysts stood firm and eventually were unconditionally accepted, though at the price of being separated from the Swedish group. The Norwegian group later held out the offer of membership to Reich. But because some among them were hesitant about this offer, Reich suggested that the matter be dropped, which it was. They, however, remained in friendly professional contact with Reich for several years thereafter.

But one of Reich's German associates, Otto Fenischel, who worked with Reich during the period of exile, eventually did an about face and became his most vicious enemy. It was primarily with Fenischel—who through books such as the *Outline of Clinical Psychoanalysis* and *Problems of Psychoanalytic Technique* became

7. Published in *People in Trouble,* p. 189.
8. Published in *People in Trouble,* p. 192.

one of the important influences in the later development of psycho-analysis—that the rumor of Reich's insanity and even institutionali-zation gained currency. These rumors were to dog Reich in the subsequent decades and to make it easy for members of the psycho-analytic establishment to discount his work in the realm of bio-psychiatric therapy; still later it was largely on the basis of these rumors that members of the scientific community were able to shrug off Reich's scientific formulations without bothering to test them.

In addition to this expulsion, and perhaps partially as a result of it, Reich could not extend the time of his Swedish visa. Forced again to move, he this time, in October 1934, settled in Oslo, Norway, where Elsa joined him.

As painful as the break with Freud and psychoanalysis was, as underhanded as was the way in which it had been engineered, it was bound eventually to come. Reich's work had by then taken him too far out of the framework of the IPA and the time was ripe for him to become independent, free of all obligations to organizations with which his own developing views came to have so little in com-mon. In looking back on this period Reich wrote that psychoanaly-sis was the mother and Marxism the father of his sex-economic work.[9] It was time for the offspring of this union to strike out on its own. "A weaker person might have completely broken under the strain of such a loss," Ilse Ollendorff writes, "but Reich, with his unbelievable energy and optimism, bounced back and threw himself into the building up of his own independent organization with the help of the few courageous and devoted people. . . ." [10]

In Oslo, from 1934 to 1937, Reich was able to pursue his work without crisis and disruption. He had access to the facilities of the University of Oslo which he made use of to test bioelectrically what previously had been his speculative belief that pleasure and anxiety constituted antithetical kinds of reactions. He started a journal. He led a psychotherapy seminar. Socially he became friendly with some of the intellectual and artistic luminaries of Norway. He founded the Institute for Sex-Economic Bio-research, which coordinated and centralized in one large building all the fac-ets of the work he and his colleagues were doing. His therapeutic method by this time had developed to the point where it was no

9. Boadella, p. 85.
10. Ollendorff, p. 32.

longer called character analysis but vegeto-therapy. Elsa, in the meantime, was advancing in her own professional work. It was a busy, productive, and fulfilling time for Reich.

But then, in late 1937 and lasting into late 1938, came the virulent Norwegian newspaper campaign against Reich and his work.

During his stay in Norway, Reich had sought to avoid any activity that might make things awkward for the Norwegian government. In spite of offers and invitations, he gave only three public lectures and refused to write for the newspapers. Moreover, the journal he and his co-workers issued (*Zeitschrifte für Politische Psychologie und Sexualökonomie*) in which articles on Reich's work and the developments in sex-economy were published, appeared only in German, which meant that only a tiny minority of the population had access to its contents. And yet in spite of these precautions, he once again became the focus of controversy.

And once again, he faced an alignment of social groupings that ordinarily had nothing in common, or were even fundamentally opposed to each other: the communists, the fascists, the psychoanalysts and psychiatrists, as well as the pillars of society from various medical sciences. For example, one of the psychiatrists who wrote most vitriolically against Reich in the newspapers during the campaign—implying that Reich's scientific work in measuring skin change during exhilaration and anxiety involved pornographic sexuality—was a Dr. Johann Scharffenberg, who became an outspoken critic of the Nazi occupation in its early years; while Dr. Klaus Hanssen, who attacked Reich's experimental work with bions as being "rubbish" and "nonsense," later served a seven-year prison sentence for major complicity with the Norwegian Nazi party.

Rumblings of this trouble-to-come could be heard in mid-1937 when Reich published the first report on his work in biogenesis in the previously mentioned German-language journal. The newspapers picked up this subject and sensationalized it in several articles. These articles, then, provoked some doctors of medicine and physiology at the University of Oslo to write official refutations—even though they had read only that single report by Reich, which did not include the details of the experimental background that led to his formulations concerning biogenesis. One of these was the above-mentioned Dr. Hanssen. Another was a Dr. Otto Louis Mohr who was, among others, later interviewed by an official of the American

Embassy in Oslo in response to a request by the FDA for details on Reich's trouble in Norway. The report of this interview states: "Professor Mohr did not describe Reich's experiments by which he claimed to have created life [which, it should be mentioned, is inaccurate, since Reich did not claim to have created life but only to have duplicated under laboratory conditions a process that was going on in nature all the time] and in general appeared not too well acquainted with this specific aspect of Reich's activities." And later this report continues: "I was particularly impressed by the violence of Professor Mohr's reaction in speaking of Reich's sexual theories. . . . It seemed to me . . . that Professor Mohr may simply have been reacting as many elderly and conservative-minded men might at what he considered to be an unnecessary and uncalled for discussion of a subject that he, Mohr, considered would be better left undiscussed." The report concludes: "It will be interesting to determine in the course of this investigation the importance of anti-Semitism in the case. Professor Mohr made such an issue of the fact that he himself was not anti-Semitic, that there may be some possibility that anti-Semitism (Dr. Reich is apparently Jewish) may have played a fairly considerable part in the case here in Norway."

This attack on Reich's scientific work was followed, in the fall of that same year, by an attack originating at several meetings of the Norwegian Psychiatric Society. According to Dr. Ola Raknes, the target of this attack was Reich's emphasis on the centrality of sex in the development of neurosis, on the right of children and adolescents to a free development of sexual feelings and on the role of society and social ideology in inducing the sexual inhibitions that led to neurosis.[11] Besides this, according to Raknes, Reich was accused at these meetings of having misused the findings of Malinowski in his book *The Sexual Life of Savages* as a support for his contention that neurosis was unknown in matriarchal societies where the love life of children and adolescents was free and uninhibited.[12] (This contention was repudiated by Malinowski in a letter to the Norwegian press at the height of the campaign. In this letter Malinowski sided with Reich and said that science would

11. Ola Raknes, *Wilhelm Reich and Orgonomy* (New York: St. Martin's Press, 1970), p. 44.
12. *Ibid.*, p. 44.

suffer a great loss if Reich, an "original and sound thinker," were prevented from carrying on his research.[13])

Following these meetings Reich was attacked by a Dr. Ingjald Niessen, a psychoanalyst who had formerly welcomed Reich to Norway, reviewed Reich's book *Mass Psychology* favorably, and referred to Reich as "one of the greatest psychoanalysts." [14] According to the Embassy report, it was Niessen who "touched off the controversy" with a newspaper article in which he wrote: "Psychoanalysis in this country has become sort of a weedy garden, where all sorts of parasites and climbers strike root and almost choke what is of value." Further, Niessen railed against the "quackery" of "psychoanalytic sectarians" who practice "some sort of quasi-medicinal relaxation analysis" that "only leads to sexual excitation." [15] Apparently his desire to discredit Reich remained unabated, for in the Embassy report he told the Embassy interviewer "That Dr. Reich was sympathetic with the Trotskyite communists, and since Trotsky had just left Norway for Mexico, leaving behind him a rather unpleasant feeling among the Norwegians for the Trotskyite persuasion of communists, Dr. Reich's outspoken support and defense of Trotsky was not viewed with much favor in Norway." However, a footnote by the interviewer at this point states: "Not confirmed by anyone else, including controlled American sources." That is, one can assume, by American intelligence information.

These two press attacks, then, became the springboard for the storm of controversy that broke out in the Norwegian press when Reich's book on bions appeared in the spring of 1938. Entitled *Die Bione,* it became—in spite of its being published in German— a catalyst for hates and resentments against Reich that had little to do with the scientific issues involved. Indeed, even the Embassy investigation states in its summary: "It is, of course, very difficult to assess with any accuracy the effect of the reaction of Reich's opponents to his sexual views on the central controversy over biology. The reporting officer, however, was struck by the frequency with which Reich's sexual views were referred to by his opponents

13. Quoted in Gunnar Leistikow, "The Fascist Newspaper Campaign in Norway," in *The International Journal of Sex Economy and Orgone Research,* Vol. 1, 1942, p. 272.
14. *Ibid.,* p. 270.
15. *Ibid.,* p. 270.

when their opposition to Reich's biological theories was the matter under discussion."

The invective in the anti-Reich articles and letters included a characterization of Reich as a quack and cast aspersions on Reich's sanity. Besides this, one attacker called into question Reich's claim to being a medical doctor and continually referred to him as "Mr." rather than "Dr." This was a matter that was easily disposed of by documentary evidence but which nevertheless also became an issue in Reich's trouble with the FDA. The fascists then entered the free-for-all, calling Reich a "Jewish pornographer of the worst kind." Other papers ran articles with scornful titles such as "God Reich Creates Life." Altogether over one hundred articles and letters—the bulk of them against Reich—appeared in the press while the open season on Reich lasted. Though the tradition of a free press in democratic Norway made the newspapers nominally open to both sides, in actual fact the press was against Reich, and often articles and letters submitted in his support by influential medical people never appeared in print.[16]

For the most part, Reich remained aloof from the controversy, leaving the task of his defense to his supporters and co-workers. At the beginning, however, he asked the public to defer judgment until his experimental work would enable him to issue a more detailed report on the matter of bions; and later he called for a public investigation of his experiments—a call that, with the exception of one half-hearted response, went unheeded. Ilse Ollendorff wrote about his reluctance to defend himself as follows:

It is one of the tragic aspects of Reich's life, and one of the most touching, that whenever he was faced with an irrational attack against himself and his work he would put absolute faith in the power of truth to win out in the end. He did not want to go down to the level of his attackers and he did not want anybody around him to defend him against what he later called the "emotional plague." [17]

This pattern was to be repeated in Reich's legal trouble in the United States, when again he refused to defend himself by means of legal technicalities and insisted on fighting his case on the basis of the principle of free scientific inquiry, which he saw as the fundamental issue.

16. Raknes, p. 45.
17. Ollendorff, p. 44.

Though remaining publicly aloof, Reich was, nevertheless, deeply affected by the campaign and released his anger among those closest to him—primarily Elsa. "I know what Elsa must have gone through in those days," Ilse Ollendorff writes, "because 15 years later [i.e., during the time of the trouble with the FDA] I went through the same experience." [18] The relationship between Elsa and Reich had so deteriorated by the end of the campaign that when Reich was ready to leave for the United States, Elsa decided not to go with him and remained instead in Norway.

Besides this, Reich's relationship with his co-workers was also adversely affected. ("Nic Waal—who, I understand, was not easily shouted down—had terrible fights with Reich, and other colleagues and associates began to be afraid of Reich's temper outbursts." [19]) Partially as a result of this, the Institute itself began to fall apart. Its work was completely disrupted after Reich left and Norway was invaded at the beginning of the war. Drs. Nic Waal and Ola Raknes were the only ones of the whole group to reestablish contact with Reich after the war. Though there was later estrangement between Nic Waal and Reich when she visited the United States in the late 1940s, she remained, to the end of her life, grateful to Reich for what she had learned from him. Of the effects of these crises on Reich, she wrote: "They made him often destructive and less and less patient, less loving as the years went on, and finally pathologically suspicious and 'socially insane' in . . . that his isolation prevented him from doing what he most loved to do. . . . He was never insane in the 'psychiatric' meaning of the concept. But the isolation in which he lived hindered him from constructing his connection with other people." [20] There is today in Oslo an institute, which she founded and which bears her name, for the treatment of emotionally disturbed children along sex-economic lines.

Ilse Ollendorff observes in her biography that during the Scandinavian period Reich's relations with his students and co-workers were very informal and almost everyone called him Willy. This was in marked contrast to the formality he was to assume in the United States, where he was always known as Dr. Reich. A couple of close

18. *Ibid.*, p. 45.
19. *Ibid.*, p. 46.
20. Nic Waal, "On Wilhelm Reich," in *Wilhelm Reich,* ed. Paul Ritter (Nottingham: The Ritter Press, 1958), p. 38.

friends—like Neill—were able to call him simply Reich. It is not difficult to see the cause of this change in the disruptive experiences he underwent during his period of exile. In writing of these events, Reich himself was to say in 1945: "The first clash with human irrationality was a gigantic shock. That I survived it without becoming mentally ill, is incomprehensible. . . . *As if with one blow one recognizes the natural-scientific nothingness, the biological senselessness and the social harmfulness of ideas and institutions which up to the moment had seemed quite natural and self-evident.* . . . I would even like to presume that the schizophrenic form of psychic illness is regularly accompanied with an *illuminating* flash of clarity about the irrationality of social and political processes. . . ." [21]

Eventually the attacks on Reich, and the public interest in them, began to wane and finally died out. They had, however, put into question the matter of the government's renewal of Reich's visa. This circumstance impelled him to accept an invitation from the New School for Social Research in New York City to take a position as associate professor of medical psychology. Though the campaign against him ended in the fall of 1938, he did not actually leave Norway until August 19, 1939—only a few days before the outbreak of World War II.

21. *People in Trouble,* pp. xv–xvi.

3

---◆---

A BRIEF SURVEY
OF ORGONOMY

On arriving in the United States, Reich began lecturing at the New School. He remained in this position for two years while he set up a laboratory in Forest Hills in order to continue the experimental work on bions that he had begun in Norway. From the time of his arrival in 1939 to the fall of 1947, when the FDA investigation began, Reich worked in relative freedom from harassment. Besides treating patients and training prospective therapists in his method of biopsychiatric orgone therapy, he also during this period—with his formulations on orgone energy—expanded his work into the realm of biophysics. He met Ilse Ollendorff in October 1939 and they married on Christmas Day of the same year. Their son, Peter, was born in April of 1944. But before this, in 1942, Reich had bought a 280-acre tract of land in the Rangeley area of Maine, where he planned eventually to establish a center for the study of the various aspects and ramifications of his orgone energy formulations. He and his family spent increasingly extended periods in this area until 1950, when he moved his laboratory there and, with his family, became a permanent resident of Maine.

In the spring of 1947, the attack on Reich began. It was launched by the publication of two articles. The first, entitled "The New Cult of Sex and Anarchy," appeared in the April issue of *Harper's* magazine; the second appeared in the May 26 issue of the *New Republic* under the title "The Strange Case of Wilhelm Reich."

Both articles were written by a woman named Mildred Edie Brady. She was an energetic and capable woman, according to *The New York Times* obituary (she died of a heart attack in 1965 at the age of fifty-nine), with an impressive background of accomplishments. In 1936, she and her husband, an economics professor at the University of California, founded the Consumers Union. She worked as the director of its western division until the outbreak of World War II, when she and her husband went to work for the Office of Price Administration. After the war she edited the consumer news column of *McCalls* magazine and at the same time worked as an industrial analyst. In 1950, she went back to the *Consumer Reports,* writing a regular column on packaging, credit, and related matters. She was often called upon to testify before Congress on consumer matters, and in 1961 wrote "The Great Ham Robbery"—an article that drew national attention to the meat packers practice of injecting water into ham to increase its weight. She worked as editorial director of the Consumers Union from 1958 to 1964 and then became its senior editor.

In the mid-1940s, while she worked as an industrial analyst, Mrs. Brady had occasion to study the beer industry, and as a result had become interested in the problem of alcoholism. Pursuit of this problem led her to books on psychoanalysis, and it was in the course of this reading that she first encountered the name and theories of Reich. This encounter, however, did not arouse her interest until she heard that a departmental colleague of her husband's, who was in the terminal stage of cancer, had had efforts made on his behalf for possible treatment by Reich. Apparently at the time Mrs. Brady had already established herself as an "authority" on Reich because she was asked by a friend of the patient for material on Reich. She refused to supply it. (She saw no reason—according to the FDA record of an interview with her on November 11, 1947—to turn "a lot of 'crack-pot nonsense' over" to the patient.) Later Brady learned that the concerned friend of the patient contacted a Berkeley follower of Reich who had a rented accumulator. Though these efforts on the patient's behalf did not lead to his being treated by Reich, they brought to Mrs. Brady's attention the extensive influence of Reich's work and apparently led her to do the articles.

In preparation for these articles, she came east in 1946 and managed to finagle an interview with Reich in his Forest Hills home-and-laboratory by telling him over the phone that she was bringing greetings from a West Coast friend. Atfer being received by Reich, she revealed that she was a writer and was thinking of doing an article on his work because it seemed so significant to her. No doubt she expected that he would welcome this opportunity for publicity. Reich, however, told her very plainly that he wanted no publicity, that he didn't usually give interviews to writers, and that he would prefer if she did not write about him or his work—a preference that she, of course, had no intention of respecting.

Reich in later years became more curt with and suspicious of curious and "interested" visitors largely as a result of several experiences of this kind. He was to write in the early 1950s that he had to overcome the restraint of his "nineteenth-century academism", apparently regretting that he had not changed it in time to show Brady the door. Even if he had, however, it would have made no difference. Her articles rely, in their content, very little on the experience of this interview. But his own courtesy and restraint, he later felt, had made him an unwitting collaborator in the distortions contained in her articles. He described their meeting in a rough draft of an article that was published in an unedited version and was therefore full of errors attesting to his imperfect command of English and the typewriter:

She . . . sneaked into my office with false pretense, driven by her evil intentions. . . . She . . . represented . . . that I promised orgastic potency through the use of the . . . accumulator. Now I knew well why she said this when I recalled her sitting there in front of me in the easy chair, with glowing eyes glowing from genital frustration, with eyes as I had seen them many thousand times in many people of both sexes, of all ages and professions. . . . I do not . . . tell public anything about the burning eyes in a woman body who expected orgastic potency from me the king of orgastic potency in the minds of so many frustrated cranks and biopaths; who expected, I say, orgastic potency from me, expressing this yearning clearly in her eyes, as she looks at me and then smearing me up and down in public with that pornographic insinuation about the accumulator . . . who is supposed to provide orgastic potency. Thus she turned her normal, natural desire into mudd which she then throws into my decent face.[1]

But what was this "crack-pot nonsense" Brady felt so strongly about, this "orgastic potency" she apparently yearned for so frustratedly, the "accumulator" she maligned, and, in general, the psychological, sociological, sexual and scientific ideas of Reich that so many people and organizations, over the years, had opposed and attacked with such vehemence? Here we must pause for a brief survey of the main elements of Reich's work.

Reich's contribution to the development of psychoanalytic thought and therapy is generally, though often grudgingly, conceded by the psychoanalytic establishment. It can't very well deny this contribution since, as has already been seen, he occupied several important posts in the early psychoanalytic movement; some psychiatrists and psychoanalysts who later became well known in Europe and America studied or worked under Reich during the early thirties; and, finally, his book *Character Analysis*—published in German in 1933 and in English in 1945—is still used as a standard text in many schools of psychoanalytic training which otherwise reject Reich's work.

Character Analysis is devoted primarily to the method of carrying out in practice Freud's idea of "resistance analysis," that is, the idea of focusing on a patient's resistance to the analysis before going on to deal with unconscious material revealed by the patient in dreams or free association.* In the process of developing this technique, Reich came to realize that resistance was less a matter of *what* a patient said and did than of *how* he spoke or acted.[2] On the basis of this observation Reich developed a theory of character in which various personality traits were regarded as forming a single defense system against feelings that experience had proven

1. *Conspiracy, An Emotional Chain Reaction* (Rangeley, Maine: Orgone Institute Press, 1954), item 381D (published in a limited edition).

* In much of what is explained in the following pages the author has relied on Dr. Ola Raknes' *Wilhelm Reich and Orgonomy,* the first book to present a comprehensive view of Reich's work.

2. Ola Raknes, *Wilhelm Reich and Orgonomy* (New York: St. Martin's Press, 1970), p. 19.

as being, in one way or another, dangerous. Reich called this defense system *character armor*.[3]

Reich further observed that there were changes in bodily behavior during outbreaks of emotion, and this led him to conclude that there was a bodily, muscular armor, consisting of tensions and spasms, corresponding to a patient's character armor.[4] From this it was a logical step to the idea that neuroses could be treated physically as well as psychically—an approach to treatment that had never before been attempted in psychoanalysis.[5]

In the course of developing the technique for loosening muscular armor, Reich found that long-repressed memories and emotions were often released and for the first time consciously experienced by the patient. But besides this, something else, quite unexpected, was experienced by the patient in the process of de-armorization: sensations of "streaming," [6] that is, an intensely pleasant sensation of tingly, current-like movement in various parts of the body, or throughout the whole organism, which he later regarded as the biophysical basis of the Freudian concept of pleasure. After encountering the phenomenon of such sensations repeatedly and regularly in his clinical work with patients, Reich came to see them as originating in the vegetative (i.e. involuntary) nervous system and constituting the basis for all thought and feeling. He called these sensations "vegetative streamings," and eventually came to call his system of therapy "vegeto-therapy."

Though Freud and the psychoanalytic movement in general spoke a great deal about genital sexuality, they assumed that it consisted of nothing more than erective and ejaculatory potency in the male and the ability to experience a climax in the female. Reich, however, discovered in his clinical work that these are not necessarily coincident with genital sexuality but only prerequisites to it. He found that as repressed feelings and sensations were released spontaneous movements appeared that were completely different from the voluntary movements of his patients. These were not jerky or clumsy but, quite the opposite, smooth, unified and,

3. *Ibid.*, p. 19.
4. *Ibid.*, p. 20.
5. *Ibid.*, p. 20.
6. *Ibid.*, p. 21.

when permitted to develop, would include the whole body in a reflexive kind of undulation which Reich came to call "the orgasm reflex." * Armoring, in other words, made it impossible for the organism to surrender to vegetative streaming sensations and the involuntary movement of the orgasm reflex, and without these there might be erective and ejaculatory potency in the male and a climax in the female but not full genital sexuality. Thus Reich endowed the term "genital sexuality" with a very specific meaning: the capacity of the organism to experience the orgasm reflex in the act of love and in the process discharge all the aroused excitation. He called this capacity *orgastic potency*. Its opposite was called *orgastic impotence;* in this condition the involuntary orgasm reflex was not experienced and as a result a residue of undischarged excitation or energy remained in the organism and became absorbed into the musculature where it formed the bioenergetic basis for neuroses as well as certain somatic ailments, which he called *biopathies*. On the social scene, Reich regarded the "energy stasis" that resulted from orgastic impotence as the basis for fascism as well as for other forms of irrational behavior. The idea of the centrality of the sexual function in the regulation of bioenergy and all the social ramifications of such regulation Reich subsumed in the term *sex economy*.

Reich's next book, *The Mass Psychology of Fascism,* came out of his work in "practical sociology," that is, the radical labor movement of the late 1920s and early 1930s. He felt then that radical politics would bring about a social structure in which repressive authoritarianism and compulsive morality would be replaced by self-regulatory freedom and natural morality; and that this in turn would make it possible for people to fulfill their basic instinctual needs. He seemed at that time to have assumed that once repressive social conditions and ideologies were overcome the change in human character structure would inevitably follow. But this view, he later came to realize, underestimated the depth of the character

* So that there will not be any misunderstanding on this point, it should be made clear that patients in whom the orgasm reflex appears during a therapy session do not, and are not encouraged to, have an actual orgasm. Sexual arousal is not a part of the therapy process itself; rather the therapy process is a loosening of characterological and body armor so that the natural capacity for sexual arousal can develop and find its fulfillment in appropriate circumstances.

armor in the masses as well as the neurotic craving for authority and the concomitant fear of freedom that this armor instilled in them. Subsequently he concluded that a free and rational social order could not be brought about through politics because the greatest obstacle to freedom was not the social order but the unfree people themselves, in whose armored character structures the values, the attitudes, and taboos of the repressive social order were anchored. Because of this, he concluded further that despite political efforts and ideological commitments to freedom, people would, in the end, perpetuate the same old repressive order regardless of the social and economic changes they might succeed in making. What happened to the revolution in Russia in the early thirties helped him reach this conclusion. Eventually he came to the belief that the only hope for the creation of a self-regulatory society—which he called *work democracy*—lay in the effort to prevent armorization in newborn infants. This he saw as a lengthy process extending over generations and possibly centuries, during which an ever growing number of unarmored people would gradually evolve freer social forms until the aberrant condition of armoring and all the social values and institutions that both supported and resulted from it would die out. To that end he set up, in the late forties, an infant research organization whose task it was to learn the precise mechanism of the beginning of armor in infants and children and to learn also what could be done in the way of child rearing and education to prevent the process of armoring. In this effort he drew upon A. S. Neill's experience in his unique Summerhill School and in turn influenced Neill's thinking on education and child rearing.

It might be wise to pause here—while this overview of the development of Reich's work and thinking has not yet gone into his formulations on matters of biology, physics, meteorology, and even cosmology—to point out the inner consistency of his development thus far, the way one discovery or conclusion led him to another; for this same chain of logical continuity led Reich, with mostly similar consistency, into his formulation of an all-pervasive life energy. It is also pertinent to point out the early evidence of Reich's urgent commitment to the task of improving the lot of man, the quality of human existence. For this commitment, which he retained from his Marxist days, carried over into his later work. In fact, his eventual decision to arrange for the rental of accumulators was a logical outgrowth of this commitment.

In exploring and elaborating upon the orgasm function, Reich at first assumed that the energy involved—to which Freud had given the indeterminate name "libido"—was bioelectricity. He saw the unimpeded orgasm process as one that developed according to what he called the *four-beat orgasm formula:* mechanical tension→bioelectric charge→bioelectric discharge→relaxation. It occurred to him that the movement of the body, when the orgasm reflex was present, resembled that of microscopically observed protozoa, which suggested to him two related possibilities: (1) that the orgasm function might be common to all living matter; and (2) that the four-beat orgasm formula might therefore be applicable to, and identical with, all life functions.

These possibilities remained in the realm of speculation for some time while Reich engaged in seemingly aimless experimentation with foods and other organic substances—boiling them, letting them sit, observing them under high-powered magnification—with the general question of the development of life processes in the back of his mind. Eventually this apparently aimless activity— Reich compared it to playing and in retrospect saw it as being less aimless than it seemed to him at the time—led to his questioning the commonly accepted idea in biology that new life forms could only develop from previously existing life forms. To check out the possibility that life could develop from nonliving matter, he set up two parallel experiments, one with organic and one with inorganic material. In the first he used dry moss or grass, sterilized it, and then put it in sterilized water. After this material became swollen, he observed that it began to disintegrate into small vessicles that showed a contracting and expanding motion suggestive of protozoic movement. These vessicles eventually massed together, surrounded themselves with a membrane, and become even more similar to protozoa.[7] The inorganic material used in the second part of this experiment was coal dust, fine sand, metal dust, and rust. This material was heated to incandescence and while still glowing put into a sterile, nutritive solution. Here, too, particles swelled into vessicles and began to move as did those developing from the organic material.[8]

7. *Ibid.,* p. 28.
8. *Ibid.,* p. 29.

The unorganized vessicles Reich called *bions,* which he defined as matter in transition between living and nonliving states. The bions resulting from both these experiments, when they became organized within a membrane, showed the same kind of movement, that is, the alternate contractions and expansions resembling the human organism in orgasm, following the four-beat formula. Reich called this movement—of which the orgasm was a particularized case—*biological pulsation,* and regarded such pulsation as being the most characteristic feature of the life process.

It occurred to him during this work that cancer cells might develop from organic tissue that had undergone the kind of disintegration that had resulted in bions. In studying sarcoma under the microscope he found many bacilli, which he called *T-bacilli,* that earlier he had found only when blood corpuscles were disintegrated. But he did not develop a method of applying these findings in a practical way until the logic of his research took him to the next stage—that of orgone biophysics.

Around this time Reich decided to test his assumption that the bioenergy he was dealing with in the orgasm was electrical. His experiments indicated that there were observable differences in the skin's electrical potential when pleasure or anxiety were aroused in a subject—the potential rising with pleasure and falling with anxiety.* Though this established experimentally his earlier formulation of pleasure and anxiety being antithetical and also constituted an important step in his eventual resolution of the psyche–soma dichotomy—a dichotomy that has not to this day been resolved by psychoanalysis—the differences involved seemed to him too slight to account for the way these two conditions were subjectively experienced.[9] Due to this and some discrepancies between the way electricity functions and the way bioenergy functions he began to entertain the possibility that bioenergy might not be exclusively or even mainly electrical. But if not electrical, then what could it be?

---

* Of this experimental work, Ilse Ollendorff wrote: "There were quite a few scientists—and analysts at that time who thought that Reich's experiments were crazy, that they were unrealistic. But looking at today's literature on experiments being conducted on various aspects of human sexual behavior, one can only conclude that Reich was some thirty years ahead in his ideas, and not so unrealistic or crazy at all." (Ilse Ollendorff Reich, *Wilhelm Reich* [New York: St. Martin's Press, 1969], p. 34).

9. *Ibid.,* p. 27.

The first clue came when he observed that the bions he had been working with gave out some form of radiation. When he began experimenting with this radiation he found that it acted in a way that was different from the action of the known forms of radiating energy. From subsequent research—described in detail in *The Cancer Biopathy*—Reich concluded that this was life-energy *per se,* the bioenergy involved not only in sexuality but in all other life processes as well. This, Reich felt, gave Freud's term "libido" a definite content. In thus endowing "libido" with concrete meaning, Reich felt that he had taken an important step in fulfilling Freud's belief that psychoanalysis would one day have to develop a foundation in the biological sciences. In still further experimentation, Reich began to see this energy as existing everywhere, in living matter as bound energy and in the atmosphere in a free state. It was on the basis of this latter postulation that he began devising ways of accumulating it for further study, and for this purpose, in 1940, he developed the first orgone energy accumulator.

The orgone energy accumulator that Reich eventually developed for human use is a box-shaped structure, all of whose six sides are filled with alternate layers of organic (i.e., nonmetallic) and metallic materials—cotton, glass wool, rock wool, or even polyethylene for the organic, and steel wool, metal screening, or galvanized sheet iron for the metallic. The outermost layer of the sides is usually made of celotex, while the innermost is of galvanized iron. The theory is that the organic material attracts and absorbs the orgone energy from the atmosphere and passes some of it through to the metallic material which radiates some of it toward the inside of the box, thus increasing the absorption and radiation of the next dual layer of organic and metallic substances until it reaches the space within the box itself. A living organism within this space then absorbs the energy through the skin and through breathing, and this has a generally healthful effect on the blood and body tissue.

Reich was aware that his concept of a specific life energy was not new. Hints of it are found in several Oriental religions, as well as in the writings of poets and philosophers. In recent times Henri Bergson, in *Creative Evolution,* described this energy in such terms as *élan vital* and *force creatrice.* Kammerer, a prominent biologist, in his book *Allgemeine Biologie* (1930), spoke of a "formative life energy" which is "neither heat, electricity, magnetism, kinetic energy . . . nor a combination of any or all of them, but an energy which specifically belongs only to those processes that we call life.' " [10]

Of related interest is the fact that in recent years Russian scientists have come up with the term "bioplasma" in their researches into parapsychology and acupuncture. "Bioplasma," states an article entitled "Parapsychology in the USSR," appearing in the March 18, 1972, issue of *Saturday Review,* "is presumed by the Russians to be a fourth state of matter that constantly interacts with other states of matter. . . ." [11] Just as Reich came to speak or an orgone energy field around all living things, the Russians now speak of a "bioplasmic field" and in fact have devised a means of actually photographing such fields. Also, they have found that these fields pulsate rhythmically—just as Reich found that orgone energy and all living things pulsate. "The ancient Chinese physicians," the article continues, "conceptualized a life energy running through the body, an energy that resembles the Soviet concept of bioplasma" [12]—or Reich's concept of orgone energy. In fact, the Russians have even developed a device called the "tobioscope" with which they can measure the intensity of the bioplasma energy field. And this device calls to mind Reich's "orgone energy field meter," described in Chapter IV of *The Cancer Biopathy* where he writes of its use for measuring the intensity of energy fields around people. The relationship—if any—between this research and the fact that in the late forties the Soviet Embassy in New York ordered a complete list of Reich's writings from the Orgone Institute Press, is, something that can only be speculated upon. Needless to say, Reich's name is not mentioned in the article.

At the start of the Korean War, Reich began to explore the possibility that orgone energy might be useful as a defense against the effects of radioactive fallout, and to that end began to investigate the relationship between nuclear and orgone energies, calling this experiment oranur—orgone anti-nuclear research. He put

---

10. Quoted in Wilhelm Reich, *The Discovery of the Orgone,* translated by Theodore P. Wolfe, Vol. II: *The Cancer Biopathy* (New York: Orgone Institute Press, 1948), p. 7.

11. Stanley Krippner and Richard Davidson, "Parapsychology in the USSR," in *Saturday Review,* March 18, 1972, p. 59.

12. *Ibid.,* p. 59.

some radioactive isotopes into an accumulator and found, contrary to his expectations, that the Geiger counter showed an incredible increase rather than a decrease. At the same time, in the course of this experimentation—all of which was written up in a softcover publication entitled *The Oranur Experiment*—the people working with him, as well as Reich himself, became severely ill. In probing these unexpected results, Reich concluded that the two energies—orgone and nuclear—are basically antagonistic and that the ill effects suffered by everyone participating in the work were due to the fact that nuclear energy excited and stimulated orgone energy and in the process made it noxious. Reich called this form of orgone *DOR*—deadly orgone. Its investigation, in turn, led Reich to other conclusions, of which the most important are:

that smog and air pollution are to a large extent the result of DOR in the atmosphere caused by the increased level of radioactivity from the rampant nuclear testing at that time;

that in the armored organism orgone energy caught up in cramped and spastic muscles is also transformed into DOR and thereby becomes life-inimical;

that by means of a special apparatus made of metal pipes pointing skyward and attached to an orgone accumulator grounded in water it is possible to remove DOR from the atmosphere so that fresh orgone could come in;

that a smaller version of this apparatus could remove DOR from the armored organism.

But perhaps the most striking development to come from Reich's investigation of DOR was his use of the apparatus to influence weather in general. As early as 1940, with the appearance of the English translation of *The Function of the Orgasm,* Reich wrote: "Cloud formation and thunderstorms—phenomena which to date have remained unexplained—depend on changes in the concentration of atmospheric orgone." [13] Later Reich put forward the idea of an orgone energy envelope surrounding the earth and the possibility that desert formation and droughts were results of stale orgone energy that had turned to DOR within this envelope. This and two other formulations constituted the theoretical founda-

13. Wilhelm Reich, *The Discovery of the Orgone,* translated by Theodore P. Wolfe, Vol. I: *The Function of the Orgasm,* (New York: Noonday Press, 1967), p. 342.

tion for extensive work in weather control in which Reich was engaged from the early fifties until his imprisonment in 1957. One of these principles is that the movement of orgone energy, in defiance of the laws governing other forms of energy, is always from the lower to the higher potential (which is in violation of the second law of thermodynamics and its principle of entropy). The second is that orgone energy has a strong affinity for water.

In Bangor, Maine, *The Bangor Daily News* of July 24, 1953, under the title of "Has Maine Scientist Answer to Rainmaking?" ran the story of one rainmaking operation, which stated in part:

Two men on the verge of losing their crops to the whims of nature, took a chance when a scientist told them, "I think I can give you some rain within 12 to 24 hours." And the chance paid off. . . .

The scientist was Dr. Wilhelm Reich, head of the Orgone Institute at Rangeley, Maine, and discoverer of "Orgone Energy, the Cosmic Life Energy of the Atmosphere."

. . .

Dr. Reich and three assistants set up their "rainmaking" device off the shore of Grand Lake near Bangor Hydro-Electric dam at 10:30 o'clock, Monday morning, July 6. The device . . . conducted a "drawing" operation for about an hour and 10 minutes. . . .

. . .

Rain began to fall shortly after 10 o'clock Monday evening, first as a drizzle and then by midnight as a gentle, steady rain. Rain continued throughout the night and a rainfall of .24 inches was recorded in Ellsworth the following morning.

A puzzled witness . . . said, "The queerest looking clouds you ever saw began to form after they got the thing rolling."

Monday, July 13, the drought was broken when heavy rain fell throughout most of the East. A total of 1.74 inches of rainfall was measured in Ellsworth—greater than any other section of the state.

Besides these offshoots of what began as an exploration of the relationship between nuclear and orgone energies, Reich's work with orgone includes several additional formulations, of which only the more important are touched on below.

One has to do with cancer, which Reich saw as primarily a social disease, the direct result of the pandemic repression of sexuality in our society that adversely affects the energy metabolism of cells in the organism and causes their disintegration. Reich did extensive experimental work with cancer patients, treating them with regular biopsychiatric orgone energy and the orgone accumulator. The results were written up in *The Cancer Biopathy*.*

Another is the motor force he saw as being inherent in orgone energy. Reich demonstrated the utilization of this potential in a specially constructed motor with a rotating armature at a conference held in his laboratory in Maine in 1949.

A third is the development of a new cosmology—described in *Cosmic Superimposition,* which appeared in 1951. By this time Reich had concluded that orgone was a cosmic energy,† not just local to earth, and he described how it was possible that galaxies and matter in general could have resulted from the confluence of two streams of cosmic orgone energy into a single system.

A fourth is Reich's exploration of gravity as an orgone energy function. There was word that he had solved the problem of countergravity on a theoretical level, but his formulations on this, together with a manuscript (entitled *Creation*) that he was working on during his imprisonment, could not be found among his effects after his death.

A fifth is Reich's formulation—in *Ether, God, and Devil*—of the principles of thinking that had led him through so many di-

* David Boadella in his book *Wilhelm Reich: The Evolution of His Work* (London: Vision Press, 1973), records significant interests in Italy in the treatment of cancer with orgone accumulators. A Dr. Bruno Bizzi, the vice-director of a hospital in Italy, used several orgone accumulators for the treatment of a variety of physical disease conditions, including cancer. Through this work he was able to obtain confirmation of several cases of tumor reduction, and to interest Professor Chiurco, the Director of the International Research Center in Pre-Cancer Conditions, at Rome University. Professor Chiurco, regarded as one of the foremost European authorities on cancer, initiated several international seminars on cancer prevention. At the second of these, held in October 1968, Dr. Bizzi was asked to present a paper on his experience in the orgone therapy of cancer. Subsequently, at the International Cancer Congress held in Cassano Junio the following month, Dr. Walter Hoppe, an Israeli medical orgonomist, was invited to present a paper on his treatment of a malignant skin melanoma with an orgone accumulator. As a result of this presentation Dr. Hoppe was, a year later chosen for membership in the Sybaris Magna Graecis Academy.

† This too is not a completely original "Reichian" concept. Nineteenth-century science postulated the existence of an universal yet indeterminate "ether" filling space as a means of explaining certain physical phenomena. Though this concept was discarded, there has been in recent years, due to new discoveries and formulations, a tendency among some scientists to question the wisdom of this rejection.

verse fields to so many new conclusions. He called this method *orgonomic functionalism*. Its essence is that subjective perceptions —the emotional no less than the ideational—constitute legitimate and, indeed, indispensable tools as well as subjects of scientific research.

And, finally, there is an aspect of his work in the latter years of his life that went together with his experiments in weather control—an aspect that was treated in a book (*Contact with Space*) published posthumously in 1957 in a limited edition. Though most of this book deals with weather-control work—including his work in the Arizona desert in the winter of 1954–55—a part of it also deals with unidentified flying objects. Reich recorded several UFO sightings and suggested that the "planetary DOR emergency" he saw as responsible for increased rate of desert formation might be caused by the presence of spaceships in the atmosphere as well as by the increase of radioactivity due to atmospheric testing of nuclear bombs. He postulated further that some of the heavenly bodies visible in the night sky might be such spaceships and recorded several occasions when he "disabled" them. That is, he directed the weather-control apparatus (he called it a "cloudbuster") at sky lights he thought might be spaceships and then several times he saw these lights blink or fade out. Carried out and written at a time when his entanglement with the law was becoming increasingly oppressive, this aspect of Reich's work often lacks the extended experimentation and logical sequentiality characteristic of his previous work, and the line between speculation and experimental conclusion is not maintained as carefully as previously. There will be occasion to discuss this matter further in a later chapter.

Reich often compared the totality of his work to an overflight over a newly discovered continent. In this exploratory overflight he did not linger over any particular area, but was always restlessly pushing onward, constantly breaking into new regions, leaving the details and refinements to be worked out by those who would come after.

4

THE
BRADY ARTICLES

The first Brady article, entitled "The New Cult of Sex and Anarchy," was only peripherally about Reich and his ideas. Primarily it was about the burgeoning bohemianism in the San Francisco Bay Area and exhibited—for all its contempt, half-truths, and outright distortions—a perceptive awareness of important cultural differences between this bohemianism and the one that followed World War I. In fact, it can be fairly regarded as the first public notice of the ferment from which the later Beat and Hippie movements were to sprout. Brady spoke about "their beards and sandaled feet," their "transportation via the thumb," and even about nascent communes "in which all social, economic and physical attributes, assets and liabilities, are shared in common. . . ." Reich's ideas come in only as one of the strands of the ideological line this "cult" had woven for itself—the others being religion, and philosophical anarchism. And though her treatment of Reich's social psychology—namely, that authoritarian society produces a population that is armored and therefore incapable of full sexual gratification—was as snide as her treatment of the "cult's" religion and anarchism, by itself, the article was not enough to warrant FDA interest.

It was the second article, appearing several weeks later in the *New Republic*—"The Strange Case of Wilhelm Reich"—that stirred the FDA to action.

The subtitle of this article was, "The man who blames both neuroses and cancer on unsatisfactory sexual activities has been repudiated by only one scientific journal." In this article Brady not only attacked Reich broadside but also raised for the first time in the United States the possibility of action against him—though she had in mind not governmental action so much as action by the American Psychiatric Association; for it was, significantly, primarily Reich's psychiatric theory and practice that she found objectionable.

This is significant because now, in the early seventies, with the number of new psychiatric schools of thought that have incorporated some aspect of Reichian therapy—such as encounter, sensitivity training, bioenergetics, primal therapy and rolfing—Reich's biopsychiatric formulations no longer seem as bizarre as they did in the forties. His identification of muscular armor with character formation, his orgasm theory, his method of attacking neurosis not only through talk but also by direct work on the body, his general emphasis on eliciting affects—i.e., expressed emotions—in therapy, have all received such wide, though often unacknowledged, acceptance that they can no longer be considered completely outside the pale of respectability. Certainly no one these days could realistically hope to arouse the APA over the growing practice or influence of Reichian therapy. This not only points up the extent to which thinking has changed in the last decades but also reminds us that in order to fully understand the course and issue of Reich's entanglement with the law we must keep in mind the social atmosphere of that period, which in large part coincided with the McCarthy era.

Unlike its predecessor, "The Strange Case of Wilhelm Reich" is poorly written, shrill in tone, and totally lacking in insight. Brady viewed with alarm the growing popularity of Reich's writings, as evidenced by favorable discussions and reviews in such magazines as *The Nation* and in Dwight Macdonald's short-lived *Politics*. Besides this, the avant-garde publications of the "growing group of anarchistically inclined literati on both sides of the Atlantic" were favorable to Reich's ideas. So that, according to her view, Reich had "already begun to collect a cult of no little influence." And yet, she chides, the American Psychiatric Association had not seen fit, with the exception of a single article in *Psychosomatic Medicine,* to come out strongly against him.

A large part of her article is taken up with an abbreviated, mostly accurate though often snide, account of Reich's career in Europe and America. In the remaining part of the article, however, there are gross distortions and inaccuracies. Some of these, one can assume, are simply the result of carelessness—such as her saying that Reich had given a town in Maine the name Orgonon, when it was actually his own estate in Maine that is so named; or when she stated that Reich's orgasm formula, which represented the basic life process, was charge→tension→discharge→relaxation, when in fact Reich had it as tension→charge→discharge→relaxation; or her sentence that "According to Reich, every living thing is surrounded by a field of orgone which keeps it charged with living energy," whereas Reich maintained that the field is a result of the organism's charge, not its cause.

But her most significant distortion—and one must assume that given an intelligent and literate reader like Brady, it was deliberate—is her assertion that Reich claimed patients automatically derived orgastic potency from the use of the orgone accumulator. This distortion was to affect the whole course of the preliminary FDA investigation. Though further on in the article Brady wrote a bit more accurately of the way Reich conceived of the accumulator's effect—"a kind of crutch to tide over the depleted tissue until the therapist has time to work on the 'character armor' to release outer rigidities"—it is the sensationalistic aspect that is emphasized in her article and which has remained uppermost in the public mind. Thus to this day—more than a quarter of a century after Brady first made the charge—one still encounters people who believe that Reich maintained that the orgone accumulator would directly affect a user's sexual potency; whereas the literature dealing explicitly with the orgone accumulator makes it very clear that aside from its use in the treatment of specific diseases the main value of the accumulator lies in its ability to charge blood and body tissue with energy and thus improve the general condition of the organism and its ability to resist disease.

But there is a more basic flaw still in the second Brady article. Reich had been expelled from the International Psychoanalytical Association in 1934, and since then, his work had taken him farther and farther afield from conventional psychiatry and psychoanalysis. How then could the American Psychiatric Association be logically expected to disown him, as Brady calls upon it to do? How could the various psychiatric publications honestly condemn a practice in which they had no experience? Brady seemed to be somewhat aware of this problem when she wrote: "To be sure, Reich himself does not belong to the association." But then, disregarding elementary logic, she goes on to say, "Undoubtedly, like members of any other profession, psychoanalysts on principle wish to avoid attacking *one of their number.*" [Italics added.]

The fact that a magazine like the *New Republic* saw fit to print an article so full of contempt and misrepresentations, so lacking not only in accuracy but in basic logical consistency would seem to suggest that the editors were more interested in discrediting Reich than in intellectual honesty. But why was this magazine so interested in discrediting Reich?

A clue to the answer is suggested in a scathing denunciation of Reich—through the vehicle of a review of the English translation of *The Mass Psychology of Fascism*—that appeared in the *New Republic* some six months earlier, on December 2, 1946. *Mass Psychology,* it will be recalled, is the same book whose original appearance in German triggered Reich's expulsion from the German communist party. The *New Republic* review was written by Fredric Wertham, a psychiatrist and author of a book entitled *A Show of Violence.* In the review Reich is condemned in terms that are not only reminiscent of the charges brought against him by the communists in 1933 but also recall the whole arsenal of denunciation used by American communists and fellow travelers throughout the thirties. Thus Reich is, typically enough, accused of having "utter contempt for the masses," because he believed that European communism had lost out to fascism by failing to consider that bourgeoise-authoritarian values and attitudes were anchored in the character structure of the masses. This condition, Reich wrote in *Mass Psychology,* "is expressed in their longing for authority, their mysticism and their incapacity for freedom." [1]

Wertham concluded his review with a call to all "progressive" intellectuals to combat Reich and his "psycho-fascism"—a term that represents a slightly updated version of the term "social-fascism" that figured so prominently in the communist rhetoric in the years prior to the Stalin–Hitler Pact.*

The *New Republic*'s publication of Brady's article, then, can be seen as a continuation not only of a previously established policy of opposition to Reich but also of the official communist party line of opposition that dated back to the early thirties.

In the months and years following the publication of the two Brady articles, they were condensed, quoted from, and recast in magazines of all kinds—slick, pulp, and professional. Reich described this process as an "emotional chain reaction." Brady, in a letter to the FDA some nine years later, on the day after Reich was sentenced to two years in prison, wrote: "There is a kind of journalistic excitement in learning that an article you wrote years ago has been instrumental in bearing such fruit."

1. Wilhelm Reich, *The Mass Psychology of Fascism,* translated by Vincent R. Carfagno (New York: Farrar, Straus and Giroux, 1970), p. 9.

* In his review of the recent edition of *Mass Psychology,* Christopher Lehmann-Haupt wrote in *The New York Times* of January 4, 1971, that "it hasn't an elitist bone in its body," that it "makes considerable sense," and that "whereas 15 years ago this reviewer contemplated Reich's theories of sex economy and orgone research with horrified shudders, reading *The Mass Psychology of Fascism* today made him wonder a little . . ." so that it may be "time to reconsider all of Reich . . . to reopen the question of cosmic orgone energy, its effect on cancer and the other theories Reich died in Lewisberg prison defending."

5

THE PRELIMINARY
INVESTIGATION

It took less than two months for "The Strange Case of Wilhelm Reich" to come to the attention of the FDA. On July 23, 1947, Dr. J. J. Durrett, Director of the Medical Advisory Division of the Federal Trade Commission sent the following letter to the FDA:

Attached is a photostatic copy of an article by Mildred Edie Brady which deals with Wilhelm Reich, who evidently is an emigree through round-about channels from Austria.

We have not investigated Reich and his activities. From the article it appears that he has set himself up as a local practitioner of psychiatry. . . . The reason I am sending this to you is that he appears to be supplying his patients with a gadget which will capture the seemingly fantastic substance "orgone" and accumulate it for the benefit of the person who occupies the space within this device. Having in mind the Food and Drug Administration's work on spectrochrome [a quack device] I thought you might want to look into this.

On August 1, a copy of this letter and article came to the attention of Mr. W. R. M. Wharton, who was Chief of the Eastern Division of the FDA. Wharton has been variously described by FDA people who had worked with him as "ruthless" and "dictatorial" as well as one of the five most powerful men in the agency at that time. But more significant from the standpoint of his involvement in the Reich case is the fact that he was known among subordinates and superiors to be pornographically obsessed with sex. He was known to keep a ceramic phallus in his office which he would put out on his desk when his secretary came in to take dictation. When he eventually got an accumulator as evidence, he kept it in his office and joked about it as a means of gaining sexual prowess, *à la Brady*. "This is a box," he wrote on August 26, "in which a man is placed and thereby becomes permeated with orgone, which is a progenitor of orgasm. . . . No kidding." Among a variety of rumors circulating about orgone therapy, Wharton, in the early weeks of the investigation he initiated, apparently heard that it involved teaching children to masturbate—this greatly disturbed him. It is no wonder, then, that Charles A. Wood, resident inspector for the state of Maine, and the first FDA agent to "investigate" Reich and his work, said of Wharton many years later: "He was crazy about that Reich case and didn't think of anything else during the whole time. He built it way up out of proportion." Nor is it any wonder that—as stated in a letter dated May 24, 1948, from the Chief of the New York Station to Wharton's replacement—"Mr. Wharon held a conviction that some of the publications distributed by the Orgone Institute Press were . . . pornographic and obscene."

He was, then, it seems by all accounts and evidence, a perfect example of what Reich described in his writings as an "emotional plague" type, *i.e.,* a person whose own sexuality is so bound up in guilt and repression that he can only regard sex as a dirty secret. Such a person cannot even conceive of natural sexuality and is, therefore, on the social scene, driven to irrational action at the merest suggestion of open sex-affirmation. It is hard to imagine a man more predisposed to accept fully the distortions in Brady's article, more ready to put the worst possible construction upon Reich's theory of character and sexuality and the technique of therapy he had developed to loosen the body armor that inhibits the orgasm reflex and causes orgastic impotence. And it was out of this predisposition that the investigation of Reich was launched as a search for evidence of a "vice ring" and a "sexual racket."

Inspector Wood, was phoned on August 27, 1947, by the Chief

of the Boston Station about Reich, who was at that time spending summers in Rangeley, Maine. Wood obtained and read the *New Republic* article on Reich and then went to Orgonon where, after some initial delays, Reich finally came to see him. "Dr. Reich is fifty years old, speaks with a German accent, and was dressed in blue dungarees and a work shirt at the time of the visit," Wood reported. He was greeted cordially by Reich, to whom he explained that he had come to find out whether the accumulator might be classified as a device according to FDA law. On being asked how he had heard of the accumulator, Wood mentioned the Brady article. "He said," Wood reported, "that the Brady article was 'rotten' and 'bitchy'." In spite of Reich's anger at the Brady article, however, he apparently was willing to believe that Wood's visit was made in good faith and without any preconceptions. He spoke openly to the inspector, explaining as much of his work as he could. He admitted that the accumulator was indeed a device, though in an experimental state, being used in the treatment of various diseases, including cancer. And he gave Wood pieces of literature that explained some of the theory behind the accumulator. Reich also explained to Wood the way and under what conditions accumulators were put at the disposal of patients and gave him a list of doctors who were associated with the Orgone Institute. "Most of the above information was given voluntarily," Wood's report concluded.

From Orgonon, Wood proceeded, after Reich made telephone arrangements, to the workshop in Oquossoc where the actual manufacturing of accumulators took place. This was to be a fateful visit—both for Wood personally and for the investigation as such. For at the workshop Wood met Clista Templeton, who some three months later was to become his wife and who, during the period of courtship, became Wood's—and through him, the FDA's—main confidential source of information about the orgone accumulator "business."

In 1942, in the early stages of Reich's experimentation with orgone accumulators, Miss Templeton's father, Herman Templeton, had contracted to build them as need arose, on a piece-work basis, in his small carpentry shop behind their home. After his death in 1944, his daughter took up his accumulator-building work and continued it until her withdrawal from all contact with Orgonon a couple months after her first meeting with Wood. That is, toward the end of 1947.

Ironically, it was through Herman Templeton that Reich first came to the idea of renting the accumulator to users as a means of making its effects easily available and, simultaneously, as a means of financing further research with orgone energy. This story is told in the concluding pages of *The Cancer Biopathy,* which first appeared in early 1948.

Reich had been concerned for some time about how to release the accumulator for general use and at the same time prevent it from becoming an object of exploitation and business profiteering. ("Orgone can be had like water or air and is present in infinite quantities. It is taken up by the body like air. All that is necessary to bring it to the consumer is a mechanism for *concentrating* it; this is what the accumulator does. Arrangements must be made so that even the poorest people can avail themselves of the concentrated orgone." [1]) But he also had to consider the future of orgone research—especially since it was most unlikely that any social institution would offer economic support for this research. ("I am still impressed by the fact that Madame Curie did not have sufficient money to buy radium for her researches . . . while at the same time the profiteers were making millions from radium." [2])

It was while puzzling over this problem that he heard that Templeton, who was close to seventy at the time, had cancer of the prostate, and that as of November 1941 was given six months, at the very most a year, to live. The old man apparently was one of that now all but vanished breed of American woodsmen who had never really come to terms with the ways of civilization—stubborn, inner-directed, strong-willed, and with an abiding suspicion of conventional knowledge. He was, in other words, the kind of man with whom, despite the vast gap in educational background, Reich felt an affinity. ("When I asked him one day whether he believed in God, he said: 'Of course, he is everywhere, in me and all around us. Just look over there,' and he pointed across the lake to the blue against the distant mountains. 'I call it *life,* but people would laugh at me, so I don't like to talk about it!" [3]) After explaining

1. *Cancer Biopathy,* p. 359.
2. *Ibid.,* p. 360.
3. *Ibid.,* p. 362.

the discovery of orgone energy to him Reich succeeded in persuading Templeton to build an accumulator for his own use. His pains left him and he gained seven pounds in the first two months of treatment. This, however, was not a cure. Templeton finally died in February of 1944—that is, some twenty-five months beyond the absolute maximum of one year of life that had been his official prognosis. During that period he was up and around much of the time and felt "rejuvenated."

Templeton was the first patient to have an accumulator in his own home—until that time patients would have to come to Orgonon or to Reich's residence and laboratory in Forest Hills, New York, to use one—and Reich was impressed by how much difference this easy availability made. It eliminated long trips and permitted the patient to experiment and tailor the use of the accumulator to his own needs. And it was from this experience—with Clista Templeton taking over the construction of accumulators in her late father's workshop—that Reich arrived at the arrangement of accumulator rentals that Inspector Wood came to investigate in 1947. By this time the Orgone Institute Research Laboratories had been established as a nonprofit organization, and the Orgone Research Fund, which handled the building, rental, and, later, sales of accumulators, was administered within the framework of this organization.

Inspector Wood learned from Clista that to that date some 170 of the large accumulators had been built—that is, the ones large enough for a person to sit in; and some 80 of the small ones—the "shooter" type, a cubic cabinet of about 10 inches on a side, with a hole into which a flexible metal tube is inserted so that its opposite end could be used for local application. Moreover, a number of names of users were voluntarily supplied by Miss Templeton. And finally, in his report, Wood enclosed exhibits of various kinds of printed literature related to the accumulator rental arrangement. One was an affidavit, which each patient had to sign and have notarized before obtaining an accumulator, stating that the accumulator was being rented on a purely experimental basis and that no cures were promised. A further provision of the affidavit was that if a patient were using it for nonprophylactic purposes—*i.e.,* in connection with a specific disease condition—he should do so under a physician's care. Another of the documents was a direction sheet entitled "How to Use the Orgone Accumulator," which came with each rented accumulator. This reiterated that no cures were promised and stated further:

Orgone is natural biological energy capable of charging living tissues and the blood, thus strengthening the resistance to disease. . . . But not all of its properties have been revealed as yet. Therefore, any observations you may make will help others. Inform the Orgone Institute about any change in your condition you may observe. . . . No mystical influence should be expected. Observe thoroughly and honestly, and form your own opinions. No profit interest is behind the distribution of the Orgone Accumulators. The chief aim is to define in the course of 2 to 4 years how many people who use the Accumulator regularly will still develop chronic colds, severe sinus trouble, pneumonia and diseases of the life system. . . .

Three days after Wood's lengthy report was sent to Wharton's office, a two page reply was returned to the Boston Station out of which Wood worked. "From our review of this material," Wharton concluded his reply, "it appears that we have here a fraud of the first magnitude being perpetrated by a very able individual fortified to a considerable degree by men of science. In order to invoke appropriate regulatory action, we must lay our foundation well and secure in the beginning considerable data and information." And this was followed by a numbered list of very explicit kinds of information Wood was to obtain on a return visit to Miss Templeton: names and addresses of all consignees—including those of people who had returned their accumulators; the names and addresses of physicians who prescribed the accumulators; literature and "promotional material" that Reich may have withheld from Wood but that Miss Templeton might have; and, above all, letters from "dissatisfied users" that may have been included in the return shipments. The term "dissatisfied users" recurs like a *leitmotiv* throughout the FDA material dealing with the investigation.

In addition to these instructions to the Boston Station, Wharton wrote to the Washington office of the FDA to obtain the FBI file on Reich in order to ascertain "the real facts" about Reich's previous career. Wharton knew that Reich had been taken by the FBI on December 12, 1941—that is, several days after Pearl Harbor—and held on Ellis Island until January 5, 1942. "The charge was, I believe, that he was an enemy alien," Wharton wrote, omitting to mention that Reich had been given complete clearance by the FBI and not been bothered again thereafter.

Wood made several more visits to Rangeley in order to obtain the information Wharton had requested. Clista, who was the main source of this information, was concerned about the use it would be put to, and worried that Reich might learn of her undercover cooperation, even though "she had come to question the whole Reich-Orgone setup and decided to discontinue this work. . . ." She informed Wood that she had built some thirty mouse cages for Reich in the spring of 1946 and that Reich had obtained cancerous mice for experimental purposes. Though Reich never discussed his experiments with her, she got the impression, Wood reported, that they were not going well. As an example of inaccurate information and misinterpretation that will characterize this and subsequent investigators, Wood wrote that Clista reported further that a "scientist" seen by Wood at Orgonon on his first visit there was "A. E. Neil [sic] from Sumner Hill School [sic] in . . . England" and that he was "allegedly associated with a children's school there." This, of course, was A. S. Neill, of Summerhill fame. In 1947 Neill made his first visit to the U.S. and spent much of his time with Reich at Orgonon. Needless to say, he was no scientist.

Clista supplied Wood with all the data she had about the mechanics of accumulator shipment, as well as with all the correspondence she had. None of it was as promising as Wharton had hoped it might be, though Wood included the names and addresses of all returnees in his report "for following up as possibly dissatisfied users." A woman in Berkeley, California, who had retained her accumulator only for the required minimum of three months, might "show ineffective use," he wrote hopefully.

The cost of accumulator rental was $10.00 a month, Miss Templeton reported. She neglected to mention that in cases of needy patients the amount was lowered, and in instances of dire need the accumulator was loaned out free of charge. But perhaps she did not know. (The financial record on the orgone accumulator—published in the January 1951 issue of *The Orgone Energy Bulletin*—shows that by 1950 there were 27 accumulators loaned out free and 20 at a reduced rate.) The cost to the Orgone Institute Laboratories was approximately $40 per accumulator—$20 for materials and $20 for Miss Templeton's labor. This means, wrote

Wood, that after the first four months of rental the income was all profit, and on the basis of the 170 accumulators built to that date an annual profit of some $20,000 could be made.

From Miss Templeton's place—where he was requested to park his government car in the garage lest it be seen by anyone from Orgonon who might be passing—Wood fanned out in several directions of investigation. Otis Bracket, postmaster of Rangeley, was contacted to keep a watch on Reich's incoming mail—that is, to note down the names and addresses of people sending mail to Orgonon. Besides this, Wood included in his report gossipy tidbits that, one gathers, were meant to substantiate Wharton's suspicion. Archie Carrigan, of the Railway Express Office, for instance, related that his daughter, several years earlier, had gone to Reich's residence to collect a bill and had been reprimanded by Mrs. Reich for not ringing the bell at the entrance to the ground; he also related that a Miss Shirley Goldenberg, who worked at the local hotel that summer, had been known to use an accumulator "in the nude"; and he referred to the Rolling Hill Farm children's school in the area—an institution started by a social worker who came to study with Reich in Maine and where Reich had sent his son, Peter —as "a children's nudist camp connected with Reich's operations."

During this investigation Wood learned that the lawyer who handled the legal details for Reich's various organizations was a Sumner Mills from Farmington, Maine. Peter Mills, the son, who at this time was working out of his father's office, was, two years later, to become the lawyer retained by Reich to handle the incorporation and subsequent legal matters of the newly formed Wilhelm Reich Foundation. Some four years after this, in 1953,—it was Wood who excitedly informed the FDA of this development— Mills was appointed U.S. Attorney for the state of Maine. As such he became, despite his previous representation of Reich's interests, one of the principals in the government's legal proceedings against Reich.

During this trip Wood revisited Reich at Orgonon to tell him that the orgone accumulator had been definitely classified as a device and that therefore complete information about it was required. (In his report he mentions, as if to further confirm Wharton's suspicion of quackery, that "the Dr. was dressed in blue dungarees and heavy wool shirt," and therefore "looked anything but professional.") During this interview an old man named Sylvester Brackett, one of Reich's charity patients, came to use the accumulator. He had been confined to bed with arthritis three years earlier, without ability to walk or use his hands, while now, Wood observed, he was able to move his fingers and walked "fairly well." "He was the real 'testimonial' type," Wood continued, "and Dr. Reich took great delight in bringing out Mr. Brackett's miraculous story of recovery by use of the accumulator."

The report of this visit is exhaustive—including not only an account of the second interview with Reich but a full description of the premises, as well as of a demonstration, by means of a Geiger-Mueller counter, of the concentration of orgone energy within an accumulator. In answer to questions about his teachings, Reich repeatedly referred Wood to his written works. When Wood broached the subject of Reich's expulsion from the International Psychoanalytic Association and the Norwegian newspaper campaign, Reich became angry and refused to discuss these matters.

In subsequent efforts to obtain "the real facts" about Reich and his work, Wood made trips to the local bank and to the Franklin County Registry of Deeds. From the information he gathered he concluded that "apparently all the spending is done by the five organizations [Orgone and Cancer Research Laboratory, Orgone Institute Laboratories, Orgone Institute, Orgone Research Fund and Orgone Institute Research Laboratories] and Wilhelm Reich cashes in on fees, rentals, contributions and everything else under the name of Orgone Institute."

In the meantime other FDA inspectors had begun interviewing orgone therapists and paying visits to the Orgone Institute Press in New York City. It was obvious in these interviews that the inspectors—accepting the Brady version of what orgonomy and the orgone accumulator were all about, and no doubt under the influence of Wharton's specific concern with the sexual aspect of orgonomy—were looking for a sexual racket of some kind. Dr. Simeon Tropp, for instance, who was interviewed by inspectors John T. Cain and Philip A. Jackman, reported that they were on the lookout for some kind of "sexy racket, mixed up with a strange box." [4] Tropp was questioned in particular about the women connected with orgonomy and what was done with them. Ms. Lois Wyvell, book-

4. Published in *Conspiracy,* item 19.

keeper of the Orgone Institute Press, was another person interviewed and subjected to the kinds of question that implied the
existence of a hidden vice ring. ("When Dr. Reich comes down
here, does he talk to you . . . about nothing but the weather?"
"You say you handle sex books?") [5] And though other interviewees
reported similar kinds of questions in letters to Reich, the FDA
reports, interestingly enough, make no references to them.

When word of this line of questioning got back to Reich, he was
not only disturbed but angry. If there was anything that could
arouse Reich to anger it was the implication that he, in his work
or writings on sexuality, advocated the kind of sexual activity these
inspectors were trying to find evidence of—that is, promiscuity,
pornography, "free love." In his writings—many of which the FDA
by this time had obtained—he repeatedly made it clear that the
genital sexuality orgone therapy sought to bring patients to had
nothing in common with the kind of sexuality the FDA suspected
him of advocating. Genital sexuality, on the contrary, he saw as
eminently moral—though not moralistic; it was selective, involved
deep feeling, responsibility, tenderness; it was, in fact, the direct
antithesis of what the FDA was expecting to find. Reich had encountered such misinterpretation before and regarded its recur-
rence as another symptom of the pandemic sexual sickness of a
society that could only interpret his message in the light of its own
distorted perceptions and fearful repressions. As part of this view
he took a strong position against pornography and deplored its
commercialization on the social sense as crass exploitation of
people's sexual misery. And now to be suspected of being part of
a sexual racket by a supposedly responsible agency of the American government—for which he had great, if not exaggerated, respect—was adding insult to injury.

Accordingly, on October 10, 1947, four days after he and his
family returned to their Forest Hills home from Maine, he wrote
a letter of complaint to his lawyer, Arthur Garfield Hays, saying
in part:

. . . our work is being confused with some pornographic . . . activities. It is too bad that inspectors in such a responsible position are not
capable of distinguishing between science and pornography, that they

5. Published in *Conspiracy,* item 33.

never heard the name of Sigmund Freud, and that they feel justified in asking hidden questions as, for instance, what kind of women we are employing or what we are doing with our women, etc. The implication is clearly that of indecent, smutty, pornographic behavior on our part. They should know with whom they are dealing. They seem to be disturbed by the insinuation in Miss Brady's article that the orgone accumulator gives the patient orgastic potency. I wished it did, but it does not. But to the average human mind, used to smutty sex activities going on everywhere, the word orgastic potency has a different meaning.[6]

And he ended the letter with a request that the lawyer submit a protest to the proper authorities.

No immediate action, however, seems to have been taken by the Hays law firm, and in the meantime Inspector Wood made several more visits to the Rangeley area in general and to Miss Templeton in particular, sending back reports loaded with an undifferentiated mass of minutiae and details. He visited Mrs. Elizabeth Hodgkins of the Rangeley Western Union Office who, saying "she had no use for the Reichs," gave him copies of fifteen telegrams Reich had recently sent out. When Wood later spoke to a Mr. Driscoll, manager of the Portland Western Union Office, he was told that copies of telegrams could only be given out by court order. "No mention was made of the outgoing message data already obtained from Mrs. Hodgkins," Wood writes—which, translated from officialese, means that Wood did not disclose the fact that he had in his possession telegrams that were illegally obtained. Wood spoke to an electrician who had done some wiring at the laboratory in Orgonon and who felt that "the accumulator device was a smoke screen for other research activities." On the basis of this remark, Wood then conjectured that this might be the "development of orgonotic power." In this latter conjecture he might well have been correct, though the suspicion that the orgone accumulators were a mere cover was ridiculous, since the motor power was, after all, "orgonotic" and since, too, Reich later sent notices of his work in developing motor power from orgone energy to a variety of governmental agencies. During one of these visits Wood had occasion to speak with Mr. Tom Ross, the caretaker at Orgonon. Ross later reported on this conversation as follows:

6. *Conspiracy,* item 20.

Mr. Wood . . . came in while I was working in my workshop, and told me spontaneously . . . that the accumulator was a fake . . . and that Dr. Reich was fooling the public with it. He said the case would break soon, and hinted that Dr. Reich would go to jail.[7]

We see in all of this not only the extent to which Wood himself had prejudged Reich's work but also the effort he was making to gather the kind of information that would support this prejudgment. He was unable to believe that Reich's work was exactly what it purported to be, with no secret skeleton hidden in any closets.

About a week after Wood's last visit to the Rangeley area, Wharton received a report of an investigation into the Reich files at the Immigration and Naturalization Service. Among all the details of Reich's personal life, his travels, his writings, the following appears in this report:

The file had many copies of letters . . . written by psychoanalysts and others in the field of psycology [sic] in Europe commenting on . . . various Reich publications. The trend of most of these comments was highly laudatory, some hailing Reich as the author of a new therapy that would revolutionize the world; others calling him a new Pasteur in the field of psychotherapy; all acclaimed his ability to describe his theories forcifully [sic], clearly and most interestedly [sic].

Yet this disclosure of some of the "real facts" Wharton was supposedly interested in obtaining apparently had no effect on his suspicions.

Reich, by the end of October having no reply from his October 10 letter to his lawyer, proceeded to outline a policy he and his co-workers would follow in the matter of the FDA investigation. No accumulator would be given to the FDA for testing unless such testing would be done with the cooperation of an orgonomist and unless the FDA made it clear what it was testing for; no dialogue could be carried on with FDA people who were not either doctors or scientists. "I would . . . rejoice . . . if the testing by the Administration would be made in a rational manner," he wrote. "[But] the one who in the name of the government will undertake the testing, will have to prove that he believes in our honesty." [8]

7. Published in *Conspiracy*, item 386A.
8. *Conspiracy*, item 22.

Apparently it was decided that a telephone call to the FDA would be preferable to the letter Reich had originally requested. Accordingly, Mr. Culver, of the Hays law firm, called Mr. Wharton on November 19, 1947.

"I told him," Wharton writes in a memorandum of the conversation, "that we had no preconceived notions concerning the value of the device for the purposes for which it was used. . . . I stated that we had not come to any conclusion because we do not yet have enough facts on which to base it." Mr. Culver was apparently favorably impressed by Wharton. "He was a typical government employee," he wrote to Reich, "very pleasant and willing to cooperate with us to some extent." He was also convinced that Wharton was acting in good faith. "They are not prejudging it and are willing to be shown that it will accomplish what is claimed for it." [9] However, Wharton insisted—when the matter of cooperative testing came up—that though "we would be perfectly willing to listen to Dr. Reich and to let him make any demonstration he cared to make with the device for its use . . . we could not and would not limit our investigation to any such procedure." When Culver mentioned Reich's feeling that there was no one in the FDA capable of making a fair appraisal without the presence of an orgonomist, Wharton replied that Reich could be assured that the FDA "felt itself capable of making a fair determination of the scientific aspects of the device." Wharton concluded his memorandum with: "I told Mr. Culver that I was very glad indeed that he had contacted us since I thought that he could be of advantage to his client in advising him of a course of action which would give us an opportunity to develop all the facts fairly. . . ." Culver's suggestion to Reich was that he allow the FDA to test the accumulator independently of him or a co-worker—since in any case the FDA could not be legally prevented from doing so—and then that Reich prepare a report to answer any findings with which he might disagree.

We come here to a central problem of orgone energy research which underlay Reich's reluctance to let the FDA test an accumulator on its own. By this time Reich had developed several experiments that he felt constituted objective proof of the presence and action in the accumulator of an energy unaccounted for in classi-

9. Published in *Conspiracy,* item 24.

cal physics; and he had no reservation about the efficacy of the accumulator in favorably affecting—not necessarily curing—certain kinds of what are commonly referred to as somatic illnesses. ("We are not afraid of tests. Our facts are firmly established. I was not afraid to let Einstein * test the orgone accumulator." [10]) His main concern was a circumstance he had already encountered in the past—namely, that the whole idea of a crudely constructed box collecting from the air a "mysterious," ubiquitously present energy seemed so ridiculous to anyone who had not worked with orgone energy that such a tester would tend, almost unconsciously, to ignore any results that did not fit in with his own conventional scientific assumptions.

From Reich's point of view, conventional science, despite its accomplishments and important discoveries, was structured in a way that precluded awareness of the existence of life energy and all its manifestations. "An organism which uses most of its energy for keeping living nature hidden from itself must of necessity be incapable of comprehending the living outside itself," he wrote in *Cancer Biopathy*. And, further:

[A] . . . requirement for one who works with orgone energy is that his organ sensations must be relatively unimpeded. The emotional structure of the researcher of necessity tinges his observations and his thinking; that is, the organ sensation is a tool in his work. This is true of myself as well as any other person who works with orgonotic natural functions. True, the experiment must confirm—or refute—the observations and work hypotheses; but the manner in which experi-

---

* Details of the 1942 meeting between Reich and Einstein are given in a pamphlet entitled *The Einstein Affair,* issued by the Orgone Institute Press. Einstein was at first very interested in and enthusiastic about Reich's demonstration and explanation and requested that Reich send him a small accumulator for testing. Einstein turned this over to an unnamed assistant who then reported that the temperature difference between the accumulator and the environment was due to convection current. Reich repeated the experiment by half-burying an accumulator and control and covering them with blankets. When he communicated the positive results of the experiment to Einstein, however, Einstein responded without any further interest. Several years later there was a newspaper account that one of Einstein's assistants, Leopold Infield, had decided to return to his native Poland. Reich assumed that this was the same assistant who had discredited his experiment to Einstein and saw this circumstance as part of the communist-inspired conspiracy to undermine his work.

10. *Conspiracy,* item 22.

ments are thought of and in which they are carried out depend on the perceptions of the researcher. . . . It would be erroneous to believe that experiments *alone* could yield new findings; it is again and again the living, perceiving and thinking organism which searches, experiments and draws conclusions.[11]

When Reich, for instance, sought in his work with bions to demonstrate biogenesis—that is, that life can, and in nature does, develop spontaneously from nonliving matter—challenging thereby one of the hallowed tenets of biology, the result of his experiment was explained away as "Brownian movement." This kind of movement is due to the impact of molecules upon larger colloidal particles in a solution. Though Reich recognized the existence of such movement, he contended that the movement appearing in his biogenetic experiment was different, that it consisted of rhythmic contractions and expansions, and was not of the angular, jerky kind of motion due to the collision of particles. He contended further that any movement due to such collision would have to be more or less constant, while the movement in his experiment was, on the contrary, irregular: sometimes present and sometimes not, and at other times present in only some of the particles and not in others.

Another objection to this same experiment was that the living, pulsating matter that he developed from sterilized, nonliving matter was really the result of "air infection." His reply to this, though it made little headway against the air-germ explanation, was that air infection requires many hours to develop, while the movement of the bions was visible immediately after the preparation was made. It was because of such experiences that Reich wrote: "Our science can be judged only from the standpoint of its own methods and techniques of thought and not from any other. This is a strict law in scientific intercourse, valid wherever scientific work is done. We expect and wish for criticism, but only *immanent* criticism." [12]

We shall see in a later chapter, when the tests eventually carried out by the FDA are examined, how valid or invalid Reich's reservations were. It may, however, be appropriate here to note what Paul Goodman had to say in this matter. "What is perceived," he wrote, "depends on the power and openness of the perceiving and

11. *Cancer Biopathy,* p. xv.
12. *Ibid.,* p. xix.

therefore the character of the perceiver. . . . There [seems] to be a limitation in principle to the objectivity of science as ordinarily understood—there is a sociology, psychology, and theology of science which is *not* irrelevant to what is discovered." [13]

At this time, however, there was also the more immediate suspicion occasioned by what Reich had already learned about the nature of the FDA investigation—that is, its attempt to find verification of the allegations of the Brady article rather than to ascertain the truth. And Reich continued to be suspicious, despite his lawyer's assurance. He felt that, failing to find the kind of evidence it was looking for, the FDA might move to get him on other grounds, for instance on an unwitting infraction of some law. He submitted all his financial records to tax authorities for inspection, to cover the possibility of being prosecuted on the basis of oversight in his tax payment. Though his records were found to be completely in order, the precaution was not unjustified since the FDA did in fact, at a later date, check with the tax authorities. But over and above this kind of danger, he felt that he was in danger of frame-up because of his open advocacy of adolescent sexuality and the right of infants and children to engage in pregenital sexual exploration and to play with their genitals—which is something quite different from Wharton's conviction that children were taught to masturbate. Moreover, he regarded the method of therapy practiced by him and medical co-workers—which required that the patient be undressed and involved a certain amount of laying on of hands to effect a release of biological energy from spastic muscles and organs—was particularly open to attack by the "emotional pest."

Reich also felt that communist forces were at work behind the investigation. At this point his suspicion was not as extreme as it was to become later but was based simply on the fact that the *New Republic* had a leftist orientation and had smeared the English translation of his *Mass Psychology* in a way that recalled the communist party denunciation of this book in Germany. Brady's article in this magazine he saw as an extension of the same leftist hostility to his work. Then, learning from inquiries made by friends that Brady's husband had been a fellow traveler and that she herself had been known to be even more pro-communist than her hus-

13. Published in Ollendorff, p. xiii.

band,* he wrote at this time that "The American State . . . which the Communists design to destroy and replace by their totalitarian regime, followed the lead given by the snipers." [14] In later years his view of the extent to which communist influence was involved in his trouble with the FDA was to become more extreme. At one point he even had a suspicion that a premeditated, Moscow-directed plot was behind the prosecutory actions of the FDA.

In any case, the upshot of his complete distrust of the FDA was that he refused to make an accumulator available for independent testing. At the same time, however, a notice was sent out from the Orgone Research Laboratories to accumulator users advising them to cooperate fully with any FDA agents that might come to question them—but only to the extent that such questioning did not relate to the users' sexual or personal life.[15]

In the meantime, Wharton, in a follow-up letter to Culver, repeated his request for an accumulator and added two other rerequests. One of these was that Reich divulge the names and addresses of cancer patients he had treated with the orgone accumulator. Culver replied, again, that he could recommend to Reich that an accumulator be loaned, but that divulging patients' names

---

* A Mr. Karl Frank wrote to Reich on December 15, 1947: "During my travels in California in early 1936, I made the acquaintance of the [Brady] family. . . . Professor Brady . . . gave me the impression of a well-meaning American liberal, impressed by somewhat 'leftist' doctrine . . . Mildred did not leave any doubt in her conversation that her communist sympathies were stronger than her husband's." (published in *Conspiracy*, item 50) In a letter, dated September 24, 1952, a co-worker of Reich's, wrote to another co-worker that in a conversation with Dwight Macdonald in May of 1949, he had been told that Brady's "husband was definitely a communist (in the sense of being a member or a close follower of the communist party) and that Brady herself was a fellow traveler and perhaps an actual party member." (published in *Conspiracy*, item 380) However in response to an inquiry made to Dwight Macdonald, this author, on December 31, 1972, received the following reply: "May have [said] . . . that the Brady's were definitely Stalinists but doubt if I said Communist and sure I never said anybody was a 'card-carrying Communist,' *i.e.*, a member of the CP, my crowd wasn't on speaking terms with CPers and except for Browder, Jack Stachel, V. J. Jerome, etc. I myself never knew a genuine party member. 'Stalinist' . . . meant anything from a party-member to a fellow traveller—'Communist' then to me wd. have meant CP members so never used it except re. Russians."

14. *Conspiracy*, item 45.
15. *Ibid.*, item 32.

was against the law. In the same letter he repeated Reich's objection to the insinuations inherent in the questions of FDA inspectors. Wharton promptly, and hypocritically, wrote back:

To correct what appears to be a misapprehension on the part of your client, permit me to say that none of our investigators has intimated in any way, at any time, to any person that the Food and Drug Administration has the opinion that the Accumulator is a "pornographic device of no value except for immoral purposes."

As regards Culver's statement that divulging the names of patients was illegal, Wharton felt that since reference had been made to the treatment of these patients for "promotional purposes" and in connection with a device shipped in interstate commerce, the principle of privileged information no longer applied and the matter of revealing the identity of patients fell into a different category from that of a practicing physician and his private practice. Culver's reply was that since the privilege originally belonged to the patient it could not be waived by any act on the part of the doctor.

The other request Wharton made was that the Orgone Institute Press be opened for an additional inspection. There had already been one inspection of the Press on Ocotber 7, 1947, when two inspectors spent some four or five hours questioning Miss Lois Wyvell who, as bookkeeper, ran the office of the Press. When they returned on November 6, Miss Wyvell refused to let them make another inspection and, following orders from Reich, referred them to Culver. The reason for the refusal was that Reich felt that since it was the orgone accumulator that was presumably under investigation there was no reason for the Press Office to be inspected; especially since the books issued by the Press were already on the open market and their purpose was scientific and not part of a "promotional scheme" related to the rental of accumulators, as Wharton had maintained.

The issue of "promotional literature" illustrates the gulf between Reich's position and that of the FDA. From his point of view as a natural scientist, Reich was completely justified in regarding his publications as scientific. At the same time, however, the FDA had the right, given the law within which it worked, to consider the possibility that Reich's writings might be part of a promotional scheme.

In other words, the fact that a publication is scientific in content does not preclude its being used for promotional purposes. Neither, from the standpoint of FDA law, is this possibility precluded by the fact that a device is distributed by one organization, while the publications are distributed by another, if the two are in some way related.

Dr. Theodore P. Wolfe—a close co-worker of Reich's, the translator of many of his works into English, and the director of the Orgone Institute Press—stated in a letter to Culver: "The Orgone Institute Press . . . has nothing to do with the orgone accumulator or its shipping, no more than the publisher of a book on child care has to do with the practice of pediatrics." [16] However, this analogy is not valid from the standpoint of FDA law, since there were connections between the Orgone Institute Press and the Orgone Research Laboratories which handled the distribution of accumulators—connections in the sense that some of the people working in the two organizations had professional contacts with each other and that both organizations had direct contact with Reich and were working in the framework of his leadership. The case of a publisher who had no connection whatever with a school of pediatric care that specializes in the method espoused by a book he issues falls, therefore, into a different category.

However, the terms "promotional scheme" and "promotional literature" have commercial and exploitive connotations that Reich justifiably objected to. Any unbiased reading of his works—quite aside from one's agreement or disagreement with his ideas—would make it clear that his intent was simply to explain his theories and record his experiments and observations. As Reich himself wrote at this time:

All I did was reporting [sic] results, positive as well as negative. The orgone accumulator may help in one case of shrinking biopathy and not in another. It did, for example, make an old farmer suffering from arthritis able to walk again; in other cases of arthritis it failed to help. . . . Did I use these "results" for "promotional purposes" when I reported so and so many cases as having died? If I had wanted to use my findings for "promotional purposes" would I have stopped working on cancer cases . . . and turned to theoretical problems of orgon-

16. Published in *Conspiracy,* item 52.

ometry? Was it "promotional" when I did not receive a penny for my efforts but, on the contrary, had to devote most of my time to the work without any compensation? [17]

And in *The Cancer Biopathy* there are many examples of the scrupulous way in which Reich recorded failures as well as successes. "I shall emphasize the . . . failures," he wrote in introducing his case histories. "It is most important for us to prevent the impression that we possess a cure all. . . . If one is to develop the beneficial effects of the orgone, an understanding of the failures is indispensable." [18]

And yet, however justified Reich's objection is, the FDA law does not consider it necessary to prove intent to defraud, only that fraud exists—from which it follows that promotional intent is irrelevant. Whether or not it existed in the relationship of Reich's writings to the rental of accumulators is an issue best deferred to a later chapter when the matter of the injunction eventually obtained against Reich is discussed. The point made here is the almost complete absence of common ground between Reich and the FDA at this early stage of the conflict, for this condition not only persisted in later stages but became even more pronounced.

No doubt one of the reasons Wharton wanted to have the Orgone Institute Press inspected further was to find legal ground for his conviction that its publications were indeed promotional. Another reason, it can be safely assumed, was his belief that it secretly issued pornographic literature. But permission for this inspection was not given and on December 16, 1947, Culver and Wharton met face to face at the latter's office.

Wharton, again hyprocritically, protested that no prejudgment had been made in the case, that the FDA was competent to test the accumulator and that no investigator had ever intimated that there was a sexual racket involved. "He produced," writes Wharton in a memo of this interview, "an affidavit signed by Miss Lois Wynell [Wyvell] . . . and after reading the first two paragraphs . . . I told Mr. Culver that I was not interested in [the] charges [of suspicion of a sexual racket]. . . . I told Mr. Culver that we are not dealing with personalities and that his client should realize that this is a Government investigation." In the matter of the names

17. *Conspiracy,* item 46.
18. *Cancer Biopathy,* p. 270.

and addresses of patients Reich had referred to in his writings, Wharton repeated that they were entitled to obtain this information. However, as regards the loan of an orgone accumulator he said that since there was no patent involved he would have one built for FDA testing. "Mr. Wharton didn't seem to think much of my claim that everything was on an experimental basis," Culver wrote. "He pointed out that . . . all persons seeking to defraud tthe public would simply distribute their drugs or devices on an experimental basis and escape the provision of the law." [19]

In the legalistic sense Wharton was correct in this view. Just because the accumulator was distributed on an experimental basis did not mean that no claims at all were made for it—as Reich mistakenly maintained and was to repeat again and again in the following years. Though the Instruction Sheet accompanying the accumulator states, as we have seen, that "we do not promise any cures," in the same paragraph it states that orgone energy is "capable of charging living tissue and the blood, thus strengthening the resistance to disease." Thus a claim *is* made as to the accumulator's efficacy in the "diagnosis, cure, mitigation, treatment or prevention of disease in man or other animals" (to use the language of the law).

What Reich was reacting to in maintaining that no claim was made were the Brady distortions. The FDA accepted these distortions and they formed the basis for a rash of subsequent smear articles—namely, that the accumulator "could lick anything from cancer to the common cold" (to use a phrase from one of these articles). This kind of claim, needless to say, Reich never made. Certainly he never claimed to have discovered a cure for cancer, though at the same time he did write: "Based on the observations to date, I consider the cell illumination which the orgone accumulator bring about the real and essential therapeutic factor. This cell illumination has . . . [a] destructive effect on cancer cells . . . " [20] So that, again, to the extent that a representation was made that the accumulator was capable of having such an effect, the legalistic assumption of a claim being made was correct.

However, it is a far cry from this claim to the alleged claim of having discovered a cure for cancer. For though Reich believed

19. Published in *Conspiracy,* item 55.
20. *Cancer Biopathy,* p. 270.

the orgone accumulator had a destructive effect on cancer cells, he made it clear that this did not constitute a cure. One of the problems that he saw as following from the cancer cell destruction was that the body had difficulty in getting rid of the dead cell tissue. Besides this, Reich regarded the tumor as the result of a disease process that had been developing in the organism for a long time prior to its actual appearance; therefore merely dissolving a tumor was not necessarily a cure; nor was it any guarantee that another tumor might not appear at a later date.

Whether the observations, results, and conclusions he recorded in his writings on the accumulator are valid or not is beside the point, for a scientist has a right to make bona fide errors in the course of experimental work. As has been earlier noted, Reich was meticulous in recording negative as well as positive results. In the light of these considerations, he was at times moved to overstate his case, writing for instance: "A mechanical, and therefore empty, application of . . . the Food, Drug and Cosmetic Act to the orgone accumulator is, practically speaking, utter nonsense. Human diseases cannot be handled by laws, but only by appropriate knowledge." [21] At the same time, in a broad sense, he was quite aware of the legitimate complexities that the FDA law posed for his work and his answer to this was that new discoveries required the enactment of new laws; and citing the laws passed for the administration of atomic energy, he called for the passing of similarly appropriate laws for the administration of orgone energy.

In December 1947, in response to an anti-Reich article appearing in *Colliers* in which some of the Brady distortions were repeated, the Orgone Institute decided to do something it had never done before: it prepared a news release explaining its work and correcting some of the slanderous allegations in the *Colliers* article. This news release was sent out to some twenty-five prominent magazines and newspapers throughout the country. None of them, however, saw fit to print it or even any excerpt from it. In other words, any publication could at will print anything critical of Reich and his work but none would give him or his co-workers an opportunity to answer these criticisms. Reich commented bitterly on the unfairness of this circumstance. It was open season on him, and orgonomy had been declared fair game.

21. *Conspiracy,* item 46.

No doubt this unfairness had something to do with the letter Reich wrote on December 20, 1947, informing his lawyer that he was no longer willing to waste time on the whole issue and was therefore transferring "all rights to the medical use of the accumulator" to the corporation and that the matter of the FDA investigation would subsequently be handled by the Orgone Institute Research Laboratories, under the directorship of Drs. Willie and Tropp and Ilse Ollendorff. "I have done my part in discovering Orgone energy, in elaborating some of its qualities and in constructing a device to accumulate it which, to my experience, has shown great possibilities in being useful as a medical device," he wrote in this letter.[22] This decision expressed as well his exasperation with the whole FDA issue and his impatience to get on with his work, from which this issue was diverting him.

From what has been said previously about Reich's work, it should be apparent that he was always addressing himself to root problems of human existence. Most of his writings are charged with a feeling of urgency: something was deeply wrong with the human race in its historical, social, and individual existence, and he wanted to rectify this condition. Originally, as we have seen, he felt that radical political action combined with sex-economic knowledge would rectify matters. Then, from his disaffection with politics, he moved into the realm of life functions within the organism to whose mastery he transferred the Marxist-conditioned hope of relieving humanity's illness. With the development of his work into the investigation of atmospheric orgone energy functions, this hope grew to include the mastery of the total human environment; that is, not only the establishment of a society rationally ordered to fulfill basic instinctual needs of the human animal but a new kind of relationship between man and his natural environment. This mastery was then to open the way to a new stage in the evolution of the human species. It was against the background of this persistent, though evolving, millenial hope that Reich experienced the FDA trouble as a nuisance, diverting time, energy, and attention from "life-important work"—a term he came to use more and more often as this trouble continued.

Six days after the letter announcing his withdrawal from the issue of the investigation, Reich wrote another letter to his lawyer

22. *Ibid.,* item 61.

stating that he would be willing to cooperate with the FDA if "a rational and honest approach to the problem of orgone research be made by any public or private institution, without hidden pestilential motivation. . . ." [23] But in such cooperation his recent discovery that the Geiger-Mueller counter was affected by orgone energy "would have to be established under strict legal conditions and protocols." [24]

Several weeks later it came to Reich's attention that FDA inspectors continued questioning patients and that the questions, again, had little to do with the accumulator and much more with the personal affairs of the patients as well as their relations to their therapists—how much they paid, how they had heard of orgone therapy, why they went into it, etc. Reich, feeling that his offer of cooperation with the FDA had not been accepted in good faith, reacted with predictable anger. On February 2, 1948, a second notice was sent to all accumulator users informing them that there would be no further cooperation of any kind with the FDA and that if inspectors came to question them they should refuse to answer and refer the inspectors to the law office of Mr. Garfield Hayes. And a few days later a letter was sent to Wharton, advising him of this decision and the reason for it. The effort Reich had initiated some time earlier to get a legal injunction against the FDA investigation had apparently not borne fruit—and, in fact, the preliminary investigation eventually came to an end by itself, without the injunction having been obtained.

During these months the interview operations of the FDA ranged far and wide, keeping inspectors busy not only in Maine and New York, but in New Jersey and Pennsylvania as well, and even in Oregon and California. Often as one reads accounts of these interviews—both those given by the agents and by the interviewees—one gains the impression that the matter had become so confusing for the agents that they themselves had lost touch with what it was they were supposed to be looking for. For instance, when Inspector Wood interviewed a mathematician working at Orgonon and living nearby, he asked the man where he kept his accumulator. On being told he had none, Wood said, "Oh, since you're not married you don't need one, do you?" [25] In Santa

23. *Ibid.*, item 64.
24. *Ibid.*, item 64.
25. Published in *Conspiracy,* item 57.

Monica, California, an Inspector Kinney asked the interviewee which members of his family used the accumulator and how old they all were. Others were asked where they were born, raised, if they paid the express charges on receiving the accumulator, why they went into therapy, when they had married. It is again and again obvious that these agents were absolutely convinced that something illicit and underhanded was going on but somehow they were missing it and did not know how or where to search for it.

Up to this point there had been only a few interviews with professional people not connected with orgonomy and not using the orgone accumulator. For instance, in the early part of this investigation, Inspector Jackman interviewed a Dr. H. M. Lehrer, who was very willing to cooperate with the FDA "because his medical partner, Simeon J. Tropp, M.D., had come under the influence of Reich to such an extent that he appeared to be in an hypnotic state." It was, apparently, through his connection with Dr. Tropp that Dr. Lehrer had learned of the accumulator. He told Jackman that sensations of warmth and the redness coming over the skin of the face and neck region had been explained to him by a physicist friend as a reaction to the shiny surface of the interior metal and the insulated exterior. The latter caused an accumulation of the body's own heat and the former caused this heat to be reflected.

But at the beginning of 1948, what with the continual failures of the FDA to find any substantiation for its conviction that Reich was involved in a fraud or racket, the investigation began to include more interviews with non-Reichian professional people. In December 1947 Wharton was informed that a Dr. Henry A. Cotton, Deputy Commissioner for Mental Hygiene and Hospitals for the state of New Jersey, had offered to testify for the FDA if necessary. Accordingly, on Janaury 14, 1948, Jackman and a colleague were dispatched to New Jersey to interview Dr. Cotton.

The inspectors found out from Dr. Cotton that there was a veritable hotbed of Reichians at the Marlboro State Hospital. Two of the resident psychiatrists—Dr. Albert L. Duvall and Dr. Elsworth F. Baker—it turned out were among the most important practicing medical orgonomists at the time. (Dr. Baker, who was at this time Senior Resident Physician in Charge of Womens Service at the hospital, was later, after the injunction against Reich was issued, to head the intervention proceedings attempted by fifteen medical orgonomists.) But besides this revelation the inspectors learned that accumulators had actually been found in the living quarters of three of the nonmedical resident professionals at the hospital— one a social worker, one the director of Social Services, and one a chaplain! It must have seemed to them like evidence of a spreading plague.

Dr. Cotton showed the inspectors a letter he had written more than a month earlier to Dr. J. Berkeley Gordon, who was Chief Executive Officer of the State Hospital for Mental Diseases in Marlboro. In this letter—marked "STRICTLY PERSONAL AND CONFIDENTIAL"—Dr. Cotton stated that he had heard about the FDA's interest in Reich though a Dr. Butz of the FDA, and he had encouraged Butz "to go ahead with his case as rapidly as possible." Further on in this letter Cotton explained that Dr. Duvall was being dismissed "because of his strong adherence to Reich's ideas and practices," but that he still did not know what to do about Dr. Baker. Though Dr. Baker had given assurance that he would "keep his unconventional psychiatric ideas completely out of his practice with the State patients," Dr. Cotton was still unsatisfied and suspicious, though there was little that could be done at that point other than to "keep a close eye on his future activities."

But the main purpose of this letter was that "this [i.e., the information that the FDA was investigating Reich] confirms all our own ideas about Reich and gives us further justification, if any were needed, in our attitude that he is a medical quack and not a qualified psychiatrist. There is no question but what we were perfectly justified in our attitude toward Duvall." In other words, the mere fact that the FDA was conducting such an investigation was enough to confirm in Cotton's mind his worst suspicions about Reich—even though, to that date, no tests or studies had been made and Wharton was at the same time giving Culver assurances that the investigation was fair and no prejudgment had been made. We also learn later in the inspectors' report that "although he [Cotton] has not delved deeply into Reich's theories," it was Cotton's opinion that Reich's work "smacks of charlatanism of the worst form." And adding to this a statement Cotton had made in the above-mentioned letter that "it is illegal to send aparatus of this type from one state to another,"—a statement so erroneous that even the inspectors found it necessary to correct him on it— what emerges from both the letter and the interview is that Cotton, the psychiatrist, and therefore one who would be expected to know better, was engaging in nothing more than rationalization. Perhaps such obvious rationalization was symptomatic of deeper trouble Cotton was experiencing, for several months later he committed suicide.

But this is not yet all. The FDA was presumably investigating Reich on the basis of the interstate shipment of orgone accumulators. Cotton, as a representative of the psychiatric profession, was condemning Reich primarily on the basis of the unorthodox technique of biopsychiatric therapy Reich had developed—to which the accumulator was not necessary and which was, therefore, outside the proper concern of the FDA. And yet, just as the knowledge of the FDA investigation constituted for Cotton justification of his attitude toward orgone therapy, so too, Cotton's condemnation—however uniformed it was—constituted for the FDA important confirmation of its suspicion. Thus this meeting, this interview could with little exaggeration be characterized as a case of the blind leading the blind. And, as we shall see, the psychiatric profession, through other representatives, continued over the next nine years not only to aid but in fact to encourage and exhort the FDA in its investigation and prosecution; while the FDA, with such encouragement and exhortation, could scarcely doubt that it was performing an important social service in disrupting Reich's work. The specific matter of the interstate shipment of orgone accumulators, it becomes increasingly obvious, was nothing more than a convenient legal means by which this disruption could be effected.

In the meantime the FDA had obtained several accumulators, built according to specifications supplied by Wood, though it appears that nothing was done with them during this preliminary part of the investigation. The issue of obtaining names and addresses of cancer patients upon whose treatment Reich had partially based his theories and observations dissolved when Wharton learned indirectly that most of these patients—who had been terminal cases to begin with—had in the meantime died. (It had been almost four years since Reich had stopped working with cancer patients. Indeed, at the time of this investigation, only 2 of the 170 accumulators built were being used by cancer patients, both of whom were under the care of doctors other than Reich.) The matter of a second inspection of the Orgone Institute Press also seems to have been abandoned. The whole preliminary investigation, in other words, had run its course—the end of which, no doubt, was influenced by the fact that Wharton was anticipating his retirement from the FDA on April 30, 1948.

A request from Wharton, made on March 16, that the Washington office have Reich's activities in Norway investigated by the State Department was eventually turned down by FDA Commissioner Dunbar since "information developed in this manner is likely to be of little or no evidential value except possibly as a basis for cross-examination"—a statement which indicates that even at the top levels, the FDA was thinking in terms of a court case at this early date, that is, before any legal violation or evidence of quackery had been found. Indeed, the facts seem to be quite the opposite—that is, of positive evidence found relative to the accumulator's efficacy: in a summary report Wharton ordered before his retirement and which was finally written in May 18, it is stated that "no dissatisfied users were located and all persons interviewed were extremely satisfied with the results which they attributed to the device. . . ."

This report is important and merits further discussion, especially as regards the matter of "accompanying literature"—that is, the problem of Reich's writings being part of a promotional scheme. "The literature relative to the accumulator," it states, "might lack the necessary prerequisite to be classed as 'accompanying literature.' Often times the receipt of the books, which were the motivation for the rental of the accumulator, occurred many months and sometimes a year or two prior to such rental." This, the report continues several pages later, "is a question that must be carefully considered. . . . Does the length of time between the receipt of the books and the order placed for an accumulator have any bearing. . . ?"

From this, the report moves on to a recommendation that "after determination that the 'labeling' is violative (if it is) the claims made therein should be referred to the Medical Division for their appraisal. It would seem that sufficient preliminary investigation has been done on this case to warrant an evaluation and appraisal, with a view to determining future action." And then, almost as a gratuitous postscript or an afterthought, the report ends with the statement that the post office "might be interested in the distribution via mail of Reich's book *The Sexual Revolution* on the ground of obscene literature (see pages 81–100 inclusive and pages 235–245 inclusive, dealing with adult and infantile masturbation)."

This report was sent to Washington headquarters with the recommendation that the matter be reviewed to decide if there were a violation of FDA law. If there were, the recommendation continued, then it should also be decided whether to proceed by way of prosecution or injunction. In either case, the report concluded, it should also be determined what preparations or testing would be necessary to insure the success of the action.

Though Reich's efforts to obtain an injunction against the investigation were not successful, he assumed that these efforts together with his decision of noncooperation had finally impressed the FDA if not with the fact that there was no fraud or quackery at least that it was useless to continue. In this mistaken assumption, he exhibited the optimism that is one of the outstanding aspects of his view of the human condition, yet which, in the context of the later legal trouble, repeatedly led him to misinterpret the drift and significance of developments and, indeed, played a part in their tragic issue.

No doubt this misplaced sense of triumph heightened the enthusiasm that marked the preparation for and the actual activities of the First International Orgonomic Convention held at Orgonon that summer. Mottoes that Reich prepared for this convention were "It Can Be done" and "Work, Not Politics."

One purpose of this convention was to enable Reich to bring his co-workers and supporters up to date on the work he had been doing. This consisted of the already mentioned Geiger-counter reaction he had found in orgone energy and the orgone energy motor he had developed. Besides this he had succeeded in illuminating a vacuum tube by means of orgone energy. On a theoretical level Reich had begun to develop his thinking on "orgonomic functionalism," which was later to be elaborated into *Ether, God and Devil,* published in the following year. *Listen, Little Man*—an angry book originally written by Reich in the early 1940s primarily to let off steam about the troubles he had undergone in Europe—had had accompanying cartoons made for it by William Steig and was in the press during the summer of 1948. The first volume of *The Discovery of the Orgone*—that is, *The Function of the Orgasm*—had been published in 1942; but the second volume, *The Cancer Biopathy,* was also in the press during this summer. English translations of an enlarged *Character Analysis* and *Mass Psychology of Fascism* had come out several years earlier. At Orgonon itself a large student laboratory had been completed—it was to be the site of the work, the lectures and seminars of the convention—and work had begun on what was called the "observatory," though it was also to become, in 1950, the Maine home for Reich and his family. All in all the time seemed ripe for an international convention to consolidate, to review, to inform, to clarify; and where more appropriately than at the 280-acre site Reich hoped eventually would house an ogonomic hospital, clinic, and experimental laboratories?

Though most of Reich's co-workers at this time were Americans, there were some from other countries as well. Neill came from England, Dr. Raknes from Norway, a Dr. Ferrari from Argentina. Dr. Walter Hoppe of Israel was, on his arrival at the airport, inexplicably detained by immigration officials. "Reich was unbelievably, frighteningly furious about this persecution of his work," writes Ilse Ollendorff.[26] After three days Dr. Hoppe was released, and on the last lap of his trip to Orgonon took a seaplane from Portland, Maine and landed on the small lake at Orgonon called Dodge Pond. The Makavejev film, *WR—The Mysteries of the Organism,* shows Dr. Hoppe emerging from the seaplane and being greeted at the small dock by Reich and many of the convention members. Brief and cinematically amateurish as this documentary sequence is, it manages, strangely enough, to convey a sense of the enthusiasm that characterized the whole convention.

Thirty-five people—scientists, doctors, teachers, students, laboratory workers—participated, including Eva Reich, who was a medical student at this time. Many of these gave reports on their own work in various aspects of orgonomy. Reich, of course, was the most important participant. He lectured on orgonomic functionalism, demonstrated some of his most recent work with orgone energy (including the operation of the orgone energy motor), showed films taken of crucial experiments, announced that the

26. Ollendorff, p. 87.

name of the therapy practiced by him and doctors trained by him ought to be changed from vegeto-therapy to orgone therapy. He spoke as well about the emotional plague, emphasizing that this term was neither a metaphor nor derogatorily intended, but was simply a diagnosis of neurotic action that, because of the general sickness of man, manages to exert noxious, life-negating influence on the social scene. In this connection he also spoke on a theme that was to become increasingly important in his subsequent thinking: safeguarding newborn infants from the emotional plague and the armoring this plague produces. It was in line with this thinking that Reich coined the term "Children of the Future"—that is, a projected generation of children who would not be afflicted with armoring. Significantly *The Murder of Christ,* which was to come out several years later, was dedicated to these Children of the Future.

One can assume that the birth of Reich's son some five years earlier had an influence on his thinking in this matter. His two earlier children had been born before he had discovered character and muscular armor or, for that matter, before his formulations concerning life processes and the development of his concept of self-regulation; and they were raised at a time when Reich was committed to radical political action as a means of improving the human condition. Peter, however, was born when Reich was still searching for an alternative solution to the problem of armor-prevention, and no doubt the observations he had an opportunity to make during Peter's infancy crystallized for Reich the theoretical solution he came to—*i.e.,* prevention of armoring in the new born. He wrote to Neil around this time that observing the development of his infant son made him feel like a tyro in psychology despite his twenty-five years in psychiatric work. Aside from the influence of Peter's birth on Reich's professional work, the child was a source of great pleasure to Reich during these years. Later, in the harassed and desperate last years of Reich's life, he would begin to lay inordinately heavy burdens of responsibility on his young son.

The author spoke with FDA officials about the preliminary investigation and the fact that it was conducted not to discover the truth but, rather, proceeded on an *a priori* assumption of guilt. One high official in the Office of Compliance, who had not been personally involved but was acquainted with the case, said: "We're cops and that's part of the cop psychology. When an inspector is told to investigate some operation, he automatically proceeds on the basis of there being something illegal involved that's he's got to find out about." This explanation is perhaps understandable, though not acceptable, on the level of the FDA field workers. It is understandable how the whole orgone energy movement, taken *in toto*—with its seemingly outlandish ramifications into such variegated fields as psychiatry, cancer work, physics, and biology and its general emphasis on sexuality—would very easily appear to inspectors with a "cop psychology" as quackery and fraud.

But then what about the automatic assumption of guilt on the part of the higher-placed officials of the FDA? The "cop-psychology" explanation does not—or at least, should not—apply to them. Here, however, there are other "explanations." In the case of Wharton it could well be psychological: his personal disturbances over the sexual aspects of Reich's work.

A former high-ranking FDA official with whom this author spoke had an *a priori* assumption of guilt explainable on other grounds. He was exceptionally open and articulate and quite levelheaded about the Reich case, being one of the few involved in the case who believed that Reich was honestly self-deluded and that there was no deliberate intent to defraud in the rental and sale of accumulators. ("For my money, all psychiatrists are crazy.") When asked about the matter of the prejudgment of the efficacy of the accumulators which characterized the preliminary investigation, his answer was: "But anyone could tell that the accumulators were a fake. You didn't have to be any kind of specialist to know that, and you didn't have to have test results for it either. Look, you have this cabinet made up of panels with nothing but steel wool and cotton in them, with no kind of hookup to any source of power and common sense alone tells you it can't work. We had it tested eventually, but only as a formality. We knew what the results would be, but we had to have actual statements by experts in order to go to court because that's the only thing a judge can go by. But these test results weren't necessary for our investigation."

But here was a man with an international reputation as a psychoanalyst, who was listed in the *American Men of Science,* who in the thirtes was even considered as a possible candidate for the Nobel

Peace Prize—didn't the fact of such impressive credentials give you second thoughts about the accumulator?

"No. We've seen this kind of thing happen before, though God knows, I can't explain it. A completely reputable, established and even famous professional man suddenly going off on this kind of nonsense. There was Ivey with his Korbiozon and more recently you have someone with a reputation like that of Linus Pauling coming out with that incredible nonsense about Vitamin C." So in the case of this official it was simply conventional common sense that explained his *a priori* judgment.

Whatever the reasons for the prejudgment were, there was surely something irrational in the eventual decision of the FDA to pursue the Reich case and to spend over a ten-year period what has been estimated by several FDA officials as something like two million dollars—that is some 4 percent of its limited total ten-year budget; especially so, since this two million dollars was spent ostensibly to stop the interstate shipment of, by 1954, some three hundred orgone accumulators, an enterprise that—making allowances for the accumulators that were loaned out free or at reduced charges—in its maximal year earned only some $30,000.

6

---◆---

"EMOTIONAL CHAIN REACTION"

The title of this chapter is a term Reich used to describe the far-reaching results of the Brady articles—of which the FDA investigation was only one, although the most important one. It is necessary to list some of the links in this long chain for two reasons. One is that it will provide a background to the development of Reich's thinking about and response to the spread of the misinformed and often slanderous opposition to his work; it will, in other words, establish that this response was to something real, however inaccurate and perhaps deluded it eventually became. The second reason is that such a listing will help explain some of the external pressure under which the FDA eventually made its decision to continue in the prosecution of Reich.

In the months immediately following the appearance of the Brady articles, they were condensed, quoted from, and recast in *Time* (April 14, 1947), *The Saturday Review of Literature* (August 16, 1947), *Everybody's Digest* (December 1947), the *McGill Daily* (December 4. 1947), and *Colliers* (December 6, 1947). *Mademoiselle* magazine of January 1948, in an article on Be-Bop, referred to the "Reichian device known as an Orgone Accumulator —a sort of Turkish bath cabinet which is claimed to build up a man's 'orgone energy.'" In March of 1948, the *Bulletin of the Menninger Clinic* reprinted Brady's "The Strange Case of Wilhelm Reich" as an accurate description of Reich's work. In January 1949 the Council on Pharmacy and Chemistry implied in an article in the *Journal of the American Medical Association* that orgone energy was used in promoting cancer cure quackery. *Consumers Report* of March 1949 reprinted part of the Brady article. In August of 1950, Dr. Rose Franzblau, in her article in the *Sunday Compass,* answered a reader's inquiry concerning Reich by drawing upon Brady's article. And some of the same Brady allegations were repeated in the January 1951 issue of *Cosmopolitan* in an article entitled "Are Psychoanalysts Crazy?"

However, this emotional chain reaction was not confined to magazines alone. It also appeared in books. Helen Walker Puner in her book *Freud: His Life and His Mind* (1947), in the chapter entitled "The Larger World of Psychoanalysis," disposed of Reich in two paragraphs, based mostly on the Brady articles. Dr. Clara Thompson in her book *Psychoanalysis: Evolution and Development* (1950) claimed in a footnote that "Some of his [Reich's] experiments have been repeated with negative results by T. Hauschka . . . (shortly to be published)." [1] (The article by Hauschka was never published. At a later date it was sent to Reich and refuted on the basis of faulty experimental technique.) Another book, entitled *The Mask of Sanity,* originally issued in the early forties, was in 1950 updated by its author—Dr. Pervey Clecklev, Professor of Psychiatry and Neurology at the University of Georgia's School of Medicine—to include, among others, a section on Reich and his formulations on orgone energy as an example of psychopathy. And then, in 1952, Putnam issued a book on science crackpots entitled *In the Name of Science* by Martin Gardner, a freelance writer, who had previously made erroneous and uninformed statements about Reich's work in an article appearing in the *Antioch Review* (Winter, 1950–51). In this case,

1. Published in *Conspiracy,* item 294.

however, the Orgone Institute got wind of the book before it was published and managed to obtain the section dealing with Reich and to correct some of its grosser factual inaccuracies—though the conclusions of the author as to Reich's mental condition and orgonomy as pseudoscience remained unchanged.

And, finally, the emotional chain reaction, this open season on orgonomy, was carried on through rumors and harassment directed not only at Reich but at his co-workers as well. *Conspiracy,* a volume of letters, statements, affidavits, and protocols related to the background of the FDA injunction action—printed in photo-offset in a limited edition shortly after the injunction was issued— lists some twenty-five incidents. Their full inclusion here would make for tedious reading, so only a few of the more significant and bizarre of these incidents are touched on below.

The already mentioned Dr. Nic Waal attested in a notorized statement that on November 9, 1948, Dr. Bergman of the Menninger Clinic, where she was working, said that "It is long recognized that Wilhelm Reich is crazy," and that Dr. Karl Menninger asked "whether the orgone business of Reich wasn't crazy." [2] "I believe," Dr. Waal wrote further, "that such an incredibly vicious attitude can only be due to personal insecurity and fear of competition." [3]

Then there was the old rumor that orgone therapy involved the masturbation of patients, this time voiced by Dr. Joseph S. A. Miller of the Hillside Hospital in Bellerose, Long Island, on November 8, 1949. However, the patient he named was contacted, and in a notorized statement said that she had never been to the Orgone Institute where the masturbation was alleged to have taken place. When confronted with these facts, Dr. Miller admitted he was only passing on rumors that he himself had heard. [4]

Dr. William Horwitz of the New York Psychiatric Institute reportedly stated on November 9, 1948, in a lecture to a postgraduate class, that "most psychoanalysts consider the more recent work of Dr. Reich as psychotic," and that in "orgone analysis . . . patients are stimulated erotically." [5]

On November 29, 1948, Dr. Herman Shlionsky—consulting

2. *Ibid.,* item 155.
3. *Ibid.,* item 175B.
4. *Ibid.,* item 173.
5. *Ibid.,* item 176.

psychoanalyst at the Lyons Veterans Hospital, Lyons, New Jersey —told a group of residents to whom he was lecturing that Reich was "either schizophrenic or a faker." [6]

On March 14, 1949, James A. Malaney, Executive Secretary of Professional Conduct of the New York State Education Department's Division of Enforcement of Professional Laws, wrote to Reich, as "Dear Mr. Reich," ordering him to come to discuss "a situation pertaining to your practice in this state as an M.D." and threatening drastic measures should Reich refuse to come.[7] Needless to say, Reich did not respond to this order.

In a letter to Reich, dated March 1, 1950, Dr. Howard Lee Wylie stated that he had heard rumors from Drs. Morris Factor and David Ferber, both of the New York Regional Office of the VA that Reich was schizophrenic, and that "he mechanically masturbated female patients and that his patients were encouraged to have sexual intercourse with each other as part of the therapy." [8]

In the fall of 1950 a Mr. William Fowler, in the town of Oquossoc, which is near Orgonon, spread the rumor that Orgonon was a "communist outfit." [9] Other local complaints were that the Orgone Institute was about "to take over the region," that one of its workers "was chasing some girls late at night," that Peter Reich— some seven or eight years old at the time—"was playing with himself in school," that a member of the town board who screened the books going into the local library had been disturbed by Reich's books.[10] A state trooper was sent, apparently on order from the Governor's office, to investigate and found all these complaints "without basis." [11] Other rumors were that the Orgone Institute was working on atomic weapons, that a group of children were locked up at the Rolling Hill Farm camp for use in experimental purposes, that all the adults at Orgonon were "promiscuous and share their sexual partners with each other," [12] and that boxes at Orgonon were used for "perverse sexual purposes." [13]

At Orgonon isetlf, telephone wires were crossed, vials at the lab

6. *Ibid.,* item 176.
7. *Ibid.,* item 187.
8. *Ibid.,* item 224.
9. *Ibid.,* item 298.
10. *Ibid.,* item 308.
11. *Ibid.,* item 307.
12. *Ibid.,* item 319A.
13. *Ibid.,* item 319A.

were found scattered, objects disappeared, a bugging device was found in Reich's car, garbage was repeatedly found scattered on the grounds. On November 5, 1952, a Mr. Anderson, the town druggist at Rangeley, led a group of children to Orgonon, shouting, "Down with the Commies!" and "Orgy, Orgy! Orgy!"

In 1952, when Dr. Alexander Lowen—whose books on bio-energetic therapy, a derivative of Reich's orgone therapy, have become very popular in the last few years—applied to the New York Board of Medical Examiners for licensure, he had to answer many questions about his moral character and counter many misconceptions about orgonomy.

On November 9, 1953, Reich was "discussed" on the "Dorothy and Dick" program of Station WOR; an excerpt follows:

Orgonomy as expounded by Dr. Wulfgang von Reich . . . [who] . . . it seems is *the* living student (or exponent) of Dr. Freud (more laughter)—But ah! Dr. Reich has gone further than Dr. Freud—in fact it seems Dr. Reich has gone *way* beyond *himself*. Dr. Reich can use his energy to bring rain forth from the heavens.[14]

On February 11, 1953, the American Psychiatric Association sent letters of inquiry about orgone therapy to five medical orgonomists. One of them, Dr. Chester Raphael, also received a letter from the Queens County Medical Society, on February 14, ordering him to appear before the Board of Censors because of his being an officer of the Wilhelm Reich Foundation.[15]

Dr. Edwin Cameron, president of the American Psychiatric Association, told a Mr. Jerry Serafin, who later went into orgone therapy, that such therapy "was a pure fake and that the American Psychiatric Association was going to bring charges of fraud against Dr. Reich." [16]

Reich sought to counteract the flow of rumors, slanders, and attacks, often writing to his lawyer advising him of developments, suggesting he write a letter or explore the possibility of lawsuit. Hays, however, consistently advised against lawsuits. "They rarely do any good," he wrote in a letter dated January 13, 1949. "I have had cases like this before, and ordinarily what is done is to give publicity to the libel." [17] A few days later Reich replied to Hays:

14. *Ibid.,* item 417.
15. *Ibid.,* item 431.
16. *Ibid.,* item 439B.
17. *Ibid.,* item 182.

The continuous attacks by emotionally sick people on our work constitutes quite a problem. I confess that though I understand a great deal of the characterological mechanisms which lead to such attacks, I feel utterly helpless in how to fight them. One cannot fight such attacks with reason since they are inaccesible to reason and argument. And one cannot fight them with their own weapons.[18]

Then he proposed that it might be possible to take legal action against his attackers not on the basis of libel or slander, but on the basis of obstruction to public health since "this is exactly what they are doing. The Brady crowd could have different motives than the pharmaceutic peddlers, but the effect is the same." [19]

Hays, however, replied that there was no law that made obstruction of public health illegal—and tried to console Reich by citing the long history of persecution against pioneers. Reich was very aware of the historical pattern the lawyer mentioned, saw it as part of the emotional plague, and repeatedly stated that he would not acquiesce to it. In fact, he felt himself committed to breaking this pattern.

Though the effort to counteract the tide of attack through publicity had been tried once before without success, Reich and his co-workers decided to try it again. Accordingly, on October 17, 1949, a news release was written up, briefly summarizing the course of Reich's work and its development from psychoanalysis to orgone biophysics, and announcing that "a special press interview for *science and medical editors and writers* will be held with Theodore P. Wolfe, M.D." [20] (italics in original) in New York City on October 21. Needless to say, the press release was not published anywhere and scarcely anyone showed up at the press interview. A short while after, another announcement was issued to the same writers and editors that Reich himself would conduct a "special laboratory tour and demonstration of certain orgone functions" [21] at Orgonon—and, again, there was no turnout worth mentioning.

In January of 1953 a group of medical orgonomists met in New York City with lawyer Harry Green who took an opposite tack to that of Reich's lawyer. He was more aggressive; he felt that

18. *Ibid.*, item 183.
19. *Ibid.*, item 183.
20. *Ibid.*, item 203B.
21. *Ibid.*, item 203C.

Brady as well as Martin Gardner, author of *In the Name of Science,* should have been brought to court and that Reich lacked a good public relations orientation. He stated further that "you can't call authorities liars—can't challenge their integrity—you create a lot of personal hostility." [22] He said that orgonomy threatened psychoanalysis, medicine and the pharmaceutic industry, and that this, together with the opposition rooted in conventional religious ideas, was the basic cause of the attacks on orgonomy. When he was told that Reich felt that work and the publication of its results, not litigation, were the most effective answers to the "plague," Green said this was not sufficient and that orgonomy needed a retained lawyer to be in touch with various agencies in Washington. Nothing, however, came of his suggestions—and one can assume that the reason was Reich's uncompromising insistence on sticking to basic issues, calling a spade a spade, and his general aversion to the element of compromise inherent in the whole idea of public relations. He no doubt felt that truth—the truth of his work and his formulations—would be diminished by recourse to such measures.

So instead, Reich and various co-workers wrote letters of complaint to the President, to the Governor of Maine, to the FBI, to magazines, to the Immigration and Naturalization Service—but all to no avail. In short, they were in the midst of a culture whose most sensitive taboos were threatened by their work and they were without defense against the slander and falsehoods this threat provoked.

And yet this is not the whole story. In the meantime the McCarthy era had begun and moved into full swing. Though its witch-hunting was directed primarily against real or imagined communists and communist-influenced organizations and activities, it created a nationwide atmosphere of hysteria and fear in which any kind of unorthodox or unconventional view was suspect. Reich's work obviously fell into this category and so his troubles were compounded.

There were several strange twists in this situation. The most obvious one was the fact that Reich not only was not a communist during this period, and for almost two decades past, but on the contrary, like many ex-communists, had become almost obses-

22. *Ibid.,* item 406B.

sively anti-communist. His anti-communism was so strong that he became increasingly a supporter of conservative political positions, voting for Eisenhower rather than Stevenson in the 1952 election.

Reich's rationale for his support of conservatism was that liberalism and leftist doctrine in general overlooked the characterological inability of armored man to function socially without restraints. He saw the inevitability with which freedom movements turned into tyrannies—as exemplified, above all, by the totalitarianism of Stalinist Russia—as an expression of this bind. He felt—to repeat —that the achievement of rationality in social organization would be a long and arduous process, a matter of developing ways of avoiding armoring in infants and children so that over generations a larger and larger proportion of the world's population would be unarmored and that this would lead to the natural evolution of a rational social environment. In the meantime, he regarded conservative thinking and the acceptance of limitations inherent in this thinking as the best insurance against the disaster of premature bids for freedom.

And yet perhaps the irony, his support of conservative politics and yet being victimized by it, is more apparent than real. For, together with his opposition to what Reich eventually began to call Red Fascism and his support of Eisenhower, he continued to advocate the right of infants to play with their genitals, social affirmation of and provision for adolescent sexuality, and the cruciality of the orgasm function in personal and social relations— ideas that represented a radicalism that went far beyond anything that political radicalism stood for. So it is not surprising that to the conservative mind Reich should have been regarded as the radical he in essence was. His expectation that his outspoken anti-communism and support of Eisenhower would in themselves establish him, during the social contraction of the McCarthy era, as a respectable conservative and patriotic American was ultimately unrealistic.

Curiously enough, Reich seemed never to have made the connection between the witch-hunting of the fifties and the persecution, slander, and harassment he and his work were subjected to. On the contrary, he came to see his trouble as being primarily the result of the very communist conspiracy that McCarthyism presumed to be fighting, and as the decade advanced he began to share more and more in the wild accusations that characterized that era.

A brief tracing of the evolution of his thinking in this matter suggests that the emotional chain reaction he saw so clearly as resulting from the Brady articles set off a chain reaction within him as well—and of this chain reaction he seems to have been much less aware.

In *The Function of the Orgasm*—published in 1942—Reich had stated that the main struggle in human society was not between various political alignments but, ultimately, between the pro-life and the anti-life forces. Then, in the late forties and early fifties, he came more and more to identify the anti-life forces with Stalinism. In *The Murder of Christ*—which appeared in 1953—he introduced the term "Modju" that he was to use more and more frequently in characterizing the continuing attacks upon him. The "Mo" particle was taken from the name of Moncenigo, who was the Italian duke who had Giordano Bruno, a luminary of the Italian Renaissance, burned; while the "dju" particle was taken from Stalin's original name—Djugashvilli. Reich defined this term as "an international affinity of evildoing character structure based on deep . . . frustration of early yearning for love." [23] On the one hand, he meant for it to represent the long history of such evildoing and, on the other, to express his belief that Stalinism—or Red Fascism, as he called it—in all its forms and influences was the modern exemplification of this historic evil. Then from this identification of the anti-life forces with Modju he eventually came to identify the United States—in spite of negative aspects of American life, of which he was aware—with the pro-life side. "Ultimately," he wrote, "in its larger scope the fight of the U.S.A. against Red Fascism is the fight of Life against Anti-life; the fight of truth against every human being who acts like a Red Fascist, whether he has political orientation for his act or not." [24] But then as the FDA investigation was resumed and led to legal action, the suspicion of communist influence behind the Brady articles and the *New Republic* broadened into a conviction of a communist plot in which the FDA was wittingly or unwittingly involved. Reich began to see himself, in his militant pro-life position, as upholding and

23. *Ibid.*, item 381C.
24. *Ibid.*, item 389N.

defending fundamental American interests. From this it was just a step to the conviction that the conflict between himself and the FDA was one of the most important foci of the cold war. "For the U.S. Government," he wrote, "to be led by Red Fascists into an attack on Orgonomy is for the U.S. Government to be tieing a rope around its own neck and putting the free end of the rope into the hands of Moscow Modju." [25] At the time Reich wrote these words he was just digging out from the disruption of the oranur experiment—about which more will be said in its proper place— and beginning to experiment with weather-control work as part of the effort to clear the atmosphere of the noxious form of orgone that he called DOR. No doubt he felt that this work, along with his more general life-affirmation, was being threatened by the communist forces he saw at work behind the FDA action against him.

It was in the context of these events—the emotional chain reaction sparked by the Brady articles and its rapid spread within the highly flammable hysteria of the McCarthy era, as well as the resulting emotional chain reaction in Reich's thinking—that the FDA investigation of Reich now resumed.

25. *Ibid.,* item 389R.

7

THE
INVESTIGATION
CONTINUES

Some three years passed from the time the report ordered by Wharton was sent to the FDA administration in Washington for "evaluation and appraisal, with a view to determining future action," and the time this determination was actually made. The exact date and circumstances of the decision are not in the FDA files because as Mr. Alfred Barnard—who was a high-ranking FDA official at that time—wrote to this author: "In the first place . . . neither policy nor decision making were reduced to writing in FDA in those days (or very much even today!). In the second place, the decision wasn't reached 'Bang' we go—it just sort of evolved as the matter progressed. . . . Larrick was the controlling person in the many conferences held with staff on the matter and, by concurrence rather than by a specific overt act, was responsible for moving forward with the case." * The FDA had recently

* Though Charles W. Crawford was Commissioner at the time, it was Larrick, his deputy, who made the decisions in such matters as the Reich

embarked upon a concerted anti-quack campaign, with Larrick in charge of it. There were, it appears, some ten or twelve outstanding quack cases that warranted action, but the resources were available to pursue only a few of these. And by some unreconstructible bureaucratic process, it seems, the Reich case came to be included among those few chosen for prosecution.

Mr. Barnard, who was in on the many deliberations as to which cases would be chosen, was one of those who opposed the idea of pursuing the Reich case. On June 6, 1951, he wrote to Larrick:

Unfortunately, we do not have any easy way of getting direct evidence of the extent to which curative claims accompanying these devices or the extent to which users are led to treat serious disease conditions with them. I believe that it would be a waste of money to arrange any expensive testing of the device itself until we have such evidence. To acquire this evidence will necessitate a widspread, time-consuming investigation initially by Boston District; later through follow-up by probably all other districts. I am somewhat inclined to doubt that such an investigation is the best way to expend funds at this time.

One would expect that where a selection among quack cases had to be made, the final decision would be based on an evaluation of the degree of danger to public health posed by individual cases, and those deemed more dangerous chosen for prosecution. With some two hundred or so accumulators in circulation at the time, the degree of "danger" posed by Reich should have been considered minimal. The reason given by Mr. Barnard for Reich's inclusion among the chosen cases was that his operation came to include so many different kinds of activities that it was difficult to determine its exact scope; and also that the "Reich operation" seemed to be growing more and more from bona fide psychiatry to "full-blown quackery." In addition to these considerations, it can be assumed that Reich's sex theories, à la Brady, played some part in the consultations and conferences. For instance, Mr. A. G. Murray, As-

case. Mr. Barnard wrote this author on January 16, 1973: "Those of us who were directly concerned with the day to day enforcement . . . actions of the agency invariably turned to Larrick when a decision needed Commissioner-level concurrence. It was Larrick who played the Commissioner role at regulatory planning conferences and during discussions involving the handling of individual . . . cases of sufficient magnitude or importance to warrant Commissioner attention. . . . Crawford's background was more in the Congressional and management-type areas. . . ."

sistant to the Commissioner, who was in on the deliberations and later played an important role in "developing" the Reich case for legal action, was, according to the above-cited letter from Mr. Barnard, ". . . very Puritanical in many ways and some of his attitudes may well have played a significant behind the scenes role in the Reich matter." Moreover, it should not be forgotten that during this time there was the continuing appearance of slanderous articles about Reich that must have, from the FDA's point of view, made him seem if not the most dangerous quack certainly one of the most notorious. And, finally, there was the support and exhortation of professional groups—primarily the psychiatric and psychoanalytic, but to a lesser extent the medical as well—that the FDA, as a representative and agent of accepted practices, could not easily ignore.

So some time in the summer of 1951, Washington FDA headquarters made the decision to continue the investigation, with a view toward initiating legal action against Reich.

In the meantime, important things had been happening in Reich's work. At the end of 1949 the Wilhelm Reich Foundation had been established and legally incorporated as an educational, nonprofit organization in Maine. This was done as a step toward establishing Orgonon as a center for all orgonomic work and studies, and to that end the Foundation acted as the umbrella for all the other orgonomic organizations then functioning: The Orgonomic Research Clinic, the Orgonomic Children's Clinic, the Orgone Institute Press, the Orgonomic Infant Research Center, and the Orgone Institute Diagnostic Clinic. The above-named organizations relating to infants and children were outgrowths of the problem of raising healthy—that is, unarmored—children that had been discussed in the 1948 conference. Neill was offered the leadership of this effort but refused, feeling that it was more important for him to remain independent as a friend and supporter rather than to be drawn into the orbit of Reich's disciples. Also in 1949 the third, enlarged edition of *Character Analysis,* as well as *Ether, God and Devil,* was published. Later, toward the end of that year, Reich had his first attacks of tachycardia (rapid heart beats).

Early in 1950 the Reichs, who had been spending increasingly longer periods in Maine, moved there as permanent residents. That summer the Second International Orgonomic Conference was held in Orgonon. This time there were fifty-five participants, including people trained in the biological sciences. Again, one of the important foci of the conference was the problem of the healthy child (later to become the title of one of Neill's books, though Neill himself was unable to obtain visa to attend). Another focus was the cancer problem—though by this time Reich was no longer involved in treating cancer patients. There had been a steadily growing interest in Reich's work both in the United States and abroad; scientists and others in many countries of the world were doing independent work and they reported on this work at the conference.

After it was over Reich and his wife took a brief ten-day vacation. "We stayed for once in a good hotel," writes Ilse Ollendorff, "and there we spent the last really peaceful days of our marriage. It was the quiet before the storm—for the storm broke that winter and never fully abated for Reich, although many new discoveries and developments were still to come." [1]

This storm was oranur—the orgone anti-unclear research project that Reich undertook shortly after the outbreak of the Korean War in the hope of finding a means to counteract radiation sickness in the event of a nuclear war. To carry out this research Reich obtained two milligrams of radium from the AEC in early 1951. He treated one milligram with orgone irradiation in his specially constructed "orgone room," while, as a control, the other was kept in its shielding some distance away. But instead of a neutralizing effect, as Reich had hoped, what resulted from the irradiated radium was a kind of chain reaction in the atmosphere in and around the orgone room. This chain reaction manifested itself in several ways. Objectively, the Geiger-Mueller count in and around the orgone room climbed to incredible frequencies, at times going over the 100,000 cpm mark so that the counter itself jammed. This was not due directly to the radium, because when it was taken outside, the count it gave off was normal; while at the same time, the count remained inordinately high in the orgone room even with the radium out of it.*

1. Ollendorff, p. 100.
* On February 3, 1951—three weeks after the first exposure of the radioactive material to orgone—*The New York Times* recorded that inordinately high background counts had been found extending from the Rangeley area to a radius of between 300 to 600 miles.

In addition, this charged atmosphere—it came to be called the oranur effect—had biological effects on those involved in the project. "[We] were immediately affected . . . by nausea, conjunctivitis and general malaise," Ilse Ollendorff recounts.[2] Many of the experimental mice that were kept in the area died—all, on autopsy, showing symptoms of radiation sickness. Eva almost died. Ilse had to undergo a serious operation shortly thereafter. Reich himself had a severe heart attack later in October. Generally, it seemed that the oranur effect aggravated specific health problems. There were, moreover, signs that some of the vegetation in the area began to die, and even the coloring of some of the rocks was affected.

The experiment was halted at the end of March. Its effects, however, remained for a long time after, necessitating the evacuation of Orgonon for a year or more. Eventually, as Reich rallied from this total disruption, he wrote up the experiment and its scientific implications in *The Oranur Experiment,* which came out later in 1951. In this account Reich postulated that nuclear and orgone energies were essentially antagonistic. When brought into proximity with nuclear energy the orgone energy becomes highly excited— and this became the specific definition of the oranur effect. In this state of overexcitation in response to nuclear radiation, some of the orgone energy undergoes transformation that makes it life-inimical. This form of orgone Reich called DOR—deadly orgone. In this context he saw radiation sickness as essentially an oranur effect, the overexcitation of orgone and the conversion of some of it to DOR. He postulated further that orgone could be turned to DOR under other conditions and that this took place in an armored organism. In this formulation he saw the biophysical basis for Freud's concept of the death instinct which decades earlier Reich had refuted in the context of psychoanalysis.

Though in the *Oranur Experiment* Reich expressed the hope that the oranur effect might yet be used as a means of immunizing people to the effects of radioactivity, he never followed up this possibility. Instead, his subsequent exploration of DOR and his efforts to clear it from the atmosphere around Orgonon led him to the work that was to engage him in the last years of his life— weather-control work. He was to pursue this work with increasing

2. *Ibid.,* p. 105.

intensity almost to the very day of his imprisonment. He called this work CORE—Cosmic Orgone Engineering.

During the remainder of 1951 the *Orgone Energy Bulletin* was begun on a quarterly basis to replace the previous *Annals of the Orgone Institute. Cosmic Superimposition* was issued. And Reich began, partially as a reaction to the effects upon him of the oranur experiment, to paint profusely. "If *art* is a disease," he wrote to Neill in June of that year, "oranur has brought out the artist in me." [3]

In the *Oranur Experiment* Reich recounted that many of his co-workers had been frightened by the effects of this work and withdrew as a result of it. Moreover, most of his co-workers were not scientists but doctors, many with psychiatric or psychoanalytic backgrounds who practiced biopsychiatric orgone therapy. Most of them lacked the background to follow Reich in his scientific work of this period. A case in point—though it occurred before oranur—was the situation with Theodore Wolfe. Reich wanted him to take charge of further orgonomic cancer research and treatment but Wolfe, maintaining that this was outside his specialty, refused. As a result an estrangement grew between the two men. Others who could not follow Reich in his scientific work cut themselves off from and even became hostile toward Reich.

Dr. Simeon Tropp, on his withdrawal from further orgonomic research, explained his situation to Reich by means of an analogy: He and Reich had been climbing a mountain the past years but now had reached a ledge where he felt comfortable and from which he liked the view and therefore wanted to remain there; he was grateful to Reich for having led him this high and knew that Reich was going higher, so they had to part; anytime, however, Reich felt like returning down for a visit he would be welcome. (Dr. Tropp was later one of the medical orgonomists to participate in the intervention proceedings.) However, Reich, for the most part, could not understand or accept the fact that others were unable to go as far as he; to make the transitions and readjustments he was capable of making; lacked the energy to pursue the many ramifications of his formulations into unfamiliar fields; were, in short, not endowed with his driving genius.

In summary, the year of the renewed FDA investigation marked

3. Published in Ollendorff, p. 106.

a major transitional point in Reich's work and in his organizational and even domestic situations. According to Ilse Ollendorff's account, the disruption caused by the oranur experiment exacerbated their relationship. "As I have indicated before," she writes, "when the outside world seemed threatening, Reich's wrath turned against those closest to him." [4] In commenting on this transitional point Boadella writes: "There was his [Reich's] work before and leading up to oranur; there was the near catastrophe of that experiment itself; and there was the period after, when Reich's work and his personality began to interact powerfully on each other." [5]

The renewed investigation was directed from FDA headquarters in Washington rather than from a district office as the preliminary one had been. Of course, various district offices were called upon to assist. It was generally a well-coordinated operation and consisted of two main and chronologically overlapping efforts. One was the effort to obtain evidence of false claims, misbranding, and quackery; the other was the actual testing of the accumulators to give a basis to the allegations of false claims, misbranding, and quackery.

The first of these efforts was embodied primarily in a renewed search for that elusive person, the dissatisfied user, and also by inducing evidence. Significantly, in the search for such users and the subsequent interviews the focus was primarily upon cure claims —no doubt the appearance of the *Cancer Biopathy* was in part responsible for this. In other words, the suspicion of a sexual racket was dropped. One of the most complete statements of this new policy occurs in an FDA memo dated August 8, 1952, where an interview with an accumulator user is suggested: "The interview," the memo states, "should purposely be kept free of any discussion regarding sex matters. As you may know, the company * some years ago charged that our investigators made uncalled for inquiries regarding possible use of this box in connection with cer-

---

4. *Ibid.*, p. 108.
5. Boadella, p. 265.
* In the FDA's use of such a term—and other terms such as "plant," "factory," and "firm"—one can already detect distortion. The FDA could not help but try to fit the organizations involved in various aspects of orgonomic work into the framework it was accustomed to in dealing with commercial organizations.

tain sex phenomena and it is desired that even no imaginary grounds for such unwarranted complaints be made available at this time to the company."

First word of the renewed investigation came to Reich on August 1, 1951, when an accumulator user wrote the Orgone Institute a brief note stating that "a man . . . called at my home July 31, 7 P.M. and took pictures of the Accumulator, took a statement of cost of rental and how I found out about it." [6] The Orgone Institute therefore, on August 3, wrote a letter of complaint to the FDA, protesting that accumulator users were again being disturbed by FDA agents, recalling the 1947–48 investigation and that the information of this investigation must, no doubt, be in FDA files, and suggesting that if further information is required the FDA get in touch with the newly formed Wilhelm Reich Foundation.[7] On the same day, the Orgone Institute sent out two other letters. One was to a lawyer of the Hays firm, advising him of the renewed investigation and suggesting that he get in touch with the FDA to protest and try to resolve its suspicions.[8] The other letter was to the accumulator user, advising him that he was not obligated to answer any questions regarding the accumulator and requesting him to refer any further inquiries to the Orgone Institute.[9] Then, some two weeks later, the Wilhelm Reich Foundation sent a letter to all accumulator users with the same advice and request. And finally, on August 25, the staff and members of the Foundation sent a long letter to the previously mentioned Mr. A. G. Murray, who at this time was apparently in charge of the investigation. This letter outlined the position of the Foundation in relation to the FDA—in effect, repeating the points made during the preliminary investigation—and it again offered to cooperate with the FDA in its effort to learn about orgone energy, but it added: "The test of your readiness to cooperate with us, a cooperation which was entirely lacking in 1947, will be your willingness to go directly to the Wilhelm Reich Foundation or its legal representative. If your Administration sincerely wishes to learn about the functions of orgone energy, we shall be glad to inform

6. Published in *Conspiracy,* item 330.
7. *Conspiracy,* item 331.
8. *Ibid.,* item 332.
9. *Ibid.,* item 333.

you." [10] Then, in the next paragraph, the letter continues: "Should you not cooperate with us in trying to understand the discovery of the life energy, we shall be forced to close access to any and all information to any and all of your agents. If necessary, we shall let the matter go to the highest court, revealing to the fullest . . . one of the most scandalous affairs in the history of science." [11] And the letter ends: "We request that you try to understand our work, its importance and our need for peace and quiet, that you do not mistake it for some 'Sex Racket' as you did in 1947 when your agents inquired into the private lives of people under bio-psychiatric treatment. We believe that it is the obligation of a responsible agency of the U.S. Government to be able to distinguish between a possible fraud and serious scientific pioneer work." [12] This last sentence touches on one of the most crucial aspects of the whole case: the fact that the FDA was not structured to make this kind of distinction, and that FDA law did not allow for it. (This condition can be regarded as a basic problem of law in general, which reflects conventional concensus, the lowest common denominator of established opinion. It is a situation that was recognized by De Toqueville in his book *Democracy in America* and by John Stuart Mills in his essay "On Freedom," in which he spoke of the need for protection of minority opinion against "the tyranny of the majority.")

This new investigation was marked by the same prejudgment that characterized the previous one, especially in the renewed search for dissatisfied users. The FDA managed—perhaps through contact with the Railway Express Agency or through the S.A. Collins Company, a workshop in Rangeley that was building accumulators for the Foundation at this time—to obtain the names and addresses of all people to whom accumulators were being sent and of all people who returned accumulators. The FDA was especially interested in the latter group since it held out the best promise of including dissatisfied users. But time after time the report came back that such and such was apparently not a dissatisfied user. As late as September 11, 1953, an FDA memo states:

10. Published in *Conspiracy,* item 341B.
11. *Ibid.,* item 341B.
12. *Ibid.,* items 341B, 341C.

Note in the attached letter that Mrs. Catapone [apparently a user of the Orgone Accumulator] feels that "we have been swindled." This may be a good dissatisfied customer case *of which we so far have very few.* If you agree that now is the time to get it, I will have N.Y. District get the full facts from her, looking towards considering her as a dissatisfied customer witness. [Italics added.]

There is no record of an interview with this party, and possibly by this time—some five or six weeks before a summary of the investigation was sent to the general counsel for the initiation of legal action—the idea of having dissatisfied users in the anticipated trial had been abandoned.

Simultaneously with this search, the FDA was also busy "inducing evidence." This meant primarily getting employees of the Administration to send for accumulators, literature, and, in a few cases, even for free medical advice. Ideally of course, it should not have been necessary to resort to such a measure; there should have been enough dissatisfied users who felt they had been swindled to supply the Administration with the evidence it would eventually require. But the absence of a sufficient number of such users is only one reason for the FDA's recourse to this action. Another was that it wanted to have documentary proof that the publications of the Orgone Institute Press constituted "accompanying literature," and the FDA obtained this proof by having its employees order all or part of the Press's publications, at the rate of one or two a week, shortly after obtaining the accumulator. Thus the literature and accumulators obtained in this way—that is, under minutely recorded conditions—could, when the anticipated court action came, be used as documentary samples of a total "promotional scheme." Besides this, both the accumulators and the "accompanying literature" would be used in the eventual testing by scientists and doctors. In this way the anticipated negative results could be used to show that the orgone accumulators had been misrepresented—i.e., "misbranded"—in the accompanying literature.

This effort was begun in August 1951. Very explicit instructions were given to various districts on how the evidence was to be induced. For instance, if the chosen consignees had "some minor pathological condition such as heart murmur or frequent colds, etc., this is all to the better." Even the contents of the letter to be

written to the Wilhelm Reich Foundation was included in the instructions: "Dear Sirs: Please send me a list of your publications.
Very truly yours." Then, after receiving the list, the designated
consignees were instructed to order the literature, a few pieces at
a time and in a certain order. A letter to be sent to Reich for the
purpose of proving that the accumulator ordered for general prophylactic purposes could also be used for a specific pathological
condition was dictated in a memo dated January 11, 1952, as follows:

Dear Dr. Reich:
I have recently purchased some of your books and last week my
Model I Accumulator arrived.
I have had trouble with my head for a long time which now and
then flares up. Last week this sinus "exploded" again. Because of this
I have not yet started to use the accumulator.
From your writings it looks like the Model I Accumulator can be
used for either general health or medical treatment and I could use it
for treatment of this sinus.
Please let me know if I can do this.

Since the same accumulator was, in the literature, recommended
for both prophylactic and specific treatment, the reply to this
letter was, of course, in the affirmative. When, however, these FDA
consignees sent in requests for specific medical advice they were
instructed, by a return letter from the Wilhelm Reich Foundation,
to consult their own doctors. (In *Conspiracy* Reich included several
letters, asking for specific medical advice, which he labeled "Catch"
letters, *i.e.,* deliberately sent in by FDA people. In reply to these
the Foundation stated that it would be sheer quackery to make a
diagnosis or recommendation without a full medical examination.
Ironically, however, none of the actually planted letters are included in *Conspiracy*.)
The result of all these arrangements by the FDA was that in
the Request for Admissions * sent to Reich on February 26, 1954,
shortly after the Complaint had been served on him, of the ten
people listed as having ordered publications and accumulators and

* A Request for Admissions is a legal document sent to a defendant
before trial in which he is asked to admit to factual details that are not
in themselves incriminating. In this way time does not have to be spent at
the trial in establishing these facts.

solicited information on the medical use of the latter, seven were FDA agents.

This kind of procedure cannot be legally considered as entrapment since entrapment means the effort to influence an individual or company to do something he or it does not ordinarily do—which was not the case here. It can more validly be considered as accepted police practice when evidence is required to establish legally a guilt that is commonly known to exist—such as, for instance, having an undercover policeman buy drugs from a known dealer. What was at fault in the FDA's use of his practice was its prior "knowledge" of Reich's guilt. But, again, given the extent of the chain reaction in the press as well as among the professional groups and the MacCarthyite atmosphere in which it occurred, its "knowledge" of Reich's guilt was almost inevitable.

For another kind of evidence to be used in the anticipated trial, the FDA felt it would be necessary to carry out a "factory inspection"—that is, to inspect the premises of the Wilhelm Reich Foundation in Rangeley, Maine, and the two-car garage premises of the S.A. Collins company building the accumulators, also in Rangeley.

Three men—one regular FDA inspector, one FDA medical doctor, and one FDA physicist—came unannounced to Orgonon on July 29, 1952, in accordance with their instructions. Reich himself later wrote up this encounter and was to refer to it again and again in the following years as an incident that exemplified for him everything that was irrational and dishonest about the FDA action against him.

To begin with—though Reich did not know this—the three visitors prepared themselves with film badges and pocket dosimeters for, the report states, "the inspectors' health protection in view of the fact that Doctor Reich had publicly indicated that his premises were radioactive as shown by his personal Geiger counter." * Then, as they entered Orgonon, they passed signs that said

* The film badges and dosimeters both showed no radiation, which was taken by the FDA as further proof of the fraudulence of orgone energy. The kind of radiation that Reich had written about following the oranur experiment, however, was the oranur effect—i.e., the unnatural excitation of orgone energy in the presence of nuclear radiation. This effect continued some time after the radioactive substance used in the oranur experiment had been removed, and was detectable by Geiger counters that had been pre-

"Danger," "No Trespassing," and "Admittance by written Appointment Only." After this they came to a chain blocking the road which they dropped in order to drive in further. Their justification for all these trespassing acts was that the Wilhelm Reich Foundation had written suggesting that if the FDA wanted more information on the accumulators it should get in touch directly with the Foundation. Since this letter, sent a year earlier, had been written in the hope of halting the harassment of accumulator users, and since this harassment had not halted, its invocation by the FDA men was little more than an excuse for their illegal trespassing in an abuse of governmental power.

Met by Reich's wife, Ilse, the inspectors were told that Reich saw people by appointment only. Yet she was eventually prevailed upon to announce their visit to Reich. When Reich sent word that he would not see them, Inspector Kenyon explained that Doctors Brimmer and Heller, his two companions, had made a special trip from Washington and would not be able to come again. Reich, who was on the second floor of the observatory, apparently heard this and changed his mind. For then, the report of this visit states: "A large, robust man of plethoric appearance, bounded down the steps. Subsequently this individual identified himself to the inspectors as Dr. Wilhelm Reich."

Reading almost like the scenario for a comic opera, the report has Reich bellowing, yelling, pacing, flailing, running, pounding on a desk, as he protested the preliminary investigation, and insisted that it would have to be cleared up before he would allow an inspection. ("He shouted, 'What right do you people have to come here and ask me whether my secretary has a lover?' He then yelled, 'What do you think we are up here, bums?' "). He insisted that they had to acquaint themselves with the writings on orgonomy before he would let them inspect the premises. He tested Heller's background by asking him to identify a Geiger counter and when Heller hesitated, in order to give his dosimeter full exposure to

---

viously exposed to orgone radiation. By 1952, however, the oranur effect was considerably diminished. That it did not affect the badges and dosimeters is therefore no surprise. Indeed, one orgonomic scientist told this author that it was questionable if the badges and dosimeters would have reacted even when the oranur effect was at its strongest.

the counter, Reich assumed that Heller couldn't recognize this piece of equipment. He accused them of being Red Fascists and insisted in a rage that the accumulator was not a device and therefore was outside the authority of the FDA. And finally he ordered them off the premises.

In the brief report of this visit that Reich wrote up, he stated, in part: "It was perfectly obvious . . . that they came in order to make trouble, since otherwise they would have proceeded in a serious and decent manner: They would have announced their coming; they would have made an appointment; they would have come fully acquainted with the literature. . . . They would, first of all, not have trespassed unlawfully on private property." [13] Subsequently Reich sent a telegram of protest to the Department of Justice, a letter to the FBI asking that the identity of these inspectors be checked out. *"How Far Has Modju Gone in the USA???"* he wrote in a statement a few days after the visit. "Once we stop using our rights . . . in a responsible manner against such uninformed and ignorant servants of the people, we would deserve no better than some Super-Modju in the White House." [14] And when Dr. Baker inquired about this incident of his lawyer, he received, on August 2, a reply that stated: "In my opinion, Dr. Reich was justified in ordering the intruder or intruders off the private property, being wholly within his legal rights. The Federal Constitution and laws and decisions of the Federal Courts are very strict in regard to same. . . . The men had no right to enter the premises, unless they had permission or they were Federal officers with a search warrant." [15] On August 13, Reich wrote a letter of complaint to the President.

For Reich this visit meant, in effect, that this time, just as in the earlier investigation, his offer to cooperate with the FDA had not been accepted in good faith, and this realization led to a hardening of his opposition. Following the abortive inspection visit Reich became more and more inclined to deny that the orgone accumulator was a device within the meaning of the FDA law. It was almost as if he was reluctant to abandon the position he

13. *Conspiracy,* item 356B.
14. *Ibid.,* item 360C.
15. Published in *Conspiracy,* item 361.

took in the heat of anger in the confrontation with the inspectors, and subsequently tried very hard to substantiate this basically untenable position.

A year earlier, Reich had written: "According to the Federal Act regulating the distribution of devices for health measures, under which the orgone energy accumulator would fall, the Food and Drug Administration has the right to investigate all devices at the manufacturing plant only to make sure it [sic] is correctly labelled. . . ." [16] A week after the attempted inspection, in a letter to Dr. Baker, Reich's position in this matter was reversed: "It is questionable," he wrote, "whether the orgone energy accumulator can be designated as a 'device.' " [17] Then, after giving several reasons for this position ("Are two palms moved toward and against each other, or two metal plates doing the same, thus eliciting orgone energy, a device?" [18]), he concluded that "Until the legal interpretation of the cosmic orgone energy in our present social law system is effectuated, and in order not to be in conflict with existing laws, I am contemplating to suggest that orgone energy accumulators be built within the respective states and not be shipped in interstate commerce." [19] This suggestion, however, was not followed. Had it been, the tragic outcome of subsequent events might possibly have been avoided.

On August 11, Reich's lawyer sent him a letter in which he defined the legal meaning of the term "device" as "instruments, apparatus, and contrivances, including their components, parts and accessories, intended (1) for use in the diagnosis, cure, mitigation, treatment or prevention of disease in man or other animals; and (2) to affect the structure of any function of the body of man or other animals." [20] But the lawyer left the decision of whether this definition applied to the accumulator up to Reich.

In order to be able to make this decision, Reich wrote to the AEC asking if the FDA had jurisdiction over the distribution of radioactive isotopes sent to hospitals for medical tracer work. He apparently hoped to obtain a negative answer and then, by analogy, apply this principle to orgone energy accumulators. The AEC sent

16. *Conspiracy*, item 335.
17. Published in *Conspiracy*, item 364.
18. *Ibid.*, item 364.
19. Published in *Conspiracy*, item 364.
20. *Ibid.*, item 369B.

his letter to the FDA and the FDA replied that it did indeed have jurisdiction over such radioactive isotopes. This, however, did not deter Reich from his effort to find grounds for denying FDA jurisdiction over accumulators. Several weeks later he cabled a co-worker who had been visited by an FDA man that "This government Agency has no authority on primordial orgone energy which is not a food, drug, cosmetic, or device in their sense according to their regulations." [21] This position, slightly different from what this effort began with, was still untenable. It was not orgone energy *per se* that the FDA had jurisdiction over but the structures that were shipped in interstate commerce for which certain medical claims were made and which therefore were devices within FDA jurisdiction. In this blurring of an important distinction it is possible to see the way Reich's effort to cope with the basic irrationality of the FDA investigation led him into his own irrationality.

During the years of this part of the investigation, right up to the time the Complaint was served on February 11, 1954, Reich and his co-workers apparently were not aware that the FDA was building up a legal case. The assumption seemed, in general, to be that the FDA was only trying to find evidence of illegality and quackery. Theories, suspicions, conjectures abounded—but no one seems to have thought that it was all preparatory to imminent legal action. For example, when Reich learned of various kinds of accumulator testing being done at the Maine General Hospital, he suspected that it was in connection with the FDA, but did not see it as a preparation to legal action. And when he heard that the American Embassy in Norway was gathering information on the newspaper campaign against him, he did not even suspect that it had anything at all to do with the FDA. Quite the contrary.

It will be recalled that a request for information on the Norwegian campaign against Reich was made during the preliminary investigation, at which time it was, in effect, turned down by FDA headquarters. But later it was deemed more important, and consequently, on November 15, 1951, a request was sent to the State Department from the FDA's Division of Regulatory Management. The investigation in Norway was carried out between May 20 and June 16, of 1952, with the summary report written on June 30.

21. *Ibid.,* item 385.

On June 2, Dr. Ola Raknes, one of the people interviewed by the American Embassy investigator, wrote to Reich informing him of this investigation. And on June 9, Reich wrote to Raknes a lengthy and completely misconceived interpretation of the State Department's interest, that stated in part:

The Red Fascists, after having held up the smooth acceptance and rational handling of the discovery of the life energy in the USA, have themselves, in their own country, worked with it, and this must have somehow come to the knowledge of the American government. It is most likely that even now, the American government wouldn't have acted, had not the *Oranur Experiment shaken everything and everybody to its very foundations.* [Italics in original.] . . . Now the "Oranur Experiment" has been ordered by more than a hundred leading institutions here and abroad, and I believe that the truths finally are coming through and can no longer be overlooked. Since the Oranur Experiment touches upon big State Affairs, such as atomic warfare and energy, and especially the grave emergency which exists in the world today, the American government naturally felt puzzled about the discrepancy between the positive results in the United States, most likely obtained by such institutions as General Electric, Association for Infantile Paralysis, etc., and the information they had, probably from the National Research Council, to the effect that I had been unmasked in Norway as a charlatan. Now, it seems they want to know what my enemies in Norway actually did.*

In 1953, a short while before the Division of Regulatory Management sent its report and recommendation to the General Counsel, an unexpected windfall occurred: Peter Mills—who had been Reich's lawyer in Maine from the late forties, having handled the legal details of the incorporation of various orgonomic organizations and been present at meetings where the FDA trouble was discussed—was to be appointed U.S. Attorney for the state of Maine. This meant that Mills would be prosecuting the government's case against Reich. FDA headquarters, learning from Inspector Wood that Mills used to represent Reich and the Foundation, initiated measures to have Mills appoint one of its lawyers as a special U.S. Attorney to handle the Reich case. In an interview

* This letter was found in the FDA Reich files, but was not included in *Conspiracy.* How the FDA came by it poses an intriguing question.

with Mills, this author learned that he had been quite embarrassed to find out, after his appointment, that one of his previous clients had run afoul of the law. He apparently was more embarrassed by this circumstance than by the unethicality—if not illegality—of prosecuting a person who had previously been his client. It was apparently this embarrassment and his desire to prove that he had no sympathy for his former client that prompted Mills to agree to the FDA's rather irregular suggestion and appoint Mr. Joseph Maguire, a lawyer of HEW's General Counsel, as his assistant in the case.

Maguire was to be one of the men on the government's side of the case to take the trouble to read some of Reich's books. A devout and practicing Catholic, he was deeply offended by Reich's writings on sex. This was, no doubt, an important component in the zeal with which, during the next three and a half years and under the aegis of Mills' office, Maguire fought the government's case against Reich.

Finally the FDA prepared a thirty-four-page recommendation against Reich—as well as against Ilse Ollendorff and the Wilhelm Reich Foundation—and sent it to the General Counsel on October 21, 1953. The test results had not yet all been received by the FDA at this date, but they were shortly forthcoming and there was, as has been pointed out, no doubt at FDA headquarters that the results would be negative. Consequently, there was no reason to delay action.

In making a recommendation of this kind it is, of course, desirable that the substantiating information be as convincingly incriminating as possible. This the FDA recommendation was, even at the expense of factual accuracy. Whether such inaccuracies were deliberate or merely a manifestation of the way bias creates its own reality is an open question.

There was, first of all, the matter of Reich's M.D. degree. The recommendation questioned whether Reich really had such a degree from the University of Vienna, as he claimed to have. It stated that the FDA had requested the State Department to check this matter, but did not mention that on June 30, 1953—that is, almost four months prior to the date of the recommendation—the

Vienna field office of the Department of State's Division of Security sent a confidential report confirming that Reich had received a medical degree from the University of Vienna on July 10, 1922.

In discussing the consignees of orgone accumulators, the report divided them into three groups. One was "Lay people who have heard of the devices through word of mouth or by reading Reich's literature and who use the devices for therapeutic or curative purposes without medical advice." Then, it stated: "Although we have not been able to determine percentage wise, it is believed that the bulk of the device shipments go to consignees of this type." There is, however, nothing in the whole FDA file on Reich, in all its interviews with patients, in its extended search for dissatisfied users that supports the latter statement. On the contrary, time after time the interviewed users told inspectors that their use of the accumulator was for nonspecific purposes, that it made them feel more fit, dissipated tiredness, built up resistance to colds, etc. Moreover, in all application forms for the purchase or rental of an accumulator, applicants were asked what they intended to use it for and were advised that if it was for a specific disease condition they should be under medical supervision.

The recommendation stated that when an accumulator was rented the prospective user paid forty dollars to begin with and thereafter ten dollars a month—thus obscuring the fact that the original forty-dollar payment was credited toward the first four months of the rental fee and that its purpose was simply to insure that the accumulator would be kept for the minimal time required.

In an article entitled "Report on Orgone Energy Accumulators in the U.S.A." (*Orgone Energy Bulletin,* vol. 3, no. 1, January 1951) it is stated that twenty accumulators were rented at a reduced rate and twenty-seven loaned out free of charge. The recommendation, in referring to the part of the article where this information occurs, stated that "the . . . accounting information . . . concerning accumulators . . . may be relied upon." Yet elsewhere it stated ambiguously: "We know of no instance in which distribution is made on this basis" (*i.e.,* reduced rates or free of charge).

The recommendation stated further, still taking its figures from the *OEB* article, that the yearly income from accumulators had progressed steadily from $4,594.00 in 1946 to $23,000.00 in 1950. However, it neglected to mention that elsewhere in the article it is stated that none of this money was taken as profit but rather that all of it was put into research work.

Perhaps the most important part of the recommendation is its treatment of the "labeling" connected with the distribution of accumulators. According to FDA law, labeling is defined as "all labels and other written, printed, or graphic matter (1) upon any article or any of its containers or wrappers, or (2) accompanying such article." In listing the labeling that would come under the second part of the definition, the recommendation included mimeographed sheets that come separately, free of charge, that had to do with the ordering, assembling, and use of the accumulators; and also—and most crucially—it included most of the publications of the Orgone Institute Press. "Although some of the literature is devoted largely to a discussion of sociological theories and political subjects," the recommendation conceded, "much of it is replete with direct and implied claims for cure of cancer and other serious diseases." This statement is false on two counts: cancer is not dealt with in "much" of the literature—only in a few articles in the journals and in the book *The Cancer Biopathy;* and—as has been stated before—Reich nowhere claimed to have found a cure for cancer or for other diseases. He recounted clinical successes and failures in varying degrees, but nowhere presented the accumulator as a "cure" device in the manner of conventional quackery.

Aside from *The Cancer Biopathy,* occasional articles on the use of the accumulator in the treatment of various somatic diseases occur in the sixteen issues of the *Orgone Energy Bulletin* published to that date, the four volumes of the *International Journal of Sex Economy and Orgone Research,* and the single volume of *Annals of the Orgone Institute.* But with the rest of the literature listed— that is, *The Sexual Revolution; The Function of the Orgasm; The Mass Psychology of Fascism; Ether, God and Devil; Cosmic Superimposition;* and *Character Analysis,* all of them hardcover publications *—the situation was, to put it mildly, rather questionable. The legal rationale for their inclusion in the complaint was that they, presumably, satisfied two conditions in relation to the ac-

---

* *The Murder of Christ* and *People in Trouble,* published in 1953 in a limited edition, had apparently not reached the attention of the FDA at this time, though they were later included in this Injunction.

cumulator: they allegedly constituted labeling in the sense defined above—that is, that they "accompanied" the device; and they constituted "misbranding" in the sense that they misrepresented the efficacy of the accumulator they accompanied. The legal basis for the accusation of misbranding was the negative test results the FDA had already obtained and those it was still expecting to obtain at this time.

The question is, however, whether the term misbranding can be applied to literature in which the accumulator is not mentioned and to other literature in which the accumulator is mentioned only briefly and in a context that is incidental to the main subject of the book.* The recommendation—and the default decree eventually obtained in March of 1954—took an extreme position in this matter. It went beyond the matter of reference to orgone accumulators and regarded the mere mention in any publication of the word "orgone" or the term "orgone energy" as tantamount to labeling and misbranding.

The recommendation concluded with a warning that, unless legal action was taken "the firm" would continue and expand the distribution of the accumulators (the evidence adduced here was that Reich had expressed the hope that eventually every family in the country would have an accumulator in its home). Of the three possible avenues of legal action—injunction, seizure, and prosecution—the recommendation urged injunction, primarily because, in

* In *Function* there is a reference to "orgone radiation" on page xvi of the Introduction, and four pages at the end of the book develop the idea that biological energy is atmospheric orgone energy. Within this section it is "claimed" that orgone energy kills cancer cells and charges living tissue. In *Sexual Revolution,* written long before Reich's formulations concerning orgone energy, the preface to the third edition mentions orgone energy and there is an additional reference to it in a footnote in the text—in neither case, however, is its therapeutic aspect touched upon. *Mass Psychology,* also written before Reich's work in orgone biophysics, contains several references in the Introduction to the therapeutic potential of orgone energy. *Ether, God and Devil* and *Cosmic Superimposition* do not deal with the therapeutic application of orgone energy. The main reason for their inclusion in the recommendation's objection is that they discuss "the false theories upon which the orgone energy accumulator is based." The reason for the inclusion of *Character Analysis* is that in the later edition it is stated that orgone energy is a "visible, measurable, and applicable energy of a cosmic nature"; and that it contains one sentence that asserts that blood corpuscles can be charged and cancer tumors destroyed by orgone energy.

the trial that the FDA anticipated, such a procedure before a judge would permit "the introduction of more diverse evidence."

Predictably, the General Counsel acceded to the recommendation, and preparations toward obtaining an injunction were initiated in a letter from the General Counsel to Attorney General Herbert Brownell, Jr., requesting that "appropriate procedures be instituted."

The FDA did not have the facilities or the trained personnel to run the tests on the efficacy of the orgone accumulator. As was common at that time—and even, to a large extent, today—it had various other institutions carry out the tests. There were two parts to the tests: one was directed to the biomedical effects of the orgone accumulator and the other to some of the experiments Reich had adduced as constituting objective, physical proof both of the existence of orgone energy and the ability of the accumulator to concentrate it. The biomedical tests were carried out by doctors at various clinics and hospitals—including the Mayo Clinic. The physical tests were carried out primarily at MIT and Bowdoin College.

With such reputable institutions involved, one would logically expect a high level of scientific work. The truth of the matter, however, is that, as conscientious as members of these institutions no doubt were in their regular scientific or medical research, when it came to testing orgonomy they performed on a level that, without exaggeration, can be characterized as unprofessional. Were such shoddy methods employed in a more conventional field it is safe to say that no scientific or medical body would take the results seriously. In the case of orgonomy the motive was obviously not to objectively test the theory behind the accumulator or the claims made for its efficacy but to provide the FDA with the kind of evidence it needed to clinch its case against Reich. This can be inferred not only from the unprofessional level of the testing itself but also from communications between the FDA and various testers.

For instance, Dr. Frank H. Krusen of the Mayo Clinic, who purported to test the accumulator for its effect on users' temperature, pulse, respiration, and blood pressure, wrote on August 24,

1953, in a letter accompanying his report to the FDA: "It was very difficult for me to bring myself to take the time to prepare this report because . . . this quackery is of such a fantastic nature that it seems hardly worthwhile to refute the ridiculous claims of its proponents."

A three-man committee on mathematical biophysics at the University of Chicago was interviewed by an FDA physicist regarding the possibility of their testing out some of Reich's biophysical formulations. The memo of that interview, dated May 12, 1952, states that the interviewer showed them some of Reich's writings and that they came to the conviction that the device was "a gigantic hoax with no scientific basis." The memo then adds: "the interview lasted 3 hours and all 3 of them were eager to aid the Government in evaluating the device and testify in our behalf if we so desired." In view of the fact that the three scientists were convinced so easily and were willing to testify in the government's behalf on the basis of the cursory glance they accorded Reich's writing during this interview, it is hardly surprising that a month later, on June 12, Dr. Nicholas Rashefsky, one of the trio, sent Heller the following:

I have studied the printed material of Mr. [sic] Wilhelm Reich and, to tell you the truth, I find myself somewhat at a loss as to how to report on it.

The material is beneath any refutation. Practically every paragraph exhibits complete ignorance of well-established facts of science. Other paragraphs contain wild speculations made without any scientific basis whatsoever.

* * *

Sometimes wild claims are . . . made by some individuals who insist that their claims are not necessarily contradicting the established facts of science. The argument of the claimant in such cases is usually that scientists must admit that they do not know everything. . . .

If, however, an individual makes claims which completely ignore and flatly contradict all established facts and concepts, facts and concepts on which we now depend in our daily life . . . then a person does not even need to be a scientist to see how utterly absurd and unfounded such claims are. It is quite clear that Mr. Reich's claims fall in exactly that category.

(The last quoted paragraph, needless to say, distorts the matter: Reich never contradicted *all* established facts and concepts. He often put a different construction on some of the "established" facts of conventional science; and just as often he gave full credit to the achievements of what he called "mechanistic" science, even though he felt that this kind of science was incapable of dealing with basic life processes.)

A third example of *a priori* scientific judgment by testers is contained in an FDA memo, dated September 20, of an interview with Dr. Kurt Lion of MIT's physics department, where it is stated: "It is quite apparent . . . that Dr. Lion has been completely won over to our side. . . ."

The shoddy quality of the tests, then, followed logically from such *a priori* convictions and contempt for Reich's work.

Common to most, if not all, of the tests is complete lack of concern with the environment within which the accumulator was tested, though orgonomic literature makes it clear that orgone energy and, consequently, the action of the accumulator is affected by proximity to X-rays, fluorescent lights, radium dial watches or clocks and all high voltage equipment. Since most of the FDA tests were carried out in hospitals, clinics, or laboratories where such equipment or materials are usually present, this in itself would make the test results highly questionable.

But besides this common defect there are specific defects peculiar to individual tests. For example, in the introduction to the test carried out by Dr. Krusen of the Mayo Clinic we are told that "the temperature, pulse, respiration and blood pressure were measured before, during and after each session" with his subject in the accumulator. An examination of the results of the tests, however, reveals that the blood pressure readings were made in the case of most of the subjects only at the first session and omitted in the subsequent seventeen sessions.

In the same test, Dr. Krusen notes, for each subject, that no subjective or objective changes were found. Yet, again, an examination of the figures in the record sheet reveals that in the majority of cases there were indeed changes of one kind or another in the pulse, temperature, and respiration of subjects using the accumulator. Perhaps these changes were not considered significant by Dr. Krusen. This, however, is something quite different from saying that no objective changes were found.

The test in which cancerous mice were treated by an accumulator at the Roscoe B. Jackson Memorial Laboratory in Bar Harbor, Maine, was no less defective: the Jackson Lab transplanted tumor cells into the mice, while Reich had worked with mice in which the tumor was allowed to grow spontaneously.

In a test at Johns Hopkins Hospital, Dr. Henry A. Malcolm used an accumulator on twenty-two patients with advanced stages of cancer and concluded that "In no instance was there any evidence to suggest this form of treatment is efficacious. . . ." But an analysis of his record sheet reveals that the average number of times each of the patients used the accumulator was 2.68. In contrast to this, the fewest number of treatments Reich recorded in his description of treatment of cancer patients in *The Cancer Biopathy* was 40. The longest was about 170.

Dr. John W. Norcross of the Lahey Clinic in Boston tested the accumulator on twelve anemia patients, though at the same time they continued to receive other forms of treatment and medication. In spite of this overlap he was somehow able to conclude that in "no case [was] the 'orgone energy accumulator' . . . of clear-cut benefit to the patient." Later, in an interview before the anticipated trial, Norcross revealed something he had not mentioned in his report—that "one or more patients treated in the accumulator said they felt a tingling sensation when they sat in the box and perhaps one or more said they felt better after sitting in it."

At the Maine General Hospital, Dr. E. P. McManamy treated four patients, some suffering from ulcers, some from burns. One patient with an ulceration of the great toe said the toe felt warm after a ten-minute treatment with a funnel accumulator. In a patient with bed sores on both hips it was found that the side treated with the funnel accumulator showed less drainage and faster healing than the other side. A third patient, who had burns all over his body, had his neck exposed to orgone irradiation; in subsequent days the neck was the only area not to show any blistering. Yet Dr. McManamy comes to no positive conclusion on the basis of these results.

Three of the five physical tests carried out by Dr. Lion of MIT were presumably also carried out by Dr. Noel C. Little of Bowdoin College. Little's report consists of a one-page letter of three paragraphs, each paragraph describing one test and its negative results. Too briefly presented to permit critical examination of methods or experimental setup, two of Little's tests, nevertheless, serve an instructive purpose when compared to Lion's corresponding tests.

Reich had observed that an electroscope discharges more slowly in an orgone accumulator than out of it. Lion did not actually test this but simply explained that given the construction of an orgone accumulator this phenomenon was to be expected, and he explained why. Little, on the other hand, claiming to have carried out this test, found that the rate of electroscopic discharge was not affected by the accumulator. Besides canceling each other out, these contradictory conclusions indicate also that two physicists cannot agree as to what constitutes normal functioning of electroscopes.

Reich claimed that another manifestation of orgone energy and its concentration in the accumulator was that, varying with humidity, the temperature in an accumulator was higher than the temperature of the surrounding air. Lion's results showed that the temperature in an accumulator was, on the average, lower than in a control box (a circumstance that, in itself, needs explaining), while Little stated there was no difference in the temperatures of an accumulator and a control box. So again the two physicists had contradictory results. Significantly, neither of these men said anything about balancing the control and the accumulator so that both boxes would change temperatures at the same rate when the environmental temperature changed.

In summary, then, if there was any significance at all to the accumulator tests the FDA had carried out it was that their deficiencies substantiated Reich's repeated assertions during the time of the preliminary investigation that the only way orgone accumulators could be validly tested was in cooperation with someone experienced in orgonomic research. Yet it was on the basis of these deficient tests that the FDA now began to set legal machinery into motion against Reich and his work.*

---

* The reader wishing a more detailed critique of these tests is referred to the Appendix where the biomedical tests are discussed by a medical orgonomist and the physical tests by a physicist with experience in orgonomic research.

8

COMPLAINT
AND RESPONSE

The Attorney General's office approved the General Counsel's request and preparations were begun for the trial. These preparations were primarily a matter of the pretrial briefing and rehearsing of the doctors and scientists who had carried out the various tests. The FDA Reich file does not show that any users of the accumulator, dissatisfied or other, were going to be subpoenaed for the trial. This does not necessarily prove that the FDA was planning to rely *only* on the testimony of the "experts," for it is possible that some of the plans were not committed to paper. But it suggests that the long search for dissatisfied users had yielded very little in the way of legally usable results.

The doctors were apparently, on the basis of their test reports, sent a list of questions they would be asked in court. Included with these questions were the desired answers. Then, between the first and the fifth of February, Maguire and John T. Cain—an inspector from the Division of Regulatory Management who was in charge of all the day-to-day details and decisions involved during the almost three-year period of the renewed investigation—made the rounds between Boston and Portland, Maine, holding personal consultations with the doctors to clarify possible problems and also to evaluate the kind of impression individual doctors would make as witnesses.

It was at one of these interviews that Dr. Norcross, who had tested the accumulator with twelve anemia patients, revealed the subjective reactions of some of his patients that he had not seen fit to include in his official report. While Dr. Carl F. Dunham, who had supervised the test for protozoal infection of the vagina, stated when he was interviewed that he was "not too much concerned about the failure . . . to get a final test on Trichomonas vaginalis in one case." Dr. Willaim F. Taylor of the Maine General Hospital in Portland, Maine, who had done the test on diabetes was concerned because he had only three cases to go on, but in spite of this the interviewers decided to use him as a witness because of his impressive appearance and manner. Dr. McManamy, who had tested the accumulator for its effects on wounds and burns, caused the interviewers some concern because he said he would have to mention in his testimony that one of his patients reported feeling temperature changes of the skin during orgone treatment. "He impressed us," the report of this interview concludes, "as a satisfactory witness but . . . the benefits of his possible testimony should be weighed against that portion of his testimony relating to the report of skin temperature changes."

The first legal step toward the trial for which the FDA was preparing occurred on February 10, 1954, when Reich and two other defendants—Ilse Ollendorff and the Wilhelm Reich Foundation—were served with a Complaint. This was done through the Attorney General's office which, on the same day, also issued a news release announcing the complaint action for an injunction against interstate shipment of accumulators. Citing "extensive investigations" that proved the nonexistence of orgone energy, it concluded with the charge that the accumulators were "misbranded under the Food, Drug and Cosmetic Act because of false and misleading claims."

The Complaint itself—most probably written by Maguire—was a twenty-seven-page document in which all the information gathered about Reich, his co-workers, the orgone accumulator in its several models, the claims made for the accumulators, the publications of the Orgone Institute Press and the finances of the Wilhelm Reich Foundation was presented in the framework of a money-

making scheme. Dr. Myron Sharaf referred to it in his article on
the trial as "The single most fantastic document available from the
history of the proceedings"; [1] while Dr. Charles Kelly, who later
made trips to Washington to protest the terms of the injunction,
wrote that "To understand the effect of the Complaint and the way
it was met by Reich, it must be realized that it was so vicious, so
false, so twisted and sick, that it was difficult to believe it could
ever be taken seriously in court." [2]

The Complaint ignored Reich's background and achievements,
the hard thought and hard work, the clinical, political, and experimental experience, the whole process of synthesizing underlying
concepts of Western intellectual history that distinguish his life and
writings. Ultimately, by reducing Reich's devotion to the cause of
human betterment to the level of vulgar quackery and swindle, the
Complaint was an attack not only upon him but also on the
highest, most persistent ideals of human civilization.

The Complaint charged that the defendants—Reich, Ilse Ollendorff and the Wilhelm Reich Foundation—responded to inquiries
concerning the accumulator "or literature and publications relating
thereto" by sending announcements describing the publications of
the Orgone Institute Press and order forms for them. In this way
the Complaint established these publications as "labeling," even
though most of them did not deal with the accumulator or, for that
matter, with orgone energy. The Complaint then quoted parts of
some twenty-five case histories contained in this literature to prove
that "despite disclaimers of a cure from the use of their device [the
defendants] resort to detailed accounts . . . describing 'cures' alleged to have been effected by the use of the device." Many of these
case histories were excerpted and quoted out of context and are
grossly misleading, most notably so the cases quoted from *The
Cancer Biopathy*.

The Complaint, for example, quoted a case history that stated
that a brain tumor was destroyed "as early as two weeks after the
beginning of treatment," [3] but omitted the conclusion to the case

1. Myron Sharaf, Ph.D., "The Trial of Wilhelm Reich," in *Wilhelm
Reich,* ed. Paul Ritter (Nottingham, England: Ritter Press, 1958), p. 55.
2. Charles Kelley, Ph.D., "The Life and Death of Wilhelm Reich," reprinted from *The Creative Process,* bulletin of the Interscience Research
Institute, Vol. III, No. 1, August 1963, p. 12.
3. *The Cancer Biopathy,* p. 277.

given in the same paragraph: "But the detritus from the tumor filled and clogged the lymph glands of the neck and the patient died. . . ." [4] A stomach tumor "the size of an apple" became "rapidly smaller," [5] the Complaint quoted further, neglecting to include the subsequent sentence: "But after eight weeks the kidneys became clogged: there was edema of the legs and the patient died of cardiac decomposition." [6] Similarly, in cases of ovarian and adrenal tumors, both showed marked improvements, according to the quotes in the Complaint,[7] but in sentences immediately following, omitted from the Complaint, we learn that both patients subsequently died: the first of kidney complications and the second of "enlargement and degeneration of the liver, apparently due to the process of elimination of the dissolved tumor mass." [8]

Going on to charge that the accumulator was advertised as a "preventive of and beneficial for use in all diseases," the Complaint contended the opposite and gave a long list of diseases mentioned in the Reich publications for whose "cure, mitigation, treatment and prevention" the accumulator was not effective. Needless to say, nowhere in any of Reich's writings does he say that the accumulator can be beneficially used in *all* disease conditions. But aside from this inaccuracy, the Complaint in this section managed to convey the impression that the mere occurrence of disease names in such books as *Cosmic Superimposition; Ether, God and Devil; Character Analysis; Sexual Revolution; Mass Psychology; Murder of Christ;* and *People in Trouble* was enough to characterize them as being concerned with disease treatment. In addition to these misrepresentations there is yet another: many of the disease names alleged to occur in these books do not, in fact, occur in them. For example, the terms "diabetes," "hypertension," "rheumatism," "fever," "ichthyosis," and "the common cold" do not appear in *Cosmic Superimposition,* as the Complaint alleged. How could they, in a book devoted primarily to a speculative exploration of the role of orgone energy streams in the formation of hurricanes, the aurora borealis, and the typical shape of galaxies? This kind of dishonesty is perhaps most extreme in the case of *People in Trouble,* written

4. *Ibid.,* p. 277.
5. *Ibid.,* p. 276.
6. *Ibid.,* p. 276.
7. *Ibid.,* p. 276.
8. *Ibid.,* pp. 276–277.

in 1937, in which the mere occurrence of the words "blood" and "tissues" is put forward as evidence of the book's concern with disease treatment.

The Complaint concluded with a three-part "prayer for relief"— to use the traditional legal term—asking that the defendants and all people working with them be enjoined from shipping accumulators in interstate commerce and from engaging in "any act whether oral, written or otherwise . . . with respect to any orgone energy accumulator . . . while held for sale after shipment in interstate commerce . . ."; and that the defendants pay for the legal expenses incurred by the government. The second part of this "prayer" —the plea that the defendants and co-workers be enjoined from engaging "in any act, whether oral, written or otherwise" in relation to accumulators—is extraordinary from a legal point of view. For this plea, if granted, would make it illegal for Reich or anyone in any way connected with him to mention the accumulator in any way, whether in conversation or writing of any kind, as long as a single accumulator that had been shipped across state lines still existed. This kind of infringement on basic constitutional freedoms of speech and press could only have been requested—and eventually granted—during the McCarthy decade, when such infringements had become common practice.

The document was signed by Peter Mills, U.S. Attorney for the state of Maine.

Up to this point, Reich's decisions had little effect on the course of his conflict with the FDA. Whether he cooperated with the FDA or not, whether he permitted inspection at Orgonon or not, whether he gave accumulators for testing or withheld them, whether he sent letters of complaint, advised users not to give information to inspectors, got angry—all this may have slowed the process but in no way effected its course. The only thing he could have done that could possibly have stopped the FDA proceedings was to halt the shipment of accumulators across state lines—that is, to have them built within the states, above all in New York State, where most of the users resided. But as has been pointed out earlier, though he briefly considered this possibility during the period of renewed investigation, nothing came of it.

Now, with the initiation of legal action, the process ceased being a one-sided affair and became, instead, one of interaction. And as his first act in this new phase of the process, Reich chose not to answer the Complaint. This was undoubtedly the turning point in the whole ten-year history of this conflict and it was to affect all further legal proceedings. By this decision Reich granted the prosecution the opportunity to obtain a default decree of incredibly broad scope. It was the subsequent violation of this decree that eventually sent Reich to prison.

The decision not to appear to oppose the Complaint was not easily arrived at. To begin with—we are told in Dr. Baker's account of this anguished time—Reich was stunned by the Complaint and incapable of any action for three days after receiving it.[9] Some sense of this shock is conveyed in a memo of a telephone conversation between Mills and Maguire, written by Maguire, on February 11, 1954—that is, the day after the Complaint was served:

He [Mills] said that he had just talked with the Marshall who effected the service. The Marshall told him that Reich wanted to know what it was all about, and what he should do. The Marshall advised him that he couldn't tell him what it was about, and suggested that he get in touch with his attorney who could explain matters to him. Reich offered the Marshall a drink.

After the initial shock, Reich sought to reason the irrational situation out, and from the accounts of those who were involved in these deliberations, he apparently vacillated for some time as to whether or not he should appear to contest the Complaint. On the one hand he felt that ". . . if the world did not want his work it could do as it pleased. . . . His responsibility was that of a scientist making discoveries but not having to defend them in court." [10] Thus the physicians could take any action they wished in the matter. At other times, however, he felt that the accumulators *were* his responsibility and that, therefore, he would conduct his own defense. People close to Reich and connected with his work divided into three groups on this issue: those who withdrew from the legal entanglement, those who urged Reich to contest the Complaint, and those who urged him not to.

9. Elsworth F. Baker, M.D., "Wilhelm Reich," in *Journal of Orgonomy,* Vol. 1, Nos. 1 & 2, November 1967, p. 47.
10. *Ibid.,* p. 48.

At one point, Dr. Baker relates, he and those who, like him, felt the Complaint had to be contested, brought an attorney to Orgonon for discussion of the matter with Reich. At this meeting Reich was swayed further than at any previous time to the possibility of appearing in court. But then, Dr. Baker writes:

Dr. Silvert, who was present and opposed to Reich's appearance in court, asked defiantly, "and what happens to the truth in all this?" The attorney replied, "It comes out of all the embarrassment each side inflicts on the other." Ignoring the attorney's answer, Reich became very angry, stopped the discussion, paced the floor, and accused us of trying to entangle him in court action. His appearance in court was no longer considered, and we waited for the inevitable injunction.[11]

Dr. Silvert had formerly been a staff physician at the Menninger Clinic, where, according to FDA records, he had the reputation of being a talented if somewhat erratic psychiatrist. In the middle forties he left the clinic to undergo thereapy and training with Reich. Up until the time of the Complaint he was one of the younger, less important members of the small group of medical orgonomists trained by Reich. But then he came to prominence in this group through his support of Reich in his most extreme opinions and actions during the three years of litigation, from 1954 to 1957. Indeed, he had a considerable influence on the course of this litigation. His involvement in the process went so deep as to cause his own inclusion in the eventual criminal contempt charges, and he was sentenced to prison at the same time Reich was, though for a shorter period. Among a small group of devoted former patients there is still reverence for the memory of Silvert's complete identification with Reich's extremist views. Many other Reichians, however, feel that had it not been for Silvert's influence Reich might have been prevailed upon to act more effectively in his own defense. (Indeed, toward the end Reich himself felt that Silvert's actions were to some extent responsible for the legal bind he, Reich, had gotten into.)

Reich's personal life was, at the time of the issuance of the Complaint, undergoing critical changes. The disruptive effects of the oranur experiment continued, leading to his further isolation and

11. *Ibid.*, p. 48.

probably contributing to the deterioration of his marriage, which was almost completely dissolved at this time, though the actual separation did not occur until several months later. During this time, Reich had begun on occasion to drink heavily.

In his work, however, Reich had been having what appears to be signal success in weather-influencing with the further development of the cloudbuster—a development that involved the connection of the cloudbuster to radioactive material that had been exposed to orgone irradiation. (Reich wrote a letter on this development to Eisenhower, outlining the great possibilities for peaceful use of atomic energy by such treatment of radioactive substances. In this communication Reich used the term "atoms for peace" and, later, when Eisenhower used this same term in his famous atoms-for-peace speech, Reich was convinced that Eisenhower not only had obtained the term from his earlier letter but also that the President was aware of his work and secretly supported it.) One of the most striking cases of apparent success occurred in September 1954 when Hurricane Edna threatened the eastern seaboard. The Weather Bureau fully expected the hurricane center to pass over New York and New England. Reich initiated an operation to divert it and Edna began to shift direction. Boston radio announced on the morning of September 10: "Last night it was said that only a miracle could prevent the hurricane from hitting New York. New York got its miracle. . . . Looks like New England may do likewise. . . ." New England got its miracle, too—Edna passed fifty miles east of Boston.[12]

By this time, too, Reich had begun to see the increase of drought and the rate of desert development in the world as a "planetary emergency." Consequently, his work with the weather became, in his view, increasingly more important to the survival of life on earth. He had concluded that atmospheric DOR (deadly orgone) was the cause of deserts which he regarded as the functional equivalent in nonliving nature of armoring in humans. In addition to this, Reich was at this time hard at work on the problem of negative, or counter, gravity, and was apparently nearing its theoretical solution. And, finally, Reich had, several months before the Complaint was served, become interested in UFO (unidentified flying object) phenomena and some two weeks earlier had, with Ilse, his

12. Boadella, p. 293.

first UFO sighting. The UFO problem was to become increasingly more important to him in the remaining three years of his life and eventually was to become a part of his overall concept of the planetary emergency.

His view of the continued FDA investigation had, in the meantime, developed into a total system with its own inner logic, along the following lines: The FDA's malevolent investigation was originally the result of a communist plot. This plot had two interrelated purposes: One was to disrupt his work in orgonomy so as to prevent the American government from using it to achieve decisive advantage in the cold war; the other was to steal his work—especially the "Y" factor in orgone energy, that is, its motor-force potential—and develop it in Russia. To effect this plan, Fredrick Wertham, a leading figure in the American-Soviet Friendship League, had, in his 1946 review of *The Mass Psychology of Fascism* in the *New Republic,* called on fellow travelers and sympathizers to oppose Reich's theories in every way they could. Subsequently, in answer to this call, Brady's articles were written and published, first in *Harper's* and then in the same *New Republic* from which the original call had come. (Reich occasionally departed from this latter interpretation. In some of his writings on the conspiracy he sometimes suggested that the original idea for the Brady articles may have come from spies in the FDA itself.) The FDA, either with the help of conscious spies within it, or with the help of characterological spies,* had responded to Brady's articles and the subsequent "emotional chain reaction" and thereby become to some extent an unwitting tool of the "red fascist" plot. But then, as it pursued its purpose, pharmaceutical interests within and outside the FDA, learning of the great healing potential of orgone energy and fearing that if this were recognized and accepted their whole industry would be undermined, lent their support to the FDA's aim of disrupting his work and discrediting his discoveries. Later, other elements were to be added to this system: Rockefeller interests were working in secret concert with communism against him, while the federal government and the air force secretly supported Reich's work.

---

* Characterological spies are people whose character structure made it impossible for them to live openly, but on the contrary, compelled them always to live underground lives, to act in secret, to spy, to "snipe" from ambush, to conspire and connive.

As we have seen, it is plausible that communist fellow-traveler influence was indeed involved in Wertham's and Brady's call for action against Reich. And, further, it is a fact that the FDA has often been—and, according to James Turner's book on the FDA, *A Chemical Feast,* still is—in close cooperation with various large drug interests with whom it often exchanges personnel. However, the system into which Reich put these facts has to be regarded as delusional and as such it lends itself to psychological interpretation.

We know from undertones in Reich's later writings and from explicit statements made by people who knew and worked with him during this period that in spite of his stated willingness to pursue his work in the absence of recognition and against the slanderous opposition it had evoked over the years, on some level he did care very much and very humanly for what he considered his due. When Neill, for instance, tried to get H. G. Wells and others interested in Reich's scientific work, Reich became angry with him. "I do not want anyone to be invited to approve of my work. I don't want you to try to get anyone interested in it," Neill quotes Reich as saying to him.[13] But, Neill continues, "I think he had some self-deception here. I noted that when any magazine published an appreciation he was much pleased. And why did he try to get Einstein interested in orgone functionalism?"[14] In this context Reich's delusional interpretation of the trouble he was undergoing with the FDA can be understood; for underlying this interpretation is the wish-fulfilling assumption that in reality his work had achieved far greater recognition and acceptance than was openly acknowledged.

This, of course, is far from a complete explanation of the complex question of Reich's state of mind during this period—the early and middle fifties. Neill wrote about it as follows:

In one of my last letters to him [Reich] I said something like this: "If Dulles and Ike and Macmillan and Kruschev are all sane then you are mad, and I'm all for madness. . . ." My own opinion is that he was so far in advance of all of us that his personality could not stand the strain of intense insight into the world's neurosis. He became a little sick because he could not fight universal sickness and remain completely normal.[15]

13. A. S. Neill, "The Man Reich," in *Wilhelm Reich,* ed. Paul Ritter, p. 23.
14. *Ibid.,* pp. 23–24.
15. *Ibid.,* p. 25.

The charge of insanity had been made against Reich recurrently by various opponents since the late twenties or early thirties, and there are still people today who are convinced that Reich had been institutionalized at one or more periods of his life. (Otto Fenischel's part in getting these rumors going in the United States has already been noted.) Anyone honestly trying to assess Reich's state of mind in the middle fifties does so against the background of these persisting rumors. It should therefore be made clear that the present consideration of a developing disturbance in Reich's judgment, discriminatory faculties, and perhaps mental balance has no relation to the earlier rumors; and that with the exception of the already mentioned *Contact with Space*—in which there is evidence of haste and insufficient regard for scientific method in the arrival at conclusions concerning UFOs—this consideration is not meant to reflect on the validity of Reich's work.*

Any effort to evaluate Reich's mental condition at this time is complicated by the simple fact that his scientific formulations have never been comprehensively tested by the scientific community. They are of such momentous import in themselves, in their practical ramifications, and in their invalidation of so many of the root assumptions of modern science, that in their entirety they constitute, in effect, a whole counterscience. It is, perhaps, no wonder that those scientists who have heard of Reich's scientific work have chosen to take the way of the psychiatrists and psychoanalysts and dismiss his formulations as nothing more than the symptom of a gigantic egomaniacal psychosis—in spite of the fact that there is much persuasive evidence in the writings of his co-workers in support of his formulations concerning orgone energy in its many, varied manifestations. However, until the scientific community meets the challenge of Reich's theories, the final word about his mental condition cannot be said. If a serious, unbiased program of testing and evaluation is undertaken in cooperation with present-day workers in orgonomy, the results are bound to affect the effort to evaluate Reich's mental condition in a most decisive way. If it is found that his formulations were wrong, that the results he claims to have obtained were figments of his imagination, that there is no basis for his belief in the existence of orgone energy, then the work

* In the discussion that follows I am indebted to an exploration of this problem in a conversation with Dr. Myron Sharaf.

of the last fifteen years of his life would have to be regarded as nothing more than symptoms of madness. And in that case his irrational, inconsistent, and inappropriate behavior in the early and middle fifties would be only an extension of the severe mental imbalance that had preceded it.

However, during the last fifteen years of his life, Reich treated scores of patients and trained dozens of doctors, many of them with psychiatric backgrounds, who later went on to practice what they had learned from him and one of whom—Dr. Baker—has by now trained a second generation of orgone therapists. It would have to be explained, assuming Reich was mad, how it was that none of the psychiatrically trained doctors who underwent treatment and training with Reich were able to detect the presence of such a severe psychosis.

If, on the other hand, it is found that there is a valid basis for Reich's scientific formulations, then his irrational and inconsistent behavior in the fifties would appear in a totally different light: the wonder would be that given the epochal discoveries he had made— and whose truth he carried alone in opposition not only to accepted views of a whole civilization but also under repeated slanderous attacks, harassment, and prosecution—he had the strength to maintain what rationality he had, that he was able to continue functioning at all.

Instead of appearing in court to answer the Complaint, Reich finally drew up a document entitled Response, and on February 25, 1954, sent it with a short cover letter to Judge Clifford of the United States District Court for the District of Maine whence the Complaint had been issued. It was a relatively brief statement— some four pages long—that, rather than dealing with specific allegations in the Complaint, stated Reich's opinions on the limitation of judicial power. Like the Complaint itself, the Response has become one of the central documents in the three-year litigation between Reich and the United States Government.

It began by establishing the basic premise upon which rests the claim of scientists "to a free, unmolested, unimpeded natural scientific activity in general and in the exploration of Life Energy in particular." This premise is established by a chain of reasoning that begins with the fact that American common law is an outgrowth of natural law. Before the development of orgonomy, the term "natural law" was interpreted metaphysically, religiously, or mechanistically, but with the discovery of orgone energy it became possible for the first time for man to investigate natural law scientifically. That is, since orgone energy is the basic entity in the universe, the study of its functions becomes equivalent to the study of natural law itself and therefore not subject to interference from the offspring of natural law—common law. In thus giving concrete meaning to what had been a nebulous concept or philosophic notion, Reich was in effect continuing a process he had begun years earlier in concretizing terms like libido (bioenergy, or organismic orgone energy), pleasure (streaming sensations), inhibition and repression (armor), genital sexuality (orgastic potency), ether (cosmic orgone), God (the lawfulness of natural functions).

From this, the Response moved on to its main point—the inherent limitation of judicial power.

According to natural, and in consequence, American Common Law, no one, no matter who he is, has the power or legal right to enjoin:

The study and observation of natural phenomena including Life within and without man;

The communication to others of knowledge of these natural phenomena so rich in the manifestations of an existent, concrete, cosmic Life Energy;

The stir to mate in all living beings, including our maturing adolescents;

The emergence of abstractions and final mathematical formulae concerning the natural life force in the universe, and the right to their dissemination among one's fellow men;

The handling, use and distribution of instruments of basic research in any field, medical educational, preventive, physical, biological and in fields which emerge from such basic activities and which, resting on such principles, must by all means remain free.

Most of the items in the list—the first, the third, and part of the fourth—however valid they might be in a general sense, had no direct bearing upon the Complaint. Reich, in other words, was in the Response reacting not only to the specific legal issue but also, and perhaps mainly, to the irrational motivation underlying this issue—namely, the desire to silence him and disrupt his work. One can assume that, however irrelevant to the specific issue, the Court did not take kindly to the third item: the one dealing with sex in general and adolescent sexuality in particular. The last item, on the other hand, was directly related to the Complaint, but it disregarded the jurisdiction of FDA law over the interstate shipment of medical devices.

In the remaining portion of the Response, Reich stated his convictions on the limitation of judicial power even more emphatically:

No man-made law ever, no matter whether derived from the past or projected into a distant, unforseeable future, can or should ever be empowered to claim that it is greater than the Natural Law from which it stems and to which it must inevitably return in the eternal rhythm of creation and decline of all things natural. This is valid, no matter whether we speak in terms such as "God," "Natural Law," "Cosmic Primordial Force," "Ether," or "Cosmic Orgone Energy,"

However, Reich himself, in earlier books, had made the point that at a certain period in human prehistory, when man became armored, society went off the natural track, and he saw the whole thrust of orgonomy as an effort to get human history back into harmony with nature. In *Civilization and its Discontents* Freud had formulated a fundamental conflict of interests between the individual's instinctual needs and the requirements of civilization. In Reich's view this was true only because our civilization was erected upon the condition of human armoring; our social organization and institutions were and are based on secondary—that is, distorted— forms of sexuality and feeling. The Response's appeal to the primacy of natural law, however, seems to disregard the distinction that Reich himself had made between the existent and the natural. For, according to this distinction, natural law did not and could not obtain in our armored civilization.

"I therefore submit," the Response concluded, "in the name of truth and justice, that I shall not appear in court as the 'defendant.' . . . I do so at the risk of being, by mistake, fully enjoined in all my activities."

In summary, much of the Response was an eminently rational effort on the part of Reich to work out an alignment between his formulations in matters of basic research and the common law structure. It is an extension of the belief he had held since the beginning of the FDA investigation that new discoveries required new laws for their administration. But his using the Response as a substitute for personal appearance in court was irrational.

One would have expected Reich to have known better. In *The Murder of Christ* (written between June and August of 1951, though not published until 1953), Reich had introduced the concept of "countertruth" as that which militates against the acceptance of truth. An example of this might be the pleasure anxiety of an armored person which makes him fear and oppose the orgasm reflex both experiencially and as a bioenergetic concept. Another example is the armored character structure of the average person that undermines all political efforts to institute a free society. "Using the truth as a weapon," Reich wrote in explication, "implies not only telling what has been found true but also, and in the first place, knowing why this particular truth had not been mentioned before. . . . Before proclaiming a truth one should know the obstacle to this truth." [16] The point being made here is that Reich disregarded the "countertruth" in the use to which he tried to put the Response; he ignored the existing obstacles—which he had previously so clearly delineated—to the acceptance of the truths it proclaimed. In the accompanying letter to the judge he wrote: "I . . . rest the case in full confidence in your hands." In other words, he exempted the judge from the countertruth obstacles to the acceptance of his work—for the judge could only have taken the Response seriously if he were capable of recognizing the merit of Reich's work—and fully expected the judge to dismiss the government's case against orgonomy.

There are other, secondary irrationalities in the Response and in Reich's refusal to appear in court. In this document Reich introduced a theme that would be repeated in almost all of his subsequent legal documents. "To appear in court as a *'defendant'* . . . would . . . require the disclosure of evidence in support of the position of the discovery of Life Energy. Such disclosure, however, would invoke untold complications and *possibly national disaster.*" But the only "evidence" that had not been previously published (and would not be published in the forthcoming years) was Reich's

16. Wilhelm Reich, *The Murder of Christ,* (New York: Noonday Press, 1969), p. 176.

work with negative gravity and the development of a motor force from orgone energy. However, to defend the validity of his formulations concening orgone energy in general and the efficacy of the accumulator in particular, it would not have been necessary to bring up these specific matters. There was in his writings, and in the writings of co-workers that appeared in various orgonomic publications over the previous years, an abundance of other kinds of evidence as to the validity of his scientific formulations.

Another irrationality was Reich's apparent belief that his mere appearance in court would mean he was ceding authority in matters of science to the judiciary. He could, of course, have appeared in court for the express purpose of challenging the court's jurisdiction. Had he done so, the court, after examining the issue, would most probably have informed him that it did have jurisdiction in the case since it was not only a matter of scientific research but of the interstate shipment of devices whose value was contested by a governmental agency authorized by law to pass judgment on such matters. At that point Reich could still have made the principled decision not to contest the complaint, but he could no longer have had any illusion about the results. Or, on the other hand, knowing what the results would be, he might then have decided to oppose the Complaint after all. Had he done this there is no guarantee, despite the shoddiness of the FDA tests, that he would have won. But there is every reason to believe that the resulting injunction would have been far less sweeping than the one obtained by default; and, too, Reich would then have been in a far stronger position in appealing the case than he was later when, after disobeying the injunction, he was brought to court on the much more serious charge of criminal contempt.

Interestingly enough, during the criminal contempt litigation, Reich attempted to argue the validity of his scientific formulations in court—thereby ceding to the judiciary that very authority and jurisdiction that the Response at this time denied. But by then it was too late. The judge ruled that Reich's formulations were no longer in question. He had had his chance to argue them at the time of the Complaint. Now the issue was only whether or not he had disobeyed the injunction.

Moreover, during this later litigation, Reich advanced other reasons than the one given in the Response for his refusal to appear in answer to the Complaint. He referred to this refusal as "a matter of *principle* and *self-defense*" in his first appeal brief; and in the Supreme Court brief he stated: "As the Discoverer of the Cosmic Life Energy, I dodged [the enemy's] initial assault by *non-appearance in Court*. This pulled the carpet from under the feet of the conspirators." [Italics in original.] This not only modifies and then replaces the original reason given in the Response but is also meaningless, in that his non-appearance had no defensive value but, on the contrary, placed him in a most vulnerable position. At the trial Reich gave yet another reason: His failure to appear was meant to test "how far such misrepresentation and falsifications of fact may reach into the judicial system of the U.S.A." And finally, in the brief to the Circuit Court of Appeals, Reich ascribed his non-appearance to the fact that the allotted twenty days was insufficient time in which to prepare his defense—a claim that is unsupportable, since he could have appeared and requested more time of the court and it would have no doubt been granted.

Though after submitting his Response, Reich fully expected a favorable decision, he also entertained the possibility of an unfavorable one. "Should an injunction be coming down from the Federal court . . . in the matter of the discovery of the Life Energy," he wrote at the time, "then the hopes of a rational outcome of many other things social would dim anyway. The basic duty of Wilhelm Reich in this case was to save the principle of the right of free inquiry and, with this, the possible further medical and educational, as well as biological right to be free of such unconstitutional and illegal acts on the part of an incompetent Government agency." [17] Had he stuck to what was implicit in this statement—namely, that he would abide by the terms of the injunction, should it be issued—then such consistency would have put his non-appearance in the clear light of heroic defiance against the forces of conventional thinking that persecutes new truths in all ages. His Response and non-appearance might then have been likened to the *Apology* and the subsequent concern for consistency of principle that led Socrates to drink the hemlock rather than escape. But in the context of his conduct in the ensuing three years of litigation, Reich must be likened to the crippled giants of Greek and Shakespearian tragedy whose misdirected struggles to escape the trap of

17. *Conspiracy,* item 487B.

character and circumstance only enmesh them more deeply. One is less moved by their courage, great as it is, than appalled by the spectacle of the rare brilliance of their energy running amok.

And yet even this comparison is not altogether complete, for the pathos and horror evoked by Reich's fate do not lead to emotional purgation. Perhaps this is due to his never having recognized the way he misconceived the nature of the conspiracy against him; as a result, he acted unwisely and inconsistently in coping with the legal form of this conspiracy. And yet, perhaps not. For basically Reich's fate, like that of Oedipus, was not the result of his misconceptions. But also here the comparison cannot be pushed, since Oedipus's fate was pre-determined, not contingent upon his actions or character, while that of Reich was. Society was after him, his vitality, his daring, his genius, his virility.

Perhaps there is no fully valid comparison to Reich's fate. His death in prison resolved nothing, settled no historical or existential issue, but only illustrated the murderous tenacity with which the established protects itself against the truly new, and with what self-righteousness it avenges itself on anyone who tries to remove the invisible glass partition that, according to Shestov's analogy, separates man from everything he has been conditioned not to touch, to believe is unknowable. In this modern enactment of an ancient pattern—in Reich's phrase, "the perennial murder of Christ"—there is no purgation; the pathos and horror remain starkly unmodulated and untransformed.

9

---◆---

THE INJUNCTION

As with the Complaint, failure to contest the contents of a Request for Admissions is tantamount to admission of its facts. Such a document was sent to Reich by the prosecution on February 26—that is, a day after Reich had sent Judge Clifford his Response. It contained 65 facts which Reich was either to admit or deny. Some of these facts had been previously included in the Complaint—such as Reich's claim that he discovered orgone energy and was the inventor of the "so-called" orgone energy accumulator, and that the orgone accumulator was not plugged into any source of power, etc. Reich did not answer the Request; had he decided to appear in answer to the Complaint he would, no doubt, have admitted most of the facts in the Request.

In the meantime, the Court received Reich's Response. There was some deliberation over it by the Court, but then, according to an FDA memo dated March 9, "it appears the decision has been reached to characterize this document as a 'crank letter'. It will not be construed as an appearance on the part of any one or all of the defendants, since . . . there is a waiver to that effect in the document." The waiver referred to—and this will be argued later in various briefs—is Reich's statement that "I, therefore, submit, in the name of truth and justice, that I shall not appear in court as the defendant. . . ."

The Court, of course, had the option of taking the Response seriously, looking into the matter of its jurisdiction, and then informing Reich that it had decided that the case did come within its jurisdiction. This may not have made any difference, but at least, as stated earlier, it would have made it necessary for Reich to confront the issuance of an injunction as a certainty and would have given him an opportunity to reconsider. The failure of the Court to take any of the other, less severe, options open to it at this juncture is a pattern that recurs time and again in the next three years of litigation: in every situation where the Court exercised its discretion in choosing between several possible alternative decisions, it almost always chose the one most damaging to Reich—down to the final decision not to suspend or reduce Reich's prison sentence.

So Peter Mills requested a default injunction, which was written up by Maguire and issued by Judge Clifford on March 19, 1954.

The injunction prohibited certain acts and ordered others. These prohibitions and orders were directed to the defendants Wilhelm Reich, the Wilhelm Reich Foundation, Ilse Ollendorff, and to people working in concert with them.

The prohibitionary part of the injunction barred from interstate commerce any accumulator which was "misbranded" * by the representation that it was effective as a therapeutic agent or that orgone energy exists, or by any representation that purported to depict an orgone energy field or that the accumulator collected orgone energy from the atmosphere.

The second part of the injunction ordered that all accumulators rented or owned by the defendants be recalled and destroyed, and that all labeling owned by them be destroyed as well. This labeling, it becomes clear at the end of this section, consisted of all the books and journals issued by the Orgone Institute Press. A later para-

---

* The Federal Food, Drug, and Cosmetic Act defines the term "misbranded" in section 502 in many and various contexts that extend over some five pages. As regards devices in general and the application of this term to orgone accumulators in particular, however, the term means simply that "its labeling is false or misleading in any particular."

graph, however, divided the journals from the books * and stipulated that the latter need only be withheld until all the offending parts were deleted. Needless to say, this provision was meaningless since it would have entailed going through all the copies of all the books and inking out the offending parts. In any case, in the end, the books were burned along with the journals.

The injunction also stipulated that all the destruction be done under the supervision of FDA inspectors and that these inspectors were to be given permission to go through the books, papers, records, and accounts of the defendants.

The unconstitutional request of the Complaint (that the defendants be enjoined from engaging "in any act, whether oral, written or otherwise with respect to any orgone energy accumulator . . . while held for sale after shipment in interstate commerce) was, however, made even more explicit and more blatant in the Injunction. There it was stated that the defendants were to be *"perpetually* enjoined and restrained from . . . making statements and representations pertaining to the existence of orgone energy." [Italics added.]

The concept of misbranding and labeling only has meaning when there is a medicine, drug, or device shipped in interstate commerce to which this misbranding or labeling is somehow related. If someone asserted in publicly disseminated literature that rocking in a rocking chair for fifteen minutes every day is one of the best ways of treating Burger's disease, this could not be considered labeling or misbranding so long as he was not also producing and purveying rocking chairs. As applied to Reich, this meant that his books and publications could only be legally considered as labeling and misbranding while there were accumulators being handled by the Wilhelm Reich Foundation. Once they had been recalled and dismantled or destroyed there would be no further legal basis for restricting his writings or, for that matter, preventing him from publishing information on orgone energy and even the orgone

---

* All but one of these—*People in Trouble*—have since then been reissued in popular softcover editions. This was legally possible because the government later took the position that the injunction was directed *in personam* against the defendants. Since Reich is dead, the Wilhelm Reich Foundation has been disincorporated and Ilse Ollendorff has dissociated herself from the work, there are no more defendants and therefore nothing to prevent the trustee of the Reich estate from having the books reissued.

energy accumulator. The injunction, however, did not state this; on the contrary, it not only made the withholding and destruction of literature that mentions orgone energy independent of orgone accumulators but it also sought to prevent Reich from publishing any information on his research with orgone energy under any circumstances, "perpetually."

Officials of the FDA seemed to be aware of this circumstance, yet, having obtained this unconstitutional power by means of Reich's default, they apparently wanted to exploit it as much as possible. From their point of view they now had an opportunity to do what members of the psychiatric and medical professions had been urging them to do for several years past—to stop Reich, to stop the growing influence of his publications, his ideas, and of orgone therapy in general. Had it really been the orgone accumulator alone that they were interested in, there would have been no need to stretch the legal definition of "labeling" and "accompanying literature" to the point of including so many writings not only unrelated to accumulators but even to orgone energy.

The FDA's position on this aspect of the injunction is expressed most clearly—that is, most hedgingly—in the memo of a meeting on July 29, 1954, between John L. Harvey, the Associate Commissioner, and Irwin Ross, a feature writer for the *New York Post.* When Ross asked Harvey whether Reich's books could be distributed if accumulators were no longer shipped in interstate commerce, Harvey could not give a "categorical statement," though he admitted that "the distribution of books or any written . . . material wholly dissociated from articles subject to the FDC [Food, Drug and Cosmetic] Act is not an offense under the Act." When Ross accused Harvey of saying that the decree prohibited the distribution of Reich's books under any circumstances, Harvey protested, invoking "the remote possibility that the distribution of the books might wind up in such fashion as to constitute labeling for a device." This, however, did not mean, he insisted, that the books couldn't be distributed under any circumstances.*

---

* In his article in the *New York Post*—which he entitled, *à la* Brady, "The Strange Case of Dr. Wilhelm Reich"—Ross did not deal with what appeared to concern him in the interview with Harvey. His article was, rather, a fairly comprehensive review—albeit with frequent snide innuendos —of the development of Reich's work.

The circular reasoning and evasiveness of Harvey's replies are too obvious to require comment. In effect, Harvey was simply defending the terms of the injunction that made the mere mention of orgone energy by the defendants a legal offense under any circumstances.

The FDA lost little time in publicizing its unexpectedly easy and complete victory. On the same day the injunction was issued, a news-release was sent out to the media. This release reviewed the course of legal events, gave a sketchy background to the theory behind the orgone accumulator, touched on the main points of the injunction, and concluded by quoting then FDA Commissioner Charles W. Crawford to the effect that the FDA had accepted the challenges "widely distributed by the Wilhelm Reich Foundation, daring medical researchers and physicists to test accumulators adequately." In such tests, Crawford maintained, orgone energy was found to be nonexistent and the accumulators worthless.

Besides the news release, and together with it, the FDA sent out letters announcing its victory to dozens of professional people and organizations that had over the past years either cooperated with the FDA's investigation or had urged it to stop Reich. To the one sent to the American Psychiatric Association,* it received the following reply signed by Dr. Daniel Blain, Medical Director:

We are delighted to hear of the successful prosecution of your action against the Wilhelm Reich Foundation, and I know that I speak for the profession at large in expressing our deep appreciation of the good work of the Food and Drug Administration.

Dr. Richard L. Frank, Secretary of the American Psychoanalytic Association, conveyed the response of his organization as follows:

We are most appreciative of your letter of March 25 relative to action taken in connection with Dr. Wilhelm Reich and his group. The American Psychoanalytic Association wishes to commend the Food and Drug Administration for their effective action in this situation.

Dr. Reich and his associates are not members of the American Psychoanalytic Association and their theories and activities are com-

* Almost a year later, on May 23, 1955, George P. Larrick, the new FDA Commissioner was to write in an office memo: "We could not have brought the injunction case against Dr. Reich except for the fact that nationally known psychiatrists gave willingly of their time and knowledge to help us perfect the case."

pletely foreign to all of our theories and practices. . . . Unfortunately, we were never in a position to exercise any control over or to influence his activities in any way.

(One can't help asking why Dr. Frank should even have wanted his organization to exercise control over Reich and his associates who were not members if their theories and practices had nothing in common with those of the American Psychoanalytic Association.)

Congratulatory replies came from other professionals and professional organizations as well. Dr. Charles L. Dunham of the Atomic Energy Commission wrote in part: "I appreciate very much your making this available to me, as you know only too well what a thorn in the side he has been to many of us." Dr. Sleeper, psychiatrist and superintendent of the State of Maine Hospital at Augusta, Maine, wrote in part on March 27, 1954:

I intend to look into the matter of what the citizens of Maine can do regarding Dr. Reich and his activities. I strongly suspect that it will be almost impossible to do anything to curtail his other activities, which I suspect . . . may not be in accordance with accepted medical practice.

Efforts on the part of Reich's supporters to mobilize opinion against the unconstitutionality of the injunction met with the same kind of failure as the earlier efforts made during the investigation period. Dr. Kelley writes:

Several individuals and small groups were . . . active in attempts to countermend the . . . injunction. Newspapers, hundreds of officials, politicians, editors, etc., were contacted and senators written. If one important politician or major publication had taken a strong stand against the Food and Drug Administration's crime at this time the worst of its effects could no doubt have been averted. None did—none has since.[1]

Several Maine newspapers and one Boston paper that was distributed in Maine reported in their March 20 issue that the injunction had been issued. However, Reich did not see these newspapers and so had no knowledge of this new development. It was only on the morning of March 22 that he finally learned of the injunction—

1. Kelley, p. 16.

accidentally, through his caretaker, Tom Ross, who himself had heard about it through local gossip. Then, at 1:00 P.M. of the same day, a U.S. marshal came to Orgonon to make official delivery of the injunction.

At first Reich was, again, shocked. But this time he did not remain shocked long. Instead, the shock gave way to anger, and within several hours a plan was developed to express his anger and register his protest. This plan was entitled OROP EP—Orgone Operation Emotional Plague. In introduction to the protocol of this plan, Reich wrote: "Established knowledge must have no authority *ever* to decide what is NEW knowledge." And this was followed by the explanation that "OROP EP was designed to protect [protest?] the intrusion of [into?] our scientific territory by individuals and organizations incompetent in our realm of knowledge." [2] The plan was to use Reich's weather-influencing technique to break the drought period of that winter and thereby to prove that orgone energy did exist. But this was to be done in a more concentrated way than was ever before attempted—namely, with a battery of several, separately deployed cloudbusters.

Accordingly, by 3:45 of that day, the following telegram was sent to Mr. Ivan Tannehill of the U.S. Weather Bureau in Washington, D.C.:

According to the Federal Food and Drug Administration Orgone Energy does not exist. We are drawing east to west from Hancock, Maine and Rangely, Maine, to cause storm to prove that Orgone Energy does exist. Consequences of this action are all your responsibility and that of Federal Judge Clifford of Portland, Maine. We are flooding the East as you are drying out the Southwest. You do not play with serious natural scientific basic research.[3]

The reason the blame for the consequences of the operation was placed on Judge Clifford is clear: He had issued the injunction. The reason for Tannehill's part in the blame is not completely clear, though one can suppose that it might be because he had been receiving communications from Reich on his weather work for the past two years or so without acknowledgment.

2. Wilhelm Reich, "OROP EP," in *Response to Ignorance,* Documentary Supplement No. 1, Orgone Institute Press, 1955. (This and two other pamphlets were published in a limited edition as supplements to *Conspiracy.*) p. 19.
3. Quoted in OROP EP," p. 20.

Tannehill's responsibility for "drying out the Southwest"—*i.e.*, the Arizona desert, which at this time Reich was planning to visit in order to test his rainmaking technique under desert conditions— is a slightly different matter. Reich may have been accusing Tannehill as a representative of the whole mechanistic-scientific establishment responsible for the development of nuclear energy that was hostile to orgone, that caused DOR, which in turn was causing desert development.

In these accusations against Tannehill there is a hint of the merging of two issues that until then had been separate: Reich's fight against the FDA and his fight against the "planetary DOR emergency." This merging will become more marked in *Contact with Space* where descriptions of scientific work are often interspersed with comments on trouble with the FDA, as if there were some actual inner connection between the two. There will be occasion to explore this matter further in a later chapter.

The above telegram was also telephoned to the weatherman— Weatherbee—of Radio Station WBZ in Boston "in order," the protocol explains, "to prevent a central silencing by saying, *'We just happened to have a storm.'* " [4]

It will be recalled that in the previous summer the *Bangor Daily News* ran a story of how Reich had, on a produce and pay basis, brought rain that broke a drought threatening the blueberry crops. It could, of course, be argued that the drought was at its end and the rain would have come even without Reich's operation. The fact that more rainfall was recorded in the area where the operation took place than anywhere else in the state could be regarded as mere coincidence. The point is that it is difficult to set up foolproof experimental controls for weather-influencing work. Reich usually tried to deal with this situation by comparing the weather following a "drawing" operation to weather forecasts. But even this is imperfect control since, as is well known, weather forecasts are often wrong even without the weather being influenced. The best answer to this problem would be a computer-monitored program that over an extended period correlated relative percentages of discrepancies between weather conditions and forecasts when the cloudbuster was and was not used. However, this would require the support of governmental agencies or scientific institutions—none of which were interested in this method of influencing weather. In 1960, Dr.

4. "OROP EP," p. 20.

Charles Kelley used Reich's method of weather control and wrote up the results in a booklet that included time-lapsed photographs of changes in cloud configuration during various operations. Though he used this booklet in applications for grants to several scientific bodies, he had no positive response. Dr. Richard Blasband, in 1965, carried out a series of rainmaking operations at times when rain probabilities were reported at less than 10 percent for subsequent twenty-four-hour periods or when no rain was forecast for subsequent forty-eight-hour periods. Under these conditions rain occurred in eight of thirty-eight separate operations. "For chance to have been responsible," writes Boadella of this experiment, "would have meant that nearly 50 percent of the weather forecasts on these thirty-eight occasions were erroneous." [5]

The first drawing of OROP EP took place between 3:30 and 9:30 P.M. of the day on which Reich was served with the injunction. Midpoint in this period—that is, at 6:30—Weatherbee, according to the protocol, reported the forecast as "fair . . . light snow possible to the north . . . the temperature 41°, wind SW, rising. Tomorrow winds freshen, no chance for fog. Tomorrow cloudy to north, sunny in Boston—fair to good weather." [6]

But by 7:00 A.M. of the following morning, Weatherbee reported: "Cloudsheet over NE. . . . *Yesterday's forecast an error.* . . . Clouds are persisting and may even cause slight snow . . . only a nucleus type of precipitation tonight . . . winds gently southerly . . . normal temperatures . . . tonight *cloudiness, scattered showers and snow flurries . . . tomorrow fair, sunny, higher temperatures. . . .*" [7] [Italics in protocol.]

A half-hour later Weatherbee reported: "The cloud blanket *looks worse* and *will hide the sun, a little* snow will fall and may turn into rain . . . this looks and sounds worse than it will be, it won't amount to much . . . no extremes in sight." [8]

A second drawing was conducted that day between 2:00 and 3:00 P.M. and snow began at Rangeley at 4.00 P.M.

Reich sent another telegram to Tannehill—with copies to the President, J. Edgar Hoover, the United and Associated Presses in

---

5. Boadella, p. 294.
6. Quoted in "OROP EP," p. 21.
7. Ibid., p. 21.
8. *Ibid.,* pp. 21–22.

Portland, Maine, and the *Bangor Daily News* in Bangor, Maine—a short while after, saying:

Snowstorm in Rangeley Region as predicted in telegram of 3/22/54. You can no longer escape responsibility for desert development in U.S.A. We shall pursue subject of desert development to last detail. Evasion no longer will work. Oranur Weather Control will have to win over forces of Chemistry-evil killing planetary life.[9]

The "Chemistry-evil killing planetary life" is possibly *melanor,* a substance Reich discovered as a result of the oranur experiment and which he later concluded was the specific agent by which deserts everywhere were produced. If not this, the "Chemistry-evil" could be a reference to the FDA, which in its connection with the pharmaceutical industry and in its effort to disrupt Reich's work would let the desert-producing process continue unchecked and thus kill "planetary life." Reich seemed to have disregarded the ambiguities in these telegrams and was unable to see that they could only be regarded as crank communications by those receiving them. On the other hand, no matter how carefully the telegrams might have been worded there was no possibility of their being taken seriously.

Perhaps the telegrams were written primarily for the historical record rather than to suit the immediate situation. In these last years of his life, Reich became increasingly concerned with the judgment of history. He often seems to be writing his own history, to be viewing his work and trouble in this period from some indeterminate point in the future when orgonomy will have won the day. Perhaps, then, the telegrams are best read in this context.

Keeping track of further discrepancies between actual weather conditions and weather forecasts, the protocol of OROP EP quotes from the March 26 issue of the *Bangor Daily News* that "U.S. Weather Bureau forecasts fair and warmer for today, but you couldn't tell it from the snow that was pelting Bangor streets last night."[10] And Reich's comment on all these discrepancies was: "It's all confused. They don't know what they are talking about."[11]

In the protocol many of these details are interspersed with com-

9. "OROP EP," p. 22.
10. Quoted in "OROP EP," p. 26.
11. "OROP EP," p. 25.

mentaries on "The Legal Game"—for instance, we are told that Reich will meet with agents of the FDA when they come to supervise the implementation of the injunction only if a state trooper and the local constable are present, only if notes are taken of everything that is said, and only if each of the FDA agents signs a statement that he is not working for red fascism.[12] Then, assuring the reader that newspaper publicity and "using the Cloudbuster with political undertones" were unusual practices for the Orgone Institute, the protocol concludes: "On March 25 rain fell from one end of the continent to the other, raining in 45 out of the 48 states—signifying a successful conclusion to OROP EP." [13]

Though the intention originally was to flood the East, Reich regarded the effects of this operation—as of previous ones—as extending over the whole country, if not the whole continent and hemisphere. Though this might well appear grandiose and megalomaniacal, such wide-ranging effects were quite consistent with the theoretical basis of the weather-influencing work: if the cloudbuster affected the orgone energy balance in the local atmosphere there was no reason why this should not act in chain-reaction fashion to affect the orgone energy balance (and, consequently, the weather) of more distant areas.

OROP EP received little if any publicity. Aside from providing Reich with an outlet for anger at the insult of the injunction, it had no practical effect on the course of subsequent legal developments.

Apparently when the injunction was issued Reich had no immediate intention of actively disobeying it. On March 30, a telegram signed by Ilse Ollendorff, who worked as the clerk of the Wilhelm Reich Foundation, was sent to Mills, advising him that "The Wilhelm Reich Foundation is far advanced in preparing full compliance with injunction . . . an exact account of measures taken and still in progress will be sent to your office for your information." However, this telegram, Reich was later to state in a letter to Dr. Silvert, dated January 8, 1955, had been sent without his agreement and under pressure from his lawyer, whose services he subsequently terminated. (He was to have increasing trouble with lawyers in future litigation, since he wanted to conduct the

12. *Ibid.,* p. 26.
13. *Ibid.,* p. 26.

legal work himself, at his own discretion, and wanted a lawyer to act only in an advisory capacity.)

The measures mentioned in the telegram were, according to testimony later given by Ilse Ollendorff in the contempt trial, mostly of a negative nature. Actions explicitly prohibited by the injunction were not continued—no more accumulators or literature were sent out. But, on the other hand, none of the things that the injunction ordered the defendants to do were done. Accumulators were not recalled, those on hand were not destroyed, nor were any of the publications destroyed. This, however, did not constitute a violation since the injunction stated that all these measures were to be carried out under the supervision of FDA people and the FDA did not make arrangements for such supervision. At one point a letter was actually prepared and addressed to every renter, advising him or her of the fact that the injunction required the recall of rented accumulators, but this letter was not sent out because, as Ilse Ollendorff testified at the trial:

I wanted to comply with the letter of injunction and the injunction stated that all measures be taken under supervision of the Pure Food and Drug Administration, and I was warned that if I sent out letters without supervision, I could not prove that I had sent the letters out.*

In the end, according to Ilse Ollendorff's testimony, the matter of the rented accumulators was left up to the renters: they were aware of the injunction, and whether they wanted to retain or return their accumulators was left to each individual's discretion. The renters, for the most part, decided to retain the accumulators and the revenue for these rentals continued to come in over the following months. Eventually, to facilitate the servicing of damaged accumulators and the acceptance and re-rental of those returned, Dr.

---

* The prosecution did not accept this, claiming that the defendants had not asked for such supervision. But since there were other, much clearer instances of violation of the injunction, this rather dubious line was not pursued. A letter dated March 24, 1954, from Washington headquarters to all FDA districts makes it quite clear that the FDA had no intention of waiting to be invited: "It is expected that the Boston district will begin inspection and other operations about March 29, 1954." This was later amended as revealed in a letter Maguire himself wrote to Mills on April 6, 1954, where he concluded: "It has been deemed advisable to allow the defendants at least a short period of time after the receipt of the decree to see just how far they will proceed on their own in the matter of compliance."

Silvert set up a distribution center in New York City. In this way—this is still according to Ilse Ollendorff's testimony—the ban on interstate shipment would not be violated when users returned their accumulators; although, she added, that for purely economic reasons some such arrangement had been contemplated even before the time of the injunction. (There is, it should be noted, something a bit specious about her reasoning, since the ban on the interstate shipment of accumulators would not apply to any such shipment that was necessary for their return to Orgonon.)

Some of his supporters suggested to Reich that he appeal and contest the injunction. Ordinarily, any decree granted by default cannot be appealed, and yet there are rare exceptions. He might, conceivably, have been able to accomplish something by appeal due to two circumstances connected with the injunction. The first is its unconstitutional aspect. The second has to do with the fact that Peter Mills, who was instrumental in obtaining the injunction, had previously been Reich's lawyer, and had handled all the legal matters connected with the incorporation and functioning of the Wilhelm Reich Foundation and other organizations in Orgonon. Besides this, he was also present when Reich and co-workers discussed the trouble with the FDA. In spite of these two weaknesses in the government's position, Reich refused to appeal the injunction.

Reich's only reaction, aside from OROP EP, was to write a couple of articles that appeared in print only in 1955, in a limited edition. Both of these are, in effect, attempts to recast certain aspects of the American law structure to bring it into alignment with his views on the human condition and life-energy functions.

In the first article, entitled "The Board of Social Psychiatry" and written in March 1954, Reich introduced a theme that he would later repeat and elaborate upon in his various briefs: the need for the establishment of a Board of Social Psychiatry empowered to deal with "the socially pathological acts of the Emotional Plague." [14] "True Justice," he wrote in this article, "must finally step out of its present, merely formalistic, legalistic procedure and include the *human,* the *emotional* . . . element underly-

14. Wilhelm Reich, "The Board of Social Psychiatry," in *Response to Ignorance,* p. 4.

ing the administration of social justice in human affairs. . . ." [15]
This new administration of social justice would have to be carried
out by physicians and educators "operating at the SICKBED OF
SOCIETY" [16] if human emotional illness is ever to be eradicated.

The second article, entitled "Supremacy of Basic Research"—
written in April 1954—was more specifically concerned with the
injunction than the first. In it Reich saw one of the basic issues
involved in his trouble with the FDA as "a showdown between
the forces of LIFE, scientifically still embryonic, and the forces of
DEATH, powerfully organized." [17] We have encountered this Life-
Death schema earlier in Reich's view of his work in relation to the
cold war. This schema could now be extended as follows:

Forces of Life	Forces of Death
U.S.A.	USSR
democracy	red fascism
U.S. government	FDA
orgone physics	nuclear physics
embryonic	well organized
fertile	drought and desert development
orgone energy	DOR (deadly orgone energy)

Moreover, in this article Reich objected to the injunction on the
grounds that it constituted coercion of citizens by "well-hidden
business interests to accept *only one* kind of treatment, dictated by
commercial horsethieves"; [18] that it was unconstitutional; and that
Mills' involvement in the matter made it "a clear case of criminal
collusion." [19]

However, Reich had no desire to pursue the matter through legal
channels, reverting instead to the previously held position that the
accumulators were, after all, the responsibility of the physicians
who prescribed them. It was this stand, belated as it was, which
enabled the physicians to initiate the intervention proceedings
that followed.

15. *Ibid.*, pp. 4–5.
16. *Ibid.*, p. 5.
17. Wilhelm Reich, "Supremacy of Basic Research," in *Response to Ignorance*, p. 9.
18. *Ibid.*, p. 10.
19. *Ibid.*, p. 11.

10

THE
INTERVENTION
PROCEEDINGS

On May 5, 1954, some six weeks after the injunction was issued, fifteen doctors, all trained by Reich and led by Dr. Elsworth Baker, applied to intervene in the case in order to challenge and, hopefully overturn, the injunction.

According to Rule 24 of the Federal Rules of Civil Procedure there are two conditions under which people not directly involved in a case are allowed to intervene in it. One, called "intervention of Right," occurs when people applying to intervene may be bound by a court decision even though their interests were not represented in the litigation process. Another, called "permissive intervention," may occur if the people applying to intervene, while not technically included in the legal decision of the main action, are nevertheless socially or professionally affected by it. The first condition is a right; the second is a matter of a court's discretion. In both, however, the timeliness of the application is a factor.

The application of the medical orgonomists was made on both

grounds: they saw themselves as being bound by the injunction though they had not had a chance to defend their interests in the main legal action; and they also saw themselves as being affected by the injunction in that, quite apart from whether or not they were legally bound by it, its conclusions and orders interfered with their ability to practice their chosen school of medicine.

To support their application, each of the medical orgonomists submitted an affidavit that summarized his professional background,* that affirmed the validity of orgonomy and the orgone accumulator on the basis of their personal research and experience and offered to argue and prove this validity in court. Moreover, the affidavits stated that the order of the injunction concerning the destruction of accumulators and literatures would interfere with their medical practice. Since the injunction applied to all persons in active concert or participating with the defendants, and since all the applicants had been mailed copies of the injunction by the government, it was obvious, their affidavits argued, that they were bound by the injunction and would be considered guilty of violating it if they recommended that a patient read some orgonomic literature, or helped a patient get an accumulator, or even if they treated a patient with an accumulator. And, finally, in order to comply with the provision of timeliness, the doctors explained the approximately six-week gap between the issuance of the injunction and their application to intervene by maintaining that they had had no prior knowledge that Reich would not answer the Complaint; once they learned that the injunction had been served they acted as swiftly as possible.

Two points about the affidavits deserve special mention. One is that Reich's principled opposition to arguing scientific matters in a court of law—the reason he gave for his nonappearance—was not adhered to by the fifteen orgonomists. They were prepared to argue the validity of orgonomy and the effectiveness of the accumulator with, it has to be assumed, Reich's approval. This, in effect, constitutes yet another inconsistency and reinforces the suspicion that Reich's original decision not to answer the Complaint was not rationally motivated.

* The author is much indebted to the cogent summary of this material by David Blasband in his article "United States of America v. Wilhelm Reich," in the *Journal of Orgonomy* of November, 1967, Vol. 1, Nos. 1 and 2.

The other point is the false reason given in these affidavits (and later repeated in various briefs) for the lateness of the application to intervene. We have only to recall the quotation from Dr. Baker's article, cited in the previous chapter ("His appearance in court was no longer considered and we waited for the inevitable injunction." [1]) to realize that the lateness was not due to absence of prior knowledge of Reich's intention.

The real reason for the lateness was that Reich expected a favorable outcome and refused to permit intervention until his expectation had proven false.* This reason, however, could not be advanced as a legal argument. When one enters a litigation with the hope of winning one must often be prepared, no matter how valid one's case is, to cut corners of truth in order to put one's case in the best possible light. It was this kind of legal Standard Operating Procedure that Reich in later stages of the litigation consistently refused to engage in. As much as he misinterpreted the drift of legal events, as much as he was deluded concerning the matter of communist forces against him, he refused to fight his battle on the only level it could be fought with any chance of success. He did not want to win the case on the basis of distortions of truth as he saw it, or on the basis of legalistic technicalities. Charles Haydon—the orgonomists' counsel during intervention who also represented Reich during part of the contempt proceedings—informed this author that at one point he presented Reich with a list of some fifteen technical points he could have used to strengthen

---

* Ilse Ollendorff told this author in an interview that Reich's co-workers should have acted to intervene without Reich's permission and even, if necessary, against Reich's wishes. David Boadella wrote—though not in specific reference to the legal trouble—that people around Riech could have helped him most by dissociating themselves from his irrational views, prepared to face his wrath and charges of betrayal even while they affirmed their support of all that was rational in orgonomy.[2] These views, however, seem somewhat simplistic. Were it known beforehand that Reich would eventually be jailed, then there might be some merit to them. But no one at the time of the Complaint could forsee such an eventuality. Under these circumstances, who can say with certainty that Reich's interests would have been best served by the kind of action that he could only have interpreted as betrayal and that would have intensified his already extreme feeling of isolation? It is doubtful that anything more could have been done than was done by those who, like Dr. Baker, urged Reich to contest the Complaint but at the same time refrained from acting against his wishes.

1. Baker, p. 48.
2. Boadella, p. 283.

his legal position and that Reich refused to use them. Reich, in other words, conducted his defense exclusively on the basis of what to him were the main principles involved.

Besides the affidavits submitted by the fifteen doctors, there were briefs and reply briefs prepared by Haydon in support of the application to intervene. The essential arguments in these documents were that: * the orgonomists ought to be allowed to intervene on both the grounds earlier mentioned because the injunction interfered unconstitutionally with the doctors' right to practice a school of medicine of their choice and it also interfered with their freedom of speech and press in that they would not be able to obtain scientific information from Reich or the Wilhelm Reich Foundation; it destroyed the physician-patient relationship since the patients' names and diagnoses were sure to be included in the records of people working with Reich that the injunction ordered be open to FDA inspectors; the court should have dealt with Reich's Response as a motion to dismiss due to lack of jurisdiction; the government had misrepresented and distorted matters in the Complaint; Peter Mills' involvement in the case violated the attorney-client privileges of the orgonomists (who were on the board of directors of the Wilhelm Reich Foundation that Mills had represented) as well as that of Reich.

The government's basic arguments, as they appear in several briefs, were that: the orgonomists were not bound by the injunction unless they acted "in concert" with the defendants and therefore they had no right to intervene; the untimeliness of the intervention application was not due to the reason given since some of the applicants knew of Reich's intention to default; permitting intervention would delay the execution of the injunction and thereby cause additional harm to people who, instead of getting proper treatment for their illnesses, rely on the accumulator. The government, in effect, evaded the delicate issue of Mills' former professional relationship with Reich by saying that this was a matter between Mills and Reich and could not be pressed by anyone else; and that the applicants were jumping the gun, since until they established their right to intervene they were not in a position to raise this issue.

* In this and the following paragraph, the author is again indebted to Mr. David Blasband's cogent abstraction of these arguments in his article "United States of America v. Wilhelm Reich."

Several of the above issues and the way they were argued by both sides are important enough to merit a closer look.

The main evidence the government adduced to prove that some of the applicants knew before the injunction was issued that Reich would not appear to contest the Complaint was a prior exchange of letters between one of the applicants and a lawyer. On February 15, 1954, Dr. James Willie wrote to attorney Benjamin Butler of Farmington, Maine, confirming an earlier telephone conversation about the possibility of retaining Butler to handle his (Willie's) interests in the conflict between Reich and the FDA. On February 18 Butler wrote back to Willie advising him that because of the eighty-five-mile distance between Farmington and Portland, Maine, where the Federal Court was located, Butler would have to decline the offer. Was the introduction of this correspondence by the government a violation of the attorney-client relationship?

Haydon claimed it was. "Such a release of confidential communication," he wrote in one of his reply briefs, "when coupled with the fact of Mr. Mills having represented both sides at different times, makes of this matter a most peculiar situation." The government denied that there was any violation of an attorney-client relationship in that the mere demonstration in court of the fact that such a relationship existed was not in itself a violation. Haydon replied that the government had done more than simply disclose the fact of an attorney-client relationship—it disclosed the subject of that relationship, namely that Dr. Willie had wanted to retain Mr. Butler to intervene in the litigation between Reich and the government.

Another issue was whether or not the court had erred in not regarding Reich's Response and accompanying letter as an application to dismiss the case because of lack of jurisdiction. Quoting pertinent parts of the Response and letter, the government's brief stated that to interpret these documents as applications to dismiss "taxes credulity, especially when the interpretation is by trained psychiatrists." And it concluded that the documents were "susceptible of no other interpretation . . . than—I shall not subject myself to the constituted judicial authority of this country." Haydon contended just the opposite. After a close analysis of the Response, his reply brief states: "It is difficult to conceive of a layman moving to dismiss a case for lack of jurisdiction and using language which would indicate that motion with more preciseness than that which Dr. Reich used." And his reply brief concluded that since the court had never officially passed on the issue of jurisdiction, the injunction should not have been served. (This must have been, on the District Court level, a delicate subject to broach since Judge Clifford, who was to pass on the application to intervene, was the same one who, according to Haydon's brief, erred in issuing the injunction because he had not first ruled on the matter or jurisdiction.)

Judge Clifford denied the application to intervene, both on the basis of right and of permission. In the decision handed down on November 17, 1954, he made no mention of either of the violations of attorney-client privilege alleged by Haydon. In arguing against the applicants' effort to intervene on the basis of absolute right, Clifford stated that they were not included in the injunction whose "sole object" was to prevent the named defendants from shipping accumulators in interstate commerce. This view of the purpose of the injunction, however, ignores the order to ban and/or destroy the publications of the Orgone Institute Press. Such banning and destruction were not necessary to prohibit the interstate shipment of accumulators. This fact as well as much of what has been presented in this study thus far makes it clear that the main purpose of the injunction was to stop Reich's work and influence—and the ban on the interstate shipment of accumulators served as a means to this end.

Though, the decision continued, the applicants could get into legal trouble if they were to act in concert with the defendants to violate the terms of the injunction, this did not change anything. They could do anything they wanted as regards the practice of orgonomy or the use of orgone accumulators so long as they did it independently of the defendants.

As regards the matter of permissive intervention, Judge Clifford's decision stated that any application to intervene made after the issuance of an injunction had to show a stronger reason for its lateness than was shown by the application of the orgonomists.

While there is an inner consistency in the position taken in this decision, and while this position provided the court with a convenient means of sidestepping many of the thorny issues raised by the briefs for the applicants, it is fundamentally inconsistent with the avowed purpose of the injunction: the protection of the public from the accumulator. There was a great deal made of this purpose in the various government briefs. In fact, it will be recalled, one of the grounds advanced by the government for denying the application to intervene was that if granted it would delay execution of the injunction and in that way endanger public health. Presumably, Judge Clifford had this consideration, among others, in mind when he passed on the untimeliness of the application. However, this apparent concern for public health was completely ignored both by the government and the judge when they stated that the applicants could engage with impunity in the independent shipment of orgone accumulators across state lines since the injunction applied only to the defendants named in it.

Shortly after Judge Clifford's decision, the fifteen orgonomists and Mr. Haydon took their effort to intervene to the next higher court. While the matter was pending before the Appellate Court, they submitted a motion for a temporary stay of execution of the terms of the injunction. On January 18, 1955, Judge Clifford agreed that the part of the injunction ordering the destruction of publications and accumulators be postponed until "final determination of the appeal . . . or . . . further order from this court." When on May 11, 1955, the Court of Appeals affirmed the decision of the lower court, another motion to postpone the destruction, this time pending the appeal to the Supreme Court, was made but turned down. This motion then was directed to the Supreme Court. Though the Supreme Court turned down the motion, a compromise was worked out: Simon E. Sobeloff, Solicitor General of the U.S. Department of Justice, promised in a letter to the Supreme Court dated July 5, 1955, that the government would only collect accumulators and publications but not destroy them while the matter of intervention was pending before the Supreme Court.

The petition of the fifteen medical orgonomists was turned down by the Supreme Court on October 10, 1955. The actual destruction of publications and accumulators, however—for whatever reason—did not take place until well into the next year.

Reich's thinking on the whole issue at this time was expressed in a letter he wrote to Dr. Baker on May 18, 1955, which read, in part, as follows:

It should be obvious by now that the issue before the courts . . . is new in its substance, that the statute books carry no provisions regarding the Emotional Plague. I would like to summarize briefly the true issues coming up before the Supreme Court.

1. Is it legally, morally, and factually, if *truth* should prevail, any longer possible that THE MOTIVE of a complaint should be kept out of the proceedings . . . ?

2. If the motive can no longer be overlooked, the question emerges whether it is any longer possible to exclude the irrational elements from the legal procedure. . . .

3. Is it permissible legally and morally that sick individuals, motivated by their own anxieties . . . should drag what they dislike into court . . . under the pretext and disguise of bona fide government action?

4. Is it legally and morally excusable that such activity be taken over, even if innocently, by a court of justice . . .? Is it, furthermore, admissible that such court action follow the line laid out by political, subversive hoodlums, subservient to a foreign power . . . ?

5. Is it true justice to omit the factual situation, to restrict the total issue to procedural, empty legalism, to force the public to believe that a device is *fraudulent* in the hands of A, but perfectly legal and *not* fraudulent in the hands of B, C, D, E, etc . . . ?

6. Is is morally and legally permissible that newly discovered facts be subjected to laws written into the statute books *before* there existed any knowledge of the . . . unknown natural phenomenon?

7. Has a court of law the right and authority to pass judgment on the validity of bona fide basic research in new territory? Has established opinion the right to decide what is new basic knowledge?

8. Has a natural scientist the right to refuse to fall prey to such criminal activities on the part of emotionally sick individuals . . . ? Or should the killing of scientists and pioneers by evil men continue forever unchallenged, unabated?

11

PRELUDE TO THE
CONTEMPT TRIAL

Shortly after the oranur experiment was discontinued, Reich noticed that one of its effects was that the granite walls of the observatory began to darken and crumble. After extensive observation, microscopic examinations of the crumbled material and Geiger-counter measurements of its background count, Reich concluded that there was a special process at work in this material. Later he came to regard this process as the result of the DOR-contaminated atmosphere which materialized in the dark substance he called melanor. Melanor, then, became the specific substance by which deserts were formed. Other results of the oranur experiment were substances Reich named "orite," "brownite," and "orene." All of these together he regarded as constituting a new scientific field—pre-atomic chemistry.

The desire to test these formulations as well as the effectiveness of the cloudbuster under more rigorous conditions, led him to undertake a trip to the Arizona desert in the fall of 1954. Armoring in man was the inner, "emotional desert" which was to a certain extent responsible for the outer desert. That is, human armoring that cut man off from his emotional depths led to the development of a mechanistic science and technology whose culmination was the discovery of nuclear energy; this nuclear energy then had a DOR-producing effect on the atmosphere which, in turn, through melanor, led to desert formation. If he could reverse the desert-forming process in Arizona, that is, de-armor nature, then he would have found an effective means of dealing with the planetary emergency.

In the context of this enormous challenge, which he called OROP Desert, the success of this experimental undertaking would make the matter of the injunction sink to the level of an insignificant nuisance. This consideration no doubt added to the urgency Reich felt about this undertaking. It was a struggle both against desert formation and the FDA—as incongruous as the juxtaposition of these two foes might seem. Later, during the experimental work, a third enemy would enter the picture.

In the meantime there was only minimal compliance with the terms of the injunction: the rental and sales of accumulators and the sale of literature was discontinued. Aside from this, nothing else was done, and since the FDA made no immediate move to gain further compliance, Reich came increasingly to feel that the injunction was unenforceable. His feeling about this was expressed in a letter to Neill written in August 1954 where he said: "We have won the case *factually*." [1]

Since money was no longer coming in from accumulator and book sales, William Steig, the prominent New York artist who had drawn the cartoons for Reich's *Listen, Little Man,* undertook to solicit funds from people interested in Reich's work. A letter he sent out at this time reflects the optimism felt by Reich and those working with him:

The world now *desperately needs* what orgonomy can do for it, especially in the field of Cosmic orgone engineering, and it will be coming to Wilhelm Reich for help. Meanwhile Reich has not been waiting to have a magnum of champagne launch his cloudbuster in an official ceremony. As a responsible inhabitant of a land, and of a world, in grave emergency situation, he is going ahead and doing what he can to understand and deal with the emergency.

Since the Wilhelm Reich Foundation is not endowed by anyone, but has suffered loss of funds through the injunction, we have undertaken to collect money not only for the legal fund, but also for OROP

1. Quoted in Ollendorff, pp. 122–23.

Desert, that is for the work of reversing through cosmic orgone engineering, the calamitous process of desert development. . . .

We hope many of you will want to participate by sending contributions either to OROP Desert, or to the Orgone Legal Fund. The work of OROP Desert is the more essential of the two, for obvious reasons: the desert is a problem compared to which the injunction is merely a nuisance. . . .

On this wave of misplaced optimism a letter went out on October 9 from the Wilhelm Reich Foundation, over the signature of William Moise, Reich's son-in-law and close collaborator in the weather-control work, informing the District Court in Portland, Maine, that "The Orgone Institute Press will continue its normal function of filling orders for books in the realm of natural science and orgonomic medicine." And, the letter continued: "This decision was made when it was ascertained, beyond any reasonable doubt, that the injunction . . . was pursued and obtained in a criminal manner by Moscow-directed American conspirators." (This ascertainment, Reich was later to explain in his petition to the Supreme Court, was on the basis of the compilation of documents for *Conspiracy*.) The letter then requested that if the court objected to this action, "information to this effect would be appreciated." The court did not respond to the letter. Reich interpreted this silence as further proof of his belief that the injunction was unenforceable.

Preparations for the Arizona trip had begun several months before the letter was sent. The expedition—consisting of Reich, his son, Peter, his daughter, Eva, her husband, William Moise, and Mr. Robert McCullough (another co-worker in the weather experiments)—set out on October 18, traveling in two cars.

On the way west, Moise had stopped off in Dayton, Ohio, to report to General Watson of the Air Force Technical Center on Reich's work with UFOs. Arrangements had been made beforehand for this meeting, but instead of the general, Moise was shunted to the deputy commander of the base, a Colonel Wertenbaker. Several pages in *Contact* are devoted to an account of the meeting as reported by Moise. Feeling that this was a significant meeting, that at last some breakthrough had been made in interesting the government in Reich's encounters with UFOs, Moise wrote that "The contact with Colonel Wartenbaker was excellent throughout the conference. He was serious, intent and looked at me while I talked. He was the only one who did. His excitement increased as the report progressed." [2] The FDA file, however, contains a letter sent by Colonel Wertenbaker several days after this meeting to the Directorate of Intelligence of the Air Force, in which he writes, in part:

General Watson did not talk personally to Mr. Moise, I am happy to say, but I interviewed this person. . . . The information given us by Moise defies description and I'll not attempt to give you the details.
. . . the Air Force will do well to avoid any intanglements [sic]
. . . but what is an absolute necessity from the standpoint of good public relations.

Thus Mr. Moise's interpretation, too, was typical of the unwarranted optimism that seemed to influence everyone working with Reich at this time. This interpretation was, too, one of the circumstances that, in the following months and until the end of his life, led Reich to believe that the air force was keeping secret watch over him, and to see in every air force plane passing overhead confirmation of this belief.

By the end of October, Reich and his party were settled outside of Tucson, Arizona, on an estate they called Little Orgonon, and had begun working on the desert problem. The project lasted until April of 1955—approximately a month before Judge Clifford issued his denial of the application to intervene that had been submitted by the fifteen medical orgonomists. When the party left Arizona, Peter—eleven years of age by then, yet upon whom Reich had begun to rely as if the child were an adult—went to live with his mother; and Reich went to Orgonon to write up the work in what eventually became *Contact with Space,* published posthumously in 1957 in a limited edition.

The results of the Arizona project appear to have been most promising. There was an unusual frequency of rain in that area during most of the period of the operation. Moreover, Reich reported the gradual sprouting of grass in the area surrounding Tucson where none of the local inhabitants could recall having seen any before. This grass came to approximately a twelve-inch height by December of 1954.

2. Wilhelm Reich, *Contact with Space* (Rangeley, Maine: Core Pilot Press, 1957), p. 86, (published in a limited edition).

Besides these results, however, *Contact* deals also with the matter of UFOs. Reich became interested in UFOs, it will be recalled, in late 1953. This interest continued and during the Arizona project became mingled with the weather-control work. *Contact* describes several "battles" with them—that is, Reich pointed the cloudbuster (or space gun, as he came to call it when used against UFOs) at lights in the sky he thought might be UFOs and observed, on several occasions, that the lights blinked out. At other times the lights seemed to dodge the effect of the space gun and a kind of celestial chase ensued.

One particular "battle" is described in extensive detail. It occurred in December, in the late afternoon. A short while earlier, Dr. Silvert had brought ORUR (a radioactive substance that had been exposed to orgone irradiation) to Tucson from Maine, having it towed on a line a hundred feet behind a hired airplane because the lead shielding could not contain its altered radiating action. The first sign of an "attack" was the formation of a huge black cloud over the Tucson area at about 4:30 P.M. It turned gradually deep purple with a somewhat reddish glow. The Geiger counter showed the incredibly high background count of 100,000 cpms. A dozen air force planes flew over the estate Reich had leased. Their jet trails quickly dissolved—a phenomenon that Reich had learned to interpret as indicating the presence of much DOR, since DOR absorbed moisture, which was what the jet trails were made of. Reich began operations with two "space guns." Shortly, the huge cloud began to shrink and in twenty minutes the sky had cleared. At 5:30 four B-56 bombers flew low over Little Orgonon, as if to salute the effort that had just been made there. Although no UFOs were actually sighted during this time, Reich called this "a full-scale interplanetary battle" and suspected that the menacing DOR cloud had been caused by the hidden presence of UFOs that might have been attracted to the area of the airfield where the ORUR had arrived.

From this and other similar experiences Reich eventually concluded that it was the UFOs in earth's atmosphere that in general produced DOR and the consequent melanor that caused deserts to develop, and he began to see his work in combatting desert development as amounting to nothing more or less than a cosmic war against invaders from outer space. Whether in this new conclusion he abandoned the earlier idea of the role that nuclear testing played in causing deserts is not made clear in the book. He concluded further that UFOs used orgone energy as their power and called the invaders CORE men—CORE being an anagram of Cosmic Orgone Engineering.

The disturbing aspect in Reich's treatment of these matters in *Contact* is that he did not present his ideas as mere speculations but as conclusively proven facts. This is in marked contrast to most of his earlier work where he maintained a clear differentiation between experimentally proven facts and speculations, and where the experiments that proved the facts were extensively developed and tested.

The accounts of and conclusions about battles with UFOs in *Contact* also raise the question of why space beings with a mastery of orgone energy functions should want to attack the earth. According to Reich's earlier writings only unarmored people had the refined perceptions that were necessary for work with orgone energy. The space beings, having mastered orgone energy functions, were therefore unarmored. But Reich had also maintained that unarmored life is not hostile, malignant, or destructive and seeks only its own fulfillment in accordance with the workings of natural law. Yet here were these unarmored space beings attacking the earth. Was it perhaps because they viewed armored man's earth technology as somehow life-inimical? If this were so, however, why then should Reich have taken the side of armored life against unarmored life and fought these battles? This question remains unanswered in *Contact* and Reich seemed never to have been aware of the contradiction.

These defects, together with the evidence of his irrationality in dealing with his legal trouble, would seem to make it valid at last to "psychologize," to see Reich's work of this period, especially as regards UFOs, as nothing more than an aspect of his loss of touch with social reality. And yet to do so would be to ignore the fact that others were present and witnessed these "battles." Dr. Baker recorded that he was once present when Reich caused a light in the night sky to blink out by pointing the space gun at it. "These were my observations," he wrote, "interpret them as you will." [3] Peter Reich, in *A Book of Dreams,* which in large part is

3. Baker, p. 41.

devoted to sorting out his childhood experiences with his father from accompanying fantasies, recounted several incidents in which he was actively involved. "I moved the cloudbuster back and forth and up and down, checking through the sighting scope," he wrote. "Sure enough the EA [Reich's code name for UFOs] was just a faint glimmer and seemed to be getting smaller and smaller as if it was being sucked up by the sky." [4] In other words, while Reich's interpretation of what was taking place might indeed be questioned and even validly psychologized, it seems as if something very definitely was taking place. After all, the last word concerning UFOs has not yet been said.

Dr. Silvert had been put in charge of affairs at Orgonon while Reich was on this expedition. In January of 1955, acting on his own discretion and without prior notice to Reich, he had a large truckload of accumulators and literature shipped from Orgonon to his own address in New York City. This was an act that eventually caused him to become implicated in the contempt proceedings and that constituted by far the most incriminating violation of the injunction.

In the meantime the FDA had begun to check up on Reich and the other defendants named in the injunction to ascertain what, if anything, was being done to carry out its terms. One of its first actions was to attempt an inspection of Reich's premises in Tucson. The immediate reason for this inspection was that Haydon, the attorney for the application for intervention, was going to ask for a stay of enforcement of the injunction, and the government lawyers wanted to have the results of such an inspection in time for the January 4 arguments in Portland. Accordingly, Inspector Holliday, of the Los Angeles District of the FDA, accompanied by a federal marshal, paid a visit to Reich's Tucson residence on December 30, 1954. Reich refused to see Holliday, but he did see the marshal for several minutes, and told him he wanted to have nothing to do with the FDA, though he had nothing against the marshal or the marshal's office. (Repeatedly Reich was to make this distinction between the FDA and other governmental agents. Even at court he would be extremely polite to the judge. He was trying in all such actions to demonstrate that essentially he was on the side

4. Peter Reich, *A Book of Dreams* (New York: Harper and Row, 1973), p. 27.

of government and supported law and order, and that he opposed the FDA only because it was, in his opinion, corrupt and spy-ridden.)

Reich later wrote about this attempted inspection in a speech he prepared for presentation to the jury for a trial that was to have taken place on December 1, 1955, but which was later postponed for several months, so that the speech was never delivered. According to this "speech," Holliday had come because "two weeks earlier some critical *pre-atomic* material, called ORUR, had been flown down . . . from Maine. . . ." [5] And it was this he was interested in when he told several of Reich's co-workers that he wanted to inspect everything. "Such intrusion," Reich continued, "had to be resisted, since obviously a foreign power was very much interested in obtaining information on the 'Atoms for Peace' work we did in Arizona." [6] Reich was not necessarily accusing Holliday of being a conscious spy for, as he wrote further, the "uncertainty of whether we were dealing with conscious, organized espionage or sick, sneaking psychopaths was ever with us." [7]

Inspector Holliday's report of this abortive inspection stated that he was unable to determine if Reich was building accumulators on his rented estate. To suspect Reich of going all the way to Arizona to make accumulators in secret was as far-fetched as Reich's suspicion concerning Holliday's motives in wanting to make an inspection. This kind of complete misunderstanding, complete misinterpretation, has been noted before. It came to mark the conflict between Reich and the FDA more and more during this period, and found its most extreme expression at the trial, where the defense and the prosecution often seemed to be speaking two different languages.

Beside this action, and while Reich was still in Arizona, two FDA inspectors, on November 29, 1954, visited Orgonon, in Maine, to see what was being done by the Wilhelm Reich Foundation to comply with the terms of the injunction. This visit yielded little information, however, for the only person at Orgonon was Tom Ross, the caretaker, and he was able to tell the inspectors

5. Wilhelm Reich, *"Atoms for Peace vs. The Hig,"* in Documentary Supplement No. 3 of *History of the Discovery of the Life Energy* (Rangeley, Maine: Orgone Institute Press, 1956), p. 12.
6. *Ibid.*, p. 12.
7. *Ibid.*, p. 13.

little of what they wanted to know. On the day following this visit, the inspectors interviewed Ilse Ollendorff who, at this time, having left Reich, was living and working at the Hamilton School in Sheffield, Massachusetts. Here, too, they got little relevant information, for Miss Ollendorff had severed her connection with the Wilhelm Reich Foundation. "When asked," the report of this visit states, "why she had severed her connection . . . she stated that her action had been due in part to personal reasons, but also because she could no longer comprehend what was being studied and done. She said that Reich is so far advanced that he is out in the cosmos much of the time. She was frightened by what might happen." In reply to repeated questions as to what she was doing to comply with the terms of the injunction, Miss Ollendorff insisted that since she had no further connection with orgonomic work there was nothing for her to do in regard to the injunction.

Finally, on March 17, 1955, while the petition of the applicants for intervention was still pending in the Court of Appeals and the Temporary Stay was still in effect, and Reich was still in Arizona, the FDA sent a letter to the Attorney General requesting that contempt proceedings be initiated against the defendants. This is a document of some six pages in which the history of the case is briefly recapitulated and then instances of noncompliance with the injunction are described. One is the refusal of Miss Ollendorff to give "any information whatever pertaining to the affairs, books, accounts, ledgers, and matters pertaining to the corporation. . . . She stated she does not intend to comply with the affirmative provisions of the decree because she is no longer affiliated with the other defendants." The November 29 visit to Orgonon is mentioned and the fact that a "factory inspection" was not permitted. The letter of October 11, 1954, sent by Moise to the District Court— informing it of the decision the Orgone Institute Press had made to continue distributing its publications—is cited. And, finally, an uncertain reference is made to the possibility that the literature being sold had been in Rangeley at the time the injunction was issued and transported to New York City thereafter. At this time, apparently, the fact that Dr. Silvert had had this material, along with accumulators, transferred to New York City was not yet definitely known to the FDA. And in conclusion, the FDA letter invokes that agency's most incriminating argument against quackery, as follows:

The fact that the defendants have utterly disregarded the judgment directive to recall devices and labeling owned by them but in the possession of laymen, is particularly reprehensible. These laymen, perhaps suffering from incipient tuberculosis, diabetes, cancer or some other pernicious disease, may be relying on the use of accumulators to the exclusion of appropriate therapy. As a result they may suffer irreversible damage and even death. These defendants should be made to answer for their contemptuous conduct.

The Attorney General wrote back on March 30, 1955, instructing the General Counsel to prepare the legal documents required for contempt proceedings, *i.e.,* what in legal parlance is called an information and application.

In the next several months the FDA initiated a third round of investigative activities, this time to get detailed information on the activities of Reich, the Wilhelm Reich Foundation, and the distribution center for books and accumulators in New York City that was managed by Silvert, for the purpose of collecting evidence of violations that could be used in the contempt proceeding.

Unsuccessful attempts were made to inspect the premises of Silvert and Thomas Mangravite, who was building accumulators to fill the orders received by Silvert. A watch was established on their incoming and outgoing mail as well as that of the Orgone Institute Press. There was even an incident of tampering with the mail when, according to an FDA memo dated May 31, 1955, a Mr. Moran of the Village Post Office Station, illegally opened outgoing letters of the Press. Eventually, the FDA turned to New York City's Department of Health, asking it to order an inspection of Mangravite's premises. As a result a minor litigation developed between Silvert and Mangravite on the one hand and the Department of Health on the other. The judge, however, deferred action until the main issue was decided. After the trial the matter of inspection in New York City ceased to be an issue and so was dropped.

Another unsuccessful attempt to inspect Orgonon—this was after Reich had returned—resulted in a memo dated June 14,

1955, that touched on the question of Reich's "insanity." The pertinent part of this memo stated:

Mr. Mills said that the deputy marshall who had been up to Rangeley with our inspectors came back with the story that Reich was a madman. Mr. Mills indicated that the court would not be too happy about having a madman in his court [syntax in original] and we might have some difficulty in fostering contempt of court procedures against Reich. Mr. Mills thought that some strong language in a forwarding letter from the Department of Justice would be helpful.

By June 16 another letter was sent to the Attorney General along with copies of the information and application that had been asked for. By this time the FDA had learned of Silvert's shipment of accumulators and literature from Rangeley to New York, so his name was added to the list of violators in this letter. In describing the investigative activities in preparation for the contempt proceedings, the letter makes every effort to make it seem that Reich and those working with him were violating the injunction in deliberately secret and underhanded ways. For instance:

Inspectors of the Food and Drug Administration located the cache [of literature and accumulators Silvert had shipped from Maine] in New York. While the premises were kept under surveillance, nocturnal activity in the traffic of orgone accumulators was observed. A resident of the neighborhood told an inspector that the windows are covered by blankets when there is activity in the building at night.

Needless to say, there is no evidence that any of the activities engaged in at the above-mentioned premises were carried out secretly as a means of concealment. Mangravite told this author that the blanket-covered windows belonged not to his premises but to that of the tenant on the floor below. In the eventual litigation, Dr. Silvert was accused of transfering the material from Orgonon to New York in "the dead of night" and employing various tactics to cover his trail. But the representative of the trucking company that had been hired for the shipment was asked at the trial: "So far as you can decide, was there anything undercover or misleading about the shipment?" He replied: "If there had been, I wouldn't have delivered it." FDA reports that sought to convey the impression that Silvert, Mangravite, or any of the people associated with them had recourse to cover up precautions were primarily reflecting the inspectors' own cops-and-robbers psychology and approach. They were unable to comprehend that though the terms of the injunction were indeed being violated, this violation was done as a matter of conviction and principle in a completely aboveboard manner.

The June 16 letter, after citing further refusals to permit inspection or furnish information, accused the defendants of showing "absolute disregard of the affirmative provisions of the decree" and concluded with the recommendation that U.S. Attorney Peter Mills be authorized to initiate contempt proceedings.

Strangely enough, the bureaucratic process can be astonishingly efficient when there is sufficient motivation: the information and application was filed in the U.S. District Court for the Court of Maine on the same day as the letter—June 16, 1955.

In the information the name of Ilse Ollendorff—who had been one of the named defendants in the injunction—was dropped. Thus Silvert, Reich, and the Wilhelm Reich Foundation were named as the parties against whom the contempt charge was to be directed. The substance of these charges was that Reich and the Foundation violated the injunction by not recalling and destroying accumulators and literature, that Reich violated it by refusing inspection permission to FDA officials at Rangeley and at Tucson, and that Silvert, "in concert with" Reich and the Foundation, "violated the injunction by transferring accumulators and literature from Rangeley to New York."

On the same day—the efficiency is still impressive—Judge Clifford issued an order to the defendants to appear in court on July 26 to show cause why legal proceedings should not be initiated against them. In response to this, Moise wired Judge Clifford requesting a private conference before the hearing. Though Maguire argued against this irregularity ("It was just another Reichian tactic to get in the back door.") Judge Clifford decided to permit it so that the defendants would not be able to say they had been discriminated against.

The main reason for Moise's request, it turned out, was to be able to ask the judge to excuse Reich from appearing at the hearing because (again Maguire's account) "Reich always tells the truth and he might say something that would be disasterous nationally." Judge Clifford insisted that Reich had to appear. (During this conference in Clifford's chamber, Moise told Mills and Maguire, who were present, that their action against Reich was tantamount to treason. Maguire challenged Moise, saying that if Moise were a patriot he would take this charge to the FBI agent on the floor below. Moise's answer was that this was a new kind of treason, and the FBI would not understand.)

One can assume that it was Reich who had sent Moise to Clifford with his request. What matter Reich had in mind, whose possible disclosure at a hearing could lead to disaster, is difficult to say. Perhaps the matter of his "battles" with UFOs. Reich was later, in his appeal briefs, to say that at the time of the trial he deliberately withheld material that could have strengthened his position. Moreover, he submitted, as part of the appendix to his Supreme Court brief, a copy of *Contact* labeled as "secret and suppressed evidence"—that is, evidence that he had considered secret and therefore suppressed. But there may have been something else involved as well.

In the course of research, this author heard that a woman working as a maid for a family in Maine who had some connection with orgonomy, saw some Reich books in the house and commented that she had been a guide with the Eisenhower party when the President came to the Rangeley area in the summer of 1955 on a fishing and hunting trip. She said further that she had witnessed a meeting between Eisenhower and Reich. Inquiry to the Eisenhower Library revealed that the President had indeed been in the Rangeley area on such a trip between June 22 and 27 in 1955. However, the library, in examining the log of Eisenhower's itinerary on this trip, found nothing about a meeting with Reich. A call to James Haggerty, Eisenhower's press secretary, brought similarly negative results. A telephone conversation with the woman ended in her saying that she was no longer absolutely certain that it had been Reich she saw Eisenhower meet, perhaps it was someone else. The Secret Service was queried but answered that it was not allowed to divulge any information it had in its records.

Yet, against this we have, first of all, the fact that Eisenhower had used Reich's phrase "atoms for peace" in his famous speech. This could, of course, have been a mere coincidence, a speechwriter's independent inspiration—and yet, perhaps not. It is not inconceivable that this term was taken from communications Reich had sent to the President. Besides this, we know from Ilse Ollendorff's biography that Reich was expecting a visit from a high-ranking government official during this period. Moreover, Mrs. Gladys Wolfe, Dr. Wolfe's widow, told this writer that Reich had mentioned to her that he was expecting a visit from the President. This might, of course, be delusional. Yet we have seen that to the extent that Reich was deluded during this period, it was mostly by way of misinterpreting events; rarely, if ever, was it a matter of inventing events. In this connection, it is pertinent to mention that in Reich's writing of this period there is a brief reference to a smiling-faced, high official of the U.S. Government who visited him. Fantastic as it may seem, the possibility of a meeting between Eisenhower and Reich cannot be completely ruled out. The point made here is that if such a meeting had taken place, it would, no doubt, have been included among the matters that Reich felt it would be disastrous to disclose at the scheduled hearing. (The possibility of such a meeting would also help explain Reich's conviction during this time, and in the remainder of his life, that he had highly placed protectors in the government.)

Reich, along with Silvert, appeared at the July 16 hearing at 2:30 P.M. Haydon represented Silvert, while Fredrick F. Fisher, Jr.—a Boston attorney newly brought into the case—represented Reich and the Foundation. The lawyers submitted two motions: one for a jury trial and the other that the order to show cause (why criminal contempt proceedings should not be initiated against the defendants) be discharged. To support the latter motion the two lawyers argued that the injunction exceeded the jurisdiction of the Court that had issued it; that, in other words, the Court had had no authority to order Reich and the Foundation to recall accumulators and literature and have them destroyed. Moreover, there was no assurance that had such a recall been attempted it would have been successful.

Judge Clifford made no decision on these motions. Instead, he ordered the defense lawyers to present their arguments in writing so that they could be answered by the governmentt. The date for the submissions of these briefs was set for September 9.

Reich was then permitted to present his views and he spoke for half an hour. Reviewing the contents of his original Response, he warned that the litigation against him, in interfering with his efforts to combat the planetary emergency, was weakening the country. He outlined his view of the conspiracy against him and accused Maguire of being an unwitting part of it. ("Looking at me," Maguire's memo on the hearing stated, "he said, 'I don't think you know what you are doing.'") He emphasized that though there was an effort to steal his equations he would not reveal anything about them since they were of crucial national and international significance. ("You will never get anything from me, jail sentence or otherwise to the contrary," Maguire's memo had him saying.) And after speaking about space travel and UFOs, he turned to Maguire with a plea that they join together in a search to expose the people and forces conspiring against him. "He bellowed and raged and at times was cautioned by both defense attorneys," Maguire wrote of this speech. "He talked about how humble he is. In the next breath indicated that he was one of the greatest scientists of the time."

Maguire's memo included a detail, insignificant in itself but eloquent of the distance between the two sides that must have made the hearing at times seem like a confrontation between two alien worlds.

At one point Reich and Silvert turned to look long and intently at Maguire. Maguire turned to a court official and said, "Are they staring at you or me?" He recorded that later Judge Clifford commented that he had observed this incident and that Reich and Silvert had tried to hypnotize Maguire. Needless to say, Clifford was completely wrong in this interpretation since neither Reich nor Silvert practiced hypnotism. What they were obviously trying to do was to make contact with Maguire, to get beyond his official role to the human being behind it.

One other matter of significance occurred at this July 26 hearing, but a brief look at what had been happening in the meantime at Orgonon is essential for its understanding. Reich had begun more and more to regard the course of events with the FDA as an attempt to get some of his formulas. He had more and more come to regard the whole prosecution effort as an assault he would have to resist in any way, at any cost, and he began to use the expression "do or die" frequently at this time to denote the determination with which he was prepared to resist. As part of this effort he and the people with him at Orgonon began carrying firearms on them and in their cars. Heavy chains were put up with warning signs. Some people who had inadvertently strayed on his land were shooed off at gunpoint, and the incident was reported to the police and eventually to the FDA. The deputy marshal received a letter from Reich advising him of the defensive measures taken against possible FDA "spies" and requesting him to call in advance should he want to come, in order to avoid a possible accident. Reich, in other words, began to regard the whole matter as a war. Thus, from his point of view, he was fighting a two-front war. The main enemy was, of course, the UFOs; but his effectiveness against this enemy was being undermined by the FDA, which did not realize that by hampering Reich in his main action it was, in effect, endangering its own interests as well as those of the whole world Reich was defending. If this view of things proceeded purely on the basis of paranoid logic, the next step would have been for Reich to make some kind of connection between the threat posed by UFOs and that of red fascism. Reich, however, never made such a connection. He saw himself as the commanding officer of an army, small as it was, consisting of his daughter, Eva, her husband, William Moise, Robert McCullough, Reich's son, Peter, and occasionally Silvert. It was a heavily embattled army whose "do or die" desperation Reich took so seriously that at one point he had his caretaker dig a grave in the event that he, Reich, should be killed. Peter Reich records that during the Arizona project they were all given military ranks. He himself was promoted to the rank of lieutenant in the Corps of Cosmic Engineers after the previously cited engagement with the UFOs.

The day before the July 26 hearing Moise had called the deputy marshal to ask about protection for Reich on his trip from Rangeley to Portland. The marshal said that no protection was planned and that any needed protection would be up to Reich and his party themselves. However, he warned them that none of Reich's people were to have guns in the courtroom. Eva Reich, who was a medical doctor, had, sometime previous to this tense state of affairs, purchased a small .38 pistol and carried it in her handbag for protection during night calls. Before the hearing, someone informed the deputy marshal that she had a pistol with her. He asked for it and she turned it over to him. This incident, together with a later incident involving firearms, was to become the basis at Washington FDA headquarters for discussions about protecting FDA agents.

In August of 1955, before the September deadline for the submission of briefs, Reich had his last orgonomic conference at Orgonon. Its purpose was to report on the Arizona project, to consider the legal situation, and to introduce the concept of "atmospheric medicine." This concept consisted of two parts. One was the idea that just as the cloudbuster could remove DOR from the atmosphere, a small version of it—which he had developed and called "a medical DOR buster"—could be used to withdraw DOR from the human organism. The other was that a DOR-laden atmosphere affected the health of whole populations. The flu epidemic that swept over the United States at that time, attributed to a virus that could not be identified and which was therefore called "virus x," Reich saw as a specific case of epidemic DOR sickness caused by a heavily contaminated atmosphere. Thus "atmospheric medicine" also meant the exploration of ways in which decontaminating the atmosphere could be used to affect people's health in a positive way.

One windfall that came Reich's way during this conference—and it was to be an important one during the remaining years of his life—was that he met Miss Aurora Karrer there. She was a biologist working in Washington—ironically, for HEW—with an interest in Reich's work. She was to be one of the main reasons why Reich spent that winter and the next (up to the time of his arrest) in Washington. She became, in effect, Reich's fourth wife.

Some time before September 9, Haydon and Fisher submitted their briefs in behalf of Reich, Silvert, and the Foundation. Both briefs dealt with the same basic issues, though in varying degrees of detail and emphasis.

Perhaps the most important issue is a repetition of the point advanced in the briefs during the intervention proceedings: that the court's jurisdiction was questioned in Reich's Response to the original Complaint but that the court never ruled on this question. Fisher's brief stated: "Upon receipt of the Response the Court should have set the question of jurisdiction down for hearing, and its failure to do so made the decree of injunction void." Haydon's brief on the same issue stated: "The question is not whether the Court decided right or wrong, but whether it ever became the duty of the Court to decide." Both concluded that since the jurisdiction question had never been decided, the original injunction was void and the defendants could not therefore be brought to court in contempt of such an injunction.

Besides this, the briefs contended by means of numerous precedent citations that the injunction itself was in excess of judicial authority and therefore void on that score too. The conclusion to this contention was that "a violation of a void court order is not punishable as contempt."

A final contention of the briefs was that the information submitted by the government was factually insufficient to justify the order to show cause.

The government's reply brief did not deal with most of the specific objections raised in the defense briefs. It based its argument on the more general contention that "an injunction decree of a Federal Court, until reversed or set aside by orderly process, must be obeyed by those enjoined regardless of their personal feelings as to its validity," for otherwise the courts would be undermined in their effort to administer justice. So if a violation occurs it is punishable even though the injunction may on later appeal be reversed.

As regards the Response, the government's brief contended both that it was not a challenge to the court's jurisdiction and that even if it was, the fact that the injunction had been issued meant that the challenge had been overruled. What this argument ignores, however, is the fact that if the court had ruled in the matter of its jurisdiction, it did not notify Reich of this decision in time to permit him to take other measures had he wished to do so.

In regards to Silvert, one of the defense briefs contended that he could not be held in contempt because he had shipped the accumulators and literature to his own address, so they were not seen by anyone else and therefore could not be considered branded; and since the accumulators had never been in interstate commerce, they were not subject to the decree. The government countered these arguments by claiming that some of the accumulators had been in prior interstate commerce (a claim it was prepared to prove), and that merely shipping adulterated devices and their labeling to oneself did not circumvent the decree, even if the sender–receiver was the only one to have access to these materials.

A third part of the government's reply argued that the information, contrary to the contention of the defense, was sufficiently detailed and therefore "completely fulfills the requirement that it completely describe the offense charged and fully apprise the defendants of the nature of the charge against them." Nevertheless, shortly after this brief was entered, the government moved, and received permission, to amend its information. The new information claimed, in addition to the previous charges, that Reich had ordered people working with him to refuse to allow FDA inspectors to see both his records and those of the Foundation; and that he and Silvert continued to violate the injunction by making the enjoined literature available for sale and collecting money for accumulators still out on a rental basis.

Shortly after this hearing Fisher withdrew from the case. His reason is set forth in a letter sent to Reich on September 12, 1955, in which he notes that in a recent telephone conversation Reich had expressed a desire to examine witnesses himself should a trial eventually take place. As a result of this, he regretfully concluded that he could not serve as Reich's trial counsel. However, he adds: "I have personally become quite interested in your case and would very much like to see you vindicated and to serve as your counsel throughout the legal proceedings. I am willing to remain as your counsel and to prepare a reply brief to the brief which the Government will file in response to my brief." However, Reich apparently decided not to retain Fisher on this basis, and on October 7—three days before the next hearing was to be held—he ceased representing Reich altogether.

This kind of situation was to be repeated during the remainder of the litigation. It stemmed from Reich's determination to prosecute his prosecuters, his desire to bring out the malice and irrationality motivating them, which he hoped to do by taking charge of the examination of witnesses. However, there was no legal framework within which this malice and irrationality could be made part of the case. Thus Haydon followed Fisher, and withdrew—or was dismissed—on October 21.

At the hearing on October 10 Haydon still represented only Silvert and the Wilhelm Reich Foundation. Reich represented himself. Many technical matters relating to the government's amended information, subpoenas, and the disposition of some of the subpoenaed material that had already been submitted, as well as motions on striking the decree and dismissing the contempt proceedings, were all handled at this hearing. The next hearing was then set for October 18. The following excerpt from the record of this hearing conveys a sense of Reich's position as well as his general posture in court.

DR. REICH: Your Honor, I am not a lawyer and I know nothing about law or law procedures. I know very well that you must not drive on the wrong side of the road. I know nothing about procedures. I have asked my lawyer to step out of the case for one basic reason, not because I think he is a bad lawyer, or doesn't know law and so on, but for one reason only—and that is, the procedure itself in this case, seems to have killed the truth and my whole endeavor from the very beginning of 1954 was only to get the truth to this Court. I shall try to do that again. You remember, Your Honor, I had sent you a response when I received the complaint. When I saw that complaint I knew from my factual point of view that illegal methods had been used to get that complaint in. . . . As a natural scientist, I denied the right to decide what is true or what is not true in basic natural science to both Court and Government and I think I am here in my good right. If we were to permit lawyers or politically minded people to decide what is true in basic research or not, then I think that the future research of knowledge would be gone to the dogs if I may express myself that way. Now, I have quite clearly in my speech of July 26th explained why that is so—

MR. MILLS: If the gentleman wishes to make a speech let him hire a hall. If he wants to address the Court, I suggest that he address the Court. [Reich had apparently turned to the government lawyers.]

THE COURT: I think that was an involuntary movement turning away from the Court.

DR. REICH: I understand. Thank you. I would appreciate very much—I was never in Court before July 26. Now the second point I had raised in the response was the effect of a conspiracy. I don't want to talk here about the political conspiracy, the background. I would like to bring in here one point, with your permission, and that is, as I understand from the documents that have been submitted to me in this case, that misrepresentation has been perpetrated upon this Court—misrepresentation of facts. This is a very serious charge, I know—

THE COURT: At this time, Doctor, we can't go into that. If you care to have a written motion prepared and filed, we will consider it.

DR. REICH: It is all prepared.

THE COURT: You can't go into that now unless a written motion is prepared and filed.

DR. REICH: Your Honor, am I permitted just to indicate closely what is meant by that?

THE COURT: At the proper time you may do that but at this time, I will have to rule it out.

DR. REICH: Mr. Haydon has just said that there may be a legal ground to bring in this matter here if it is important or crucial to the decision of whether the jurisdiction was in the Court or not.

THE COURT: I will rule it out for the time being.

DR. REICH: For the time being. I would appreciate it very much if you would permit me to ask a question as to whether or not a matter can be brought in later.

THE COURT: I won't be able to advise you. You will have to go to your attorney about that.

DR. REICH: I understand that. Your Honor . . . I have only to add a few words. . . . I have been presented to this Court as a crook and as a swindler—

THE COURT: I wouldn't quite say that.

DR. REICH: I would like to stress the point that I am a very experienced and well-acknowledged man of standing.

THE COURT: I think they have already stated that to the Court, themselves, that you are a very well-known, qualified psychiatrist and honored in your profession. So you have no worry on that point.

DR. REICH: Then I don't understand how this whole thing came about.

THE COURT: Well, that is beside the point. Anything further, Doctor?

DR. REICH: Thank you, no.

The next hearing was scheduled for November 4. Reich prepared several motions regarding the matter he had been unable to bring out at the October 18 hearing. He still acted as his own attorney in preparing these motions and signed them not only with his name but also as a representative of EPPO—The Emotional Plague Prevention Office, a name he coined for an organization he had thought up, but which existed only on paper. In one of his motions he charged that illegal misrepresentation of facts, illegal concealment of facts, and illegal procedural maneuvering "contrary to fact, truth and justice" had been resorted to by the government, both in obtaining the injunction and in obtaining the show cause order for criminal contempt.

Another motion Reich prepared was "to dismiss the case against orgonomy completely and to replace the contempt of court charge by the recommendation to establish 'Boards on Social Pathology' in the court of the U.S.A." As in so many of Reich's attempts to deal with his legal entanglement this motion is both fundamentally right and, at the same time, inappropriate to the technical realities of the situation.

He attributes the FDA's success in obtaining the injunction and barring the application to intervene not to any factuality but to the mere skillful use of procedural technique. If the FDA case against him continued in this way he would land in jail; but if he should succeed in bringing his factual evidence—i.e., the misrepresentation and concealment of truth—into court, the complainants would be the ones to land in jail. However, "As a physician at the sickbed of society, and as a scientist," he is not interested in jailing even guilty people, since jail "is an antiquated institution" and suitable only for keeping criminals "out of social circulation." He does not approach this matter with any vindictiveness, with any desire to punish enemies—the FDA or those behind it—who are out to kill him and his discovery, Reich states. This lack of vindictiveness stems less from pity than from the simple practical consideration that jailing his enemies "would not accomplish anything useful for society and a better handling of human affairs in the future upon this suffering planet." He therefore submits "that the available evidence in the hands of both FDA and Orgone Institute be opened up for inspection in public hearings"; furthermore, that the total legal issue involved be handled publicly, as a *"master example of Social Pathology."* Much of this, while true, was at this point in the case irrelevant. The time to have exposed the FDA's dishonest methods was when the Complaint was issued. This motion was submitted, Reich stated, as an attempt to settle affairs in open court hearings by means of "Social Biopsychiatry," wherein he and Silvert would work in their "professional capacity as scientific workers representing EPPO. . . ." Again, we see here an attempt on Reich's part to deal with the developing litigation in social-psychiatric terms rather than in legal terms.

A third motion which Reich prepared for the November 4 hearing had to do with the conventions of legal phraseology. In a letter to Reich from his newly engaged lawyer, James St. Clair, Reich was advised of the October 10 hearing and that "We will, at that time . . . present . . . motions to dismiss and arrange for a trial date." Reich's objection—and this might have had something to do with the fact that Reich did not have St. Clair represent him at the October 10 hearing—was to the word "and" in the letter and in the court record. According to him, the word should have been "or." "A seemingly insignificant word 'AND,'" he wrote, was "interpolated between the provision of the opportunity for the defendant to FREE HIMSELF of the charge of contempt of court OR (NOT 'AND') the further legal privilege to present his evidence to a jury." He was later to belabor this issue repeatedly and even attribute his arraignment to this imprecise use of words.

But before the November 4 hearing the second incident involving firearms occurred. It illustrates Reich's desperate state of mind at this time and also the way the FDA exaggerated and distorted in its constant effort to put Reich in the worst possible light.

A. Harris Kenyon—the FDA inspector from Boston who had unsuccessfully tried to inspect Orgonon in June of that year—met Maguire in Massachusetts, and after some investigative activity the two of them signed in at a motel in Rangeley. In the evening, Kenyon—according to his memo, written on October 20—drove out to see Tom Ross, the caretaker at Orognon, to discuss with him the matter of Silvert's shipment of the literature and accumulators from Orgonon. While he was talking with Ross, Reich passed by in his car. Kenyon cut short the interview, apparently wishing to avoid an encounter with Reich, and left. But while Kenyon was discussing this episode with Maguire at the motel, Reich drove up. Obtaining the number of his suite, Reich knocked on Kenyon's door, but Kenyon and Maguire did not reply. Reich left and returned, left and returned until Kenyon decided to open the door. Reich then asked Kenyon to wait until another person came and in the meantime accused Kenyon of being a spy. William Moise drove up shortly, parked his car among other parked cars so that Kenyon was able to see only his head and shoulders as Moise got out of the car. Reich then called—this is all according to Kenyon's memo—"You can leave your rifle in the car, Bill, you won't need it." So Moise returned to the car, opened the door then shut it as if putting something in. Then he joined the group. Reich introduced Kenyon to him and Moise accused him of being a spy. There

Observatory at Orgonon, where Reich both lived and worked from the middle forties on.

Research work at the steel-lined laboratory at Orgonon.

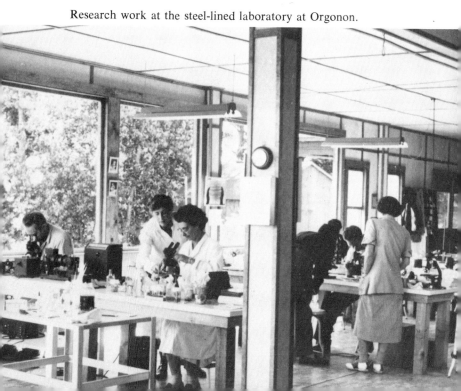

The completely metal-lined room where an observer, after sitting a while in complete darkness, could observe orgone energy.

Mildred Eddy Brady, whose 1947 articles in *Harper's* and the *New Republic* marked the beginning of the American campaign against Reich. COURTESY OF CONSUMERS UNION OF UNITED STATES, INC.

Reich mausoleum at Orgonon. The bust of Reich was made by sculptor Jo Jencks.

Wilhelm Reich in 1956, after
the trial.   JOE COVELLO

Dr. Michael Silvert in 1956, some two years before his suicide, after his release from prison.   JOE COVELLO

The orgone accumulator "factory," where accumulators were built from the later forties to early fifties. One man, working part-time, was able to fill all the orders for accumulators. The FDA spent some two million dollars to halt this accumulator "business."

Reich (center) and Silvert working with the cloud buster at Orgonon in 1956.
JOE COVELLO

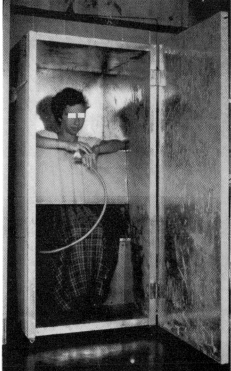

e large-sized orgone accumulator in use.
KARI BERGGRAV

Ilse Ollendorff, Reich's thir
circa 1950.   KARI BE

A scene at the first international orgonomic conference, Orgonon, August, 1948. Reich at center rear, A. S. Neill at right rear.   KARI BERGGRAV

e John D. Clifford, Jr., who officiated
e issuance of the injunction, the in-
ntion proceedings, and the hearing
minary to the contempt trial.

A. Harris Kenyon, chief FDA inspector of
the Boston district, whom Reich ordered
off Orgonon property on several attempted
inspection visits.

Charles W. Crawford, FDA commissioner
from 1951 to 1954. It was during his
administration that the decision was made
to seek legal measures against Reich.

George P. Larrick. As assistant
missioner under Crawford, he
ated the "anti-quack campaign
the framework of which the a
against Reich was taken. He
ceeded Crawford in 1954
remained FDA commissioner
1966.

Reich being taken to prison by deputy marshall William C. Doherty in
March 1957.

followed a heated exchange, Reich wanting Kenyon to sign some kind of protocol. Kenyon refused and shut the door. More pounding. Whereupon Kenyon opened the door and Reich is reported to have said to him: "Mr. Kenyon, I warn you. Don't ever set foot on Orgonon property again. If you do, you will see something—you will experience something." (What Reich had in mind by this threat is difficult to say—perhaps some effect of cloudbusters on the property. It does not sound like a threat of direct physical violence.)

Later the motel owner and a friend who had been present when Moise had driven up told Kenyon they were positive that Moise didn't have a gun when he left his car. "They considered the actions of Reich and Moise," Kenyon's memo concludes, "as a big act put on in an attempt to make an impression."

These two "gun" episodes—this one and the one of Eva surrendering her .38 pistol before the July 26 hearing—together with testimony given in the trial resulted in a strange letter. Dated August 10, 1956, written by Milstead of the FDA's Division of Regulatory Management and directed to the FDA's Division of Administrative Management, this letter stated that the successfully completed Reich case had been "fraught with danger." The defendants testified at the trial that they always carried firearms and would have fired at trespassing FDA men, the letter asserted. (This is another exaggeration. Robert McCullough, who was not one of the defendants, testified that in a situation of extremity he might have been compelled to fire at trespassing FDA men.) Moreover, the letter continued, one of Reich's "fanatical supporters surrendered a loaded .38-caliber revolver to a deputy marshal before entering the courtroom." And Kenyon and Maguire, "in a remote section of the Maine woods," had a "loaded deer rifle 'pulled' on them" by William Moise. Significantly, when speaking of this incident at the trial, Kenyon made no mention of the fact that observers had told him Moise did not really have a rifle in his hand.

So much for the gun incidents.

All the motions Reich submitted were denied at the November 4 hearing. Silvert's prior motion—that the amended information be dismissed since "illegal procedural maneuvering with misrepresentation of facts" had been used in the charge of contempt brought against him—was also dismissed. The judge explained to Reich in the "and/or" matter that "Only in the event . . . that you did not prevail in your motion to dismiss would trial be set. . . . In the event your motion was granted, that was the end of it. . . . Does that clarify it?" Reich's reply was in the affirmative, yet he went on expounding on the matter. At one point he interrupted himself with the request that the Court "admonish my opponents not to make fun of me." To which the judge replied: "I am certain they are not. Perhaps you are oversensitive. I don't believe Counsel for the Government has any desire to do anything that will embarrass you, and I of course would not tolerate that if it was so attempted." At which point Maguire commented: "I would like for the Court to inform both defendants . . . that Mr. Mills and I have the privilege of conferring with one another here at the counsel table. . . . Certainly, when we confer, we are not poking fun at anyone."

In regard to Reich's motion that illegal misrepresentation of pertinent facts, illegal concealment of pertinent facts, and illegal procedural maneuvering had been perpetrated upon the court in the way the injunction had been obtained, the following exchange took place:

THE COURT: The only trouble with this is, Doctor, that you had the opportunity to come in and defend and you chose not to do so. You will remember that in your letter addressed to me—

DR. REICH: I remember. My response mentioned two things. . . . One was the lack of jurisdiction on basic natural science. The second point was conspiracy. This is a serious point now, the conspiracy which is really behind these things, and I could not possibly come then to be crushed here without having prepared anything, within twenty days.

THE COURT: You would have been afforded the opportunity to come in later, to have a continuance later.

. . .

DR. REICH: Yes, I could have come, but the reasons for not coming go very deep, and if all this evidence—

THE COURT: I can't consider the motive. The only thing that I know is that you defaulted and there was no recourse left for the Court but to proceed accordingly.

DR. REICH: May I be permitted to show now that the original complaint, 1056, the civil complaint—

THE COURT: I am afraid I can't grant that request, Doctor, as much as I would like to do so.

. . .

DR. REICH: May I ask this question: If such fraud has been perpetrated on this Court, can that be resumed?

THE COURT: Not now. You see, apparently, Doctor you have been proceeding . . . upon the theory that this Court has determined, by the issuance of the Decree of Injunction, that "orgonomy" is merely a pseudo-science; that "orgonomy" does not exist or is not valid. This Court has not at any time made any determination regarding the existence or validity of orgonomy. . . . Now, had you defended, instead of having defaulted in the original proceeding, I would have excluded any evidence tending to prove or disprove the existence or validity of orgonomy because that evidence would have been regarded by this Court as being immaterial and irrelevant to the main issue.

This last statement of Judge Clifford's is rather hard to believe. The original complaint alleged that orgonomy was a pseudoscience. The judge could conceivably have excluded that aspect from the court proceedings. But the FDA would have had to present the medical tests and the people who conducted them. Reich would have questioned them and offered the results of his own clinical work in rebuttal. The question as to the therapeutic value of the orgone accumulators would inevitably have arisen, and from this would have risen the question of the reality of orgone energy. The judge could not very well have excluded this question nor the pro and con argumentation it would have provoked—with the FDA then introducing its evidence, based on the MIT tests, and Reich introducing his. But even aside from all these considerations, had there been a trial and the accumulator adjudged adulterated—that is, falling below the level of effectiveness claimed for it—that in itself would have been tantamount to deciding that orgonomy was a pseudoscience. In simple logic, a decision on the accumulator constituted a judgment on orgonomy—the two could not be separated. However, once the default decree had been entered, separating the two apparently became for Judge Clifford a convenient way of avoiding the complicated legal implications of a court passing on matters of science.

Aside from the argued issues, what emerges from the transcript of this hearing is the extreme courtesy Reich showed the judge and the judge's consideration, at times rather patronizing, toward Reich, his determination to let Reich have his full say even in matters that had already been decided or that the judge deemed irrelevant. For instance, when Reich's Response and the matter of the court's jurisdiction was being argued, the following exchange took place:

THE COURT: I have already indicated to you my ruling, but you go right ahead. I want to afford to you full opportunity.

DR. REICH: Thank you very much. Exactly here the basic issue appears . . . and that is, first that jurisdiction was denied. . . . Now, our lawyers have moved correctly to establish first the jurisdictional question, and that was not done.

THE COURT: I held that I had jurisdiction.

DR. REICH: May I ask now: Did you, Judge, ever pass on that jurisdictional question then at that time?

THE COURT: Oh, yes, the mere fact that I accepted it and proceeded would indicate that I had passed upon the question of jurisdiction. . . .

DR. REICH: Now may I raise this very same basic question again?

THE COURT: Go ahead. I am not going to prevent you from talking and presenting your issues.

DR. REICH: I understand your position, Judge, fully, but I appreciate it if you understand my position fully.

THE COURT: Yes, absolutely. There is no question in the mind of the Court or any of the officials that you are absolutely sincere and honest in your contention.

DR. REICH: If the Court considers me as being a true scientist in this and having done something important, then I would request the privilege of believing me that that I could not possibly at the present moment . . . bring forth certain facts, certain situations, because of certain involvements of national importance. . . . As I said on July 26th, I would have to refuse at the risk of going to jail. . . .

THE COURT: Of course that is up to you, Doctor.

DR. REICH: That is just what I wanted to make clear. There are certain things I could not do now. I can only indicate what it is.

THE COURT: Well, I don't think we will go into that any further, Doctor.

DR. REICH: Thank you.

There followed next an exchange between Silvert and the judge in which Silvert pleaded that since in the intervention proceedings he had been exempted from the terms of the injunction, he had an absolute right to ship the literature and accumulators from Maine to New York—especially since he did so without the knowledge of Reich, who was in Arizona at the time. Maguire's answer was that neither Silvert nor anyone else had ever been exempted from the terms of the injunction since these terms prohibit anyone from acting in concert with Reich—and the government was prepared to prove that Silvert had acted in concert in the shipment he undertook.

The trial date was then tentatively set for December 1. Reich in preparation for it wrote his speech "Atoms for Peace vs. the Hig." (Hig stood for Hoodlums in Government). Though this speech was never delivered, it represented Reich's most complete expression of his feelings and attitudes toward his legal entanglement at the end of 1955 and therefore merits some examination.

The introduction to the speech states: "It is with deep regret and with disgust that such an address to an American Jury had to be conceived and prepared for trial of the discoverer of the Life Energy. . . ." [8] And then it opens on one of the fundamental legal issues of the contempt proceeding—whether illegal laws have to be obeyed or not. The case for the affirmative—namely, that illegal laws must be obeyed—was, it will be recalled, previously argued in one of the government's briefs. (Later, to anticipate, this position will be repeated by the Court of Appeals' decision.) Reich, however, maintained just the opposite at this time and throughout, namely, that illegal laws should not be obeyed. Since the injunction was obtained by illegal means, it was unlawful and its terms did not have to be obeyed. "Judicial opinions," Reich wrote, "if not based on factual evidence are unlawful opinions; therefore, they are not 'The Law' no matter whether proclaimed by judges or attorneys of any kind." [9] But besides being unlawful the injunction was also unobeyable, Reich maintained. "It is as if I were requested to grow within 10 days green elephant tusks—or else. . . . Nothing could illustrate better the request that I stop the world

8. *Ibid.*, p. 1.
9. *Ibid.*, pp. 1–2.

from talking, thinking, acting, reading about cosmic orgone energy." [10] This, of course, is somewhat of an overstatement since the injunction did not make Reich responsible for what the world did about orgone energy, so long as this was done independently of any act on his part.

The speech then went on to state that Reich and his co-workers didn't deny having disobeyed the injunction and that this disobedience would be repeated "under the same circumstances." [11] It was for this reason that everyone at Orgonon was armed. But contrary to the secret procedures of the "drug agents," Reich and his co-workers "kept everything in the open," [12] informing the authorities of every step taken and sending all pertinent documents about the discovery of orgone energy and the conspiracy against it to the FBI and the CIA. "We are, as scientific workers in *Basic, Pre-atomic Research* as well as professional citizens, responsible to the world community for what happens to the Discovery of the Life Energy." [13]

In accounting for his refusal to appear in the original Complaint proceeding, Reich wrote: "He [The Discover of the Life Energy] did not appear because he refused to take orders from Moscow Higs through an American Court. . . ." [14] And later he stated that this nonappearance was part of the "civic duty of the discoverer and his assistants to resist the assault on the discovery, and to set a precedent to the effect that never again should such infamous conduct be permitted to harass discoveries." [15] Then, Reich reiterated two of his central contentions: that the fact of human irrationalism had to be recognized in the law structure; and that crucial discoveries, like that of orgone energy, had to be written into the law structure.

What is repeatedly apparent in this "speech" is that Reich was capable of very lucid thinking, but that when it came to the matter of the motive behind the FDA's prosecution this lucidity would be replaced by wild, irrational charges. Thus, he wrote a bit further on that, "Already in August 1952 FDA agent Kenyon . . . ap-

10. *Ibid.*, p. 2.
11. *Ibid.*, p. 2.
12. *Ibid.*, p. 3.
13. *Ibid.*, p. 3.
14. *Ibid.*, p. 3.
15. *Ibid.*, p. 4.

peared with two alleged scientists *to find out what the Oranur experiment was all about."* [16] [Italics in original] And that he knew these agents were really "pharmaceutic agents representing American industrial interests who were ready to sell out the country . . . via Moscow affiliations." [17] The reference in the last sentence is to the idea that Reich got from reading a book of Emanuel M. Josephson that came out in 1952, entitled *Rockefeller Internationalist: The Man who Misrules the World,* which purported to prove that the Rockefeller family was working in secret alliance with the USSR.

Later, still pursuing the matter of political motivation, Reich saw an ominous conspiratorial significance in the fact that Kenyon had come on the 1952 inspection visit with Heller and Brimmer only a short time after Panyushkin—"the GPU Terrorist" [18]—had returned from Moscow. This visit came, too, three months after Orgonon was stricken with DOR and two months following the invention of the cloudbuster. "Strange, is it not, this coincidence taken together with the curiosity of Holliday in Arizona soon after the transportation of ORUR from Maine to Arizona?" [19]

It was, then, with the convictions and in the state of mind expressed in this "speech," that Reich, some six months later, came to defend himself against the charge of criminal contempt at the trial held in Portland, Maine. The "speech" itself was sent to Judge Clifford.

16. *Ibid.,* p. 9.
17. *Ibid.,* p. 9.
18. *Ibid.,* pp. 13–14.
19. *Ibid.,* p. 14.

12

---◆◆---

THE TRIAL

Reich moved to Washington, D.C., in late 1955. Besides his desire to be with Miss Karrer, who worked in the capital, another reason for this move—Miss Ollendorff suggested—was that he liked the idea of being close to the center of governmental power at a time when he was involved in litigation with the government. He rented a suite at the Alban Towers Hotel, and to avoid people he did not want to see he used the alias Walter Roner. His daughter, Eva, and her husband, William Moise, moved to Washington shortly afterward to be with Reich, to help him in his preparation for the trial and with the weather work he did there—about which, however, there are only a few details available.

Reich appears to have been comfortable in this new situation and even considered the possibility of buying property somewhere in the environs of the capital. Peter came there to spend vacations with his father. In the account given in his book, there is conveyed a sense of the growing closeness between him and his father during this time. The son, little as he was, was apparently a source of great comfort to Reich. In spite of Reich's telling Peter that he wanted him eventually to go out and make a life of his own, Reich seems to have reposed many of his hopes for the future of his work in his son. In March of 1956, for example, Reich wrote to Neill: "He [Peter] is my best 'little' friend. He visited me twice here in

Washington. He partook fully, consciously and enthusiastically in our Desert work in Arizona. He knows much already about natural science and about DOR emergency." [1] Peter recorded that at some time during the contempt litigation Reich took him in his arms and, giving way to fear and despair, quietly wept. Most of the time, however, he impressed on Peter the necessity to be very strong and very brave in the face of the "conspiracy."

After several date changes—from December 1, 1955, to March 6, 1956—the trial was finally set definitely for April 30. In the meantime, Judge Clifford, pleading overwork and family difficulties, was replaced by Judge George C. Sweeney.

The trial, however, still did not begin as scheduled. This time because of Reich. He maintained that the notice of the trial he received had not been properly signed—that is, the U.S. Attorney's (Mills') signature was not on the notice, instead the U.S. Attorney's name had merely been typed in. This issue, of course, was a matter he could easily have verified by consulting a lawyer. Ilse Ollendorff did that. On receiving word from Reich that she should not honor the notice she received because of the "improper" signature, she consulted a lawyer, was told the notice was perfectly in accordance with courtroom protocol, and appeared at the designated time. Thus, she escaped being brought in in handcuffs later—as Reich, Silvert and Mangravite were.

The issue Reich made of this matter seems similar to the issue he had earlier made, and was to make again, of the "and/or" wording. That is, in the strictest technical sense he was right, but he refused to accept the fact that legal matters often went not according to technical correctness but according to traditionally established practice. Thus, Reich was not above making an issue of technicalities, but such technicalities had to have a principled basis —however misconceived—and not be pursued solely for the purpose of gaining legal advantage.

The matter of the signature had been first raised by Reich when the trial date was set for March 6. On March 3, William Moise, as clerk of the Wilhelm Reich Foundation, wrote to the clerk of the court in Portland: "Under ordinary routine legal circumstances it would have occurred to no one . . . to be petulant about signa-

1. Published in Ollendorff, p. 130.

tures and similar things. The case of the FDA, however, most regretably, is not of such kind. With a criminal conspiracy in the background of the FDA action, with the illegal procedural maneuvering . . . and with several mistakes having occurred in what you termed 'customary routine matters,' it is felt that all legal papers, orders, etc., should be executed, not according to custom but according to law." And the letter concluded with the statement that "only legally correctly signed and executed documents will be accepted by the Counsel for the Discovery of the Life Energy."

When the trial date was postponed to April 30, there was, again, an exchange of correspondence between Reich (either directly or through Moise) and the court. This time Reich insisted not that Mills' manual signature be on the order to appear for trial but the judge's personal signature; and he put the court on notice that no orders without the judge's signature would be honored. As late as April 24 * Reich wrote to Judge Sweeney that if a "proper" order were not received in time, he would assume that he did not have to appear for trial. "I wish to assure you," he explained, "that I . . . prefer . . . to take the grave risk of these extraordinary precautionary steps and to feel *clean* like mountainbrook water, rather than to act against our conscience . . . and to feel dirty like sinking into a *swamp*." [Italics in original.]

In the meantime, on April 23, Reich had sent a telegram to Mills urging him "for reasons of national planetary security to help reaching [*sic*] peaceful solution of embarrassing legal tangle by withdrawing contempt charge." (It is difficult to determine if Reich was so out of touch with the legal realities of his position that he was hoping in this way to be able to avert the trial or whether he sent the telegram for the sake of historical record, about which, as has been noted, he was very concerned. Perhaps both possibilities were involved.) When he received no reply from Sweeney by April 30, Reich jubilantly phoned Dr. Baker to tell him that the case had been won. But he had scarcely put down the phone when a federal deputy marshal appeared at his hotel suite, put Reich into handcuffs and took him to Portland, Maine. Silvert and Mangravite,

* The letter is actually dated October 24, 1956, but this is surely an error since the contents make it clear the trial had not yet taken place. Moreover, since there is mention of the telegram having been sent on April 23, 1956, the letter could not have been sent in an earlier month.

who, on instructions from Reich, had also failed to appear, were also brought to Portland in handcuffs. They all spent a night in the Portland jail and were later found in contempt. Reich was fined $500, Silvert $300 and Mangravite some smaller sum.

The trial began at 10:00 A.M., on Thursday, May 3, 1956, and ran for three consecutive days. It was concluded the following Monday, May 7. Reich and Silvert represented themselves and William Moise represented the Wilhelm Reich Foundation. The government was represented by Mills and Maguire. There were few people in the public seating area, a dozen or so Reich supporters, except for the last day—Monday—when the verdict was to be brought in. At that time some twenty or thirty Reich people were present, most of them having made the trip from the New York City area. "Reich seemed in good spirits," Dr. Myron Sharaf, who was present at the time, stated in his account of the trial, "and looked well in spite of what must have been a tremendous ordeal in the days preceding the trial. He rubbed his wrists at the beginning of the trial, as if indicating that it was a relief to be out of the hand cuffs." [2]

Sharaf described Judge Sweeney as "a round-faced man who looked like a cross between Senator Mundt and Winston Churchill." [3] He was a stronger and more independent man than Clifford, but also less kindly. Thus he did not allow as much latitude as Clifford had in the prior hearings. At the beginning he was impatient with both Maguire and Reich; with Maguire for drawing out the process of proving the obvious, and with Reich for trying constantly to introduce "irrelevant" issues. But as the trial proceeded, Sharaf wrote, Sweeney "softened toward Reich . . . and the 'out of order' rulings were done . . . with less impatience, as though he were following the law more than his inclination. . . ." [4]

The jury selection went quickly—only one juror was challenged. The jury members "looked like a movie jury—extremely typical . . . down to one Negro." [5]

The transcript of the trial makes, for the most part, tedious read-

2. Myron Sharaf, Ph.D., "The Trial of Wilhelm Reich," in *Wilhelm Reich*, ed. Paul Ritter (Nottingham, England: The Ritter Press, 1958), p. 66.
3. *Ibid.*, p. 63.
4. *Ibid.*, p. 64.
5. *Ibid.*, p. 63.

ing. The bulk of it is devoted to the government's development of its case, proving in minute detail, through its subpoenaed witnesses, the various ways in which the injunction had been disobeyed by Reich, how Silvert had shipped literature and accumulators from Maine to New York, and how Reich had later accepted funds from Silvert that Silvert had collected on the basis of sales and rentals of the material he had shipped. But in the second part of the trial, when Reich was permitted to present his case, things livened up a bit. The judge resolutely refused to permit Reich to bring in matters that did not relate specifically to the government's charges. Reich wanted to speak about the prosecution's motivations, the "conspiracy," misrepresentation, and the unconstitutionality of the original injunction. The judge, however, held repeatedly that Reich could bring these matters in only in his final address to the jury. Yet Reich continued to be at all times most courteous to the judge, often thanking him even when the judge stopped him from pursuing "extraneous" matters, or when the judge overruled some objection Reich wished to raise.

Legally, Reich had no defense. The verdict was a foregone conclusion almost from the beginning. It was because of this that the judge was often impatient with the lengths to which Maguire went in substantiating what was hardly ever contested by Reich and was often freely admitted by him. Most of the witnesses answered the questions put to them in a clear and unambiguous way. There was no attempt on the part of those who had been connected with Reich or Silvert to hide or mitigate anything, although they did from time to time resist some particular construction Maguire sought to make. The only time there was hedging to avoid straightforward answers was when Mills and Maguire were put on the witness stand.

The first witness called by the government was Morris Cox, Clerk of the U.S. District Court for the District of Maine. Through his testimony it was established that the injunction had been entered and signed by Judge Clifford on March 19, 1954, at 2:45 P.M. Eastern Standard Time. The fact that Reich had no defense in legal terms came out while Cox was still on the stand. Silvert was asked by the court if he admitted to having been one of the applicants for intervention when the following exchange ensued:

DR. REICH: We never denied that we did not obey the injunction. We
    never denied that.

THE COURT: Well, what are we trying here?

DR. REICH: I would like to shorten the procedure.

THE COURT: In what way?

DR. REICH: We never denied that we did not obey the injunction.

THE COURT: May I ask if you have violated this injunction?

DR. REICH: I did not violate the injunction.

THE COURT: You just said that you never denied it.

DR. REICH: I will put on witnesses later.

These remarks reflect the contradiction in Reich's legal position.
He was willing to admit not having "obeyed" the injunction, but
to admit that he had "violated" it implied that the injunction had
some binding force—which Reich was not willing to concede. From
his point of view, the injunction was illegal and unconstitutional to
begin with, so it could not be violated by the mere disobedience
of its terms. From the point of view of the court, of course, this
distinction was meaningless, and what Reich admitted this early in
the trial made it clear that the government would win the case.

The next witness was Ilse Ollendorff. She and Reich had been
separated for some two years at this time, and though they were in
frequent contact by telephone—mostly in matters relating to their
son—the meeting at the trial was probably their first since the
separation. In spite of the pressures that had made it necessary for
her to leave Reich, she displayed an admirable loyalty to him and
his work at the trial. Of her testimony, Sharaf wrote: "She was a
fine witness, perhaps the clearest and most secure of any that took
the stand during the trial." [6] Her testimony referred to only a few
months of the post-injunction period when she was still at Orgonon.
Nevertheless, it was important from the standpoint of the government's desire to prove that certain of the injunction's provisions
had not been complied with from the very beginning.

When Maguire proceeded to read off the names of all the books
listed in the injunction and asked her if they "were employed in
connection with the sale, rental, and distribution, generally, of Orgone Energy Accumulators . . ." the following dialogue took
place:

6. *Ibid.,* p. 64.

MISS OLLENDORFF: None of these books were used in connection with the sale of accumulators.

MR. MAGUIRE: Isn't it a fact, Miss Ollendorff, that these books could be ordered by anybody who submitted the order to the Wilhelm Reich Foundation or any one of its affiliates?

MISS OLLENDORFF: Yes, but independent of the Orgone accumulators. They were issued and published by the Orgone Institute Press and were shipped to people who ordered them from the Press, but they were not in connection with Orgone Energy Accumulators.

THE COURT: Are they banned in the injunction decree?

MR. MAGUIRE: Yes.

THE COURT: Well, what is the sense of going over that? You have the books and you have the injunction.

From her testimony Maguire showed that after the issuance of the injunction none of the accumulators had been recalled and that money for their rental continued to be collected. Then he moved on to establish a connection between the Wilhelm Reich Foundation and the Orgone Institute Research Laboratory which, under the directorship of Silvert, began renting and selling orgone accumulators while Reich was in Arizona. In this way Maguire was proving that Silvert's involvement with accumulators was in concert with both the Wilhelm Reich Foundation and with Reich, its director.

Reich's questioning of Miss Ollendorff was brief and had almost nothing to do with any of the information Maguire had so laboriously elicited. This was to be typical of his cross-examination of all the later government witnesses. He was not interested in denying any of the specific charges of violation that Maguire was developing. His cross-examination, in other words, did not constitute any kind of legal defense, though it was consistent with the way he conceived of the basic issues involved in the case. He sought to gain from Miss Ollendorff and subsequent witnesses testimony that would establish the importance of his work and the consequent necessity to disobey any terms of the injunction that would interfere with it.

The prosecution then called a Mr. Paul Berman to testify that he had rented an accumulator in 1952 from the Foundation and that in December 1954 he had sent his monthly rental to the Orgone Institute Research Laboratory at Silvert's address in New York. This further strengthened the government's contention that Silvert had worked in concert with Reich. In his cross-examination, Reich attempted only to establish whether the accumulator had had good effects on Berman, an attempt that Sweeney promptly cut short. This and other attempts later in the trial seem to indicate the Reich had forgotten his original contention that he would not argue the validity of his scientific formulations in a court of law since no court had jurisdiction in scientific matters.

The deputy marshal who had come with the FDA man to inspect Little Orgonon was called to testify that the FDA had not been allowed to carry out the inspection—thereby scoring another point for the prosecution, since the injunction ordered that inspections be allowed. Reich's cross-examination attempted to make one point— that the FDA man had said he came to inspect "everything." This, of course, was in line with his belief that the FDA was out to discover his secrets for the communists and was, at this particular visit, motivated by the news of the arrival of the ORUR material some time earlier.

So it went, with most of the prosecution's witnesses giving new details and proofs of injunction violations and Reich rarely contesting these details and proofs in his cross-examinations. In general, Maguire sought to establish that after the injunction was issued accumulators were not recalled, that accumulators were rented and sold, that literature was sold, that inspections were not permitted and—the most important point—that in transferring accumulators and literature from Maine to New York, Silvert was acting in concert with Reich.

As regards this last matter, both Reich and Silvert sought to establish through testimony of witnesses that Reich had not known that Silvert intended to make the shipment. The simplistic assumption in this was that if Reich did not know of this act before it was carried out, Silvert could not have done it in concert with Reich. From a legal point of view, however, the fact that Reich did not dissociate himself from this act after he found out, the fact that he continued to accept funds that came from the sales and rentals of the shipped accumulators and literature after he found out, constituted action in concert. The judge made this clear, yet

Reich and Silvert persisted in their position and continued gathering testimony to support it. Later they repeated this attempted exculpation in the appeals.

It was at the end of the first day of trial that Reich, Silvert, Mangravite and one or two other subpoenaed witnesses were fined for their failure to appear in court when ordered. Sharaf wrote that Reich insisted he had no intention of disobeying the court's order, but only wanted to make sure, with so much subversion around, that everything was properly done. "It was a mistake," he told Mills. "And Mills gave him his usual hostile, willfully uncomprehending look." [7]

Some time during the next day's session Reich submitted a letter to Judge Sweeney in which he offered a solution to the "legal jam" created by the fact that "on the one hand . . . I am innocent and could not act differently . . . [and] on the other hand the merely legal procedural formulations binds the jury to find whether or not I have violated the injunction." Saying that he felt that "everybody concerned" wanted to find a way out of the tangle without committing a judicial injustice, Reich suggested in this letter that it could be accomplished by changing the charge to the jury. Instead of having the jury decide "did" Reich violate the injunction, the wording should be changed to "had" Reich to violate the injunction. "I am asking for this privilege," the letter concluded, "on the basis of the fact that during the pre-trial procedure I had been arraigned on the basis of an error when instead of dismissal *or* trial the formulation was dismissal *and* trial. . . ."

Perhaps, once again, the most striking fact about this letter is that there is so much that is right about it, especially Reich's distinction between factual and legalistic guilt. Certainly, on the basis of what has been presented in this whole account thus far—the predetermined assumption of guilt that marked the beginning of the FDA's investigation, the long search for dissatisfied users and the dismissal of what was said by satisfied users of the accumulator, the shoddy quality of the tests the FDA had conducted, the distorting selectivity of material in the Complaint concerning claims for cures as well as the misrepresentation of the whole field of orgonomy as a vulgar moneymaking enterprise, the classification of all of Reich's writings as part of a promotional scheme for this

7. *Ibid.*, p. 69.

enterprise—certainly, on the basis of all of this, it can be validly maintained that in any but the narrowest legalistic sense Reich was factually innocent.

But against this, there stands the pathetic first sentence of the second paragraph where Reich assumes that "everybody concerned" wants to find a decent way out of the legal tangle. Perhaps this could apply to the judge—there is some evidence, as will be later shown, that Judge Sweeney was quite disturbed over the legal predicament Reich had gotten into. But the letter says "everybody concerned"—which includes Mills and Maguire. Reich's deceiving himself to the extent of including them among those wishing to avoid a judicial injustice—that is the pathos. Reich had said before that they and the FDA and the "espionage" they were a part of were out to get him, to destroy him and his work. And now Reich was, in effect, appealing to their decency; blocking out of his awareness the hatred he was the brunt of; blinding himself to his own vulnerability as if he lived in a decent world where even in official intercourse people acted with consideration for each other. The pathos here lies in the circumstance that Reich—who had looked so deeply into human irrationality and its subsequent evil, who had taken the full, unflinching measure of man's misery and still was able to see beyond it the promise of fulfillment inherent in the nature of things—should have reached a point where this vision became intolerable and he was compelled to take refuge in such delusion to try to reduce the danger he was in to the level of an easily rectifiable semantic error.

In the context of these two considerations—Reich's essential rightness together with his self-deception—the actual request of the letter becomes insignificant. The request, of course, could not be granted. Sweeney promptly turned it down.

The testimony presented on the following days was as tedious, repetitive, and unnecessary as that of the first. Reich's cross-examinations were for the most part just as irrelevant, as far as the court was concerned. He himself became bored by most of the procedure and at one point commented: "Your Honor, we would like to object to this. It is kind of lengthy and complicated and a sleepy examination." Even the judge became impatient. When Maguire went into meticulous detail concerning the expenditure of funds by Reich in Arizona, Sweeney broke in with: "How far are

you going in this thing—buying cigarettes, cigars and such things?"
There were, however, occasional moments of heightened interest
when fundamental issues came into open conflict.

When Reich, in one of his cross-examinations, sought to establish what he considered an important legal issue—*i.e.,* that the decision in the matter of the intervention proceedings meant that the
fifteen medical orgonomists were exempted from the terms of the
injunction—Sweeney explained: "Judge Clifford, when he wrote
the opinions, on the question of intervention, pointed out that the
action was against three people and, therefore, the injunction ran
against three people. It did not effect the rights of any others to
deal with this unless they acted in concert with the defendants."
This issue was to arise again later in the trial.

Finally, on the third day of the trial, it was the defendants' turn
to call and question witnesses. Judge Sweeney, in his instructions,
cautioned them to stick to facts and to the issue of whether or not
the injunction had been violated. "We cannot go into wherefores,"
he pointedly said. "Now you have a right to make an opening to
the Jury, telling them what you have to prove, but only on the
question of violation, and I hope that I won't have to stop you."

Reich's opening statement is inexplicably omitted from the
transcript of the trial. But it and the entire defense case lasted
about an hour and a half, according to Sharaf's estimate.

Again, as in the cross-examinations, Reich attempted, despite
the judge's instructions, to establish not that the injunction had
been obeyed but that there were weighty reasons for disobeying it.
He ran into trouble in this attempt during his questioning of his
first witness, William Moise:

THE COURT: The only question here is whether you disobeyed or did
    not disobey the Injunction. The Court does not recognize any
    excuse for not obeying it after it was issued.
DR. REICH: May I reenforce my statement that I have disobeyed the
    Injunction?
THE COURT: Then what are we trying here?
DR. REICH: That is not my question.
THE COURT: If you have admitted that you have disobeyed this injunc-
    tion then you are really wasting our time here. I cannot listen to
    why you disobeyed it or why you had to. The fact is that if you
    admitted you disobeyed it your case is about over. I said to you,

today, we are producing facts. When the case is argued by you, you have a greater range of variation to argue to the jury. You can argue, for instance, any inference that would naturally arise from the facts that have been produced. You can argue motives. You have a greater range on argument, but until you have entered a plea of guilty, we will go on with this case.

DR. REICH: I do not plead guilty.

Yet a short while later the following exchange took place:

DR. REICH: Was the Injunction violated?

MR. MOISE: Yes, sir, we had to.

DR. REICH: Was it violated in a strong manner and very defiant with great determination?

MR. MOISE: With great determination.

DR. REICH: Did we have a reason to do so?

MR. MAGUIRE: I object to that, Your Honor.

DR. REICH: Was it?

MR. MOISE: Yes.

THE COURT: I will sustain the objection.

When Maguire was called to take the stand it was obvious from the very beginning of his testimony that he would use his experience and Reich's inexperience in court to be as difficult a witness as possible:

DR. REICH: Mr. Maguire, you conducted the case against Orgone [sic] for how long—since when did it begin?

MR. MAGUIRE: Well, in the first place, I have conducted no case.

DR. REICH: Well, you have presented it?

MR. MAGUIRE: I have conducted no case against Orgone, at any time.

DR. REICH: But you were the lawyer.

MR. MILLS: I object, Your Honor, as entirely irrelevant.

THE COURT: I will allow it. I am going to give him a little more latitude than a lawyer would have.

Maguire next denied ever having seen two works Reich showed him: *Conspiracy and Emotional Chain Reaction* and *The Red Thread of a Conspiracy*. Ilse Ollendorff wrote in her biography that she was very shocked by this false statement since she had seen both volumes in Maguire's office when, earlier, she had been called there to identify Foundation records. During a recess she went to the judge's chamber and told him of the falsehood. Judge Sweeney, she wrote, "advised me to tell Reich about it, to have

Reich put me on the witness stand and to question me about this incident." [8] And, she added: "I think that Reich was very pleased with my role in the trial which made me, the government witness, one of the best witnesses in his behalf. I remember he gave me a big hug when I told him about Maguire." [9] The follow up to the judge's advice will be presented later.

In the meantime, continuing to question Maguire, Reich sought to bring his view of the conspiratorial background of the case— that is, his belief that he was the target of a communist plot—by asking Maguire if he were aware that in August of 1954 some 230 people working for HEW were suspended as subversives. However, the judge ruled the question out.

Then there was the following exchange between Reich and Sweeney:

THE COURT: Would you like some time to organize?
DR. REICH: Yes, and I would like to object to the procedure.
THE COURT: No, but I want you to have every chance you can.

. . .

DR. REICH: Your Honor, may I call another witness. Just as a fact that we have not obeyed the injunction?
THE COURT: Surely.

There is something surreal and Kafkaesque about this exchange and others like it: The judge seeking to help the defendant but preventing him from presenting his defense; then the defendant politely asking permission to help prove the prosecution's case and the judge courteously acquiescing.

A rather touching situation developed when Mr. Tom Ross, the caretaker at Orgonon, took the stand. A relationship of deep mutual respect had developed between him and Reich. Consequently, Ross found it difficult, out of loyalty to Reich, to give the kind of answers Reich wanted:

DR. REICH: Mr. Ross, will you tell the jury whether we have ignored the Injunction?
MR. ROSS: I could not answer that question for you.
DR. REICH: Did we obey it,—tell the truth please?
MR. ROSS: I cannot answer that question.

8. Ollendorff, p. 140.
9. *Ibid.,* p. 140.

THE COURT: Have you seen something done that would be a violation of the Injunction?

MR. ROSS: Yes.

THE COURT: Well, that is the answer he wants.

The subsequent exchange probably constitutes the strongest demonstration of one of the points Reich sought to make—the determination with which he was resolved to resist the FDA:

DR. REICH: In connection with our being armed certain happenings occurred at Orgone [Orgonon] last July which were very dangerous in connection with not obeying the Injunction. Do you remember that we had chains and we were armed?

MR. ROSS: Yes.

DR. REICH: Did you prepare a grave for me during those two weeks?

MR. MAGUIRE: I object to that.

DR. REICH: That is not ridiculous if you are in it.

THE COURT: All right, did you prepare the grave?

MR. ROSS: Yes.

THE COURT: You did not use it?

MR. ROSS: I prepared it.

DR. REICH: Do you think it was serious then?

THE COURT: Not what he thinks.

A very brief cross-examination followed:

MR. MAGUIRE: Don't you mean you dug a hole?

DR. REICH: I object. It is a serious thing.

THE COURT: I will sustain the objection.

It was almost as though, in sustaining the objection, the judge was trying to counteract his own, probably involuntary, facetiousness of a moment earlier when he had asked Ross if he had used the grave.

Reich next called Robert McCullough. McCullough, it will be remembered, had accompanied Reich on the Arizona expedition. Through his testimony Reich again established that the commitment to resisting the injunction was so great that everyone at Orgonon was instructed to be armed at all times against possible intrusion by FDA agents. At which point the judge intervened and the following dialogue (later to be cited by the FDA as proof of the danger involved in the case) took place:

THE COURT: Do you mean to say that had the United States Marshal sought to do something you would have shot him?

MR. MCCULLOUGH: No, Sir. I would say I was armed to prevent trespass.

THE COURT: Would you have shot a Pure Food and Drug Inspector?

MR. MCCULLOUGH: I would not have shot, but I might use it to stop trespassing.

THE COURT: Well, suppose he kept coming?

MR. MCCULLOUGH: Well, I am big enough.

THE COURT: Well, suppose he was big, too? You wouldn't shoot anybody, would you?

MR. MCCULLOUGH: Well, I wouldn't say that. Under some conditions, I might have shot somebody, yes.

Reich then elicited from McCullough the information that during the Arizona desert work McCullough developed an injury in his right side that made him limp. The purpose here was to demonstrate the potency of DOR. Judge Sweeney, again giving way to flippant irony—perhaps occasioned by his knowledge that in effect the case was over, had long been over—asked: "That wasn't caused by a Pure Food and Drug Inspector?"

When Silvert took the stand Reich's questioning was, again, directed to demonstrating the seriousness of his determination to resist the injunction and the FDA:

DR. REICH: Did we violate the Injunction?

DR. SILVERT: We did.

DR. REICH: We were determined to disobey it and ignore it?

DR. SILVERT: Yes.

DR. REICH: At the risk of our lives?

DR. SILVERT: Yes, Sir.

DR. REICH: It is very serious, Your Honor. It was extremely serious.

THE COURT: I have told you it was.

Here Judge Sweeney interpreted Reich's comment in a way obviously not intended, referring it to the disobedience of the injunction rather than the reason for this disobedience.

Following this, Maguire, by astute cross-examination, put Silvert in a logical bind. On the one hand Silvert had just admitted complicity with Reich in disobeying the injunction; yet earlier he had maintained that his shipment of the material from Orgonon had been done at his own discretion, not in concert with Reich, and did not constitute a violation of the injunction; besides this, he had also maintained that he could not disobey the injunction since in the intervention proceedings it was decided that he was exempt from the terms of the injunction. Consequently, he was compelled to do what must have been an embarrassing about-face and retract his prior admission:

MR. MAGUIRE: When you said "We violated it," you mean you personally have violated the Injunction?

DR. SILVERT: I would certainly have been willing if I had, but I was never covered by the Injunction myself.

MR. MAGUIRE: Have you violated the Injunction?

DR. SILVERT: I am not named in the Injunction.

MR. MAGUIRE: Have you violated the Injunction?

DR. SILVERT: I would like to say yes, but actually I don't believe I have.

One of the more dramatic moments of the trial occurred shortly thereafter when Reich went back to Silvert in redirect examination to establish what he considered a basic contradiction in the way the injunction had been interpreted—again with reference to the intervention proceedings:

DR. REICH: Dr. Silvert, will you tell the story of how you were in the Injunction and out of the Injunction again?

THE COURT: He never was in the Injunction.

DR. REICH: Oh, yes, Your Honor, he was, everybody was in it.

THE COURT: No, they were not either. It merely said it was not limited to those enumerated in the Injunction proceedings.

DR. REICH: The Injunction was against all books, all activities, all associates, even my foreign publishers.

THE COURT: I will tell the jury who was covered by the injunction.

Reich, of course, was in error on this point and the judge, concerned lest the jury be confused, clarified the issue. He maintained that people not named in an injunction are not therefore excluded from its terms if they act in concert with those that are named. "For example," he said, "if Dr. Silvert took accumulators from Maine to New York, if he did that in the interest of anyone named in the injunction, no matter what the relationship was between them, then he comes within the injunction because he is acting in concert with them. If, on the other hand, it had no connection whatsoever with the people not named [this must surely be an error in transcription; the word "not" makes nonsense of the whole point Sweeney was attempting to elucidate] in the injunction, then he is not covered."

When Reich called his next witness—Peter Mills—to the stand the atmosphere became a bit charged. Reich tried to elicit testimony to show that Mills had acted out of improper motives, unethically, and with bias in prosecuting the case. He began by presenting Mills with a list of the legal activities Mills had performed for Reich and the Foundation,* and asked him to acknowledge its accuracy.

MR. MILLS: I am presented, Your Honor, with an eight-page list of items and dates and I am in no position to verify or deny.

THE COURT: Do you have any reason to challenge any of it from your memory?

MR. MILLS: No, I have no reason to challenge it but I haven't any reason to confirm it either, Your Honor, as they are listed. I could state, generally, that I would try to be responsive to any question that the examiner asks.

The judge, calling a recess, advised Mills to use the time to check through the list. Very likely it was during this recess that Ilse Ollendorff saw Judge Sweeney in his chambers and pointed out to him Maguire's false testimony. In her biography she wrote of a further exchange that took place between her and Judge Sweeney at this time, on the matter of a psychiatric examination for Reich. Judge Sweeney told her that this would be the only way for Reich to escape a guilty verdict. However, Miss Ollendorff took a strong stand against the judge's suggestion—because, on the one hand, it would have enraged Reich and his co-workers, and on the other, "whatever Reich's delusions may have been in regard

* In the appendix to Reich's brief to the Court of Appeals there are some fifty items of correspondence in which Mills was involved. These include matters concerning the Wilhelm Reich Foundation, accumulators, Orgone Institute Laboratories, etc. Moreover, Mills witnessed, and had deposited in his law office statements concerning, the working of the Orgone Energy Motor (August 1, 1947) and the illumination of "vacor" tubes and the Geiger counter reaction. In a letter Reich sent Mills on February 27, 1950, the following sentence is included: "It is essential for you to be informed that this Institute is . . . entering a major struggle against vested pharmaceutical interests . . . which obstruct . . . the development of Orgone Therapy of cancer and other biopathies." He became legal clerk of the Wilhelm Reich Foundation on August 31, 1951.

to the conspiracy or the secret nature of his work . . . he was absolutely rational . . . so far as his basic premises were concerned, namely that scientific research should be free of any kind of politcal interference. . . ." [10]

When, after the recess, Mills resumed his testimony, he claimed that the list of activities was not accurate, though he admitted that many of the items on the list "appear to be authentic." The next logical step was for Reich to request him to point out the items he objected to—which Reich did. But Mills gave an evasive answer, Reich's questioning was diverted and this point was never followed up.

In the final part of the testimony Reich tried to explore the matter of Mills' switch from being friendly—when he was Reich's and the Foundation's lawyer—to being his enemy. Mills denied that he had had anything but a professional relationship with Reich. Of this Ilse Ollendorff wrote: ". . . Mr. Mills . . . shocked me . . . since I remembered that on more than one occasion he had brought his wife along to Orgonon and we all had friendly, personal chats." [11] This subject was then pursued as follows:

DR. REICH: Now, Mr. Mills, the problem which is before us here, in this legal case—I think the Court will permit me, as a human being, to ask one central question which pertains to the Injunction since you are the counsel for the opponent.

MR. MILLS: Are you asking me a question or testifying?

DR. REICH: I am leading up to my question. My question is now why you changed from our counsel to be the counsel for the opponent?

DR. REICH: This problem, Your Honor, I submit to you to be admitted in Court.

THE COURT: Well, what is your question?

DR. REICH: My question is, under the circumstances, what reasons or what facts induced Mr. Mills after being our counsel for three years, and I regarded him as a good friend, to be our opponent's counsel and the one to prosecute me and Dr. Silvert as criminals?

THE COURT: That is a fair question if there is anything.

MR. MILLS: The question is, what prompted me?

DR. REICH: What made you change your mind?

10. *Ibid.*, pp. 140–41.
11. *Ibid.*, p. 140.

MR. MILLS: I have never changed my mind. I am not conscious of changing my mind.

THE COURT: Wait a minute. The original question was, what prompted you to change sides.

MR. MILLS: I never changed sides. I first made my connections, I believe, with you on August 29, 1952. [This date is off by several years.] I never advised you on matters concerning the Pure Food and Drug Administration. I did not read the law with respect to the Pure Food and Drug Administration. I did not know it had any application in this business. You did not advise me.

As mentioned earlier, it was very likely that Mills was embarrassed, after becoming U.S. Attorney, to learn that he had represented someone in legal trouble with an agency of the federal government. This may well have influenced him to direct the prosecutory action against Reich instead of withdrawing from it and letting someone else direct it. It may well have been the reason, too, why in his testimony at this time he denied that there had been anything but a strictly professional relationship between him and Reich. His denial of any prior knowledge of Reich's trouble with the FDA further served the purpose of exonerating him from embarrassment. But it at the same time was intended to protect him from the charge of having served as the lawyer of two sides to a legal conflict, a practice that is not only unethical but illegal as well. Thus in the subsequent part of his testimony Mills denied having been present at one particular meeting at Orgonon in 1952 when the matter of the renewed FDA investigation had been discussed. At the next trial session the minutes of this meeting were brought and they clearly showed that Mills had indeed been present when the matter of the FDA had been discussed. Thus he had seemingly committed perjury in his testimony. No doubt a skilled lawyer could have exploited this circumstance to good use, made an issue of it which may not have averted the eventual verdict but certainly could have delayed and complicated it. Reich, however, did not pursue this matter.

Mills' position on the witness stand must have been uncomfortable for him. Sharaf recalled that he "was extremely defensive and at moments seemed to be spitting pure hate." [12] This defensive discomfort must have intensified when Maguire's attempt, in a brief

12. Sharaf, p. 70.

cross-examination, to bail his colleague out backfired. Maguire
tried to establish that Mills had no choice, once the matter was
referred to him by the Department of Justice, but to direct the legal
action against Reich. The question he finally put to Mills was:
"Did you have any discretion pursuant to orders of the Attorney
General as to whether or not you could proceed or not proceed?"
But before Mills could answer, Sweeney exposed the dishonesty of
the question by saying: "That is not a fair question. We all know
he may have assigned it to someone else if he did not care to sit
on it."

Reich next called Ilse Ollendorff. She testified that Maguire had
lied when earlier he had stated under oath that he had never seen
Conspiracy and Emotional Chain Reaction. Maguire denied having
denied that he had previously seen the volume shown him and
demanded that the court reporter read the relevant testimony back.
The judge, however, said: "The jury will be the people to decide.
The jury has heard your testimony, and now they have heard this
testimony, and they will decide." Perhaps with the verdict such a
clearly foregone conclusion he did not want matters to get unnecessarily sidetracked.

Maguire, when cross-examining Ilse Ollendorff, attempted to
defend his earlier testimony by eliciting from her the fact that since
Conspiracy was compiled in a loose-leaf binder, it was possible
that the volume shown him on the witness stand may have had
some pages removed and therefore there was no way he could
assert he had had previous occasion to see that publication. This
technically was not very convincing and an experienced lawyer
might well have made a serious issue of Maguire's lying. Reich,
however, ended his whole presentation at this point without pursuing this particular matter any further.

When the trial was resumed on Monday, May 7, there were only
brief testimonies by Silvert and Miss Sheppard, his assistant, on
financial transactions, and then Reich and Silvert rested their case.

There followed what the trial transcript calls "Summations by
Mr. Maguire for the Government and Dr. Silvert for the Respon-
dents." The transcript does not give the content of these summations and, strangely enough, it fails even to mention that Reich
also gave a summation. Silvert's summation consisted of reading a
shortened version of Reich's "Atoms for Peace *vs.* The Higs."

"Silvert read well, but his voice did not carry either the authority or emotional resonance of Reich's. One felt that the statement did not make too much of an impression on the jury and that its main significance lay in its historical value," [13] Sharaf writes. Reich spoke next. Sharaf continues:

Reich . . . concluded with a very few words to the jury. He pointed out, among other things, that he had given $350,000 . . .* to orgone energy research which made ridiculous Maguire's efforts to prove who had paid a $21.50 . . . bill. He told of his difficulties in fighting the case, how one had the feeling that whatever one did it was wrong—wherever one turned there was a closed door. He told of his experimental nature, how he wanted to see how this case would develop, how he even went to jail briefly to see what jail was like though he could have been released on bail earlier. He found out, he said, it was barbarous and inhuman and the people should do something about it. He thought it would be a good idea if every member of a jury, every member of the bar, including Maguire and Mills, would spend a little time in jail to see what it was like. He had found out because it was his way to study at first-hand what he dealt with. He wished his opponents had also found out what they were dealing with, had read the orgonomic literature and sat in the accumulator.

His words were simple and sincere and left a deep impression on me and others.[14]

Reich finally turned to the judge, and, saying something like, "I'm not sure it's proper for me to say this," turned next to the jury and told them how much he had enjoyed seeing their "open, honest faces" the past days of the trial. (If Reich was, at this time, paranoid—as some have claimed—then it was a paranoia that existed alongside an astonishing degree of naïve trust.) Then, as he returned to the defendants' table, Deputy Marshal Doherty, who had brought him to the trial in handcuffs—and who would eventually take him, again in handcuffs, to prison—rose and warmly shook Reich's hand.

Of Maguire's summation, Sharaf wrote:

---

* This money came from royalties Reich earned from the sale of his books and fees from his personal practice. Ilse Ollendorff points out in her biography that Reich put so much money into research that there was seldom any for elaborate vacations or any kind of opulant living.

13. *Ibid.,* p. 72.
14. *Ibid.,* p. 72.

Maguire gave a short rebuttal, concentrating on material presented in the Hig address. To Reich's statement that orgonomy was in the realm of basic research and that the Atomic Energy Commission had consented to this, he claimed that he had a letter from the AEC indicating otherwise. To Reich's charge that the FDA agents were "hoodlums," he countered with the years of government service of these agents and accused his opponents of being "hoodlums" for keeping the agents at gun point. But perhaps the most searing, stunning moment of the whole trial—the moment when the very fundamental issues were joined, though they were . . . not issues to be decided in a court room—came when Maguire scoffingly said: They talk about pre-atomic energy! What's that? We've moved way beyond that—we've got A-energy and now we are getting H-energy! (the H-bomb)! What worlds upon worlds were contained in these sentences! [15]

Judge Sweeney's final charge to the jury was relatively short and simple, but not without some eloquence. He said at the beginning:

Now this case should be decided free of any sympathy, any bias, or any prejudice, and should be decided purely on the evidence produced before you. Justice is best achieved in the Courts where the jury, using their common sense and ordinary intelligence and the experience of their past lives, ascertain what the facts are in the case. . . . As I waive my right to comment on the facts, I expect you to leave the law to me and to apply the law as I give it to you regardless of how unfairly you think I interpret the law or how bad you may think the law is.

Next, he briefly reviewed the history of the case and the contents of the injunction. The only question, he stated, was whether the injunction had been disobeyed. Outlining the various ways the injunction might have been disobeyed, he went on to explain the matter of a reasonable doubt. Such doubt ought not to be aroused by mere sympathy for a defendant in his misfortune or by the reluctance of a jury to accept the responsibility for convicting anyone. "If having weighed the evidence of both sides," he said, "you reach the conclusion that the defendant is guilty to the degree of certainty that would lead you to act on it in the most . . . critical affairs of your life, you may properly convict." The degree of certainty, in other words, did not have to reach the point of mathe-

15. *Ibid.*, pp. 72–73.

matical certainty; if such were the requirement then "most criminals would go unwhipped of justice."

He said further that the case was essentially simple and had been
well presented. The central issue was that a court was authorized
to enforce its decrees. "It would be a sorry state . . . of affairs,"
he continued, "if the court made an order and somebody says:
'Well, I am not going to obey it.' " Then, echoing the position
previously maintained by Judge Clifford, Sweeney asserted that the
"merits of Orgone" was not the issue, that the only issue was to
"justify the dignity of this court . . . if anyone has violated its
order." And, he concluded: "Now I leave it to you to say whether
there has been a violation of the order and who did it."

In other words, in accordance with the position Sweeney maintained from the beginning of the trial, he now excluded from the
jury's consideration everything that Reich saw as being the essence
of the case. Given such an order it is not surprising that the jury
returned after a deliberation of some ten or fifteen mintes, with the
verdict that Reich, Silvert and the Wilhelm Reich Foundation were
all guilty.

"Reich looked deadly serious as the jury filed in," Sharaf wrote,
"and his seriousness persisted after the foreman announced the
jury's decision." [16] Reich had fully expected a not guilty verdict,
and he "left the courtroom in a very active, serious mood; he said
that a 'legal scandal' had been committed, that this was just the
beginning and that he was glad that at least certain issues had been
expressed in the courtroom." [17] Sentencing was deferred to May 25.

Thus the trial ended. Reich had never had the opportunity to
present what he considered to be the essence of the case: the
reasons why he had to disobey the injunction. But even if he had
had such an opportunity, it is doubtful that the verdict would have
been any different. There are cases where laws or court orders are
deliberately disobeyed for the specific purpose of contesting their
constitutionality. Reich's case, however, did not come within this
framework. Challenge through disobedience is recognized by
courts, if at all, only after all possible legal channels have been
tried—and Reich, as we have seen, never went to court to contest
the injunction. Moreover, the manner in which he disobeyed the

16. *Ibid.*, p. 73.
17. *Ibid.*, p. 74.

injunction made it clear that his disobedience was not done as a preparation to a legal challenge but as an act of open defiance that went far beyond the token disobedience necessary for legal challenge.

Sharaf's final remarks on the trial merit quotation, since they constitute the only account in print of the situation which Reich and his followers were in at the time:

There was something of the atmosphere of Calvary about the whole business and Reich may have been provoked into doing something parallel to what Christ had done when he in desperation asserted: "I can destroy your temple in three days," and then all his enemies could gloat and say: did you hear him? Now we have him! He was surely wrong there. And he was wrong on one level, but not on another, the "followers" huddled around then and they huddle now. Can he really destroy the temple? Is there really espionage? Do they want all the top secret information? Will he be able to show them the importance of it all? And the Maguires smirk and win for the moment, the jury goes home and lives as it lived, the judge feels concerned and worried, but what can you do? and everybody is as they were, or are they? [18]

* * *

I hope he doesn't become another martyr for people to enjoy in the mirror. If people ever come through really, they won't need such martyrs-in-the-mirror. And if they don't come through, another one is senseless. . . . Maybe the image of someone dying for his truths stirs on the young, fires the imagination of new seekers of truth, maybe it has some point. But we have had many of them and it doesn't seem to have done much good in the long run. I hope Reich will live out his days. He had done and suffered enough and it is time others took up the brunt of that burden. The work stands, they can burn books, but the books are out, the accumulators are out in the world, they can't touch it. [19]

18. *Ibid.*, p. 75.
19. *Ibid.*, p. 77.

13

THE APPEALS

On May 11, two weeks before the date set for sentencing, Silvert and Moise, in the FBI offices in New York City, lodged an oral complaint of perjury against Mills and Maguire. According to the memo of a telephone conversation between Mills, Maguire, and John McGuire, of the Washington FBI headquarters, dated May 31, 1956, the complaint was forwarded to an FBI agent in Portland. There, no action on it was taken, and no further reference to it occurs anywhere in the records.

Silvert and Moise, at the same time, also lodged a complaint of perjury against Mangravite—the man who had been building accumulators for Silvert. On Silvert's advice, Mangravite had refused to obey the subpoena to appear for the trial and, as a result, was also taken to Portland in handcuffs and had spent the night in jail with Silvert and Reich. We know the basis for the perjury complaint against Mills and Maguire, but in regard to the complaint against Mangravite "no statement of any facts pointing to the perjury was made. . . ."

The complaint against Mangravite is an indication of the degree to which Reich was out of touch with the realities of his situation—since, one must assume, this accusation originated with Reich. But this complaint also shows the extent to which Moise and Silvert were at this time committed to Reich's most irrational ideas—

Silvert especially, since he had grown to know Mangravite well during the past year and a half and had become very friendly with him. This kind of blind commitment was later to become almost grotesque, as evidenced by this footnote to Reich's brief in the Supreme Court appeal: "Dr. Silvert has conceded that he may well have been unknowingly induced by subversive conspirators to do this [ship the material from Rangeley] in order to provide 'proof' of interstate shipment *after* the injunction was issued."

A few days before the sentencing, a letter sent by William Steig to solicit funds from friends and supporters further illustrated the degree to which even at this critical juncture in the litigation Reich's co-workers went along with him in his unrealistic assessment of his situation. The letter opens with the statement that despite expectations that "simple life-affirmative logic" would rule in Reich's favor, the court had instead, by its verdict, restricted Reich's work against deserts and DOR. But this was only "the beginning of a long fight which we *hope* will eventuate in an environment in which people . . . can live, love, work and learn to understand their place in the cosmic order without fear of being crushed by the pestilential robots who foster desert development in humanity." Reich and his co-workers, the letter continues, emerged from the trial "clean and strong," and now though orgonomy had to fight "in the opponents' own area, an evil with some thousands of years of practice behind it," orgonomy was in a strong position for this battle because of its "scientific understanding of what the evil is." (This evil, of course, was what Reich years earlier had called the "emotional plague"—that is, people using social and institutional power to support their pathological life-hating activity.)

However, Reich's distance from the realities of his legal situation was not a permanent condition. Dr. Sharaf has told this writer that in his conversations with Reich there were times of great lucidity interspersed with misjudgment and perhaps delusion. Once in a discussion concerning the "communist conspiracy" against him, Reich entertained the possibility that the prosecution by the FDA was nothing more than the grinding of bureaucratic machinery, and then added something like: "In that case we're really lost."

On the sentencing date, May 25, Maguire asked for three-year prison terms for Reich and Silvert and a fine of $50,000 for the

Foundation. This figure, Maguire maintained, represented the approximate amount illegally obtained by the Foundation since the issuance of the injunction. Reich and Silvert made no comment on this, and instead handed Judge Sweeney a letter. Judge Sweeney, however, did not at once read the letter. He simply announced the sentences: two years for Reich, a year and a day for Silvert, and a fine of $10,000 for the Foundation. Only then did he read the letter aloud, and so it became part of the court record:

Your Honor:

We have lost, *technically only,* to an incomprehensible procedure treadmill. I and my fellow workers have, however, won our case in the true, historical sense. We may be destroyed physically tomorrow; we shall live in human memory as long as this planet is afloat in the endless Cosmic Energy Ocean as the Fathers of the cosmic, technological age.

Already today every decent soul knows that truth and wells of new knowledge are on my side. I have won the battle against evil.

One day the motives and legalistic maneuvers of the technical winner of today, the drug and cosmetic Hig, will emerge from the archives and see the clean light of day.

I certainly prefer to be in the place where I am instead of being in the shoes of the Hig. I may suffer physical disaster, but shame and dishonor are *not on my face.* It is on the face of the XXth Century Judas Iscariot, Peter Mills, who betrayed his former friends and clients when the Oranur experiment struck us in 1952, and when the Red Fascist Hig, under Moskau [sic] order, was out to get our experimental secrets while, at the same time, they spread poison and slander in our peaceful village about us. Judas hurriedly left the apparently sinking ship; in addition he covered up his tracks by accepting the role of prosecutor for the Moskau inspired drug Hig against his former friends and clients.

In a deep sense, too, we are all guilty, bar none. We were and still are on trial, without exception, in one of the most crucial test crises in the history of man.

This important subject has been presented by me in 1953, during the grave planetary DOR Emergency, as if in anticipation of the Hig assault. Here, the Murder of Christ, 2,000 years ago has been taken as an historical example of the method used by the Emotional Plague of Man to kill Life and Truth.

This time, however, Judas has betrayed and the Hig is killing the scientific hope to cope with the planetary disaster that is upon us.

I wish to thank you, Judge Sweeney, for the fairness shown us, within the given bounds. I know you know the truth. May your knowledge help to improve the American judicial system to secure factual truth.

Reich and Silvert announced their intention of appealing the case and moved for a stay of sentence. Judge Sweeney granted the stay, but with the warning that they would have to cease their violative activities, and that if they did not he would vacate the stay, even if the Court of Appeals had not yet made its decision. The defendants had ten days in which to give formal notice of their intention to appeal, and forty days in which to file the necessary documents. They were released on $15,000 bail each.

The FDA lost no time announcing its victory. During the injunction period, but especially after the trial, Reich supporters had been sending letters of protest to congressmen and senators who, in turn, had made inquiries about the case to the FDA. Many of the FDA letters announcing the victory—they were form letters—now went out to such senators and congressmen, which included Humphrey, Fulbright, Margaret Chase Smith (of Maine) and Lehman. Besides this, letters were sent to various publications as well as to various governmental agencies—such as the Weather Bureau and the FBI—and, of course, to the leaders of the professional organizations of psychiatrists, psychoanalysts and the AMA. These letters recounted briefly the history of the case, stated that "we have made extensive investigations of various Orgone Energy devices—tests made by the best medical clinicians available; outstanding physicists were also engaged to . . . determine whether any energy such as Orgone exists," and that as a result Reich had been "thoroughly discredited."

Aside from the local Maine papers, few publications carried the news. *The New York Times* announced it in a very short article; but the *New York Post* ran a longer article under the title of "Let's See the Orgone Cure a Two Year Jail Sentence." Besides this, the FDA Commissioner on June 13, sent a self-congratulatory letter to all the FDA districts that had been involved in the case, commenting that the "gratifying outcome was made possible by . . . brilliantly executed field investigation and . . . most careful planning." Citing the complications arising from the fact that Reich and Silvert were psychiatrists, and the threat of gun play, the letter concluded that "It is most gratifying to know that we have employees . . . that possess the intelligence and determination to deal with charlatans of the type involved in this case."

The sentences and fine probably came as a shock to Reich—somehow, again, he had hoped that the court would see the essential rightness of his position. Mr. Robert McCullough recalled that on the morning before the sentencing, at breakfast, Reich and his new wife, Aurora, were making plans for the future, with Reich trying to cheer up the glum and apprehensive half-dozen people who had come to be with him in court.

Some people connected with Reich, though not active in his work of this period, tried to influence him after the sentencing to avail himself of conventional legal measures. Ilse Ollendorff wrote him a letter urging this and assuring him that "neither your name nor your honor would be in any way sullied by using all possible conventional legal means." [1] Reich replied to her as follows: "My personal fate may well be doubtful. But I have powerful backing. Many great people have died for far less than I am risking. . . . Somehow, I feel I have won and shall win further. You are right: I would not take well to a penitentiary, and—most likely —would be killed there." [2] In his feeling that he had "won" so far, Reich was referring to the fact that he had remained loyal to his beliefs, had refused to compromise. He was talking about his image in the mirror of history, about which he was more concerned than his personal fate.

Strong urging also came from Neill. In a letter written to Reich on October 22, 1956, he stated in part:

. . . If you didn't attend the second summons [i.e., the order to appear at the trial; the first was the order to come to court to answer the Complaint] because someone said the summons wasn't properly signed, then I am sure you got the wrong advice. Such a point cannot fight a battle whereas your original trumpet call—No court has the right to judge a matter of science—was right and powerful. . . .

Reich, I love you. I cannot bear to think of your being punished by an insane prison sentence. You couldn't do it and you know it. I wish to God that you'd simply let some good lawyer take up your case from the legal angle. Why should anyone waste breath and time trying to ex-

1. Ollendorff, p. 144.
2. Published in Ollendorff, p. 144.

plain to a judge and jury what your work is? They can't possibly understand. . . . I think you are all wrong in thinking that the trials are instigated from Moscow. . . .

The Tatsache [fact] is that you are being crucified fundamentally because you are the first man in centuries who has preached pro-lifeness, because you were the one and only man to assert the right of adolescence to love completely. The majority in USA, Britain, Russia, in the whole world are anti-life, so that you do not need to look for specific enemies like the FDA; they are only the shot that was fired at Sarajevo, not the basic cause of the attack on you. In any court your defence should be in big letters I AM FOR LIFE AND LOVE, not I am the victim of Russia or red fascism or anything else. I confess to a feeling that you have imagined motives when the big motive of hostility was there plain to be seen. . . . To think that the great man who has advocated rationalism all his life would now embrace irrationalism is a terrible thought. Terrible because when you are up against the hard rationalism of the law courts you must be super-rational to win.

. . . Get that lawyer and fight them with their own legal weapons, for your weapons are invisible to them.[3]

But by this time Reich, still acting as his own counsel, had already prepared and submitted his brief to the Court of Appeals. And he replied to Neill several days after his appearance at a hearing in the Appeals court: "The Appeal hearing went well in our favor so far. But, the enemy is tough, a killer." [4] He again expressed this optimism in a letter he sent to Steig sometime toward the end of the year, and before the Appeals decision, which was handed down on December 11. This letter, which Steig in turn sent out to all those who had contributed to his previous appeal, stated in part: "The battle could not have been conducted in our favor, as it has been, without the manifold kindnesses of people, close and distant alike."

This optimistic mood continued to infect the people who were closest to Reich even after the Appellate Court's ruling in support of the decision of the lower court. In a letter William Steig wrote in January 1957, soliciting more funds for weather work and legal expenses, he stated that this decision only seemed to be a setback. In reality, "developments are in our favor" because "courtroom procedure has seen a new development in which malevolent, psy-

3. *Ibid.*, pp. 148–49.
4. Ollendorff, p. 149.

chopathic behavior is directly confronted as such" so that "How the Court continues to handle this case has become what amounts to its own personal problem."

In short, Reich, who had earlier been wrongly convinced that the injunction would not—indeed, could not—be enforced, now seemed just as convinced, except for occasional moments of faltering optimism and despair, that the sentence would never be executed. His son, Peter, reports him as saying one day at Orgonon while they were out getting target practice: "I hope the appeal will be accepted, because I think the trial made it clear what we stood for." But then he added: "You must understand that I might die. Someone might try to kill me." [5]

Three briefs were submitted in October 1956—one by and for Reich, one by and for Silvert, and one for the Foundation prepared by the now re-engaged Charles Haydon. Reich's own brief was accompanied by several volumes of appendices—a transcript of the trial, a copy of *Conspiracy,* of "Atoms for Peace *vs.* The Higs," and a volume of all the documents he had submitted to the Circuit Court. He tried also to submit a copy of *Contact with Space,* but the book was not yet printed and the court refused to allow an extension of time that its submission would have required. (*Contact* was later submitted as part of the appeal to the Supreme Court.) The government submitted a single brief, and then Reich and Haydon each submitted a reply brief to counter the government's argument.

Of all these submissions perhaps the most interesting is Reich's first brief, which he submitted as "Chief Counsel for Discovery of Cosmic Life Energy." Its fifty-two pages were primarily devoted to a summary of Reich's scientific work of the previous few years, and to the new paths into the future this work opened. Its legal aspect emphasized Reich's contention that his discoveries were of such an unprecedented nature that they did not fall within the framework of old laws and required new laws for their proper social administration. There was—as with his other legal writings —much that was true in this brief, but also much that was misconceived and wrong and even inaccurate.

5. Peter Reich, *A Book of Dreams* (New York: Harper and Row, 1973), p. 53.

Again, Reich believed such a piece of writing would be accepted as valid legal argument. In doing so, he overlooked the "countertruth"—that is, all the social and psychological factors he had in earlier writings so eloquently elaborated upon as militating against the social acceptance of his ideas and formulations. Indeed, he devoted a part of the brief to a completely new—and, to this writer, unconvincing—interpretation of these "countertruth" factors. Reich seemed also to have assumed that the judge, reading this brief, would be immune to the "countertruth," that he was somehow part of a superior world in which it did not apply.

There is much evidence that the brief was hurriedly written—it is often rambling, repetitive, poorly edited, and at times contradictory. It consists of two main parts—"Appeal to Fairness" and "Appeal to Reason." The first part opens as follows:

The judgment against the Discoverer of the Life Energy of May 7th, 1956, was obtained under Legal conditions and social circumstances which are without precedent in the history of jurisprudence. These extraordinary conditions and circumstances blocked the defendants *technically* in clarifying fully the issue before the jury. The jury rendered its verdict uninformed. Had the full factual evidence involved in the case been presented, the verdict would have been *"not guilty."* However, this evidence was submerged in and blocked by *top secret* involvements of the basic research work of *Wilhelm Reich, M.D., the discoverer of primordial, massfree cosmic energy* (also Life Energy). [Italics in the original.]

Besides evidence that he himself withheld at the trial because it was "top secret"—evidence that Reich apparently decided, at least in part, to reveal now in his appendices—the verdict was invalid also because "the trial court did not permit testimony as to the motives, the 'why' in this case. . . ."

The "substantial matters of a top secret nature, without precedent in fact and law" that he omitted from the trial but which he now included, were: The Oranur Experiment, The Problems of Invaders from Outer Space, The Integration of Oranur and Space Problem. (The last point refers, no doubt, to his conclusion—as presented in *Contact with Space*—that UFOs were, on the one hand, powered by orgone energy and, on the other, the cause of the atmospheric conditions that led to desert formation.) The brief does not attempt to answer the question of what enabled Reich to reveal in early 1957 matters that were so secret that he could not even mention them in the May 1956 trial.

In making his point that "Neither Social Administration nor Courts . . . have or can have jurisdiction on things unknown and scientific opinions as yet unformed, uncertain and full of possible error," Reich gave the example of an automobile driver wanting to fly a jet plane—the jet engineer would, of course, refuse to give the automobile driver permission, but this could not be construed as contempt.

Then, in explaining his failure to appear in answer to the Complaint, Reich gave a list of reasons, some of which had little to do with the reason originally given.

Next, however, Reich made a point that, in the light of what has been presented in the earlier chapters, and in the light of Reich's experience, appears eminently valid:

There is . . . no *precedent in legal history* to the effect that a basic discovery in natural science should, at the same time . . . involve such fearful emotions in man, fear and rage toward being threatened in his deep, emotional constitution. The total problem of *human irrationality* ("Emotional Plague") in all its social, judicial and political unheard-of aspects could not possibly be dragged into a legal dispute on the validity of a new technical device.

But this too, valid as it may be in itself, raises the question of why Reich felt, in this brief, that he now could bring in the problem of human irrationality which he could not bring in at the time the Complaint was issued.

In the subsection entitled "Legal Situation Without Precedent" Reich, by analogy, implied that the FDA really knew that his work had been classified by the government as "top secret" but failed to reveal this to the court. But this outlandish accusation is then followed by another point that, in spite of its grandiose language, could well turn out to be true:

The injunction did not concern a routine case of fraudulent production to deceive the public. It was, on the contrary, the most crucial discovery ever made in natural science by an acknowledged, widely-known scientist and physician, arbitrarily misrepresented to the court as a quack and fraudulent crook.

So unprecedented was this situation, the brief then went on to argue, that no lawyer could be found who could adequately handle the case. "Every one among the half dozen lawyers of known ability and good reputation chosen to represent the case was helpless in comprehending what went on. Each of them admitted that a 'conspiracy' was afoot, but none acted in accordance with this conviction in open court."

Reich next argued that the case was also without precedent in terms of science—and there is a brief summary of what Reich regarded as the "DOR Emergency"—that is, the pollution of the atmosphere and the effect of this on desert formation.

Reich argued that against the background of the crucial work and discoveries he was engaged in—all of which proved that orgone energy existed—the injunction made no sense and therefore the criminal contempt verdict should be dropped. This argument, despite its legal ineffectiveness, might eventually turn out to be the most important point to be made about the whole litigation. Reich was consistent in trying to serve a higher law, hidden from the eyes of the pillars of society—a circumstance in which tragic heroes have often found themselves.

In the next section, "Morally Without Precedent," Reich argued that the trial was inadequate to the real issues in two ways: on the one hand, the defendant could not introduce important information because it would have been deleterious to national security; on the other hand, the court did not allow the defendant to introduce the matter of motives, which would have proven "an underground conspiracy on the part of the powerful food and drug industry." Always concerned not to appear to be criticizing the court or the legal system as a whole, Reich added: "The court had, as the counsel for the defense saw it (he may be wrong), to be careful not to cause a landslide in ugly revelations of the backstage affairs of American industry and government."

And Reich's conclusion to this "Appeal to Fairness," Part I of his brief, then was:

Free men are those who refuse to yield under sentence of death what they are ready to yield of their own free will. Let us acknowledge this expression of freedom as one of the basic characteristics of free people.

Part II—"Appeal to Reason"—begins with an introduction in which it is stated that "The momentous nature of the deceit perpetrated on honorable U.S. Courts of Justice by pathological individuals can only be explained in terms of the essence and the dimension of the Discovery of the Life Energy." And much of the remainder of this Part seeks to substantiate this contention—that is, to present "the essence and the dimensions" of his formulations concerning orgone energy.

First there is a discussion of the problem of UFOs, which, he maintained, only a knowledge of orgone energy functions was adequate to deal with. However "the characterological make-up of mankind turns out to be the one obstacle in the way of exploring and coming to grips with the technology of the space invader. Man, having armored his organism against his bodily sensations, especially those centered in his genital orgastic-function, fails to be free of fear in touching the Ea [Reich's code letters for UFO phenomena] subject." This is the new "countertruth" factor: man's fear of confronting UFO phenomena.

The U.S. Air Force was fully aware, the brief continued, of the presence of UFOs in earth skies as well as of Reich's discovery of a motor force in orgone energy because—and the logic here is a bit obscure—"without this new force there seemed to be no hope to cope with the invader . . . in an adequate technological manner." However, the discovery of cosmic orgone energy was so revolutionary an event that it was "more dangerous than the H-bomb," and as a result it would take many years of cautious progress before this discovery was fully assimilated. "All actions taken by the Discoverer were based on this version of the secret events." Here too the logic is unclear—the "secret events" ordinarily did not refer to the discovery of orgone energy but, among other things, to Reich's work with UFOs.

Then Reich outlined seven ways in which orgonomy would effect basic changes in the world. This was of particular interest since it constituted a summary of what he must have considered at that time the most important aspects of his work. One of these was the "biological revolution," that is, the development of a way of child rearing that would permit children to grow up unarmored and thus lead to a "new type of man." This was the only one of the seven areas to which Reich applied his method of biopsychiatric therapy. The next was the mastery of gravity—Reich had been working on the theoretical aspect of this problem for a year or more—which would lead to the third area: space travel. The fourth way in which orgonomy would bring about crucial changes in the world would be through the "Cosmic Energy Motor" which would replace conventional types of motors and would enable future space ships to carry their gravitational fields with them and thus usher in the "cosmic age." The fifth would be the introduction of "atmospheric medicine." Since diseases are fundamentally "the pathogenic effects of Life Energy gone stale," they can be treated by draining off this stale energy by means of the medical DOR-buster. The next area would be that of pre-atomic chemistry which through orene, one of the substances that developed from the oranur experiment, would make it possible to produce organic soil from rocks and thus grow all kinds of foods artificially. And, finally, the seventh way in which orgonomy would effect a basic change in the world would be that of desert fructification.

This section then concludes:

The Discoverer is well aware of the implications of the discovery for such industrial empires as the Rockefeller Empire or the massive chemical industry. They shrivel in the face of the Cosmic Energy Ocean. Not protection of old financial or political privileges but safeguarding the planet Earth and transforming its technological structure is the task of today. [How far ahead of his time Reich was in his ecological concern!] Let us hope that the great industrial powers of our planet have retained their pioneering spirit; that they have not sunk to the low level and the shabby method used against the discovery of the Cosmic Energy by a corrupt U.S. Administrative Agency.

In arguing "Why the Case Should be Entirely Dismissed," Reich began with the description of a pledge he made to himself when he began studying natural philosophy in the early 1920s: because scientists made so many mistakes in their old age he would stop publishing scientific information when he had reached the age of sixty. Less than six months away from his sixtieth birthday at the time of writing this brief, he was now, however, uncertain if he would be able to fulfill this pledge because his discovery of orgone energy "seems persistently to become the pivot on which the turn of the age hinges." Without, however, developing this problem further—there are several such abrupt discontinuities in the brief —Reich went on to discuss the "Invasion from Outer Space" and to raise the question of how mankind could hope to survive a crisis so unprecedented that it made the present mechanistic age obsolete. And, again, instead of exploring the new problem, Reich asserted that "the mechanistic Enemy of Man" cannot be convinced of the reality of life energy by any amount of proof and that the FDA's action in asserting that orgone energy didn't exist was, in effect, part of the effort of "frightened souls" to deny the onset of the Cosmic Age.

Abrupt discontinuities appear again in the section entitled "Terror Stricken Men of Science." Asserting that when it came to knowledge of the future there were no authorities, he could therefore not yield such authority to anyone without betraying the future. Despite his adhering to this principle, however, intruders sought to force their way into his laboratory, clinic and office in an effort to discredit him and his work. (Even here one can observe logical discontinuity: the implication is that his determination to adhere to his principle should of itself have deterred the intruders.) This kind of behavior, the brief continued, was mentioned because it "fits so well with the reports by Ruppelt, the head of 'Project Bluebook' . . . of the U.S. Air Force until 1952." Then indicating that he would list five ways in which Ruppelt's persecution (because of his writings on UFOs) and his own were similar, Reich seems to have forgotten this intention and instead listed the ways in which he and his work were obstructed and attacked by "The Enemy of Man" and the way the public, by its silence, supported such obstruction and attacks.

He then concluded:

Nothing will convince them [the terror-stricken men of science]. *They are frightened.* Orgonomy would have long since gone under had it not resolved to let the "authorities" come to the pioneers in cosmic research *to learn*, before they could judge. . . . Before Humanity can hope to cope with the space problem it will needs have to *reconstruct itself* and its society.

Reich then asserts in a section entitled "Revelation," "Delivery" that even though man has longed and prayed for revelation for ages now, when his biological structure is revealed to him, he runs amok. This revelation of biological structure came about through his book *Character Analysis,* for with this, repression was no longer an effective way of hiding anything. In effect this book, by its analysis of the emotional expression of the organism, exposed man.

The very depth of the person, its secrets, were threatened to be revealed. . . . The structural spy, who hid behind a veneer of docil-try . . . ; the student who appeared devoted to his teacher . . . but was really out to steal knowledge and to kill the giver; the legal counsel who became a U.S. Attorney and impounded scientific litera-ture without having read this literature, later cringing like a worm on the witness stand from bad conscience. The power to read expression from movement and behavior was bad enough. But now the menace to be revealed was driven to fearful proportions by Oranur.

The oranur experiment, Reich explains, left his co-workers un-able to hide anything in their depth, and as a result some of them fled, even though they carried what they wanted hidden with them. "There was a force acting in them that pressed these hidden things out into the open." Then he explains the effect of the oranur experi-ment in greater detail:

Oranur had charged the core of the bio-system in everyone to the utmost. The core energy now was pushing outward, expanding ir-resistibly. The characterological armor broke down. . . . Until then, the well-built armor block had been sufficient to prevent the breaking down of the dam that held the secret. Now the core energy flooded the armor, broke through the barriers, flooded the whole person and threatened to flood even the consciousness to the degree of insanity.

Perhaps Reich in these lines, was, without being fully aware of it, also describing a process he underwent himself. Ilse Ollendorff, in her biography, dates the beginning of what she considers Reich's "breakdown" to the early fifties—that is, the time of the oranur experiment.

After this section Reich reached his seven and a half page con-clusion. "If the U.S. Government," he began on a conciliatory note, ". . . intended for reason of national security to stop the publications of the Discovery of the Life Energy, it should have said so frankly." He would gladly have complied and much money would have been saved. It was not necessary to resort to "harass-ment and imprisonment." The case against him should be dropped because its continuation might be counterproductive in that it might make him into a matryr. In these considerations, Reich was apparently trying to reconcile his high regard for the American government and his conviction that it supported his work with the fact that that same government, through the FDA, had permitted the legal action against him to continue to the point of his being found guilty and sentenced to prison.

He has always been aware, the brief continued, of the social dangers inherent in his orgonomic work and the revolution in human existence it presaged. In fact, he himself, out of loyalty to the U.S. Government and the Air Force and CIA, with which he had cooperated for years in crucial work, refused to bring certain evidence into court. (One must assume that this reference to cooperative work was an exaggerated interpretation of the polite letters these agencies had sent him in response to his communications.) Then, calling for an inspection of all the pertinent evidence, the brief stated: *"The Injunction had to be violated* because the discoverer of the Cosmic Energy had during 1954–1955 . . . fought under the very eyes of the Air Force the First Battle of the Universe."* This was a reference to the "battle" described in a previous chapter. (See p. 174.)

The real contempt of court, the brief argued, was committed not by Reich but by "the complainant who had deceived the . . . judge; who had in a subversive manner done everything to keep the lie in and the truth out of court; who has from the very beginning falsified facts in his presentation to the court in the first complaint for injunction." Thus the dignity of the court is best secured by its not permitting the practice of deceit in legal matters. In this connection the following points were made:

If procedure is so designed that it *kills* truth and fact, then procedure, and not factual truth, must yield to revision.

If law is practiced in such a manner that quite obviously to everyone, the guilty one goes free and the innocent and decent one faces imprisonment, then the law practice must be changed. . . .

The long brief and its long conclusion finally ended on this impassioned note:

. . . The discoverer has dissolved all his organizational power in order to demonstrate that he does not want power; that he should not be feared. His power is his—may this be told candidly—unprecedented natural skill and training in functional thinking, practiced in endless efforts ever since his early childhood. It was this skill which empowered him to discover the basic cosmic force; it was the same skill that brought him trouble from the anxieties this accomplishment aroused.

. . .

The dignity of the court, never insulted by the discoverer or his assistants, never even doubted in any way, more: protected wherever possible, will only be enhanced in the eyes of the international public if the court of appeals will open the doors wide to . . . full, factual enlightenment of the discovery and its social consequences.

After Reich's brief, the others, which deal only with legal matters, seem somewhat anticlimactic. Haydon's brief for the Foundation argued primarily that the original injunction had been obtained by fraudulent means. Silvert's brief opened with the argument that the conspiracy against Reich was tied in with "one of the most virulent centers of American dictatorial growth and corresponding subversive espionage." From this it went on to argue that Silvert had not acted in concert with Reich in shipping the material—repeating the already cited simplistic position; that the prosecution had lied at the trial in trying to prove that Reich profited personally from the income from literature and accumulators; and that the literature of the Orgone Institute Press did not constitute labeling.

The government's opposing brief argued that even if the injunction had been obtained by fraud, which it hadn't, it would, according to the law, have to be obeyed all the while it was in force. Besides this, it contended that Silvert had acted in concert with Reich and that Reich and Silvert both had admitted in their briefs that they had not obeyed the injunction.

These contentions and countercontentions were then argued further in the reply briefs, and finally, on December 11, 1956, the Court of Appeals issued a four-page decision supporting the verdict of the District Court. Predictably, this four-page document completely ignored the contents of Reich's brief. In answering Silvert's contention that he had not acted in concert, the Appellate Court's decision stated that since he knew of the injunction and its terms, he had knowingly abetted in its violation. As regards a court's jurisdicton in matters of science, the decision stated that this matter "does not deserve much comment or discussion. Its refutation is obvious from its mere statement. . . . The United States Government has power to forbid and . . . to prevent the transportation in interstate commerce of devices of alleged therapeutic value if they are adulterated and misbranded." In the matter of fraud being involved in the way the injunction was obtained—which deserved "only slightly more extended consideration"—the decision stated that according to law even such an injunction had to be obeyed while it was in force and because of this the District Court had acted correctly at the trial in preventing the defendants from presenting evidence to substantiate their charge of fraud.

Reich's reaction to this negative decision was similar to his reaction at the end of the trial: he was shocked, upset, and yet rallied to new hope in the immediate plans made to appeal to the Supreme Court. Another stay of execution of the sentence was obtained pending the result of this appeal.

Much of the argumentation in the new briefs submitted by Reich, Silvert, and Haydon—who again wrote the brief for the Foundation—as well as the counterarguments in the government's brief, were restatements or further refinements of points already made in the previous appeal. Beyond this they included comments on the opinion of the Court of Appeals. The most significant of all these briefs is Haydon's, since he undertook in it to contest in conventional legal terms—as Reich's and Silvert's briefs for the most part did not—the decision of the Court of Appeals. Because of this, Haydon's brief comprised the furthest legal ramifications of the Reich case within the accepted American law structure. If this case is ever to be re-opened—some people interviewed by this author were considering this possibility—the point of departure for such an action would no doubt be this final, professional brief by Haydon.

Haydon's brief argued that the Supreme Court should allow a writ of certiorari—that is, a review of the case—because the Court of Appeals—in maintaining that a federal agency could obtain an "enforceable injunction" through fraud, and that the District Court had done right in preventing the defendants from exposing this fraudulence at the trial—had arrogated to itself the authority to decide a question of federal law which only the Supreme Court was empowered to pass on. Then after extensive substantiation of this contention Haydon's brief concluded:

Concern for the administration of justice requires that public officials charged with that administration refrain from perverting justice to their private and individual purposes. In this case such a perversion occurred and the result of the judgments below [i.e. the lower courts] is that those perversions have received judicial sanction by the sacrifice of reality to form. The dignity of the courts of the United States of America cannot be served when decrees, obtained by the fraud of public officials, are enforced by contempt proceedings. No citizen of the United States should be deprived of his liberty as the result of the connivance and fraud of public officials.

But before the Supreme Court decided whether or not it would review the Reich case—in fact, even several months before the Court of Appeals had announced its decision—the FDA moved to have two basic provisions of the injunction enforced: the destruction of accumulators and the destruction or withholding of the enjoined literature. Its unwillingness to await the results of the two appeals was, no doubt, an indication of the degree to which the FDA was certain what the results of these appeals would be.

14

---◆◆---

DESTRUCTIONS

The publications of the Orgone Institute Press were destroyed in five separate operations—four in 1956 and one in 1960. There was nothing Reich or Silvert could do to prevent the four 1956 acts of destruction. The stay of execution of sentence that had been granted pending the outcome of the appeals was, explicitly or implicitly, contingent on their compliance with the terms of the injunction. Had they persisted in opposing the execution of any of these terms, they would, no doubt, have been immediately imprisoned.

Today, this author was recently told by a high-ranking FDA official, the FDA would be most careful about destroying literature because of the "book-burning mystique"—that is, presumably, because such a mystique would make book destruction bad public relations. The FDA was aware of this mystique in the fifties but apparently felt less need to make concessions to it during the McCarthy period. Indeed, FDA Commissioner Larrick, in a speech to the American Bar Association at Dallas, Texas on August 28, 1956—that is, almost a week after the last of the destruction operations of that year—defended the FDA burning of Reich's books by contending that "if one may call this labeling a book and thereby escape from the provisions of the law, a glaring loophole exists." Defining a book as printed material contained between hardcovers, Larrick then maintained that there was a definite difference between a court order to discontinue false labeling and book burning as "the suppression of the spread of knowledge." As an example of this difference he cited the fact that a few years earlier when a certain brand of molasses was represented as a panacea for illness, both the molasses and hardcover books that made the claims for its effectiveness were destroyed. "We are all familiar," he concluded, "with the fact that many well meaning people seem to do their thinking in terms of slogans and catch words. . . ."

There are several errors and contradictions in Larrick's statement. The first is that he seems to have been unaware that no books of Reich, in the simplistic sense of printed matter between hardcovers, were ordered destroyed by the injunction; they were only ordered withheld. The second, following the first, is the implication in Larrick's statement that hardcover books by Reich were actually destroyed. This is an error only in a formalistic sense: FDA records showed that no books were destroyed and according to the terms of the injunction they should not have been. In actual fact, however, Reich's books *were* burned. Larrick was closer to the truth than the official FDA records were—but only because he was confused about the actual terms of the injunction and because he did not know what actually happened. The third is that the analogy made between Reich's books and the books on the curative power of molasses is inappropriate since most of Reich's books do not mention the device that was supposed to make them labeling—namely, the orgone accumulator. Even those that do mention the accumulator, with the exception of *The Cancer Biopathy,* do so most briefly and peripherally to other matters. From this it is possible to conclude that the destruction of the publications of the Orgone Institute Press—both the hard and soft cover—was an act of book burning precisely in the sense that Larrick rejected, that is, "the suppression of the spread of knowledge."

The first act of destruction took place on June 5, 1956, at Orgonon, when three accumulators and a set of panels sufficient to make another accumulator were chopped up. This operation began with Inspector Kenyon calling Mills to find out if Reich and Moise were at Orgonon. Mills phoned Orgonon, spoke with Reich and asked if there would be anyone there in the next few days. Reich said there would be and wanted to know why the inquiry was being made. Mills' reply was ambiguous: there would be "some visitors" coming. Reich asked if they would be communist FDA agents and went on to speak with anger about the whole course of the conspiracy.

When Kenyon, accompanied by inspector Niss and Deputy Marshal Doherty, drove to Orgonon on the fifth of June, there were no barriers up. They were met by Moise, who quite civilly told them that two lawyers from Lewiston, Maine, whom Reich had contacted, had arrived only a few minutes earlier and were in conference with Reich and Silvert. They were asked to wait until the conference was finished.

After a short while they were ushered into Reich's study and were introduced to the two attorneys, Platz and his associate, Scolnik. The group of them then went carefully over the whole injunction. The inspectors were told that all the accumulators out on rental had in the meantime been sold to the renters and that Silvert had ten accumulators and damaged panels for an additional twenty-five or thirty stored in a public warehouse in Manhattan. Reich informed them that there were three accumulators in the students' laboratory on the estate.

Then there followed some discussion as to who would actually carry out the destruction. Reich and Silvert refused, insisting that the FDA people do it. The inspectors insisted that the decree ordered that the defendants themselves do it under the supervision of FDA agents. Finally Reich and Silvert gave in on this point. Then there was further disagreement about the accumulators in New York—the FDA inspectors insisting that they should be recalled to Rangeley for destruction. But it was the FDA inspectors who conceded on this point, agreeing that the latter accumulators could be destroyed in New York under FDA supervision. No doubt from Reich's point of view all this discussion must have seemed like a negotiation of surrender terms between two warring countries. Though he made an effort to remain calm and reasonable, occasionally he broke out into bitter accusations, got up, paced about, went out of the room briefly and returned. "Their attitude," the FDA memo of this operation stated, "seemed to be that of martyrs. The Food and Drug Administration could take and destroy everything they had."

There were two other matters of contention. The agents asked that the accumulators that had been sold be recalled. Platz, however, maintained that this did not have to be done since Reich and Silvert had already been penalized by their sentence for these sales. When the agents asked about the ten books listed in Section 5 of the injunction—that is, the section where the literature ordered withheld was listed—Reich gave his assurance that these books would remain impounded in New York pending the result of the appeal that was at that time being prepared.

Then the action began. The three accumulators and the set of panels were taken from the students' laboratory and piled on the ground. An attempt to burn them proved unsuccessful, so Peter Reich—who was twelve years old then—joined Moise and the caretaker, Tom Ross, in chopping up the accumulators and panels with axes. There followed some discussion over some fifty copies of journals that Reich wanted to retain for his library. Attorney Platz said he would need time to look into the matter and would give the inspectors his answer within seven days.

In his book, *A Book of Dreams,* Peter Reich gives a moving, child's-eye view of this incident, in which he describes the tense discomfort of the marshal and of the two FDA inspectors, and Reich's restrained, impersonal bitterness. Reich asked them at the beginning, according to his son's account, "How is it to be done . . . ? Shall we use our bare hands?" [1] Then, after the panels had been sufficiently chopped up, he asked them if they wanted the wreckage burned; indeed, he almost insisted on it, saying, "We have gasoline! It would make a nice fire, no?" [2] And though they refused this offer, Reich went on, offering them books to burn and his scientific equipment, continuously staring at them so hard that they could not meet his eyes. One of the inspectors, as the three men got into their car, said he was sorry and Reich's reply was, "Yes, you're sorry. Of course. Aren't we all. Good-bye, gentlemen. Someday you will understand." [3]

1. Peter Reich, *A Book of Dreams* (New York: Harper and Row, 1973), p. 53.
2. *Ibid.,* p. 57.
3. *Ibid.,* p. 58.

The following day the inspectors learned from Mills that the clerk of the court had called Mills and relayed the hope of Judge Sweeney that FDA agents would "keep away from Reich and his group." Though no explanation for this is given in the memo, one can infer that Judge Sweeney was, in this, attempting to protect Reich from exposure to people who he knew Reich considered his enemies. At this meeting between Mills and the inspectors it was decided that, despite Platz's contention that Reich and Silvert had already been penalized for it, pressure would be brought to bear for the recall of all the accumulators that had been sold since the issuance of the injunction.

Later that same day, Inspectors Kenyon and Niss met with Platz about this matter. He now objected to the idea of recall on a different basis, saying that "he could visualize the defendants sending a letter to a customer only to be told that the customer had paid his money for the device, it was his, and the defendants could go climb a tree." To which the inspectors replied: "Let the defendants send out the recall notices and we'll see what will happen. At least the defendants could thus evidence good faith." This seemed to impress Platz. He agreed to discuss this matter as well as the destruction of the fifty journals with Reich, after which he would call Kenyon.

There were, it appears from a later FDA record, eighty-two orgone accumulators that had been sold from the time of the injunction. The total income from these sales came to $8,264.75. Though the records in the file do not state anything further in this matter—except for a notation that by July 18 Silvert had still refused to attempt such a recall—it is quite clear that few if any of the sold accumulators were ever recovered.

The next destruction—this time of books—took place at Orgonon just three weeks later, on June 26. The record is not altogether clear as to where the literature that was burned came from. The June 7 memo had mentioned the 50 copies of various journals in the students' laboratory that Reich wanted to keep for his library; the FDA "Record of Partial Compliance with Injunction 261" lists a total of 251 pieces of literature that were burned on June 26 at Orgonon, and the memo by Inspector Niss, in which the June 26 burning is described, states that "We went into the students' laboratory and Dr. Reich said, 'There they are, burn them.'" The apparent discrepancy between the earlier 50 and the later 251 pieces of literature in the laboratory could not be resolved by this author on the basis of the material available to him.

As in the earlier instances of destruction, so now, too, the FDA representative insisted that he would not perform the act of destruction but would only supervise it. Attorney Scolnik, who was present, in an effort to mediate the disagreement, volunteered to carry the literature out and have it burned. But while the matter was still being discussed, a man from the S.A. Collins company appeared. It seems that Reich had earlier arranged with the company to send out a man to do the job. No doubt his not informing Niss of this arrangement and the subsequent unnecessary disagreement reflected Reich's own conflicting feelings in that situation.

During the time of the operation, Scolnik was worried about remaining in the laboratory because Reich had warned him of the heavy DOR contamination in it. To minimize its possible effect on him, Scolnik left the laboratory from time to time. Reich, in a touching display of concern for Niss, suggested that he too leave for a while since he did not look well. Niss, however did not follow this suggestion. "I told him that I felt fine and preferred to finish the counting," his report stated.

"During the burning," Niss's report stated further, "Dr. Reich found himself just about to throw some of the literature on the fire. He stopped short and remarked, 'I promised myself that I would have nothing to do with the burning of this literature.' " Reich told Niss that his books had been burned in Germany but he had never expected it to happen again. But apparently this was said without personal bitterness toward Niss. "The conversation was pleasant during my visit," his report continued. One can assume that had Inspector Kenyon been along the visit would have been less pleasant. There was something about Kenyon that made Reich see him as an integral part of the "conspiracy."

The breakdown of the 251 pieces of literature was:

Orgone Energy Bulletin—166 copies
The Orgone Energy Accumulator—2 copies
International Journal of Sex Economy and Orgone Research— 47 copies
Emotional Plagues versus Orgone Biophysics—19 copies
Annals of the Orgone Institute—11 copies

> *The Oranur Experiment*—2 copies
> *Ether, God and Devil*—4 copies

Of these publications, the last one—*Ether, God and Devil*—should, technically not have been burned since it is listed in Section 5 of the injunction along with the other hardcover books that were to be withdrawn rather than destroyed. Reich, however, wanted these four copies burned; they had become contaminated with DOR.

Niss's memo ends:

Upon completion of the discussion Dr. Reich shook hands with me and then went up to the observatory. He soon returned and left the premises in his car waving as he went by. Mr. Scolnik remained behind in order to drive the employee of S. A. Collins Co. back to his place of business as the literature was still burning in the incinerator. I left the premises when I was satisfied that all the material had been destroyed.

Perhaps the emotional impact of the destruction had worn off somewhat after the first operation.

On July 9 the ACLU, in a letter to Commissioner Larrick, protested these destructions. Stating that it was primarily concerned with safe-guarding civil liberties and not with the validity or invalidity of Reich's formulations, the letter took issue with the FDA's considering as labeling "comprehensive books of serious scientific intent." Had the FDA legal action against Reich been challenged, the letter continued, there was no doubt that such a broad injunction would not have been issued. As it was, the injunction was now making it possible to destroy two particular books —*The Sexual Revolution* and *The Mass Psychology of Fascism*—that made no reference to orgone energy. And, it concluded:

It is a serious challenge to the freedom of scientific inquiry and to the freedom of the press, principles of free thought on which our democratic government is based, for any agency of government to take advantage of such a dragnet injunction to thwart the dissemination of knowledge—however eccentric or unpopular that knowledge may be. Certainly the Food, Drug, and Cosmetics Act contemplates no such result. . . . Many students and professors have come or written to us concerning the Food and Drug Administration's action, which they see as a governmental attempt to shut off the circulation of scientific knowledge. The American Civil Liberties Union agrees with their contention and urges that the Food and Drug Administration act immediately to put an end to the destruction of Dr. Reich's books by seeking on its own initiative to modify the injunction which it has obtained.

The ACLU was also not accurately informed about the injunction: the injunction did not call for the destruction of *The Sexual Revolution* and *The Mass Psychology of Fascism* nor any of Reich's other hardcover books. Moreover, as of the date of the above letter no copies of *The Sexual Revolution* and *The Mass Psychology of Fascism* had been destroyed.

FDA Commissioner Larrick replied to the ACLU on July 16. Enclosing a copy of the injunction, Larrick began by taking refuge in a technicality: The FDA itself did not destroy anything, it only supervised "compliance with the terms of the injunction." In answer to the objection to the burning of the two books mentioned in the ACLU letter, instead of clarifying the issue and stating that these books had not been destroyed and were not even slated for destruction—apparently he still had not bothered to read the injunction—Larrick justified the destruction on the ground that these books were part of a "distributional scheme of offering the Orgone Energy Accumulators as therapeutic devices." Then after summarizing the history of the Reich case, Larrick concluded:

While we share your concern about any encroachment violating our cherished freedom of thought and press, this freedom is not a license to distribute false and misleading labeling in promoting a worthless device. Our courts have enunciated this doctrine time and again.

In this he was, of course, begging the question: the whole point of the ACLU letter was that most of Reich's writings did not constitute labeling.

On August 15 the ACLU responded to Larrick's letter in part as follows:

We have reviewed the injunction carefully and believe that it does not adequately explain or justify the assumption of responsibility by a federal agency to enforce an order for destruction of books which have not been alleged or adjudged to be obscene.

No further communication between the FDA and ACLU took place. A December press release by the ACLU protesting the burning of Reich's publications was not picked up by any major newspaper in the United States. The same kind of silence prevailed in England. There a letter of protest signed by Neill, Sir Herbert Read, and others was not printed in any of the important newspapers.

The reason there was no further exchange between the ACLU and the FDA becomes clear from a February 1, 1957, letter the former wrote to Reich. Urging Reich to give serious consideration to the ACLU's offer of help in the case, it stated:

I [the writer is Rowland Watts, staff counsel of the ACLU] realize some of the factors that influenced your decision not to discuss this matter with us in the past. I think, however, you should keep in mind that in the same way that you deem you have a responsibility as a scientist to refuse to condone the attempted judicial evaluation of your theories, you, and we, have a like responsibility to uphold the right of free speech and free press, regardless of the scientific merits of what is being said or printed.

It then concluded by asking Reich for permission to see the file of the case in Haydon's office and requesting him to send a copy of his petition to the Supreme Court.

The copy of this letter which was sent to Haydon contained the following notation by hand at one side: "2/7/57 Reich called Att[orney]—Told Att to have nothing to do with ACLU as far as R[eich] is concerned." The reason for this refusal, of course, was that the ACLU was, for Reich, tainted with leftist-liberal doctrine.

This rejection of the ACLU's offer of help constitutes one of the clearest examples in the whole ten-year process of how Reich's view of a widespread communist conspiracy against him and the concomitant, almost McCarthy-like, suspicion of any kind of liberalism, weakened his position in the litigation. Probably the ACLU could not have had the injunction changed. Yet it was the only non-Reichian organization to express an interest in Reich's side of the case and its support may have improved Reich's position in his final, pre-arrest court appearance by the simple fact of its involvement and the possible publicity that such involvement was capable of arousing.

The third act of destruction took place on July 23, 1956. The locale of this destruction was discussed by Silvert and the FDA—the FDA inspectors insisting that they were authorized by the injunction to supervise destruction only at Rangeley, Maine, and Silvert seeking to avoid the expense of shipping material back from New York to Rangeley. If he wanted to have the destruction take place in New York, he was told, he would have to get permission for this from the District Court. Apparently on his own discretion then, Silvert decided to ship the accumulators in New York to Rangeley for destruction.

The accumulator material was shipped on July 18, and reached Rangeley on July 23. This shipment consisted of accumulator panels—enough for some fifty accumulators—and of two crated accumulators, five shooter boxes and seven accumulator seat boxes, which were all the accumulators Silvert had stored. It omitted only two private accumulators that he kept at his own premises, and which he was in the following months to refuse, in spite of continued requests by the FDA, to surrender.

Dismantling so many accumulator panels presented a problem, as this would take several days. It was finally agreed that Mr. Collins of S.A. Collins, would "on his honor" have the panels dismantled, and that the FDA inspectors would then return and check that this had been properly done. "Dr. Silvert," the memo dated July 30, 1956, states, "was pleasant throughout the interview. He did mention at one point that he would rather be found guilty of contempt of court than of fraud."

The next act of destruction—and by far the largest of them all—took place in New York City on August 23. Six tons of orgone literature, valued at something like $15,000, were burned at this time.

Where the literature would be burned was again a problem, the FDA still insisting that it was necessary to have it shipped back to Rangeley, where alone it had authority to supervise destruction. Silvert, apparently deciding to force the issue, made plans to have the literature burned in New York City and on August 21, he called the New York district office of the FDA to inform Inspector Ledder that he had arranged for a cartage company to come and pick up the literature at eight o'clock on the morning of the twenty-third. When Ledder asked whether the literature listed in Section 5 would be included in the destruction, Silvert insisted that this Section had been complied with since the material ordered there for withdrawal from circulation had in fact been withheld from circulation since the trial. Silvert did not ask that any FDA representative should be present to supervise but was only advising the FDA of his intention.

Ledder promptly forwarded a copy of his memo of this telephone conversation to Maguire in Washington. Maguire had the FDA advise Silvert that the hardcover books originally ordered withdrawn had subsequently been shipped from Rangeley and therefore now came within the terms of Sections 1 and 3 of the injunction—that is, the Sections ordering the destruction of labeling literature. His reasoning was that the fact of their shipment had somehow changed the status of these books. In making this decision, apparently at his own discretion, Maguire illegally arrogated to himself the function of interpretation that properly belonged only to the court that had issued the injunction.

This interpretation was also passed on to Ledder along with the order that he witness whatever Silvert did with the books and other literature but that he make it clear to Silvert that he was there simply "as an observer and that our position is that they should have been returned to Maine as required by the decree." Thus the FDA was attempting to have it both ways: On the one hand, to be present in an unofficial capacity simply as observers rather than as official supervisors; and on the other hand, in this unofficial capacity to impose a new interpretation of the terms of the injunction that would compel Silvert to burn the hardcover books. One can speculate that the reason the FDA followed this arrangement was that it would later have a legal out if its interpretation were contested.

Dr. Victor Sobey, a medical orgonomist who witnessed this destruction, recorded it in a letter on September 24, 1956, partly as follows:

I arrived at the stockroom at 7:30 a.m. on August 23. Present were Dr. Silvert, Martin Bell, Miss Shepard [sic], myself and two FDA agents, a Mr. Ledder and a Mr. Conway. All the expenses and labor had to be provided by the Press. A huge truck with three in help were hired. I felt like people who, when they are to be executed, are made to dig their own graves first and are then shot and thrown in. We carried box after box of the literature. . . .[4]

When Inspector Conway told Silvert that the literature listed in Section 5 was now to be included in Sections 1 and 3, Silvert asked for clarification—was Conway saying the books too had to be burned? Conway replied by shrugging his shoulders and saying that "This was their opinion." Dr. Sobey's letter then continues:

So again they were laying a trap. If the Press decided to destroy the books . . . then the FDA could say they are blameless, because the Press agreed. . . . If the Press didn't destroy the books, the FDA could serve the Press with a complaint for not complying with the injunction, and then everybody is in court again.[5]

Ledder described the actual burning briefly in his memo:

The truckload of the literature . . . was transported to the incinerator of the New York City Sanitation Department, Gansevoort Street Destructor Plant. We accompanied the truck to the incinerator and witnessed the destruction of the literature. The truck dumped the material in the dumping area and the overhead crane picked it up and dumped it into the fire.

Ledder's tabulation of the burned items showed no record of any of the books listed in Section 5. It showed only those items listed in other Sections for destruction:

Orgone Energy Bulletin	12,189
International Journal of Sex Economy and Orgone Research, Vols. I–IV	6,261
Emotional Plague Versus Orgone Biophysics	2,900
Annals of the Orgone Institute, Nos. 1 & 2	2,976
The Oranur Experiment	872

This writer asked Dr. Sobey, Miss Sheppard, and Mr. Bell whether any of the hardcover books listed in Section 5 of the injunction had been destroyed in the August 23 burning. He was emphatically told that they had been. Informed that according to the FDA record of this operation no such books had been de-

4. Quoted in *The Jailing of a Great Scientist in the U.S.A.,* 1956, a pamphlet by Raymond R. Rees and Lois Wyvell.
  5. *Ibid.*

stroyed, Dr. Sobey replied: "That's ridiculous." He recalled that he himself had tried to salvage a hardcover book out of one of the cartons but had been told by an FDA inspector that this was not allowed. Mr. Bell recalled clearly that he himself had loaded boxes filled with hardcover books onto the truck. Miss Sheppard, when told that the FDA record showed that no hardcover books were destroyed, said: "That's a coverup."

If anyone were in a position to know what literature had been loaded on the truck it was Miss Sheppard. The Ledder memo, in this connection, stated: "Miss Sheppard prepared a tally sheet in duplicate on which she entered the tally as the cartons were removed and loaded onto the dump truck. The original of this tally is attached hereto."

However, the talley sheet was, in fact, not attached to the report—nor was it found anywhere else in the entire FDA file on the Reich case. It is therefore entirely possible that a coverup was involved; that, in other words, because Maguire had no legal authority to revise the terms of the injunction as he did, there had been a doctoring up of the record against the possibility of future legal complication.

It was in this way that the FDA destroyed not only the journals issued by the Orgone Institute Press but Reich's ten hardcover books as well—*Character Analysis; The Mass Psychology of Fascism; The Sexual Revolution; The Murder of Christ; The Function of the Orgasm; Listen, Little Man; The Cancer Biopathy; People in Trouble; Ether, God and Devil;* and *Cosmic Superimposition.*

Dr. Sobey's letter on this burning ends with these words: ". . . I . . . suggest that you do not lose the true issue here; the burning of these books is not the whole issue but is only one aspect of the murder of the truth." [6]

The burning that took place in 1960 occurred at the initiative of Miss Mary Boyd Higgins, the trustee of the Reich estate. She had had this material in storage for some time and wanted to dispose of it. The burning itself, under FDA supervision, occurred on March 17 of that year. The FDA record of this event does not include an actual tally of the number of items.

6. *Ibid.*

15

---◆---

IMPRISONMENT

During most of the appeal period Reich lived in Washington in the same hotel as before and under the same pseudonym. Some time in January 1957 he and Miss Karrer drew up a marriage contract that, besides dealing with practical matters of property and settlement in the event of the death of either partner, contained also the kinds of provisions that have since come to be included in the concept of open marriage. Miss Karrer would retain sole ownership of any assets she had, which she would be free to dispose of as she wanted; neither of the partners to marriage were assuming any kind of financial obligations toward the relatives of the other; Reich would support Miss Karrer and any children born to them during their marriage. Perhaps the most striking part of this agreement is that dealing with the possibility of an eventual divorce: since both parties were aware of human growth and development, and divorce may, as a result, become eventually mutually desirable, it would not be carried out in anger and they would go their separate ways as good friends. All of these terms were based on Miss Karrer's awareness of Reich's devotion to scientific work and on her desire that the marriage arrangement would not interfere with it. The level-headed sanity of the terms of this contract, as well as the originality of the idea of such a contract, assumes particular significance in the context of official psychiatric reports on Reich's mental condition that were issued some two months later, and which are discussed below.

Besides these marriage plans, Reich continued to be active in his work—mostly with weather and atmospheric conditions, the UFO problem and the theoretical problem of countergravity.

It was a month or so after the marriage contract was drawn up that, on February 25, the Supreme Court decided against taking up the Reich case. Reich and Silvert immediately filed motions for reduction and suspension of sentences. Judge Sweeney ordered a hearing on these motions for March 11.

In the meantime Reich, Silvert, Moise and his wife, Eva, had all been exploring other possibilities of ameliorating the critical legal situation. Calls were made to the office of the FBI both at Washington headquarters and at various field offices. On February 2, Reich himself appeared at an FBI field office and on February 14 he went to J. Edgar Hoover's office insisting on a personal interview. The interview, of course, was not granted. Two days later Reich mailed directly to Hoover all the documents connected with the case. Two days after that Silvert attempted to see Hoover. On February 27, Eva went to FBI headquarters. The purpose of all these visits was to try to convince the FBI that there was espionage involved in the case and that Maguire and Mills had perjured themselves at the trial. Needless to say, nothing came from these attempts and meetings, except that they were all promptly reported to Maguire.

The day before the March 11 hearing Reich and his party came to Portland and engaged a ten-room suite at the Lafayette Hotel. William Steig and Moise, carrying documents with them, then went to the local police headquarters and, according to an FDA memo written by Maguire, asked if there were a cell available for a citizen's arrest that they planned to make. Though Mills and Maguire were not specifically named, there can be no doubt that it was they about whom the inquiry was made. The desk sergeant referred them to the county attorney, who tried to dissuade them from their stated intention, warning them of possible unpleasant consequences. Though they did not seem to be dissuaded by the county attorney, nothing further developed in this matter. One can see this abortive effort as a measure of the feeling of desperation that must have prevailed among those close to Reich as the critical hearing neared.

One wonders, however, why Steig and Moise felt it necessary to first check on the availability of a cell. Perhaps the whole move was planned not so much with the intent of carrying out the arrest as with the purpose of convincing the police that there was illegality involved in the case—with what desperate shred of hope in mind one cannot begin to guess.

Mills, however, when informed of this inquiry by the FBI—who kept a close watch on the Reich party and followed their every move outside the hotel—was not taking any changes. Contacting Maguire in Washington, Mills told him to come directly to his (Mills') home and spend the night before the hearing there rather than in a Portland hotel. Maguire reached Mills' home that night, finding all the doors locked and bolted. Admitted in, he learned that Mill's wife and oldest son had been warned not to answer door knocks or telephone calls.

This incident together with the past incidents of "gun play," led the government to ask for special security arrangements at the hearing. A federal marshal and his three deputies, a deputy and guard from Bangor, Maine, two FBI agents, a number of employees in the Federal Building and men from the Immigration Division were consequently interspersed among the people in the spectator seats. Besides this precaution, Maguire, after the hearing, was escorted by two FBI agents to the Maine Turnpike for his trip back to Washington. Needless to say, all these precautions were grossly overreactive: Reich and his party were not planning any kind of violence.

At the hearing each side was given fifteen minutes to present its argument. Maguire, again taking refuge in a technicality, objected to Silvert's representing the motion made on behalf of the Foundation since Moise was the Foundation's authorized representative. Judge Sweeney, however, overruled Maguire's objection. Silvert then began to speak, but his voice was hoarse so he had to stop. Reich then spoke, confining his remarks primarily to the matter of his own possible imprisonment. The *Portland Evening Express* of March 11 reported his words as follows:

He pleaded against being imprisoned, saying that if the sentence were carried out, it inevitably would deprive the U.S. and the world at large of his equations on space and negative gravity.

These equations, he said more specifically in his written motion, "are carried only in my head, known to no one on this planet. This knowledge will go down with me, maybe for millenia, should mankind survive the present planetary DOR Emergency.

"It would mean certain death in prison of a scientific pioneer at the hands of psychopathic persons who acted in the service of treason against mankind in a severe planetary emergency.

"It would amount to gross neglect of duty of the court with regard to all legal facts on official record in this case."

Maintaining further that his arrest would be a violation of the constitution that would end the role of the United States as a "beacon of . . . planetary social development as it has been heretofore" and that would "lead to the downfall of the U.S.A. as a self-governing society at the hands of a few conniving master minds," Reich asserted that he and Silvert were devoted to the promotion of new knowledge, not a cancer cure. "We are not crooks, not criminals," he concluded, "but courageous people." One can assume that the dire national consequences Reich saw resulting from his arrest were, on the one hand, in line with his view of the importance of orgone research in the cold war and, on the other, its crucial role in combating the planetary DOR and desert emergency.

Maguire then rose to speak but Judge Sweeney restrained him; it would not be necessary. The motion to strike sentence was denied, he announced; the motion for reduction of sentence would not be passed on at this time. He ordered that Reich and Silvert undergo psychiatric examinations within sixty days, after which the motion would be decided.

After arrangements were made to pay the $10,000 fine imposed on the Wilhelm Reich Foundation, Reich and Silvert were handcuffed and led out by deputies. As Reich passed Mills he said to his former attorney: "You won't live through this, Mills." Moise—according to Maguire's report of this hearing—told a reporter, "or some other habitue of the Federal Building," that he, Moise, was going to flood the country with rain. There is, however, no record of any rainmaking operation immediately following Reich's and Silvert's arrest. The threat to do so, like the previous threat of a citizen's arrest, must have come from the state of extremity that prevailed among Reich's supporters.

Though Reich at times foresaw the possibility of his being imprisoned, he could not get himself to fully believe in it. No doubt, until the handcuffs were actually placed on him, he expected that somehow he would escape the sentence—if not by Sweeney's ruling on the motions then by some kind of intervention by high-placed federal officials, perhaps the President himself. Though this expectation was not realized, he continued to believe that the federal government was really, secretly sympathetic to him and his work. Throughout his prison stay he continued to believe that every air force plane flying overhead was intended as a sign that he had not been forgotten or abandoned.

After a night in the local jail Reich and Silvert were driven the next day to the federal prison in Danbury, Connecticut, by two deputy marshals. Miss Karrer was at the local jail when the party left and wanted to be at Danbury when they arrived there. Deputy Marshal William Doherty—who had brought the Complaint, who had served the injunction, who had accompanied FDA agents on abortive inspection visits to Orgonon, who had brought Reich handcuffed to the trial, who had been present at the first act of destruction, and who had over these years developed a relationship of mutal respect and liking for Reich—arranged for Miss Karrer to follow his car to Danbury. In the car, with Doherty driving, Reich and Silvert sat handcuffed in the back, discussing weather conditions and observing the state of the vegetation that they passed.

Reich was kept at Danbury for ten days. During this time he underwent a psychiatric examination, and it was on the basis of the psychiatrist's subsequent recommendations that on March 22 he was moved to the federal prison in Lewisberg, Pennsylvania, where there were more extensive psychiatric treatment facilities. Silvert remained in Danbury.

Judge Sweeney's deferment of the ruling on the motion to reduce sentence pending the result of the psychiatric examination must be seen in the context of the exchange that had taken place between him and Ilse Ollendorff during a recess in the trial. Judge Sweeney had then, it will be recalled, suggested a plea of insanity as the only means by which Reich could escape the consequences of his violation of the injunction. His ordering a psychiatric examination at the final hearing was, no doubt, a further effort in this direction. Judge Sweeney was much disturbed by the case and by the sentence he felt that the legal circumstances made it necessary for him to impose. Dr. John Murray, a Boston psychiatrist and friend of Sweeney (and who, coincidentally, had been a student of Reich's in Vienna), found the judge, during the rounds of golf he played with him, much preoccupied by the Reich case and upset by the fact that he had had to send Reich to prison. In ordering the psychiatric examination Sweeney must, therefore, have been fairly certain, or at least hopeful, that the results woud give him an excuse for absolving Reich of legal responsibility.

Sweeney's order took Mills and Maguire by surprise. The degree to which they were surprised and, in fact, upset—especially Mills —is evidenced in exchanges between them on the matter.

On March 18, Mills wrote to the Assistant Attorney General in the Criminal Division of the Department of Justice that in regard to the ordered psychiatric examination he had "had no reason to doubt the mental competency of the defendants to understand the proceedings against them or assist in their own defense and at the trial [I] had no indication that the Court was disposed to cause the accused to be examined as to mental condition. . . ."

One must doubt Mills' honesty in both parts of this statement. In Maguire's memo of a telephone conversation he had had with Mills on June 14, 1955, it will be recalled, the following appears:

Mr. Mills said that the deputy marshal who had been up to Rangeley with our inspectors came back with the story that Reich was a madman. Mr. Mills indicated that the court would not be too happy about having a madman in his court and we might have some difficulty in fostering contempt of court proceedings against Reich. Mr. Mills thought that some strong language in a forwarding letter from the Department of Justice would be helpful.

The reason for Mills' concern with Sweeney's order is that—according to a March 18, 1957, memo of a conversation with Maguire—"he seemed to feel that it would be a reflection on him if these prisoners were found of sufficient unsound mind to harve stood for trial." Though the syntax of this sentence is somewhat off, it is clear that Mills felt he would be put in a bad light if it was found that he had prosecuted men who were mentally incompetent.

Maguire sought to reassure Mills by saying that he himself had never had any cause to think Reich and Silvert not competent to stand trial. The fact that they acted so erratically in engaging and then dismissing various attorneys was merely a matter of "tactics . . . artfully and cunningly conceived . . . to garner something."

In this Maguire too was being somewhat less than honest. In the matter of Reich's mental condition it seems to have been generally accepted in the FDA that there was something wanting. In a 1955 hearing before the subcomittee of the Commitee on Appropriations of the House of Representatives, Commissioner Larrick testified in relation to the "orgone case" that "There was a very noted psychiatrist who . . . had recognition throughout the world as a leading psychiatrist, but apparently he became mentally disturbed." Moreover, measures that continually left Reich and Silvert more legally vulnerable—as Maguire the seasoned lawyer must surely have realized—could hardly be called "tactics" for the purpose of garnering something.

Maguire and three members of the Department of Justice— Kernan, Birely and Gottschall—met on March 27 to discuss the matter of the mental competence of Reich and Silvert to have stood trial. The first psychiatric examination had already been held, but reports of these examinations had not yet reached these people. At this conference, one of the men from the Justice Department said that "it would be unusual for a psychiatrist . . . to make a finding that a defendant was incompetent who had stood for trial a year previously." Maguire told the others that his personal opinion, after having been legally involved with Reich for some years, was that Reich was perfectly sane and that he would welcome such a finding by the psychiatrists in order to avoid a relitigation of the case. "The writer feels sure," Maguire significantly concluded his memo, "that those persons at the conference well understood our feelings and motives."

Reich and Silvert were examined at Danbury on March 22 by Dr. Richard C. Hubbard, a psychiatrist who was not a member of the prison staff but worked only in a consulting capacity. The examination consisted of an interview lasting about an hour. A young psychiatrist at the time, Hubbard had heard of Reich, was particularly well acquainted with Reich's *Character Analysis* and so it was for him not a routine examination. They spoke for some time—with Reich dressed in prison clothes—about Reich's work, his scientific formulations and the "conspiracy." At one point, in the midst of conversation, hearing the sound of an airplane, Reich rose and went to the window to spot it. Then he turned to Hubbard and informed him that the plane was flying overhead because of his presence in the prison, as a sign that he was being protected. Hubbard did not know what to make of this. He had had prisoners in examinations deliberately say outlandish things to be thought unbalanced so as to invalidate a sentence. He could hardly believe, however, that someone like Reich would try such a trick. At the same time, with his background Reich must surely have realized, Hubbard thought, that what he had just said could only be interpreted as a psychopathic symptom of some kind. It was only through further discussion that Hubbard was able to conclude that Reich really believed what he had said about the air force plane.

Toward the end of the interview Reich asked him what his diagnosis was going to be. Hubbard was most deferential and apologetic in explaining that given his background and training he could only conclude that there was a definite disturbance. Reich's response to this was a thoughtful nod, as if in agreement—not with the conclusion itself, but with the preliminary to it: that Hubbard with his background could not evaluate Reich's condition in any other way. Reich must, no doubt, have appreciated Hubbard's honesty in this matter.

Dr. Hubbard's brief report on Reich was as follows:

Diagnosis:
Paranoia manifested by delusions of grandiosity and persecution and ideas of reference.

The patient feels that he has made outstanding discoveries. Gradually over a period of many years he has explained the failure of his ideas in becoming universally accepted by the elaboration of psychotic thinking, "The Rockerfellows [sic] are against me." (Delusion of grandiosity.) "The airplanes flying over prison are sent by air force to encourage me." (Ideas of reference and grandiosity.)

The patient is relatively intact in the greater part of his personality though there is enough frank psychotic thinking to raise the question as to whether the diagnostic label might more appropriately be Schizophrenia Paranoid type. In general his emotional responses and behavior are consistent with his ideas. No hallucinations were elicited.

Discussion:
In my opinion the patient is mentally ill both from a legal and psychiatric viewpoint, hence should not stand convicted of a criminal charge.

Treatment:
Observation in a mental hospital.

Interestingly enough, in this report there is implicit "psychologizing"—that is, the outstanding discoveries Reich felt he had made are seen as part of his aberrant mental condition.

In the case of Silvert, Hubbard's report was:

Diagnosis:
The condition of the patient is probably best described as "Folie à deux." That is, by contact with Dr. Reich he has absorbed Dr. Reich's ideas including the delusional ones. During the interview he expressed some doubt concerning the truth of Dr. Reich's ideas (persecution and ideas of reference) but ended up with the statement that he believed them. His personality is well preserved. Affect and behavior were normal and consistent with the ideas expressed.

Discussion:
It is doubtful if the patient could be considered legally insane. Though theoretically his conception of the criminal charge against him would be the same as Dr. Reich's, namely a part of a plot against them.

Treatment:
Separation from the primary psychosis is probably sufficient. He could follow a normal routine in prison.

On Dr. Hubbard's suggestion, then, Reich was removed to the federal penitentiary in Lewisburg, Pennsylvania. There Reich was again examined. The report, dated March 28 and signed by Dominick J. Lacovara, Senior Surgeon and Chief of Psychiatric Service at the prison, stated in part:

During the interview, Reich's emotional responses and general demeanor were consistent with his expressed ideation. On occasions he elaborated upon certain theories which are not accepted generally by scientific circles but are adhered to by certain groups which appear to be in the minority. Reich circumvented interrogation when pursued, often expounding nebulous concepts. He considered himself endowed with a superior or, at least, unique ability to isolate orgone energy from the atmosphere by means of a special "accumulator" he devised.

In his discussions he unraveled a rather intricate and somewhat logical system of persecutory trends, particularly regarding the Rockefeller Foundation "which made me a tool of its socio-economic interpersonal relations."

The following represents the consensus of the Board of Examiners: In our opinions

    1. During the interrogation, Reich gave no concrete evidence of being mentally incompetent. He is capable of adhering to the right and refraining from the wrong.

    2. Although he expressed some bizzare ideation, his personality appears to be essentially intact.

    3. In our opinion, it is felt that Reich could easily have a frank break with reality, and become psychotic, particularly if the stresses and environmental pressures become overwhelming.

In other words, the report from Lewisburg, though also psychologizing the matter of Reich's scientific work, came to a conclusion opposite to Hubbard's: Reich, though a borderline case, was legally sane and therefore by implication, had been competent to stand trial.

All the reports—including another one on Silvert, the contents of which is substantially the same as that of the report on Silvert that was quoted earlier—were sent to the Bureau of Prisons of the Department of Justice. Shortly thereafter, Warren Olney III, the Assistant Attorney General of the Criminal Division, wrote a letter of evaluation on the matter. The FDA file contains only the second page of this letter so it is not possible to say definitely to whom it was sent or when. It is, however, more than likely that it was sent to Maguire since he was the one who had been in touch with the people in the Criminal Division; and the date must have been sometime between April 18, the date of Silvert's second examination, and April 25, the day when Judge Sweeney passed on the motion for reduction of sentence. The pertinent part of page two of this letter states that "the Danbury report, which concludes that Reich is 'mentally ill both from a legal and psychiatric viewpoint' represents the conclusion of a single psychiatrist not resident at the institution." Citing the fact that such psychiatrists are not in a position to observe prisoners daily as resident ones are, the paragraph states that the Lewisburg report is the more satisfactory of the two. Besides which, in the latter report there is common agreement among three doctors. "We are authorized by the Director of Prisons to add," the paragraph concludes, "that the general policy is to accept the conclusions of the resident psychiatrists in the event of differing views between him [sic] and the consulting psychiatrist."

In an interview with Dr. Hubbard this author learned that there had been no question in Hubbard's mind that Reich was legally insane. He felt that his professional competence had been impugned by the opposite diagnosis made in Lewisburg and consequently called Lewisburg to discuss the matter. One of the doctors on the Board of Examiners which had examined Reich told Hubbard that the members of the Board had had no doubt but that Reich was "nuttier than a fruit cake." ("Or some such phrase," Hubbard said.) Their diagnosis was essentially not a psychiatric but an administrative one. There was no point in following through with a diagnosis of legal insanity since this would only mean that the whole case would be relitigated—which was exactly what Maguire had represented to the men from the Department of Justice. It was to avoid this legal and administrative rigamarole, the doctor at Lewisburg told Hubbard, that the Board decided in favor of legal sanity, not because they, as professional men, disagreed with Hubbard's diagnosis.

Whether or not concurrence in the matter of Reich's legal insanity and the possible earlier release from prison on that basis would have been more beneficial to Reich than what actually occurred in an open question. It is entirely possible that he would have interpreted a suspension or reduction of sentence for reason of a declared insanity as more of a defeat than the imprisonment he was sentenced to, as the final act in an almost twenty-five year effort to pin this label on him. It was, of course, not these considerations that motivated the concern and the efforts—whatever they were—of Mills and Maguire to have Reich declared legally sane. In the light of what has been revealed in this account about his actions, suspicions, and expectations in the last three years of litigation, it should be clear that Reich qualified fully for the status of legal insanity in the specific technical sense and in terms of the conventionally accepted criteria—however questionable their merit —used to determine this condition. He was therefore unjustly deprived by backstage machinations of whatever consideration or immunity such a diagnosis entitled him to. The fact that he, and possible those close to him in his struggle at the time, might have preferred it this way does not alter the fact of this injustice.

It is one among the many ironies of Reich's life that all the while he exhibited no symptoms of imbalance, of loss of touch with social reality, he was considered insane by officialdom; yet when he began, after decades of harassment, slander and persecution, to show such symptoms officialdom declared him sane.

Before April 25, the date set by Judge Sweeney for the hearing on the motions by Reich and Silvert, there was one other detail of some importance in regard to Reich's disposition: The FDA received a letter from J.C. Taylor, Warden of the Lewisburg prison, requesting a report on Reich's offense, his history, and any additional information which might throw light on the case. This information, the warden wrote, would be used by the classification committee to decide what kind of treatment Reich would receive in prison—this did not refer to medical treatment—and also would be used at a later date when the matter of Reich's parole would arise. The reply to this request—an eight-page letter—was written by G.S. Goldhammer, who was Assistant Director of the Division of Regulatory Management of the FDA.

It begins with a capsule history of Reich's professional activities in Europe. In summarizing Reich's trouble in Norway, Goldhammer states:

Characteristically, Reich was involved in an extensive Norwegian newspaper controversy for several years before he left Norway, at which time a number of apparently well-established Norwegian doctors and scientific organizations seriously questioned his work. They inferred that his sex-economic theories and his other alleged scientific research were not sound and the impression received from this period of his life is that Reich fled Norway under pressure from the scientific and medical authorities there.

This distortion suggests that, at best, Goldhammer did not bother to read the State Department reports very carefully. It also sets the pattern for several other distortions in subsequent paragraphs of his letter, such as: "Reich sold or rented about 1,000 of these models [the box type] in this country, the sale price was about $225 each." In point of fact the Foundation had, altogether, built only about three hundred box model accumulators over the years. "Reich and his followers distributed much literature in connection with the devices, representing them to be of value in the treatment of cancer, diabetes, hardening of the arteries, heart trouble, and all other disease conditions." The distortions here are too obvious by now to require refutation. As regards the tests the FDA had had carried out, Goldhammer might well have believed in their validity when he wrote that "the best medical clinicians" and "outstanding physicists" proved that the accumulators were worthless and that no energy such as orgone existed.

This lengthy reply to Warden Taylor, then, is like the machinations related to the psychiatric reports—an attempt to make sure that Reich would serve as much of the two-year sentence as possible.

The April 25 hearing was held in Boston. Reich and Silvert were not present. Though Olney's prior communication settled the matter of whether Reich had been competent to stand trial, the psychiatric reports did, as has been shown, indicate some mental disturbance. Maguire apparently wished to make sure that Judge Sweeney would not use the fact of such disturbance to reduce the sentences. He therefore argued that if there were a question of mental illness the welfare of Reich and Silvert would not be served best by their early release since the facilities of the Bureau of Prisons provided for excellent psychiatric treatment. Besides this, Maguire argued further, Reich and Silvert would continue selling and renting accumulators if they were released without punishment.

Judge Sweeney decided not to change the sentences. On April 29 he sent a letter to the U.S. Board of Parole saying that though he "was strongly inclined to reduce the sentences," the government asserted that Reich and Silvert would continue in their "business" so he decided to let the sentences stand. Then, in an obvious effort to mitigate the effects of his decision, Sweeney added: "While I seldom recommend either for or against parole, in this case I recommend for it if they are satisfied that they have learned their lesson and will [not?] continue the adjudicated practice." *

* There is an important detail in this matter that can only be mentioned but not fitted meaningfully into the context of these events. This author learned during his research that at some point in the beginning of his imprisonment Reich signed a statement that he would not, if sentence were reduced or suspended, do anything connected with the sale or rental of accumulators. A query to Mr. William Moise on this matter brought the

Among prison officials, the Lewisburg Federal Prison has the reputation of being a country club. The dining hall floors, they will tell you with something like astonishment, are washed after every meal. The facilities for psychiatric care are second to none in the country. To this prison are sent convicted men who, like Reich, were not considered hardcore criminals but who somehow, in the course of professional or public life, ran afoul of the law.

Reich seemed, in his own way, to have made a good adjustment there. Since he had been declared legally sane there was no attempt made to give him psychiatric treatment—which, in any case, he would doubtlessly have refused. Because of his heart condition he was given the job of checking out books in the prison library. He had little contact with the other prisoners, Mr. Harvey Matusow, who had been imprisoned there several years earlier on the charge of perjury committed in his testimony during the McCarthy hearings, recalls in his article, "The Day Reich Died." During exercise time, Matusow writes, Reich would simply stand apart in the courtyard and, with a hand shielding his eyes, turn his face to the sun—one assumes, to expose a skin condition that had been with him for many years to the sun rays. When other inmates tried to talk to Reich about his imprisonment Reich would say that the matter was too controversial to discuss.

Much of his free time Reich spent working on his book entitled *Creation,* which dealt with mathematical orgonometry and his theoretical formulations on countergravity—and which was never found after his death. Besides this he did a lot of reading. Ilse Ollendorff records that he was particularly interested in Sandburg's massive, four-volume biography of Lincoln and the essays of Emerson. No doubt Reich felt a close affinity with Emerson's thinking, mystical and abstract as it often is. Emerson's concept of the Oversoul of which every individual soul is a part could

following reply: "Reich did sign such a statement. It was given to me by Aurro [Aurora] Karrer supposedly from judge sweeney. [sic] WR signed it and ig [I] gave it to Aurro. Nothing ever happened." Requests for further details went unanswered. It is difficult to know what to make of this piece of information. Its clarification, together with the clarification of other murky areas in the Reich case, will have to wait until the people most closely associated with Reich during this period make their experiences public and until the relevant material in the Reich archives is made available for study.

readily be interpreted as a philosophical perception of the relationship Reich postulated between the orgone energy in the organism and that of the atmosphere and cosmos in general. Emerson's statement that "society everywhere is in conspiracy against the manhood of its members" must have struck a particularly responsive chord in Reich during this time. Emerson's exhortation to people to open themselves to the universe and let the "ethereal tides" flow through them (*i.e.,* orgonotic streaming), his emphasis on self-reliance, the primacy of the truth of an individual's own experiences and perceptions over commonly accepted attitudes and interpretations, his concept of temperament being a function of a man's "immersion in nature," his general view of Nature—with a capital N—must all have meant a great deal to Reich in his reading.

Reich himself was somewhat surprised by the adjustment he was able to make to prison life. "I am taking it better than I thought," Ilse Ollendorff quotes him as writing.[1] He was allowed to name three people who would be his visitors and three with whom he would correspond. These were Eva, Peter, and Aurora. Eva and Aurora visited him often. ("Did you see that beautiful young girl who used to come and visit him?" Matusow quotes one of the prisoners saying of Aurora.[2]) Apparently during part of the time of Reich's imprisonment Aurora was living near Lewisburg to be able to visit him more frequently. Apparently, too, on particularly "bad" days—*i.e.,* when the atmosphere was more than usually contaminated with DOR—Eva and William Moise came with a cloudbuster mounted on a truck and conducted decontaminating operations over the area around the prison. (In the *Oranur Experiment,* written, it will be recalled, in the early fifties, Reich had theorized that many prison riots were caused by the effects of atmospheric DOR being intensified by the metal of prison cells.)

There were several curiously contradictory elements in Reich's thinking concerning his imprisonment. On the one hand, he came to regard his imprisonment as a deliberate measure of protective custody on the part of high officials in the government. This, of course, was a means of reconciling the fact of his continued

1. Ollendorff, p. 155.
2. Harvey Matusow, "The Day Reich Died," in *East Village Other,* February, 1–15, 1966, p. 10.

imprisonment with his conviction of Eisenhower's interest in his work. But on the other hand, he repeatedly wrote in letters that in spite of his imprisonment he had won his battle. In one particular letter to Peter he expounded on this idea in detail, saying that his imprisonment was an honor since it was on the basis of an "unlawful court order" and this put him in the proud company of people like Socrates, Christ, Bruno, Galileo, Dostoyevsky, and Gandhi.[3]

Moreover, in spite of his occasionally viewing himself as being in protective custody, he feared that arrangements were made to have him killed in his cell. And besides this, he made several efforts toward an early release.

One of these was in May 1957, when he appealed for a Presidential pardon. Reich fully expected that it would be granted and on the basis of this expectation was far advanced in making plans to spend that summer at Orgonon. Nothing, of course, came of this appeal. The second effort was his application for release in October when his time for possible parole came up. Here, again, he was certain that the release would be granted and he made plans to meet with Peter at a Howard Johnson restaurant near Peter's school and to spend Thanksgiving with Eva and her husband.*

However, during the time he was waiting for the parole hearing he began to feel ill. Fearful that his illness might delay his release, he kept his condition a secret from prison authorities. And it was this illness that resulted in his death. He was found dead on his cot in his cell on the morning of November 3—two days before the time set for the parole hearing.

To forestall suspicions or rumors of foul play, the prison authorities called in an outside pathologist to conduct the autopsy and also to test for possible poisoning. No toxic substances were found, but gross pathology was. His death was attributed to heart complications—"myocardial insufficiency with sudden heart failure."

Often in past years Reich had maintained that a heart attack was a biophysical manifestation of emotionally heartbreaking ex-

---

* The Russian sputnik had been shot into orbit about this time. Reich was not impressed by this feat. He wrote to Peter that it was a "nice stunt like a ball thrown upon ocean waves and tossed about helplessly. It will never be an active navigation vehicle." [4]

3. Ollendorff, p. 155.
4. *Ibid.*, p. 156.

perience. His own fatal heart attack can certainly be seen as such a manifestation. Beneath the brave external optimism he managed to maintain during most of his prison term and in the years prior to it, a deep despair must have been eroding his vital resources. There is only so much the human spirit can do, so much abuse it can take, and in the end, when pitted against a whole hostile world, the strongest life system must succumb. Reich had hoped to break the millennia-old oppression of what he called the "emotional plague," of everything that made human history the bloody tale it is, that has consistently killed human potential and thereby kept human existence restricted to the level of minimal survival. His death essentially was martyrdom. Whether it also meant failure and defeat remains yet to be seen.

There was little official notice taken of his death. *The New York Times* ran a short obituary, as did *Time,* adding its own special brand of snide innuendo. The same occurred in England, with the *Manchester Guardian* declining to publish a letter about Reich that Neill sent in. The only mass publication that tried to do justice to the event of Reich's death was the *Village Voice.*

The funeral was held in Orgonon on a cold, blustery day and proceeded according to the way Reich himself had previously provided: no religiosity, a recording of Marion Anderson singing Schubert's *Ave Maria.* Some thirty or forty people—mostly from the New York City area—attended. Dr. Baker delivered a short, quiet, low-keyed speech, as follows:

Friends, we are here to say farewell, a last farewell, to Wilhelm Reich. Let us pause for a moment to appreciate the privilege, the incredible privilege, of having known him. Once in a thousand years, nay once in two thousand years, such a man comes upon this earth to change the destiny of the human race. As with all great men, distortion, falsehood and persecution followed him. He met them all; until organized conspiracy sent him to prison and there killed him. We have witnessed it all. "The Murder of Christ." What poor words can I say that can either add to or clarify what he has done? His work is finished. He has earned his peace and has left a vast heritage for the peoples of this earth. We do not mourn him, but for ourselves, at our great loss. Let us take up the responsibility of his work and follow in the path he cleared for us. So be it.

Reich's will was an extension of the effort of his life. Aside from a few minimal bequests, his whole estate was to be administered by the Wilhelm Reich Infant Trust Fund, whose function was to be threefold: to prevent distortion of his work and slander of his life, and yet to make the facts available to the future, the trustee of the Fund was to seal and store away all his unpublished writings for fifty years; to set Orgonon up as the Wilhelm Reich Museum in "order to preserve some of the atmosphere in which the discovery of the Life Energy has taken place over the decades"; [5] and to devote the income that accrued from his discoveries to "the care of infants everywhere; toward legal security of the infants, children and adolescents in emotional, social, parental, medical, legal, educational, professional or other distress." [6] The reason for this last provision, Reich's will explains, is that throughout his life he loved young people and was in turn loved by them. "Infants used to smile at me because I had deep contact with them and children of two or three very often used to become thoughtful and serious when they looked at me." [7] The third provision of his will, in other words, was an expression of his gratitude to his "little friends" for the love they had shown him during his life.

5. Wilhelm Reich: *Selected Writings* (New York: The Noonday Press, 1960), p. viii.
6. *Ibid.*, p. ix.
7. *Ibid.*, p. ix.

16

---◆---

EPILOGUE

Normal time for possible parole is ordinarily one-third of a prison sentence. This is why the matter of Reich's parole had come up in November—when eight months of his twenty-four-month sentence had been served. By this rule, Silvert, who had been sentenced to a year and a day, should have been eligible for parole some time in July. Instead, for reasons this author could not ascertain, he was not released until December 12, 1957—that is, after he had served some three-quarters of his sentence.

With his medical license revoked by the State of New York, he could not resume his former practice. He took a job as a bellhop captain in a hotel, where he worked for the next several months, keeping aloof from almost all of his former acquaintances and fellow orgonomists. On May 2, 1958—almost on the exact date of the second anniversary of the trial—Silvert took poison in Van Cortlandt Park in the Bronx. A note found on him after his suicide stated that the reason for his act was that he was suffering from an incurable disease. Whether this was meant to be taken literally or as a metaphor for his whole situation and, possibly, guilt over Reich's imprisonment and death, has never been determined.

For the FDA, however, the Reich case did not end yet. The FDA continued to be concerned over the matter of possible accumulators in interstate commerce and the influence of Reich's ideas. On June 23, 1959, FDA headquarters sent a letter to Dr. Theodore R. Robie—a high official in the New Jersey Psychiatric Association who over the years had urged and abetted the FDA effort against Reich—stating that some of the medical orgonomists in the New York–New Jersey area were still using the accumulator and requesting Robie to pass on any information he obtained relating to this matter. "Let me again extend our appreciation," the letter concludes, "for the part you played in bringing this difficult case to a successful conclusion." (It should, of course, be clear that from the standpoint of legal consistency—since the courts had ruled, in connection with intervention proceedings, that the injunction was directed *in personam* against the defendants named therein and since Reich and Silvert were by then dead and the Wilhelm Reich Foundation had long been dissolved—that the FDA no longer had any right to take any further action in relation to accumulators. Indeed, in the intervention proceedings, the judge had made it clear that anyone not working in concert with the named defendants had an absolute right to build, rent, sell and ship accumulators in interstate commerce.)

Some two years after the letter to Robie, the FDA received a letter from Oliver Field, the director of the American Medical Association, in which the Wilhelm Reich Museum established in Orgonon is described:

The museum shows some of his paintings, but his scientific equipment is limited to a very small laboratory with a few glass slides (as he left it), with photographs, scales, oscilloscope, Geiger counter and telescope. The impression one receives is that this man, in the prime of a possible medical discovery, was clamped into prison. The library is apparently stocked with recent editions referring to his work.

His body lies in a sarcophagus next to his home, and the trustees are raising money for a monument to be erected on the premises

. . .

I believe an investigation should be instituted to determine for what purposes the money is being collected through the public sale of tickets. While I realize no medical problem is now involved, there could be a possibility of a renewal of Reich's former teachings on Orgonomy.

This letter is one of the most explicit expressions of what was only implicit in all the legal proceedings: that the main purpose of the FDA action was not the concern for the health of people using the accumulator, but the spread of Reich's "teachings on Orgonomy."

In response to this letter, an inspector was dispatched from the Boston district to conduct an "establishment inspection" on October 26, 1961. The inspector learned from Tom Ross, who was still the caretaker of the estate, that the museum was open to the public two days a week during July and August and that—according to his memo—"funds were collected by the sale of tickets to the museum." Ross told the inspector that 80 percent of the proceeds went to the Wilhelm Reich Infant Trust Fund, but he could not account for the remaining 20 percent. However, Ross assured the inspector, that "no 'accumulators' were present on the premises."

The next day the inspector returned but was prevented from inspecting the premises by Miss Higgins, the newly appointed trustee of the Infant Trust Fund.

As late as February 4, 1963—that is, almost six years after Reich's death—Milstead of the Bureau of Enforcement of the FDA, wrote the following intra-administrative referral:

I am told that Reich's books are being published in paperback form and there is still considerable support for his theories. Do we know what is going on at Reich's old headquarters at Rangeley, Maine? If not, we suggest that the Boston District be requested to inquire into this matter when convenient. We, of course, are primarily interested in whether or not there is any present distribution of any of Reich's devices.

And in response to this suggestion, FDA agents were asked to interview the Barnes and Noble bookstore regarding its sales of Reich's books, as well as Mr. Thomas Mangravite, Dr. Baker, and Miss Lois Wyvell to find out if they were in any way involved with accumulators. Needless to say, no traffic in accumulators was found in the subsequent interviews and investigations.

For the FDA the Reich case seems to have ended at that time.

Most of the principals are now dead. The only survivor is Peter Mills, who has recently been serving again as U.S. Attorney for the state of Maine. On a visit to the Federal Building in Portland, Maine, this author sought an interview with Mr. Mills. Mills ac-

ceded to the request for an interview and appeared with his son—
a clean-cut, bright-faced young man studying law at Harvard—
who put his arm around his father's shoulder and said with an
engaging smile, "Here he is, the twentieth-century Judas Iscariot."

Mills is a short, roundishly built man with an easy, ready smile
on his full face within which small sharp eyes sparkle with suspicious alertness. He was quite pleasant during the hour-long
interview, his manner conspicuously informal as he settled on the
edge of a conference table and began to speak. Referring to himself as a "simple country lawyer," he insisted on randomly reminiscing on the Reich case rather than answering specific questions.
This reminiscing, however, was not really as random as his manner implied; beneath its apparent randomness there was apparently
some anxiety, a desire to exculpate himself. Claiming he was a
long-standing "civil libertarian," Mills was shocked and surprised
when told that *The Sexual Revolution* and *The Mass Psychology
of Fascism* had indeed been included in the injunction. But after
half an hour, apparently forgetting his earlier surprise, he said
with heavy emphasis that he had sat down with Maguire (who had,
according to Mills, written up the injunction and handled all the
legal details of the case) and Judge Clifford and argued strongly
but to no avail against banning of all of Reich's books. At the
end of the interview, when asked for a picture of himself, Mills
refused, saying with a look of confidentiality, that he was up for
reappointment. The implication was that the inclusion of his picture
in this study might somehow jeopardize his reappointment.

All of which points up one of the most significant aspects of the
Reich case: that many of the people involved in the effort to disrupt Reich's work, to burn his books, to discredit his ideas and
slander his name, to imprison him and break his heart were of the
kind one usually thinks of as being ordinary, decent law-abiding
citizens, people concerned for their families, their religious beliefs,
their mortgages, insurance policies and careers. The term Hannah
Arendt coined to refer to Eichmann at his trial—"the banality of
evil"—applies as well to these people. In perpetrating the persecution and injustice against Reich, they were—like Eichmann ar-
ranging the technical details for the annihilation of European
Jewry—doing nothing more than what was normally expected of
them, only fulfilling their social and professional duties. They were,

in other words, merely executing the implicit or explicit mandates of the society they were part of.

Reich wrote in the final paragraph of *Listen, Little Man* (written in 1948): "Whatever you have done to me or will do to me in the future, whether you glorify me, put me in a mental institution or hang me, sooner or later necessity will force you to comprehend that I have discovered the laws of the living and handed you the tool with which to govern your life, as heretofore you were able only to govern machines." [1]

With the growing interest in Reich's ideas and formulations during the past decade, it is inevitable that the challenge of these formulations, as concerns orgone energy particularly, will eventually be confronted by the scientific community. Such a confrontation will not only be a test of Reich's view of his accomplishment as expressed in the above quotation. It will also finally determine who was really on trial in all that has been presented in this book: Reich or the world of conventional thinking as represented by the FDA and the American legal structure.

1. Wilhelm Reich, *Listen, Little Man* (New York: The Noonday Press, 1972), pp. 125–26.

APPENDIX 1

The Complaint *

Complaint for Injunction
[Filed February 10, 1954.]

The United States of America, plaintiff herein, by and through Peter Mills, United States Attorney for the District of Maine, files this Complaint for Injunction and respectfully represents unto this Honorable Court as follows:

1. This proceeding is brought under Section 302(a) of the Federal Food, Drug and Cosmetic Act [21 U.S.C. 332(a)], hereinafter referred to as the "Act", specifically investing the several United States District Courts with jurisdiction to enjoin and restrain violations of Section 301 of said Act [21 U.S.C. 331] as hereinafter more fully appears.

2. The defendant, The Wilhelm Reich Foundation, is a Maine corporation, hereinafter called the Foundation, having its principal place of business at Rangeley, Maine. The defendant Wilhelm Reich is an individual who resides at Rangeley, Maine. The said defendants manufacture and have been and now are introducing and causing to be introduced, and delivering and causing to be delivered for introduction into interstate commerce in violation of 21 U.S.C. 321(a) orgone energy accumulators, devices within the meaning of 21 U.S.C. 321(b), which are adulterated within the meaning of 21 U.S.C. 351(c) and misbranded within the meaning of 21 U.S.C. 352(a), and further, said defendants have been and now are causing said devices to be adulterated and misbranded within the meaning of 21 U.S.C. 351(c) and 352(a) while held for sale after shipment in interstate Commerce in violation of 21 U.S.C. 331(k), all, as hereinafter appears. The defendant, Ilse Ollendorff, also known as Mrs. Wilhelm Reich, is an individual who resides at Rangeley, Maine, who holds and has held responsible managerial positions in the conduct of the business and affairs of The Wilhelm Reich Foundation, such as, member of the board of trustees, treasurer, secretary, and administrator of the Foundation, administrative director of Orgone Institute Research Laboratories, Inc., an affiliate of the Foundation; supervisor and in charge of the distribution of said orgone energy accumulator devices and the Orgone Research Fund.

* This document constitutes the opening of the legal case against Reich some seven years after the beginning of the FDA's investigation.

3. The orgone energy accumulator device is available in several styles and models. The box style orgone energy accumulators are designed to stand upright and are large enough to permit an adult to sit inside. (See Exhibit A attached). The height, width, and depth are each several inches less than those of the ordinary telephone booth. The top bottom, sides, and door are similarly constructed. Each is made with alternating layers of organic and metallic material. The outer layer may be of celotex or plywood, then alternating layers of steel wool and rock or glass wool and the inside layer is galvanized sheet metal. In recent years plastic wire mesh has been used as a substitute for the sheet metal. A device with six layers is called a three-fold energy accumulator. One with two additional layers is called four-fold and progressively so as the layers increase. The door is hinged to one side, and usually either has an open window or has portions cut out at the top and bottom for ventilation. There is a two-section removable seat made in layers as described above. A small section is cut out at a corner of the seat for the insertion of a length of B-X type hollow cable into the other end of which a funnel may be placed. The drop section may be used as a chestboard by placing it upright in front of the chest of a person sitting in the box. Chestboards are also made and sold separately. Attached and marked "Exhibit A" is page 31 of a booklet entitled THE ORGONE ENERGY ACCUMULATOR Its Scientific and Medical Use showing a box style orgone energy accumulator device, equipped with a two-section seat chestboard, and funnel arrangement.

4. A "Shooter" type orgone energy accumulator device is a box about one cubic foot in size, all sides of which are made in the manner described in the preceding paragraph. It is equipped with a B-X type hollow cable into which a funnel may be inserted. Attached and marked "Exhibit C" is page 37 of the booklet from which Exhibit A is taken, showing a "shooter" orgone energy accumulator device.

5. The blanket style orgone energy accumulator device is constructed of wire mesh with several alternating layers of organic and metallic material covered on the outside with plastic. It is made in three portions which may fold down flat. It is for use in bed or local application. One section may be placed under the mattress and the other two over the patient. Attached hereto and marked "Exhibit B" and "Exhibit D", respectively, are pages 32 and 38 of the booklet described in Exhibit A, which pages show how the said blanket style may be used in bed and for local application.

6. The funnel style orgone energy accumulator device is also constructed of wire mesh with several alternating layers of organic and

metallic material covered with plastic. An example of the use of said funnel style is shown on page 39 of the above described booklet, which is attached hereto and marked "Exhibit E". The picture shows an earlier style metal funnel orgone energy accumulator device insulated on the outside with cotton and tape.

7. The orgone energy accumulator device is not connected with or plugged into any source of electrical or any other type of energy or power.

8. In the interstate distribution of the orgone energy accumulator device the said defendants offer them for sale at the following prices:

Style	Price
Cabinet	$225.00
Chestboard	15.00
"Shooter"	40.00
Funnel	25.00
Blanket	60.00

The said defendants also offer for rent cabinet style orgone energy accumulator device for an advance "contribution" of $40 plus a $10 monthly "contribution" payable in advance. The said defendants recommend unless a person has used an orgone energy accumulator device and is well acquainted with its effects that he rent for a three months trial period. If it is decided then to purchase, the $40 "contribution" and $30 rental are credited to the purcase price. At the end of a two year rental period reapplication is to be made for the rental of the device or it is to be returned to the defendants.

9. Prospective purchasers of the device may learn about it in several ways. They may hear of it in conversation with persons acquainted with the device; through advertising campaigns conducted by the defendants in newspapers, journals, and in magazines which promote the sales of books, periodicals, booklets, journals, bulletins, and other publications of the defendants. Such advertising announces the existence, availability, and prices of defendants' publications on the discovery and medical use of orgone energy by employing the orgone energy accumulator. They may also learn of the same by such announcements appearing on the removal covers of defendants' said books and on the inside and outside permanent covers of said booklets, pamphlets, and journals; by exhibitions of defendants' publications at booksellers and library association conventions and conferences; by listings in book reference sources; by the use of a mailing list containing approximately 7500 names; by means of 10,000 copies of a

catalogue describing the contents of each book and periodical of the defendants, 7000 of which were mailed by the defendants to prospective customers. Purposes of the promotional and advertising campaigns, by such means, and the said publications, is to acquaint the public with the alleged discovery and medical use by means of said device of the alleged orgone energy; to acquaint the reader concerning specified stated uses therefor; to furnish certain specific instructions and directions for the use of orgone energy accumulators; to create a demand for the purchase or rental from the said defendants of said orgone energy accumulator devices. Lacking certain of said publications the purchaser or lessee of such a device would be without information concerning instructions and directions for the use of said device in various diseases and disease conditions.

10. The said defendants distribute and cause to be distributed in interstate commerce various items of written, printed, and graphic matter which relate to said devices and which written, printed, and graphic matter is printed and distributed through the Orgone Institute Press, a department and the publishing house of The Wilhelm Reich Foundation, located at Rangeley, Maine. Such written, printed, and graphic matter consists of books, book covers, booklets, periodicals, journals, pamphlets, bulletins, brochures, order blanks, announcements, catalogues, catalogue sheets, form sheets, application forms for the rental or purchase of orgone energy accumulators, sheets containing instructions for their use, among others. Said items of written, printed, and graphic matter accompany said devices when they are introduced into and delivered for information into and while in interstate commerce, and constitute labeling of said devices. Said written, printed, and graphic matter contains instructions for the assembly of the large box models and directions for the use of the various models, both as a prophylactic and for use in the cure, mitigation, and treatment of various symptoms, conditions, and diseases, and misbrands the said devices in that said written, printed, and graphic matter represents and suggests that said devices, when used as directed, are effective in the cure, mitigation, treatment and prevention of said symptoms, conditions, and diseases, whereas, the said devices are not effective in the cure, mitigation, treatment, and prevention of said diseases. The false and misleading statements and representations contained in said written, printed, and graphic matter are hereinafter more particularly set forth and alleged in this complaint.

11. When written inquiries are received by the said defendants pertaining to the prophylactic and medical uses of orgone energy accumulator devices or literature and publications relating thereto, the

said defendants in actively promoting the sale and rental of said devices, and their distribution in interstate commerce, respond by sending through the United States mails, catalogues and announcements containing descriptive material, and the prices, with order blanks therefor, of the following, among other, publications:

The Discovery of the Orgone by Wilhelm Reich	
Vol. I—The Function of the Orgasm	6.00
Vol. II—The Cancer Biopathy	8.50
The Orgone Energy Accumulator Its Scientific and	
Medical Use	2.00
Orgone Energy Bulletin	
A quarterly publication	4.00
Ether, God and Devil by Wilhelm Reich	4.50
Annals of the Orgone Institute, No. 1	2.00
Listen Little Man by Wilhelm Reich	3.00
The Mass Psychology of Fascism by Wilhelm Reich	4.50
Character Analysis by Wilhelm Reich	6.00
International Journal of Sex-Economy and Orgone	
Research (Published 1942 through 1945)	7.50
Emotional Plague versus Orgone Biophysics	1.00
Internationale Zeitschrift Fur Orgonomie	1.00
Orgone Energy Emergency Bulletin	.40
The Murder of Christ by Wilhelm Reich	
People in Trouble by Wilhelm Reich	(20.00)
	(for)
	(the)
	(set.)

12. The defendant, Wilhelm Reich, in the aforesaid written, printed, and graphic matter claims to have discovered a form of energy which is present in the atmosphere and for which he coined the term "orgone energy". He claims that this alleged energy is life energy, has therapeutic value, and is beneficial in the cure, mitigation, treatment, and prevention of disease.

13. The defendant Reich in said literature claims to have invented, in 1940, a device which collects from the atmosphere this alleged energy and accumulates it in the device, where it is usable for scientific, educational, and medical purposes. Approximately 10 of these devices were made in New York State from 1940 to 1942; from then until 1949 they were made by Herman Templeton, a Maine hunting and fishing guide, and after his death were made by his daughter, at

Oquossoc, near Rangeley, Maine; for a short time thereafter they were made in New York again; and since 1950 they have been made by S. A. Collins & Son at Rangeley, Maine.

14. The defendants claim in said literature that this alleged energy is demonstrable, useful, and measurable. They attempt to prove the existence of such energy and its presence in the device by employing well-known scientific instruments and by resorting to the use of phenomena such as light, heat, radio-active measurements, and electro-magnetism.

15. The said defendants state in said literature that organic material, which should constitute the outermost layer of the accumulator, attracts and absorbs the alleged orgone energy, that metallic material, though it attracts said energy, quickly reflects it; that by layering the accumulator as described in paragraph 3 hereof, always with the organic matter on the outside, a direction is given to the said energy from the outside to the inside, where the alleged energy is collected and concentrated.

16. The said defendants maintain that the medical use of their box style device is accomplished by sitting in it. The manner of use of the other styles is shown in Exhibits A through E attached hereto.

17. The defendants maintain, as stated in said literature, that the enclosure within the device constitutes an alleged orgone energy field and the person in the enclosure another such field; that the energy fields of the two systems make contact; that both the person and the energy field of the accumulator begin to "luminate"; they become excited and, making contact, drive each other to higher levels of excitation. The defendants maintain that the user of the device becomes aware of this alleged phenomenon through feelings of prickling, warmth, relaxation, reddening of the face; further that body temperature increases from one half to one and one half degrees, Fahrenheit.

18. The said defendants state in said literature that the box style device should fit the size of the person who uses it; that the body surface should be no more than about 2 to 4 inches away from the metal walls.

19. The said defendants state in said literature that the blanket style device may be used by bedridden individuals in place of the regular box type device.

20. The said defendants state in said literature there is no mechanical rule as to the length of time a person should sit in the accumulator. They suggest that on the average a person requires from 5 to 30 minutes daily; that with regular use the time may be shortened from 30 minutes to 10 minute sessions; that the necessary time for sittings

will be decreased in accordance with the greater number of layers the device has; that the patient may sit in the accumulator clothed or unclothed; that woolen or too heavy clothing is not recommended as it is alleged that such prevents quick contact and lumination; that it is better for a person to indulge in 2 or more short sittings than one protracted sitting as the latter could cause serious damage.

21. For local application of the alleged orgone energy using the "shooter" style device with funnel attachment which is applied to the area to be treated, the defendants recommend approximate irradiating times, examples of which are as follows: heart region 2 to 5 minutes; root of nose, 4; mouth cavity 5; closed eyes 1; ears, 2; solar plexus, 3; wounds, burns, cuts and bruises, 5 to 20 minutes; using a glass tube filled with steel wool instead of the funnel attachment, with the tube inserted in the vagina, 1 minute; using a smaller glass tube so filled and placed inside the nose, no time is specified.

22. The said defendants, despite disclaimer of a cure from the use of their device, resort to detailed accounts of case histories in the said literature describing "cures" alleged to have been effected by the use of the device. Outstanding results are alleged to have been accomplished in inordinately short periods of time. Some examples of such claims are as follows:

ORGONE ENERGY BULLETIN

Vol. 1. No. 1   *January 1949*

Page 13   A woman, aged 30, suffered a leg injury. The wound suppurated and did not heal for several weeks. After 3 sessions in the orgone accumulator, the wound closed * * *

Page 13   * * * cutaneous abscesses; even after only one treatment the abscesses receded, and after five further treatments they had completely disappeared. In the meantime, the child developed some new abscesses; again they began to recede rapidly after the first orgone treatment.

Page 13,   A woman, aged 46, with a carcinoma of the liver, came for
14   orgone treatment in the last stage of her disease. Shortly before the appearance of the liver metastasis, she had been operated on for carcinoma of the left breast. She had lived in complete sexual abstinence for 17 years. Her menstruation was very weak and always lasted only two days. The patient came for treatment twice daily for half an hour and after two days of treatment she felt much better, as her appetite increased and she was able to walk with greater

ease. Three days later, menstruation occurred which, although still as weak as before, lasted four days for the first time. Her hemoglobin content arose from 75% to 85% within a week and her weight increased by 2 lbs. * * *

Page 14 A patient, aged 56, with pseudomyxoma peritonei * * * had been constipated for half a year * * * After the first treatment, bowel movement was copious * * *

Page 15 A man, aged 56, with angina pectoris had his first attack eight years ago and had had no trouble whatever since then. A week before the beginning of the orgone treatment new attacks set in, some of them of a serious nature. Consciousness was partly clouded. The attacks occurred with varying intensity several times a day, up to the first orgone treatment. After the first treatment, there were no more attacks. * * *

Page 16 A patient, aged 62, with an arteriosclerotic heart disease became sick 5 years ago. He had been repeatedly hospitalized and his doctors had given him up on several occasions. After a few weeks of orgone treatment, he felt strong enough to take a walk of several miles in the glare of a tropical sun at noon against medical advice, a thing which he had been unable to do for years. * * *

Page 16, 17 A woman, aged 65, suffered from a myodegeneratio cordis for 7 years. Two years ago she was hospitalized for several weeks because of her heart disease. Since all internal medication failed, and since the patient, after returning from the hospital, was no longer able to leave the house, her family decided to try orgone therapy in spite of the skepticism of the physician in charge of the case. Her heart condition improved so much that the patient, after 3 weeks of orgone therapy, could do without any internal medication. Several weeks later, she was able for the first time to walk outside again, for half an hour. * * *

Page 17 In a case of chronic bronchitis in a woman aged 20, an improvement was visible after only 5 orgone treatments. Previous slight increases of temperature disappeared. * * *

Page 17, 18 A patient, 60, was suffering for years from a duodenal ulcer. He was severely constipated during almost all of his life. The ulcer especially caused serious painful attacks which increased after the patient's wife died several months ago. The constipation improved immediately after the first treatment. In the course of one month of treatment, the constipation, after first alternating with normal bowel movements, was completely eliminated. The pains disappeared after the fourth session. In addition to these results, 3 warts on the left hand and a corn became smaller. The treatment is being continued.

Page 18   A patient, aged 20, with anemia was treated with the accumulator for a fortnight. The number of erythroyctes rose from 3.7 million to 4 million and her hemoglobin content rose from 70% to 80%.

Page 18   An inflammation of the eyeball after the removal of a splinter disappeared altogether after having been subjected to radiation from an accumulator tube.

Page 18   A patient, aged 39, had a hemorrhage of the throat which lasted for hours and which ceased immediately following the first orgone treatment.

Vol. II, No. 1   *January 1950*

Page 16,   A 53-year-old-woman one year before the beginning of
17   orgonic treatment had a thrombophlebitis of the right calf. * * * After 1 week of orgone treatment, a reaction of very severe, almost unbearable, pain occurred. (In some other cases, we have also observed that the pain increases at the beginning of orgone treatment. The transformation of lifeless tissue into living tissue is of an inflammatory nature, and hence the cause of the pain is understandable.) After 11 days of irradiation, the first significant improvement took place, manifested in the reduction of pain and also improved walking. The improvement continued. When she had had 1 month of treatment, she could walk quite freely, even "run," * * *

Page 17   Buerger's disease.* * * One Patient, a 40-year-old man, had suffered from this disease for the last 16 years. * * * When he came for orgone treatment, there were wounds of a gangrenous nature on several of his toes and the surgeon urgently recommended amputation. Instead of amputation, the patient decided to try the orgone accumulator. After the first irradiation, he felt a strong prickling sensation on his feet, * * * After the second, third, and fourth irradiations, the same phenomena appeared. After the fifth, the wounds were dry for the first time in 8 years. When he had had 8 irradiations, entirely painless intervals occurred, whereas formerly the patient suffered constant pain. * * * The legs, which were ice cold before the therapy, became warmer. Previously the patient took about 2 dozen pills daily to combat the pain; now he could get along with 1 or 2. The wounds started to close.

Page 18   * * * A second patient, aged 35, had been suffering from Buerger's disease for 10 years. * * * After 14 years of irradiation twice daily his walking was already very much improved. He no longer needed a cane and the healing of his wounds progressed rapidly. * * *

Page 18   A 43-year-old patient suffered for many years from Buerger's disease. * * * After orgone treatment for 1 month, he again wished "to exercise and to jump" (the patient is a gymnastics instructor). * * *

Page 20   A 39-year-old woman had been suffering for 4 years from chronic sneezing; a specialist diagnosed her illness as asthmatic sneezing." * * * After 3 weeks of orgone irradiation, her sneezing stopped. * * *

Vol. II, No. 3   July 1950

Page 133   Re: Breast Cancer * * * The patient was only able to use the accumulator one half hour a day, six times, over a period of three weeks and then she left for the country. Very soon after that she noticed that the lump had disappeared. When I saw her on her return six weeks later, the tumor had entirely disappeared and the chronic cystic mastitis had almost gone. Both breasts were of normal consistency. In spite of the fact that I have seen many remarkable results from the orgone accumulator, and that I knew small, malignant breast tumors disappear after 2 to 4 weeks of orgone irradiation, what I saw here was still unbelievable.

Page 135   Re: Cancer of the Breast. There was a mass in the outer upper quadrant of the right breast. The outer edge of the tumor was sharp and about 2 inches in width. Proceeding medially, the tumor could not be differentiated from the rest of the tissue. Both breasts showed signs of chronic cystic mastitis. * * * Two weeks later I saw the patient after she had been using the orgone accumulator twice a day. The color of her skin was better and she seemed generally improved. The sharp edge of the tumor was gone and there remained only some enlarged gland tissue which was not differentiated from the rest of the breast tissue. Both breasts were much softer. Three weeks later the tumor had completely disappeared.

Vol. III. No. 3   July 1951

Page 165 Re: Ichthyosis * * * The patient began to use the orgone energy accumulator on September 15th for daily thirty-minute irradiations. Within 2 weeks he reported a marked decrease in the itching and scaling. The skin began to assume a healthier pink color * * * Within 1 month after beginning to use the accumulator he was free of itching and the scaling of the skin was present only on the legs.

THE DISCOVERY OF THE ORGONE
Volume Two   The Cancer Biopathy

Page 140-143 Our orgone therapy experiments with cancer patients consist in their sitting in the orgone accumulator. The orgone energy which is concentrated in the accumulator penetrates the naked body and is also taken up by way of respiration. * * * I began with sessions of 30 minutes. * * * During the first session the skin between the shoulder-blades became red; * * * During the next session, the redness of the skin spread to the upper part of the back and chest. * * * During the third, she began to perspire, particularly under the arms; she related that during the past few years she had never perspired. All these reactions of the organism to the orgone radiation are typical in all cancer patients. * * * Our patient came with a hemoglobin of 35%. Two days later it was 40%; after 4 days, 51% after a week, 55%; after 2 weeks, 75%, and after 3 weeks, 85%, that is, normal.

(The foregoing also appears in International Journal of Sex-Economy and Orgone Research, Vol. 1, 1942, at page 138 et seq.)

Page 171-173 The patient had a swelling the size of a bean at the outer margin of the right breast. * * * I refrained from having a biopsy done. Since the patient wished to undergo the orgone therapy experiment, there was no reason why I should not wait to see whether the tumor would disappear after a few irradiations. If it would disappear rapidly, it would have been a malignant tumor. If it took many weeks or even months to disappear, or if it neither receded nor grew, it would have shown itself to be a harmless glandular enlargement. * * * definitely established the diagnosis of an advanced carcinomatous shrinking biopathy. * * * The patient started with daily orgone irradiations in my laboratory. Later she ordered an orgone accumulator and took two daily irradiations of half an hour each; * * * After 10 days of orgone irradiation, the tumor was no longer palpable. (Observation of earlier cases had shown that orgone therapy eliminates breast tumors of medium size in the space of two to three weeks).

(The foregoing also appears in International Journal of Sex-Economy and Orgone Research, Vol. 2, 1943, pages 4, 5.)

Page 199 * * * In the case of orgone energy, * * * the tumor can be easily destroyed.

(The foregoing also appears in International Journal of Sex-Economy and Orgone Research, Vol. 2, 1943, page 20.)

Page 275, 277 In many cases of biologically debilitated blood and severe anemia the attack on the tumor is preceded by the formation of a great number of young erythrocytes, as can be observed microscopically. Breast tumors disappear in the course of 2 to 3 weeks. Observation to date shows that the tumors always become soft, no matter what their location. * * * In one case of brain tumor the destruction of the tumor occurred as early as two weeks after the beginning of treatment. * * *

Another woman with a tumor of the stomach the size of an apple, also reacted rapidly to the orgone therapy. The tumor, which was palpable, became soft and became rapidly smaller. Similarly, a third woman, with ovarian tumor, who had reacted to the orgone therapy with an improvement of her general condition and with a decrease in size and a softening of her tumors, * * *

In a boy of 5 with an adrenal tumor and metastases in the spine, X-ray showed calcification of the bone defects after 4 weeks. The primary adrenal tumor was no longer palpable after 2 weeks' treatment. * * * The fact should be remembered that none of our cases came to us shortly after the discovery of the tumor. They all had tried other methods for several years, and when they came to us, they had been given up as hopeless and were on the point of dying.

(The foregoing also appears in International Journal of Sex-Economy and Orgone Research, Vol. 2, 1943, pages 57, 58.)

Page 283 Anemias were eliminated within 3 to 6 weeks.

THE ORGONE ENERGY ACCUMULATOR
Its Scientific Use and Medical Use.

Page 35 * * * Painful burns, cuts, bruises will stop smarting after a few minutes. * * * One can follow the healing process as it runs its course. * * * According to the size of the injury, five to twenty minutes will suffice to set the healing process into rapid motion.

Page 36 The wounds heal in a matter of a few hours; severe ones need a day or two.

Orgone energy also sterilizes the wound. Microscopic observation shows that, for example, bacteria in the vagina will be immobilized after only one minute of irradiation through an inserted glass pipe filled with steel wool.

23. When the said defendants cause the devices to be introduced or delivered for introduction into interstate commerce, and while the devices are being held for sale after shipment in interstate commerce, the labeling thereof, consists in part, of a small metal plate affixed to, or, an ink impression stamped on, the side of the device. In addition the defendants mail from Rangeley, Maine, addressed to the consignee other items of labeling which are usually received within a few days, either before or after, delivery of the device. Some of these items are as follows:

    a. Application For Use of The Orgone Energy Accumulator— on which the purchaser specified whether he desires the device for medical, non-medical or experimental use.

    b. How To Use The Orgone Accumulator—which contains some directions for use of the cabinet style device, "shooter", seat box and chestboard.

    c. Instructions For Assembling The Orgone Accumulator—which contains directions for assembling the cabinet style accumulator.

    d. Catalogue sheet—which lists and partially describes the various styles of accumulators.

    e. Physician's Report.

    f. A form letter entitled To All Users of The Orgone Energy Accumulator".

    g. Instructions for the Use of the Orgone Energy Accumulator Blanket.

24. The defendants have devised a jargon stemming from their coined word "orgone" and utilize words having "orgone" as a base in the promotion of the pseudo science which they call "orgonomy."

25. That said defendants have been and now are representing and suggesting in the labeling of said devices, in particular on page 3 of the mimeographed sheets entitled HOW TO USE THE ORGONE AC-CUMULATOR, under the heading PLEASE READ CAREFULLY, that said devices be kept at least three rooms away from an operating X-ray machine; that said devices should not be used in proximity to operating X-ray equipment; and against experimenting with radio-active materials in combination with the alleged orgone energy because "it is dangerous to life", which representations and suggestions in said labeling are and were false and misleading and misbrand said devices within the meaning of said Act, 21 U.S.C. 352(a), since such repre-sentations and suggestions convey the impression and belief that the alleged orgone energy is a powerful form of energy, particularly when in contact with emanations from radio-active material and Koetgen rays, whereas, the alleged orgone energy, as claimed to have been discovered and its existence proved by the said defendant Reich as stated in the labeling for said devices, is not a powerful form of energy, is non-existent, and is not "dangerous to life".

26a. The aforesaid orgone energy accumulator devices have been and now are further misbranded when introduced into, while in, and while held for sale after shipment in interstate commerce, within the meaning of 21 U.S.C. 352(a) in that their labeling, namely, the book-let (outside cover) entitled THE ORGONE ENERGY ACCUMU-LATOR—Its Scientific and Medical Use, the booklet (page 198d) entitled THE ORANUR EXPERIMENT, and book (page 66) entitled COSMIC SUPERIMPOSITION, and the frontispiece of ORGONE ENERGY BULLETIN, Vol. 1, No. 1, the book entitled THE MUR-DER OF CHRIST, and the bulletin entitled "Internationale Zeitschrift Fur Orgonomie April 1950", contains written printed and graphic mat-ter, namely a photograph with caption, which is false and misleading in that such written, printed, and graphic matter conveys the impres-sion that the photograph is an actual photograph depicting the alleged orgone energy, whereas, the alleged orgone energy is not thereby depicted.

26b. The aforesaid orgone energy accumulator devices have been and now are further misbranded when introduced into, while in, and while held for sale after shipment in interstate commerce, within the meaning of 21 U.S.C. 352(a) in that their labeling, namely, the book (pages 198a and 198b) entitled THE ORANUR EXPERIMENT, contains written, printed, and graphic matter namely, photos 1 and 3 captioned as showing an excited orgone energy field between the palms of the hands and from an alcohol flame, respectively, which is false and misleading in that such written, printed, and graphic matter conveys the impression that the photos show excited orgone energy fields, whereas, said photos do not show excited orgone energy fields.

27. The orgone energy accumulator, in all of its styles and models, is a device within the meaning of 21 U.S.C. 321(b), and is and was further misbranded when introduced into, while in, and while held for sale after shipment in interstate commerce, within the meaning of said Act, 21 U.S.C. 352(a), in that its labeling, namely, the printed matter mentioned in paragraph "23" hereof and the written, printed and graphic matter hereinafter identified, accompanying said device, represents and suggests that the device is an outstanding therapeutic agent is a preventive of and beneficial for use in all diseases and disease conditions, is effective in particular in the cure, mitigation, treatment, and prevention of the diseases, conditions, and symptoms hereinafter mentioned, which representations and suggestions are false and misleading since the device is not an outstanding therapeutic agent, is not a preventive of and beneficial for use in all diseases and disease conditions, is not effective in the cure, mitigaton treatment, and prevention of the diseases, conditions, and symptoms hereinafter enumerated. Examples of the diseases, conditions, and symptoms, and the items of written, printed, and graphic matter wherein they appear, which constitute the labeling referred to above, are as follows:

THE ORGONE ENERGY ACCUMULATOR

Its Scientific and Medical Use.

cancer
anemia
headaches
cancer tumor of breasts
acute and chronic colds
hay fever
rheumatism
arthritis

varicose ulcers
chronic illnesses
bruises
cuts
lesions
abrasions
wounds
burns
sinusitis
migraine
vascular hypertension
high blood pressure
decompensated heart disease
brain tumors
arteriosclerosis
apoplectic attacks
skin inflammation
conjunctivitis
sterilization of wounds
immobilization of vaginal bacteria
chronic fatigue
undernourishment
diabetes

ORGONE ENERGY BULLETIN

cancer
angina pectoris
constipation
high blood pressure
low blood pressure
Hasedow's disease
abscesses
chronic diarrhea
chronic bronchitis
gastric ulcer
putrefaction of the intestines
inflammation of the eyeball
paradeutosis
anemia
lichenoid eczema
osteoporosis
arteriosclerotic heart disease

duodenal ulcers
thrombophlebitis
compound fracture
Buerger's disease
purulent frontal sinusitis
diabetes
ichthyosis

INTERNATIONAL JOURNAL OF SEX-ECONOMY AND ORGONE RESEARCH

cancer
angina pectoris
asthma
cardiovascular hypertension
epilepsy
multiple sclerosis
choria
cancer pains
raising hemoglobin
elimination of cancer tumors
tumor easily destroyed
lung cancer
tumor of the breast
high blood pressure
low blood pressure
brain tumor
inoperable cancer of esophagus
prevention of metastases
leukemia
fistula
trichomonas vaginalis
colds
cutaneous abscesses
healing of wounds
underweight
anemia
in pregnancy

ANNALS OF THE ORGONE INSTITUTE

cancer
angina pectoris
common cold

The Discovery of the Orgone Vols. I & I'

tumors
anemia
wounds, burns, bed sores
colds
grippe
infection
trichomonas vaginalis
cancer
angina pectoris
arteriosclerosis
varicose ulcer
common cold
pneumonia, prevention of
high blood pressure

Emotional Plague Versus Orgone Biophysics

arthritis
colds
sinusitis
anemia
cancer
leukemia
angina pectoris
vascular hypertension
varicose ulcer
cancer tumor
arthritis

Listen, Little Man

cancer

Ether, God and Devil

cancer

The Sexual Revolution

cancer

Character Analysis

cancer tumors

The Cosmic Superimposition

cancer
common cold
ichthyosis
rheumatic fever
hypertension
diabetes

The Mass Psychology of Fascism

cancer

The Oranur Experiment

colds
cut finger
influenza
tissue degeneration
blood degeneration
cancer

Internationale Zeitschrift Fur Orgonomie

cancer
diabetes
wounds
duodenal ulcer
pernicious anemia
Basedow's disease
high blood pressure
low blood pressure
paradentosis
lichenoid eczema
osteoporosis
angina pectoris
arteriosclerosis
myodegeneratio cordis
prostatitis
myocardial infarction
intestinal trouble
mediastinal malignancy
sinusitis
burns
diabetic neuritis
colds

ANNALS OF ORGONE INSTITUTE

common cold
angina pectoris
cancer

ORANUR PROJECT

counteracts nuclear radiation
chronic colds
chills
low resistance
pneumonia preventive
healing of wounds and burns
old resilient ulcers
prevention of burn blisters
relief of pain in cancer
rheumatism
migraine
neuritis
cuts
shock
atomic warfare
epidemics

THE MURDER OF CHRIST

cancer

PEOPLE IN TROUBLE

cancer
blood
tissues

28. The orgone energy accumulator device, in all styles and models, is adulterated within the meaning of 21 U.S.C. 351(c) in that its strength differs from and its quality falls below that which it purports and is represented to possess, since it is not capable of collecting from the atmosphere and accumulating in said device the alleged orgone energy as claimed to have been discovered and its existence proved by the defendant Reich.

29. The plaintiff is informed and believes that unless restrained by the Court, the said defendants will continue to cause the introduction or delivery for introduction into interstate commerce, of the said orgone energy accumulator device, in all its styles and models, mis-

branded within the meaning of 21 U.S.C. 352(a) and adulterated within the meaning of 21 U.S.C. 351(c). The plaintiff is also informed and believes that unless restrained by the Court the said defendants will continue to cause the said orgone energy accumulator device, in all its styles and models, to be misbranded and adulterated within the meaning of 21 U.S.C. 352(a) and 351(c) while held for sale after shipment in interstate commerce.

WHEREFORE PLAINTIFF PRAYS:

That the defendants, The Wilihelm Reich Foundation, a Maine corporation, Wilhelm Reich and Ilse Ollendorff, individuals, and each of their officers, agents, servants, employees, attorneys, all corporations, associations, and organizations, and all persons in active concert or participation with any of them, be perpetually enjoined from directly or indirectly introducing or causing to be introduced or delivering or causing to be delivered for introduction into interstate commerce in violation of 21 U.S.C. 331(a), any orgone energy accumulator device, in any style or model, and any and all accessories, components or parts thereof, or any similar article, in any style or model, which is misbranded within the meaning of 21 U.S.C. 352(a) or adulterated within the meaning of 21 U.S.C. 351(c):

AND FURTHER PRAYS:

That the aforesaid defendants, their officers, agents, servants, employees, attorneys, all corporations, associations, and organizations, and all persons in active concert or participation with any of them, be perpetually enjoined from directly or indirectly doing or causing to be done any act whether oral, written, or otherwise in the manner aforesaid or in any other manner, with respect to any orgone energy accumulator device, in any style or model, or with respect to any similar article or device while held for sale after shipment in interstate commerce, in violation of 21 U.S.C. 331(k), which results in said article being misbranded within the meaning of 21 U.S.C. 352(a), or adulterated within the meaning of 21 U.S.C. 351(c);

AND FURTHER PRAYS:

That the plaintiff be given judgment for its costs herein and for such other and further relief as to the Court may seem just and proper.

/s/ PETER MILLS

United States Attorney

Address:

Federal Court House,
156 Federal Street,
Portland 6, Maine.

The Response *

OROP DESERT

NO. 1   FEBRUARY, 1954

Love, work and knowledge are the well-springs of our life.
They should also govern it.

RESPONSE

Regarding the Request of the Food and Drug Administration (FDA)
to Enjoin the Natural Scientific Activities of Wilhelm Reich, M. D.

In order to clarify the *factual* as well as the *legal* situation concerning the complaint, we must, from the very beginning, distinguish concrete *facts* from *legal procedure* to do justice to the facts.

Technically, legally the US Government has filed suit against the natural scientific work of Wilhelm Reich.

Factually, the FDA is *not* "The US GOVERNMENT". It is merely one of its administrative agencies dealing with Foods, Drugs and Cosmetics. It is not empowered to deal with *Basic Natural Law.*

ORGONOMY (see BIBLIOGRAPHY on the HISTORY OF ORGONOMY) is a branch of BASIC NATURAL SCIENCE. Its central object of research is elucidation of the Basic Natural Law.

Now, in order to bring into line the legal procedure with the above-mentioned facts, the following is submitted:

The common law structure of the UNITED STATES rests originally on Natural Law. This Natural Law has heretofore been interpreted in various ways of thinking, metaphysically, religiously, mechanistically. It has never concretely and scientifically, been subjected to natural scientific inquiry based upon a discovery which encompasses the very roots of existence.

The concept of Natural Law as the foundation of a secure way of life, must firmly rest upon the practical concrete functions of LIFE itself. In consequence, a correct life-positive interpretation of Natural Law, the basis of common law, depends on the *factual* elucidation of

---

* Instead of appearing to answer the Complaint or to challenge the court's jurisdiction, Reich submitted this Response. It was considered a "crank" letter by the court.

what Life actually is, how it works, what are its basic functional manifestations. From this basic premise derive the claims of natural scientists to a free, unmolested, unimpeded, natural scientific activity in general and in the exploration of the Life Energy in particular.

The complaint of the FDA is factually intimately interconnected with a basic social issue which, at present, is reverberating in the lives of all of us here and abroad.

Abraham Lincoln once said: "What I do say is that no man is good enough to govern another man without that other's consent. I say this is a leading principle, the sheet anchor of American republicanism."

At this point, I could easily declare "I refuse to be governed in my basic natural research activities by the Food and Drug Administration." But exactly here, in this constitutional right of mine, the basic conclusion in the interpretation of Natural and Common Law becomes apparent.

There are conspirators around whose aim it is to destroy human happiness and self-government. Is now the right of the conspirator to ravage humanity the same as my right to free, unimpeded inquiry?

It obviously is NOT THE SAME THING. I shall not try to answer this basic dilemma of American society at the present. I shall only open an approach to this legal and factual dilemma. It has a lot to do with the position of the complainant, trying to enjoin the experimental and theoretical functions of Life in its emotional, educational, social, economic, intellectual and medical implications.

According to natural, and in consequence, American Common Law, no one, no matter who he is, has the power or legal right to enjoin:

> *The study and observation of natural phenomena including Life within and without man;*
> *The communication to others of knowledge of these natural phenomena so rich in the manifestations of an existant, concrete, cosmic Life Energy;*
> *The stir to mate in all living beings, including our maturing adolescents;*
> *The emergence of abstractions and final mathematical formulae concerning the natural life force in the universe, and the right to their dissemination among one's fellow men;*
> *The handling, use and distribution of instruments of basic research in any field, medical, educational, preventive, physical, biological, and in*

fields which emerge from such basic activities and which, resting on such principles, *must by all means remain free.*

Attempts such as branding activities and instruments of such kind as "adulterated," in other words as fraud, only characterizes the narrowness of the horizon of the complainant.

No man-made law ever, no matter whether derived from the past or projected into a distant, unforeseeable future, can or should ever be empowered to claim that it is greater than the Natural Law from which it stems and to which it must inevitably return in the eternal rhythm of creation and decline of all things natural. This is valid, no matter whether we speak in terms such as "God", "Natural Law", "Cosmic Primordial Force", "Ether" or "Cosmic Orgone Energy".

The present critical state of international human affairs requires security and safety from nuisance interferences with efforts toward full, honest, determined clarification of man's relationship to nature within and without himself; in other words, his relationship to the Law of Nature. It is not permissible, either morally, legally or factually to force a natural scientist to expose his scientific results and methods of basic research in court. This point is accentuated in a world crisis where biopathic men hold in their hands power over ruined, destitute multitudes.

To appear in court as a *"defendant"* in matters of basic natural research would in itself appear, to say the least, extraordinary. It would require disclosure of evidence in support of the position of the discovery of the Life Energy. Such disclosure, however, would invoke untold complications, and *possibly national disaster.*

Proof of this can be submitted at any time only to a duly *authorized* personality of the US Government in a high, responsible position.

Scientific matters cannot possibly ever be decided upon in court. They can only be clarified by prolonged, faithful bona fide observations in friendly exchange of opinion, never by litigation. The sole purpose of the complainant is to entangle orgonomic basic research in endless, costly legal procedures a la Panmunjon, which will accomplish exactly NOTHING rational or useful to human society.

Inquiry in the realm of Basic Natural Law is *outside the judicial domain,* of this, or ANY OTHER KIND OF SOCIAL ADMINISTRATION ANYWHERE ON THIS GLOBE, IN ANY LAND, NATION OR REGION.

Man's right to know, to learn, to inquire, to make bona fide errors, to investigate human emotions must, by all means, be safe, if the word FREEDOM should ever be more than an empty political slogan.

If painstakingly elaborated and published scientific findings over a period of 30 years could not convince this administration, or will not be able to convince any other social administration of the true nature of the discovery of the Life Energy, no litigation in any court anywhere will ever help to do so.

I, therefore, submit, in the name of truth and justice, that I shall not appear in court as the "defendant" against a plaintiff who by his mere complaint already has shown his ignorance in matters of natural science. I do so at the risk of being, by mistake, fully enjoined in all my activities. Such an injunction would mean practically exactly nothing at all. My discovery of the Life Energy is today widely known nearly all over the globe, in hundreds of institutions, whether acclaimed or cursed. It can no longer be stopped by anyone, no matter what happens to me.

Orgone Energy Accumulators, the *"devices"* designed to concentrate cosmic Orgone Energy, and thus to make it available to further research in medicine, biology and physics, are being built today in many lands, without my knowledge and consent, and even without any royalty payments.

On the basis of these considerations, I submit that the case against Orgonomy be taken out of court completely.

Wilhelm Reich, M.D.

Chairman of Basic Research

of THE WILHELM REICH FOUNDATION

Date: February 22, 1954

APPENDIX 3

The Injunction *

IN THE UNITED STATES DISTRICT COURT FOR THE DISTRICT OF MAINE SOUTHERN DIVISION

UNITED STATES OF AMERICA,

Civil Action
No. 1056

PLAINTIFF

V.

DECREE OF INJUNCTION

THE WILHELM REICH FOUNDATION
A MAINE Coporation, WILHELM
REICH AND ILSE OLLENDORFF,
DEFENDANTS

Plaintiff having filed a Complaint for Injunction herein to enjoin the defendants and others from further alleged violations of the Federal Food, Drug and Cosmetic Act; and each defendant having been duly served, on February 10, 1954, with a summons and copy of the Complaint; and no defendant having appeared or answered in person or by representative, although the time therefore had expired; and each defendant having been duly served, on February 26, 1954, with a copy of Requests for Admissions; and no defendant having served any answer to said requests, although the time therefor has expired; and the default of each defendant having been entered herein; and it appearing that the defendants, unless enjoined therefrom, will continue to introduce or cause to be introduced or deliver or cause to be delivered into interstate commerce orgone energy accumulators, devices within the meaning of the Federal Food, Drug and Cosmetic Act, 21 U.S.C. 301 et seq. which are misbranded and adulterated, and in violation of 21 U.S.C. 331 (a) and (k); and the Court having been fully advised in the premises:

IT IS HEREBY ORDERED, ADJUDGED, AND DECREED that the defendants, THE WILHELM REICH FOUNDATION, WILHELM REICH, and ILSE OLLENDORFF and each and all of their officers, agents, servants, employees, attorneys, all corporations, associations, and organizations, and all persons in active concert or partici-

* Obtained by default, due to Reich's failure to appear and answer the Complaint, the injunction includes provisions for the banning and destruction of Reich's writings.

pation with them or any of them, be, and they hereby are, perpetually enjoined and restrained from doing any of the following acts, directly or indirectly, in violation of Sections 301 (A) or 301 (K) of the Federal Food, Drug, and Cosmetic Act (21 U.S.C. 331 (a) or (k) with respect to any orgone energy accumulator device, in any style or model, any and all accessories, components or parts thereof, or any similar device, in any style or model, and any device purported or represented to collect and accumulate the alleged orgone energy:

(1) Introducing or causing to be introduced or delivering or causing to be delivered for introduction into interstate commerce any such article or device which is:

(a) Misbranded within the meaning of Section 502 (a) of the Act (21 U.S.C. 352 (a) by reason of any representation or suggestion in its labeling which conveys the impression that such article, in any style or model, is an outstanding therapeutic agent, is a preventive or and beneficial for use in any disease condition, is effective in the cure, mitigation, treatment, and prevention of any disease, symptom, or condition; or

(b) Misbranded within the meaning of Section 502 (2) of the Act (21 U.S.C. 352 (a) by reason of any misrepresentation or suggestion in its labeling which conveys the impression that the alleged orgone energy exists; or

(c) Misbranded within the meaning of Section 502 (a) of the Act (21 U.S.C. 352 (a) by reason of any photographic representation or suggestion with a caption, or otherwise, which conveys the impression that such is an actual photograph depicting the alleged orgone energy or an alleged excited orgone energy field; or

(d) Misbranded within the meaning of Section 502 (a) of the Act (21 U.S.C. 352 (a) by reason of any other false or misleading representation or suggestion; or

(e) Adulterated within the meaning of Section 501 (c) of the Act (21 U.S.C. 351 (c) in that (1) its strength differs from or its quality falls below that which it purports or is represented to possess or (2) it purports to collect from the atmosphere and accumulate in said device the alleged orgone energy; or (3) doing any act or causing any act to be done with respect to any orgone energy accumulator device while such device is held for sale (including rental, or any other disposition) after shipment in interstate commerce which results in said device becoming misbranded or adulterated in any respect; and

IT IS FURTHER ORDERED:

(1) That all orgone energy accumulator devices, and their labeling, which were shipped in interstate commerce and which (a) are on a

rental basis, or (b) otherwise owned or controlled by any one of the defendants, or by the defendants, be recalled by the defendants to their place of business at Rangeley, Maine; and

(2) That the devices referred to in (1) immediately above, and their parts, be destroyed by the defendants or, they may be dismantled and the materials from which they were made salvaged after dismantling; and

(3) That the labeling referred to in paragraph (1), just above, except those items for which a specific purchase price was paid by their owners, be destroyed by the defendants; and

(4) That all parts or portions of the orgone accumulator devices shipped in interstate commerce and returned to Rangeley, Maine, or elsewhere, and awaiting repair or re-shipment be destroyed by the defendants, or, they may be dismantled and the materials from which they were made salvaged after dismantling; and

(5) That all copies of the following items of written, printed, or graphic matter, and their covers, if any, which items have constituted labeling of the article of device, and which contain statements and representations pertaining to the existence of orgone energy, and its collection by, and accumulation in, orgone energy accumulators, and the use of such alleged orgone energy by employing said accumulators in the cure, mitigation, treatment, and prevention of disease, symptoms and conditions:

> The Discovery of the Orgone by Wilhelm Reich
>> Vol 1—The Function of the Orgasm
>> Vol 2—The Cancer Biopathy
> The Sexual Revolution by Wilhelm Reich
> Ether, God and Devil by Wilhelm Reich
> Cosmic Superimposition by Wilhelm Reich
> Listen, Little Man by Wilhelm Reich
> The Mass Psychology of Fascism by Wilhelm Reich
> Character Analysis by Wilhelm Reich
> The Murder of Christ by Wilhelm Reich
> People in Trouble by Wilhelm Reich

shall be withheld by the defendants and not again employed as labeling; in the event, however, such statements and representations, and any other allied material, are deleted, such publications may be used by the defendants; and

(6) That all written, printed, and graphic matter containing instructions for the use of any orgone energy accumulator device, instructions for the assembly thereof, all printed, and other announcements and order blanks for the items listed in the paragraph immediately above, all documents, bulletins, pamphlets, journals, and booklets entitled in

part, as follows; CATALOGUE SHEET, PHYSICIAN'S REPORT, APPLICATION FOR THE USE OF THE ORGONE ACCUMULATOR, ADDITIONAL INFORMATION REGARDING SOFT ORGONE IRRADIATION, ORGONE ENERGY ACCUMULATOR, ITS SCIENTIFIC AND MEDICAL USE, ORGONE ENERGY BULLETIN, ORGONE ENERGY EMERGENCY BULLETIN, INTERNATIONAL JOURNAL OF SEX-ECONOMY AND ORGONE RESEARCH, INTERNATIONALE ZEITSCHRIFT FÜR ORGONOMIE, EMOTIONAL PLAGUE VERSUS ORGONE BIOPHYSICS, ANNALS OF THE ORGONE INSTITUTE, and ORANUR EXPERIMENT, but not limited to those enumerated, shall be destroyed; and

(7) That the directives and provisions contained in paragraphs (1) to (6) inclusive, above, shall be performed under the supervision of employees of the Food and Drug Administration, authorized representatives of the Secretary of Health, Education and Welfare; and (8) That for the purposes of supervision and securing compliance with this decree the defendants shall permit said employees of the Food and Drug Administration, at reasonable times, to have access to and to copy from, all books, ledgers, accounts, correspondence, memoranda, and other records and documents in the possession or under the control of said defendants, including all affiliated persons, corporations, associations, and organizations, at Rangeley, Maine, or elsewhere, relating to any matters contained in this decree. Any such authorized representative of the Secretary shall be permitted to interview officers or employees of any defendant, or any affiliate, regarding any such matters subject to the reasonable convenience of any of said officers or employees or said defendants, or affiliates, but without restraint or interference from any one of said defendants; and

(9) That the defendants refrain from, either directly or indirectly, in violation of said Act, disseminating information pertaining to the assembly, construction, or composition of orgone energy accumulator devices to be employed for therapeutic or prophylactic uses by man or for other animals.

March 19, 1954
   2:45 P.M.

                    /s/ John D. Clifford, Jr.
                    United States District Judge
                    for the District of Maine

A true copy of original filed at 2:45 P.M. on March 19, 1954
Attest:

        Morris Cox
     Clerk, United States District Court

APPENDIX 4

*Appendix to Reich's Reply
Brief to the U.S. Court of
Appeals October 1956* *

APPENDIX

PRINCIPLES INVOLVED

*Love, Work and Knowledge
are the wellsprings of our Life
—They should also govern it.
They are neither "left" nor
"right," but* Forward *directed.*

1. On Free Men

Free men refuse to yield under sentence of death what they are
ready to yield of their own free will. Let us acknowledge this expression of freedom as one of the basic characteristics of free people.
(Brief for Wilhelm Reich, M.D., p. 20.) †

2. Ten Basic Principles of Truthful Conduct in Both Basic Research and Jurisprudence

(1) Battle for Truthful Procedure.
(2) Jury must render verdict fully informed.
(3) There are no authorities on new knowledge, that is "Knowledge of the Future."
(4) Government must not interfere with basic research.
(5) Scientific literature must not be ever impounded or burned.
(6) Non-appearance in Court as self-defense against fraudulent
complaints is a lawful means to avoid legal entrapment by
master connivers.
(7) Bona fide scientists must not be dragged into Court to be

* This is a summary of Reich's original brief to the Court of Appeals. It
is a succinct expression of the point of view from which he regarded his
entanglement with the law.

† Briefs for Wilhelm Reich, M.D., Michael Silvert, M.D., and The Wilhelm Reich Foundation are from Case 5160, Wilhelm Reich, et al., v.
U.S.A. [Footnote in original. Ed.]

harassed to death by competitive commercial or political interests.

(8) Disclosure of scientific information, especially if secret, must not be forced by Court action or by administrative invasion of property and records. There are peaceful ways via conference and agreement.

(9) New knowledge requires new administrative laws.

(10) Judicial errors must be realized and corrected. They must not be perpetuated. (Brief for WR,* pp. 1–2.)

3. Principles of Good Government

On Lawfulness of Laws: Government must never arrogate to itself the right to decide what is and what is not Knowledge of the Future. Government must not falsify facts in presentations to the Court in order to usurp such authority. We do not wish to be governed nor do we wish our civil affairs to be administered by impertinent administrators.

"The dignity and authority of the court must be guarded against disobeyance of its orders; its laws, even if they are not statutory laws, must be obeyed." [In Charge to Jury of Trial Court, Case U. S. A. vs. Wilhelm Reich et al.] True, very true. But the orders themselves must be LAWFUL orders or be based on statutory laws. The courts are guarding over their dignity best by not permitting deceit of the court as was done in this case to happen at all. (Brief for WR, p. 48.)

On Procedure and Law: If procedure is so designed that it kills truth and fact, then procedure, and not factual truth, must yield to revision.

If law is practiced in such a manner that quite obviously to everyone, the guilty one goes free and the innocent and decent one faces imprisonment, then the law practice must be changed as quickly and as radically as possible.

These are the ABC's of justice, obvious a priori. (Brief for WR, p. 49.)

On Responsibility of Science and Medicine: It is the duty of courts of justice to guard over the dignity of the court and against the abuse of privileges of freedom of action and speech. However, scientists and medical men in high position have the terse duty to watch over the independence of scientific inquiry into the laws of nature from any inference whatsoever, especially from ignorance, arrogance, prejudice, political or commercial interests. Science meets with jurisprudence at the very roots of man's existence in fact, reason and functional logic. Let us not, however, neglect those common roots. We have painfully

* Wilhelm Reich. [Footnote in original. Ed.]

learned what replacement of such principles by arbitrary interference has done to destroy security and human happiness. (Brief for WR, p. 49.)

On Security of Natural Science: It is crucial to demonstrate the principle of security of basic research. The very security of Natural Science is in question. (Brief for WR, p. 49.)

On Duties of Public Officials:

(a) "A prosecutor is supposed to be an impartial representative of public justice * * *. A society cannot suppress lawlessness by an accused through the means of lawlessness of the prosecution. A society cannot inspire respect for the law by withholding its protection from those accused of crimes. It was and is the prosecuting attorney's duty to assist in giving a fair trial to a defendant." *Read* v. *United States,* 8 Cir., 42 Fed. 636; *Berger* v. *United States,* 295 U.S. 78, 55 S. Ct. 629, 79 L. Ed. 1314.

(b) "A prosecutor must, to be fair, not only use the evidence against the criminal, but must not willingly ignore that which is in an accused's favor. It is repugnant to the concept of due process that a prosecutor introduce everything in his favor and ignore anything which may excuse the accused for the crime with which he is charged."

(c) "Corruption is an act of an official or fiduciary person who wrongfully acts contrary to duty and to the rights of others. *State* v. *Shipman,* 202 N. C. 518, 163 S. E. 657, 669. Its effect vitiates the basic integrity and purity negativing that which is vital to the due course of justice."

(a), (b) and (c) cited from *United States* v. *Ragen,* 86 F. Supp. 382 (D. C. Ill.).

(d) It is no defense on the part of the prosecution to the charge of suppression of evidence and fraud that the defendants did not appear to contest the entry of the decree. Such an argument might be made by a private litigant, but certainly cannot be set up by public officials. In *United States* v. *Saunders,* 124 F. 124 (8th Cir.), Circuit Judge Sanborn stated at page 126:

(e) "Whatever public officials are empowered to do for the benefit of private citizens, the law makes it their duty to perform whenever public interests or individual rights call for the performance of that duty. *Supervisors* v. *United States,* 4 Wall 435, 446, 18 L. Ed. 419; *City of Little Rock* v. *United States,* 103 Fed. 418,424."

(f) The public officials who prosecuted the action for a civil injunction were required not to impose upon the court by suppression of evidence and bad faith. This rule of adhering to fair dealing and lack of fraud on the part of public officials has been applied mainly in criminal cases.

(g) The appellants in the case at bar and the defendants in the main action had the absolute right to rely on their respect for American institutions and their knowledge that the prosecutors could not honestly prove the allegations of the complaint. They had the absolute right to rely on the cloak of purity which surrounds public officials and the presumption they will perform their duty honestly.

When that cloak has been used to defraud a court for the purpose of making it seem it has jurisdiction in a case where none exists, the court should set the entire proceeding aside under Federal Rule of Criminal Procedure 12. [(a) to (g) from Haydon, Brief for The Wilhelm Reich Foundation, pp. 8–10.]

4. Common Principle of Basic Natural Science and Jurisprudence

The following is a self-evident truth in natural science and its derivative, the judicial common law: *Results obtained by unlawful means are themselves unlawful,* invalid in the technical sense of jurisdiction. The legal profession adheres to these basic self-evident principles of all jurisdiction, since it does not wish to forsake the very foundations of the administration of justice. Conscious, systematic deviation from this principle constitutes the "shyster," defined in Webster's dictionary and in the Encyclopedia Britannica as the "pettifogging lawyer." (WR in Brief for Michael Silvers, M.D., p. 10.)

The court whose jurisdiction is attacked for fraud upon it or for any other cause, must itself, make the inquiry and determination. The question is not whether the Court decided rightly or wrongly, but whether it ever became the duty of the Court to decide at all. (Haydon, Brief for The Wilhelm Reich Foundation, pp. 10–11.)

5. Disclosure of Motivation

The *kind of appearance* discloses automatically the motive and the nature of action. And the motive of action discloses again automatically the purpose of action. It is a priori obvious, what a person was up to, if his entry through a window in the dark of night is secured. The judgment of the action follows from this behavior "a priori," as it were.

The thief reveals himself as does the potential murderer through the manner in which he enters a home. (WR in Brief for Michael Silvert, M.D., p. 10.)

6. On Discovery of Life Energy

(a) *On Oranur Medicine:* Disease is basically no more than the pathogenetic effect of Life Energy gone stale in various forms and phases according to the organ where it happens. Disease can therefore be "drawn out from the organism," as it were, via the Medical DOR-Buster. This principle was well applied to the old type of medicine which used the wet compress, diuretics, laxatives, blood transfusions, etc.

By drawing dead or deadly life energy from the diseased organ, an entirely new principle of medicine, incalculable in its potentialities, is being practiced.

(b) All disease is basically *DOR sickness*. It will be fought at the very roots of disease: by removal of DOR from both atmosphere and organism. Since bacterial or infectious diseases are end results of decaying life, the medical axe is thus also put to the roots of the known diseases of classical medicine.

(c) *On Classical Medicine:* Oranur Medicine is not in disagreement with or antagonistic to classical medicine. On the contrary: It fills the classical concepts of "disease" with a concrete meaning by introducing tangible facts of "Disposition to Disease." The animosity expressed toward Oranur Medicine is not emerging from factual scientific principles, but from commercialized interests in a mass production and sale of artificial drugs and adulterated foods.

(d) *On Orene:* Orene plus mass emerges from atmospheric OR energy, which is a massfree function of the cosmic energy. The planet is in constant metabolic exchange with the energy system of the universe. The so-called galactic and the equatorial OR energy streams are the practically limitless sources of Orene, of Life Energy. Orene is the formative life principle per se. (Brief for WR, pp. 28–29.)

(e) *On Oranur:* A government of nations, bent on abolishing the threat of atomic warfare, on securing peace in the world and bringing health and happiness to people everywhere, could do untold good. Cosmic energy could finally serve useful purposes, since *slowness* of chain reaction and *medical efficiency* have been found in the *cosmic primordial forces*. Such humane efforts would command respect and secure the deep confidence of people in our endeavors everywhere. No single man or organization could accomplish this end; only allied social institutions could do it—from the nursery school to the institute of higher learning, from the professional organization to the military Pentagon in every land. (Record Appendix, Vol. I, "Atoms for Peace vs. The Hig," p. 15.)

7. Entering the Cosmic Age

(a) *My Pledge, 1920, and Dilemma, 1956:* As a young student of medicine, early in 1920, embarked on the study of natural philosophy,

I was impressed by mistakes made by scientists in old age. It was then that I pledged myself to stop publishing scientific information once I reach the age of 60 (March 24, 1957). The best, then, I could do, so I reasoned with myself, would be to live as straight as I could continue to do under the given circumstances. Then let my fellow men decide for themselves what they wished to do with my way of life: imitate it, emulate it, ignore it, or punish me for it by imprisonment for two years. However, I was firmly resolved not to yield to any power on earth in what I called *"my way of life,"* which was to be a life of dedication to knowledge, truth, work and love; to be rather killed than yield to principles other than those enumerated. I would have shaken my head in disbelief had anybody told me at that time that I would actually have to face extinction of my life, work and honor in 1954. I succeeded in discovering the primordial cosmic energy, with it the Life Energy on our planet, and this was my ill fate. The "Pledge" still holds. It has been vindicated:

Having become responsible to a certain extent for the outcome of of the present struggle of mankind for cleanliness, clarity and self-preservation in the cosmic DOR emergency, I am facing the dilemma between my pledge of 36 years ago to stop advising mankind at 60 and the new fact that the discovery of the Cosmic Life Energy seems persistently to become the pivot on which the turn of the age hinges: The turn from the passing age of Mechanism and Mysticism to the functional Cosmic Age.

(b) *On Foundation of Cosmic Age:* The Cosmic Age seems to develop from two basic foundations: The restructuring of the Human Character in newborn ones and the entering into our lives of a technology of the primal, massfree, cosmic energy that fills the universe.

(c) *On Threat to Human Race:* Mankind is facing the most crucial, most dangerous development in its history: The planet on which we live and breed our race together with other living species is being visited, so many reliable observers, including myself, say, by living beings from outer space. These beings are superior technologically to ourselves in the use of motor force, speed, in nearly everything, including intelligence. They have conquered the pull of gravity that keeps us down to earth.

We are approaching crossroads in our existence, in every type of existence, excluding none. Upon our timely and correct decision will depend the fate of our future existence: whether we shall continue to exist at all or shall vanish forever, leaving only a dead planet behind, like the moon which is covered with white ORITE.

(d) *Crossroads Ahead:* We are approaching crossroads of sound versus cowardly judgment in Science, Technology, Religion, Education, Social Administration, and—last but not least—in everyday personal behavior. Survival in good form will depend on how well we manage to read and to pass by the many confusing road signs. And let us not be mistaken: Confusion is the uppermost objective of the old road signs. Let us with Nietzsche's Zarathustra put up *new* road signs.

(e) *On Everybody's Responsibility:* Something strong, true and pregnant with future knowledge will take charge if we are to emerge from those crossroads ahead alive and whole. The responsibility is Everybody's. There are "Fuehrers" no longer. They perished with their age. Everybody, without exception, is on trial. Everybody has been found guilty by the Highest Court, Life, of gross neglect of duty to Truth and its offspring; of treason to The Living. Only a few good guides as in old pioneering times of 1492 or of 1770 have remained. (Brief for WR, pp. 31–34.)

8. Outlook on Pre-Atomic Physics

Science: All human existence rests on some kind of knowledge, no matter how primitive or incomplete; our future, with the past dead, will rest on a *new* kind of knowledge. The present battle raging in the U. S. A. between the commercial forces of "atomic" chemistry and the embryonic knowledge of "pre-atomic," (primordial, massfree) cosmic energy is a part of the dilemma with regard to which road ahead to take: the atomic or the pre-atomic one, or, as in Oranur, a combination of both. Are matter and mass the primary constituents of the Universe, as the mechanico-mystical view demands? Or, is massfree energy before matter the primary source of Existence? "Matter," "Particle," thus are reduced to secondary natural functions in our existence. They will no longer rule our lives. And with the "particle" or "atomic," i.e., chemical view of life, also the rule of chemistry monopolies, artificial drugs, unnatural adulterated foods, noisy, smoky motors will end, never to return. Those who kept the Enemy of Man going hard against orgonomy know that this is the fate awaiting them.

The battle between the material atom and the massfree orgone energy unit in the cosmic energy ocean has been raging for quite a while, subterraneously since about 1924, openly since 1937. There can be little doubt as to the outcome, who is the stronger power and who will win. Will mankind realize this and practice it in its institutions, laboratories, courts, legal decisons, administrative regulations to the fullest extent possible as soon as possible? Before we reach the crossroads ahead, we must have made up our minds in the right, not the wrong direction.

Technology: The OR-Motor was the first step in the technological development toward noiseless, smokeless, smooth-functioning loco-motor machines of the future. Inevitably, the Cosmic Energy Motor will replace the steam engine and the electrical motor. It will be fed by the practically limitless power resources contained in the Cosmic Orgone Energy Ocean. It will be the motor that will carry our Space Ships into vastnesses as yet unimaginable. This motor will finally and irretrievably free man from the so very futile effort of overcoming gravity by way of mechanical thrust, the jet-engine-type of motor function. Both mechanical gravity, theoretical gravity and the machine to carry its own gravity field with itself, the Cosmic Energy Field will be ours in a not too far remote future.

The Cosmic Energy Motor will be the lever which will turn our present civilization into that of the coming *Cosmic Age.* The Cloud-buster and the Spacegun are the twin brothers of the OR motor. The Cloudbuster rests on the principle of the "Orgonomic Potential" from low to high and on the affinity of cosmic energy to water, its "thirst." It is the device that will basically be used in shifting and changing Cosmic Energy potentials, in destroying and creating clouds, in drawing in energy from the cosmic (galactic) energy streams of the universe (see "Space Ships, DOR and Drought," 1954), in the coming utilization of these streams as thoroughfares for the space ships, as it were. (Brief for WR, pp. 34, 26, 27.)

Space and Gravity: The discovery of the Cosmic Life Energy will inevitably lead toward the mastery *of gravity. Gravity* within the confines of our planetary atmosphere, i.e., mass attraction in accordance with the laws of Newton will be practically mastered, as electricity or magnetism today. The technological mastery of *positive* gravity will further lead to the elaboration of tools which will open up the vast field of *negative gravity* or *counter-gravity,* already known today in a theoretical orgonometric manner. A point will be reached in human knowledge regarding the gravity functions where *positive* and *negative* functions will balance each other; in other words, technologically speaking, where *"Hovering"* in the field of gravity of our planet will be made practically possible without the use of mechanical force.

From the functions of negative and neutralized gravity a logical path of research will lead into the technological problems of *Space Travel,* inevitably, just as the discovery of galvanic electricity led to today's electric motor.

The appearance of visitors from outer space, superior to us technologically, forces point-blank, off-the-bat action with regard to our mechanistic scientists before we reach the crossroads ahead and not while we are passing through the tangle: the mechanistic physicist, astronomer and biologist will needs have to realize the change and resign or he will integrate his work within the valid realm of mechanistic thinking, into the total effort of humanity to conquer outer space.

It is necessary to clean up the field of operations regarding space technology before we approach the task itself. Otherwise, to judge from past experiences, we shall be crushed to pulp by those who obstruct our efforts by every means available, in terror of their emotions and orgonomic realities from mere biopathic reasons.

"Authorities": There are *no Authorities in New Realms of Basic Research.* The mechanistic mind is not only not trained to think functionally; the mechanistic mind thinks contrary to most basic qualities of the primal cosmic energy. This is the reason why the mechanicochemistic mind had so consistently and accurately bypassed the existence of this energy in the universe; it is also the reason why it had used the most elaborate methods of evasion, interpreting away, laughing or slandering away all manifestations of the massfree cosmic energy.

- A. The earth planet has been invaded by a powerful intruder from outer space.
- B. The mechanistic physicists are incapable of coping with the problem. Earth's scientists are not equipped methodically or factually to understand how craft can travel through "empty" space with such speed and efficiency. Mechanistic, classical physics knows nothing of the Primal Cosmic Energy.
- C. Frightened and confused, some present-day mechanistic scientists obstruct rational progress in this matter by ridicule, persecution, shabby means of argumentation, cowardly gossip behind the back, slander and outright threat of putting the pioneers of the Cosmic Age into penitentiaries or lunatic asylums.
- D. The so-called ordinary people seem to know the truth or want to know it; but as usual in such struggles it stands by passively, either admiring the pioneers helplessly or supporting the slander of good work by The Enemy of Man. However, their sympathy seems in general to be on the side of the development forward. (Brief for WR, pp. 25, 34, 37, 38.)

9. On the Enemy of Man

Murder by Proxy: The techniques employed by Stalin-Hitler Principles in attempted murder by proxy consist of the following:

(1) Paralysis of the victim through an assault based on an "incredible lie," according to the well-known Hitlerian principle, "The bigger the lie, the easier it will penetrate and be accepted": "Orgone Energy, UFOs, Cosmic Energy *do not exist.*"

(2) Conniving, Conspiring and Confusing (CCC) the legal environment of the victim.

(3) Invading completely the victim's personal and social existence without his consent or knowledge.

(4) Relying on the reluctance of ordinary people to get into trouble while hiding their own little secrets themselves.

(5) Using others, mostly biopathic individuals in psychiatric care, to carry out their conniving, conspiratorial activities.

(6) Accusing the victim of the very crimes the killer has himself committed: Contempt of Court; Fraud.

(7) Obtaining the consent of the victim in major operations designed to kill him.

(8) Letting the victim carry the expenses for the CCC acts. The U. S. public has paid to the Black-Red Fascist combine all expenses of the assault.

(9) Letting the victim confess to a crime never committed.

(10) The goal: Harassment, Confusion and Paralysis before the final kill is delegated to somebody else and is executed by proxy.

(11) Making organized murder appear as suicide. (Beria's method of harassment into insanity or suicide a la Masaryk.)

It does not matter whether the single particular agent of *Treason to Mankind* is aware of his or her role or not. Consciousness of such functions is not necessary to its efficient fulfillment. On the contrary: The less conscious the conspirators, the better the purpose of espionage is served. (WR in Brief for Michael Silvert, pp. 7–9.)

The Enemy of Man never succeeded in eradicating the structural knowledge in man of the Life Energy, and he knew it. The fight of the mechanistic Enemy of Man against functional natural research simply refused to accept proof. Their present catastrophic predicament in the interpretation of the planetary emergency is of their own design and making. There was no amount of proof, no degree in accuracy of observation, and no limit in the exactness of presentation of facts that would have convinced the mechanist whose emotions were set against any proof like the hindlegs of a stubborn mule against the ground. (Brief for WR, p. 36.)

10. On Laws Needed for the Protection of
LIFE IN NEWBORNS and of TRUTH

(From Wilhelm Reich: "The Murder of Christ," 1951, given to Judge
Sweeney on May 7th, 1956.)

A careful study of the realm of social pathology reveals the fact
that there exists no law in the U. S. A. which would directly protect
factual truth against underhanded lie and attack motivated by irrational
interests. Truth is at present at the mercy of chance. It depends entirely on whether a law officer is personally honest or dishonest, emotionally rational or irrational, subjectively inclined toward or against
factual functions. It is most difficult to operate as a pioneer in new
fields of human endeavor, if any emotionally sick individual anywhere
on the social scene can—unhampered—destroy work or knowledge he
dislikes, and if truth is in no position to defend itself against underhanded attack. It is obvious that the future of the U. S. A. and the
world at large depends on the rational upbringing of the newborns in
each generation which will enable them to make rational decisions as
grown-ups. (See Wilhelm Reich: *Children of the Future,* OEB,* October, 1951.) There do not exist any laws as yet to protect newborns
against harm inflicted upon them by emotionally sick mothers and other
sick individuals. However, there are many old laws rendered obsolete
long ago by progress in the understanding of the biology of man, which
threaten progressive educators with extinction if they transgress technically these old laws. These facts, together with the operation on the
social scene of emotionally sick individuals, block progress and the
search for better ways in medicine and education. Although laws which
are serving the welfare of people at large can never accomplish factual
changes, life affirmative laws can protect those who strive practically
for betterment of the fate of humanity. Therefore, two laws, one to
protect Life in Newborns, and a second to protect Truth against underhanded attacks (beyond the scope of libel laws which are not suited
for this purpose), should be studied and formulated by legislatures,
institutions of learning and foundations whose work is primarily devoted to securing human welfare and happiness.

To illustrate: Truthful and thorough investigation of natural love
life in children and adolescents, one of the most crucial tasks in present
day mental hygiene, is held up and rendered helpless by the single
fact that any biopathic individual who himself has been emotionally
warped in childhood or adolescence through frustration of his needs
for love, is in a position to put in a complaint to an Attorney Gen-

* Orgone Energy Bulletin. [Footnote in original. Ed.]

eral's Office to the effect that those who investigate the subject of love life in childhood and adolescence, and make certain suggestions as to its solution, are committing a crime, the crime of "seduction of minors." If the attorney happens to agree emotionally with the complainant, the investigation of fact is completely at the mercy of chance. There exists, according to rich experience in actual situations, no provision on the statute books to prosecute the biopathic individual on the basis that his motivation is not truth-seeking, or helping children or adolescents, but only hate of such scientific procedures. The motivation of an accusation should always be taken into consideration, just as the motive for a murder is taken into consideration.

This example must suffice to illustrate the situation. The Archives of the Orgone Institute contain enough factual evidence to prove that the situation is bad indeed where pioneering efforts are burdened with the rather hopeless struggle with such irrationalism in addition to the factual difficulties entailed in the pioneering job.

(This is the text of a proposal made to the Congress of the U. S. A. in November, 1952 by The Wilhelm Reich Foundation.)

APPENDIX 5

Court of Appeals Decision
December 1956 *

The Wilhelm Reich Foundation
Rangeley, Maine
(AF 1-962)

UNITED STATES COURT OF APPEALS

For the First Circuit

No. 5160

WILHELM REICH ET AL.,
Defendants, Appellants,

v.

UNITED STATES OF AMERICA,
Appellee,

Appeal from the United States District Court
for the District of Maine.

Before MAGRUDER, Chief Judge, and WOODBURY and
HARTIGAN, Circuit Judges.

Wilhelm Reich, pro se; Michael Silvert, pro se; and Charles Haydon
for The Wilhelm Reich Foundation, appellant.

Joseph Maguire, Attorney, Department of Health, Education and
Welfare, with whom Peter Mills, United States Attorney, and Warren
E. Whyte, Attorney, Department of Health, Education and Welfare,
were on brief, for appellee.

OPINION OF THE COURT.
December 11, 1956.

WOODBURY, Circuit Judge. The United States, on February 10,
1954, filed a complaint under § 302 (a) of the Federal Food, Drug, and
Cosmetic Act, 52 Stat. 1043, 21 U. S. C. § 332 (a), in the United

---

* Upholding the decision of the District Court, this decision ignores most
of the thinking submitted by Reich in his briefs.

States District Court for the District of Maine asking for an injunction restraining the Wilhelm Reich Foundation, a Maine corporation, and Wilhelm Reich and Ilse Ollendorff, individuals residing in Rangeley, Maine, from violating § 301 (a) and (k) of the above Act by either introducing, or causing the introduction into interstate commerce, or, while being held for sale after shipment in interstate commerce doing anything resulting in the misbranding of, certain devices known as "orgone energy accumulators," * which it was alleged were adulterated within the meaning of § 502 (c) of the Act and misbranded and summons was duly made on the defendants on the same day that the complaint was filed.

The defendants entered no appearances and filed no answers. Indeed, in a letter to the judge of the court below dated February 25, 1954, the defendant, Dr. Wilhelm Reich, indicated unmistakably that he, at least, had no intention of filing either an appearance or an answer. Dr. Reich wrote to the court in part:

> "My factual position in the case as well as the world of science of today does not permit me to enter the case against the Food and Drug Administration, since such action would, in my mind, imply admission of the authority of this special branch of the government to pass judgment on primordial preatomic cosmic orgone energy."

On the day after this letter was written requests for admissions were propounded by the United States and served on each of the defendants. These requests were ignored, and on March 19, 1954, upon request of the United States, the default of each defendant was entered by the clerk of the court below. On the same day the United States moved for default judgment, its motion was granted, and the court immediately entered a decree of injunction as prayed for in the complaint. By the terms of this injunction the named defendants, and "each and all of their officers, agents, servants, employees, . . . and all persons in active concert or participation with them or any of them" were "perpetually enjoined and restrained" from indulging in the practices set out in detail in the complaint. Furthermore all orgone energy accumulators out on a rental basis or otherwise owned or controlled by the defendants were ordered recalled to the defendants' place of business in Rangeley, Maine, and there either destroyed or dismantled for salvage under the supervision of employees of the Food and Drug Administration, and

* In their commonest form these are box-like structures in which the patient sits for treatment. It is asserted by the Government that these devices were being falsely held out to the public at large by the defendants as at least beneficial in the treatment of a great number of human ills ranging from cancer to the common cold. [Footnote in original. Ed.]

in addition all printed labels and order blanks for orgone energy accumulators, and certain listed descriptive literature pertaining thereto, were ordered destroyed.

Certified copies of the decree of injunction were served on the named defendants on March 22, 1954, and at the same time copies were either served or mailed to several other persons in the Rangeley area who were either employees of or contractors for the defendants in the manufacture and distribution of the devices. At the same time copies of the decree were also mailed to a number of duly licensed physicians in the New York, New Jersey, and Philadelphia area, most of whom specialized in psychiatry, who were known to have used orgone energy accumulators in the treatment of their patients. Included in this group was the appellant herein, Dr. Michael Silvert.

On March 30, 1954, the defendant Ilse Ollendorff as clerk of the corporate defendant sent a telegram to the United States Attorney for the District of Maine stating:

> "The Wilhelm Reich Foundation is far advanced in preparing full compliance with injunction of March 19, 1954 Stop An exact account of measures taken and still in progress will be sent to your office for your information."

No further account of measures taken to comply with the injunction was ever sent to the District Attorney, nor does it appear that in fact any such measures ever were undertaken.

Next, on May 5, 1954, the doctors in the New York-Philadelphia area referred to above, including as we have already noted the appellant Dr. Michael Silvert, applied to the court below for leave to intervene. Their application was denied on November 17, 1954, in accordance with an opinion of the court below of that date reported in 17 F.R.D. 96 (1954). This court affirmed on that opinion *sub nom Baker v. United States*, 221 F. 2d 957 (1955).

We turn now to the case before us which was initiated by the United States Attorney for the District of Maine on July 15, 1955, when, acting under § 302 (b) of the Act, he filed in the court below an information charging the Wilhelm Reich Foundation, Dr. Wilhelm Reich and Dr. Michael Silvert with failing and refusing to obey the injunction of March 19, 1954, and asking for an order to show cause why they should not be adjudged in criminal contempt for their misbehavior. The defendants appeared and filed motions to dismiss, which were denied; the United States moved to amend, its motion was allowed, and the defendants again moved to dismiss and their motions were again denied. They also filed several other motions, all of which were denied, and do not require description or discussion. It will suffice to say that the defendants were given full opportunity for hearing on every occasion.

Eventually, on May 3, 1956, the defendants, in accordance with their request, were put to trial by jury on their pleas of not guilty. They were found guilty by the jury and thereafter sentenced by the court, the corporation to a fine and the individuals to terms of imprisonment. These appeals are from the respective judgments of sentence.

The defendants did not contend below and do not urge here that the injunction of March 19, 1954, had in fact been obeyed. On the contrary, they admitted at the trial that no attempt had been made to comply with its terms. Their contention is that the court below had no jurisdiction to issue the injunction. The individual appellants say that they, both individually and acting through the corporate defendant, of which Dr. Reich was the moving and guiding spirit, were engaged in basic scientific research which no agency of the Government had jurisdiction to interfere with or control, and that furthermore and more specifically, the court below had no jurisdiction to issue the injunction for the reason that it had been procured by fraud and deception practiced upon the court by officers and agents of the Food and Drug Administration. In addition Dr. Silvert contends that he is not bound by the injunction because he was not a defendant in the original suit in which it was issued and had not been served with process therein.

None of these contentions have any merit.

We turn first to Dr. Silvert's separate contention. It has been settled law for a long time that one who knowingly aids, abets, assists, or acts in active concert with, a person who has been enjoined in violating an injunction subjects himself to civil as well as criminal proceedings for contempt even though he was not named or served with process in the suit in which the injunction was issued or even served with a copy of the injunction. *In Re Lennon,* 166 U. S. 548, 554 (1897); *Alemite Mfg. Corp.* v. *Staff,* 42 F. 2d 832 (C. A. 2, 1930) and cases cited. See also Rule 65 (d) F. R. Civ. P. The question then is whether Dr. Silvert had actual knowledge of the injunction of March 19, 1954, issued against the Wilhelm Reich Foundation, and Dr. Wilhelm Reich and Ilse Ollendorff personally. There can be no doubt that he did. He was mailed a copy of that injunction when it was issued, he admitted at the trial that he read the injunction when he received it, and moreover he was one of those who moved to intervene in the suit in which it was issued. Thus it is abundantly clear that he knew of its existence and knew its terms.

The appellants' first jurisdictional contention does not deserve much comment or discussion. Its refutation is obvious from its mere statement. Of course the United States Government has power to forbid and power to take appropriate steps to prevent the transportation in interstate commerce of devices of alleged therapeutic value if they are adulterated or misbranded.

The appellants' second jurisdictional contention deserves only slightly more extended consideration. There can be no doubt whatever that Congress in § 302 (a) of the Federal Food, Drug, and Cosmetic Act gave the District Court jurisdiction over the subject matter of the original suit. Nor can there be any doubt that the District Court obtained personal jurisdiction over the defendants in that suit by legal service of process upon them in Maine. This jurisdiction, once obtained, certainly would not be terminated by any fraud practiced upon the court by the successful litigant. On the contrary, the Court's jurisdiction would necessarily have to continue in order to permit the court to entertain an application by the victims of a successful litigant's fraud to vacate the injunction through the remedies and procedures for relief outlined in detail in *Hazel-Atlas Glass Co.* v. *Hartford-Empire Co.,* 322 U. S. 238 (1944).

And the remedies and procedures available to a defrauded litigant certainly do not include refusal to obey an injunction. It is too well settled to require a lengthy citation of cases that an injunction, temporary or permanent, must be obeyed as long as it is in force and effect. *Howat* v. *Kansas,* 258 U. S. 181 (1922); *United States* v. *United Mine Workers of America,* 330 U. S. 258, 289, et seq. (1947) and cases cited. Nor is this rule a mere technical quirk of procedure, for as the Supreme Court pointed out in *Gompers* v. *Bucks Stove & Range Co.,* 221 U. S. 418, 450 (1911):

> "If a party can make himself a judge of the validity of orders which have been issued, and by his own act of disobedience set them aside, then are the courts impotent, and what the Constitution now fittingly calls the 'judicial power of the United States' would be a mere mockery."

See also the remarks made by Mr. Justice Frankfurter at the bottom of page 311 and the top of page 312 of his concurring opinion in the *United Mine Workers case, supra.*

It follows that the court below did not err in refusing to permit the defendants at their trial for contempt to show in their defense that officers and agents of the Food and Drug Administration had procured the injunction of March 19, 1954, by fraud perpetrated upon the court.

Although the court's refusal to permit the defendants to show fraud in procuring the injunction is the only error asserted by them to have occurred at their trial, we have nevertheless, because the defendants were not represented by counsel in the court below and only partially on appeal, examined the record with particular care. We find ample evidence that Dr. Reich and the Wilhelm Reich Foundation deliberately refused to obey the injunction and that Dr. Silvert aided and abetted them in flouting it. Nor do we find any erroneous rulings of law. Indeed, it is evident from the record that throughout the trial the presiding judge solicitously protected the appellants' rights and gave them full opportunity to present every defense available to them under the law.

Judgment will be entered affirming the judgments of the District Court.

APPENDIX 6

*Appendix to Reich's Brief in Appealing to the
U.S. Supreme Court (January 1957)* *

NEW LAWS NEEDED TO RESTRAIN PATHOLOGICAL POWER DRUNKENNESS

Proposed by Wilhelm Reich, M.D.

> *Wisdom gained in clouds
> is clouded wisdom—
> True wisdom is rooted in
> seething reality.*
>
> *WR 1956.*

First: On Lawfulness of Laws

All new laws proclaimed to govern human conduct in a growing and developing planetary society are designed to secure life, liberty and happiness for all. They must be *Lawful* laws. They must not be unlawful laws. Laws msut be based on facts, not on opinions: on truth, not on falsehood. Unlawful orders are automatically null and void.

Second: On Wellsprings of Social Existence

Love, Work and Knowledge are the wellsprings of our existence. They are the wellsprings of our life, liberty and happiness with equal justice for all. They shall govern the future planetary social organization.

Third: On Life-Necessary Work

Life-necessary work and *naturally grown interhuman relationships* shall determine the lawfulness of laws, social responsibility and social guidance. Life-necessary work and natural interhuman relationships comprise *Natural Work Democracy.*

Fourth: On Unlawful Laws

Laws and orders which contradict, impede, destroy or otherwise en-

* Here Reich expands on one aspect of the changes he felt were necessary to bring the American legal structure into rational conjunction with his view of the human condition. The Supreme Court turned down the appeal.

danger the development of self-determination and violate peaceful development, shall be null and void.

Fifth: On Protection of Truth

Social battles for truthful procedure are lawful battles. Procedures for elimination, evasion, eradication or falsification of factual truth are unlawful.

5-1. Juries, judges, magistrates and other judicial persons or bodies must render their verdicts fully informed on all pertinent facts involved in the case. Verdicts based on untruth, suppression or falsification of evidence are unlawful and intrinsically void.

5-2. Social administrations must not interfere with the search for factual truth and basic new knowledge.

5-3. *Learning is the only authority on Knowledge of the Future.* There are no authorities in undisclosed realms of nature or New Knowledge. Learning and improving ability to find and correct one's own mistakes are, among others, true characteristics of bona fide basic research.

5-4. Scientific tools and publications based on learning and search for new knowledge must never be controlled, censored or in any other way molested by any administrative agency of society. Such acts are unlawful, only perpetrated in dictatorships.

5-5. Bona fide scientists, i.e., men and women engaged in learning and searching for new knowledge must not be ever dragged into courts of justice for their opinions or be harassed by commercial or political interests of the day.

5-6. The citizen has the constitutional right to ignore complaints against him *IF* he can prove to the satisfaction of the court that:

A. He has informed the court of his reasons for ignoring the complaint;

B. His reasons to ignore the complaint were weighty, based on proof of fraudulent presentations of fact, on motives to complain other than bona fide grievance, on a competitive conspiracy using illegal means, etc.;

C. The Judge has been victimized, misled, or otherwise prejudiced;

D. Responding to the complaint would have meant inevitable undeserved disaster.

"A" in conjunction with either of "B," "C" or "D" constitute sufficient reason lawfully not to appear in court as defendant.

5-7. *Disclosure of scientific information must not be forced* under any circumstances, by anyone or for whatever reasons.

5-8. *New knowledge requires new administrative laws.* Laws applicable in one defined realm cannot be applied in a different realm of social or natural functioning.

5-9. *Judicial errors must be realized and corrected.* They must not be perpetuated to the detriment of justice. Perpetuation of judicial errors for whatever reason is unlawful.

5-10. *Judicial procedures which are shown to hamper truth and fact and run counter to the very meaning of due process of law,* which is to safeguard indivisible factual truth, *are to be revised or abolished.*

a) Judges acting in courts of justice are responsible for the safety of truth and fact from any interference by expediency, negligence, political or commercial interests. Judges are administrators of truth and justice, and nothing else.

b) *There is no excuse whatever for judicial error.* The innocent must not fall prey to faulty procedure. Judges are as law officers subjected to the *Boomerang Law* in case of gross neglect of justice. They shall suffer what they meted out unjustly.

c) Judges are to be appointed on the basis of their judicial expertness, not on any other, political, racial, commercial or similar grounds.

d) Judges may only interpret statutory laws. They may not legislate themselves under our Constitution.

e) Judges must not be beneficiaries or advocates of religious, commercial or political enterprises. Their only realm of functioning is jurisprudence and jurisdiction under the Constitution of the U. S. A., in pursuit of common law decency, truth, fact, above-board activity, absence of deceit, etc.

Sixth: On Enemies of Mankind

Individuals, legal persons, organizations and social groupings which advocate or operate on lines adverse to common natural laws or laws under the Constitution, or I to IV of the "New Law," shall be excluded from determining the course of society. They may *talk* against work democracy, but they may *not act* against the socially-organized rule of Love, Work and Knowledge. As *ENEMIES OF MANKIND,* they may not be elected to public office. Those lawfully declared to be Enemies of Mankind, if insisting on acts of fiendship against the self-rule of Love, Work and Knowledge, shall be subjected to the Seventh Law.

Seventh: On Boomerang Justice

Officers of the law, officials of a self-governing society and other highly placed responsible citizens (of the Planet Earth) shall be, if necessary, called before courts of justice to answer charges of *"treason to mankind."* If convicted upon *factual* evidence of treason, they shall be subjected to the *BOOMERANG LAW:* They shall suffer themselves whatever they may have planned against the planetary citizens who through safeguarding *Love, Work* and *Knowledge* as the natural foundations of a self-governing social system have secured true justice at the very source of social life.

Eighth: On Striking Obsolete Laws

In order to secure social rational progress and to prevent the development of irrational human adherence to untimely or hampering tradition, statutory laws which are no longer representing or reflecting living, actual reality shall be stricken from the statute books ("Statutory Rape").

Ninth: On Safety of Natural Love

Natural love functions leading up to and expressed in natural courting mating shall be considered *natural functions at the very basis of man's bioenergetic existence.* They shall be protected and secured by special laws. Human activities adverse to this basic natural function shall be prohibited by lawful procedures insofar as they tend to impede or destroy these natural love functions in infants, children, adolescents and grown-ups. Abuse of natural love functions for political, conspiratorial, commercial, pathological (unnatural) and similar purposes is in violation of this law.

Tenth: On Supervision of Unlawfulness
of Legal Procedures

A special legislative body in Congress shall be established by way of amendment of the Constitution to constantly survey and supervise judiciary and law enforcement procedures. This committee shall be responsible to the people and their organizations of life-necessary work, not only for security of justice, truth and fact; it shall safeguard the constitutional laws which guarantee the development of society to ever more complete self-government of nations, organizations and responsible citizens.

APPENDIX 7

*Appeal to the U.S. Supreme Court on Behalf of
Reich, Silvert, and The Wilhelm Reich Foundation
Written by Charles Haydon (January 1957) ***

SUPREME COURT OF THE UNITED STATES

October Term 1956

WILHELM REICH, THE WILHELM REICH FOUNDATION,
and MICHAEL SILVERT,

Petitioners,

–against–

UNITED STATES OF AMERICA,

Respondent.

PETITION FOR A WRIT OF CERTIORARI TO THE UNITED STATES COURT OF APPEALS FOR THE FIRST CIRCUIT.

Petitioners above named pray that a writ of certiorari issue to review a decision and judgment of the United States Court of Appeals for the First Circuit which affirmed judgments of the United States District of Maine, Southern Division, entered on May 25, 1956, (Petitioners' Rec. App. Vol. IV, pp. 160a–165a), adjudging petitioners guilty of contempt of court and sentencing the petitioner Wilhelm Reich to imprisonment for two years, the petitioner Michael Silvert to imprisonment for one year and the petitioner The Wilhelm Reich Foundation to pay a fine of $10,000.

OPINIONS BELOW

The United States Court of Appeals for the First Circuit delivered an opinion by Woodbury, Circuit Judge. That opinion has not yet been

---

* This document constitutes the final statement of Reich's case in its furthest legal ramifications in terms of established legal structure. As such, it would be the point of departure for any attempt to reopen the case.

reported and is printed as an appendix to this petition. There was no opinion in the District Court.

JURISDICTION

The judgment of the Court of Appeals was dated, made and entered on December 11, 1956. The jurisdiction of this Court is invoked under 28 U.S.C. 1254 (1), 62 Stat. 928.

QUESTIONS PRESENTED

1. Whether, in a proceeding to punish for contempt of a decree of injunction entered by default in a case brought in the name of the United States of America, the contemnors may show, in defense, that the injunction was procured by deliberate fraud perpetrated upon the the court by federal officials and agents.

2. Whether such a decree so obtained is void.

3. Whether United States District Courts have jurisdiction to determine questions of scientific opinion.

STATUTES INVOLVED

Federal Rule of Criminal Procedure, Rule 12,

subdivision (b) (2): "Lack of jurisdiction or the failure of the indictment or information to charge an offense shall be noticed by the court at any time during the pendency of the proceeding."

subdivision (b) (4): "A motion before trial raising defenses or objections shall be determined before trial unless the court orders that it be deferred for determination at the trial of the general issue. An issue of fact shall be tried by a jury if a jury trial is required under the Constitution or an act of Congress. All other issues of fact shall be determined by the court with or without a jury or on affidavits or in such other manner as the court may direct."

REASONS FOR ALLOWING THE WRIT

The decisions in the courts below are warrants to federal agents and officials to perpetrate fraud and deceit in the name of the United States of America upon District Courts for the purpose of achieving private ends through injunctions in civil cases.

This case presents a novel question of law and an unusual set of facts. The subject matter is without precedent.

The Court of Appeals has held that officers and agents of the Federal Food and Drug Administration could procure a valid and enforceable injunction in the name of the United States by the perpetration of a fraud upon a United States District Court. It held further that the District Court did not err when it prevented those afflicted by the fraud from showing it to a jury which tried them for contempt.

The Court of Appeals has thus decided a question of federal law which has not been, but should be, settled by the Supreme Court.

The manner in which the Court of Appeals decided the question gives judicial approval to fraud and is so far a departure from the accepted and usual course of judicial proceedings, and is a sanction of such a departure by the District Court, as to call for the exercise of the Supreme Court's power of supervision.

STATEMENT OF THE CASE
Background

Petitioner Wilhelm Reich is a world renowned scientist. Among his books, those entitled The Function of the Orgasm, Character Analysis and the Mass Psychology of Fascism, were pioneer works and are now accepted and standard texts in the fields of psychology, social science and natural science.

There grew out of his works, his experiments and the medical journals to which contributions were made, the science of Orgonomy. It is not within the scope of this petition to give a complete exposition of Orgonomy which may be obtained only from a study of the literature. This scientific literature reveals that Reich laid bare in psychiatry the concept of character and physical "armoring." Armoring comprises the sum total of character and muscular attitudes which an individual develops as a defense against emotional disturbance which result in anxiety and the like. Examples of such armoring are character rigidity and muscular spasms. These are universally accepted concepts in psychiatry given to the world by Dr. Reich's great works.

It was Dr. Reich's concept that the armoring of a human organism in a given case might be such that it resulted in an inability to absorb its necessary energy or to employ the necessary energy in the organism's living functions.

Prior to the commencement of the proceedings which have given rise to this petition, Reich for a long time had been experimenting to seek this same energy in cosmic forces. He had postulated the theory that the energy, called Orgone energy, might be a contributing factor to the occurrence of hitherto unexplained natural phenomena, such as the Aurora Borealis and hurricanes. Further, if such were the case, this energy would be harnassable for use in the commercial and economic interests of society.

The petitioner, The Wilhelm Reich Foundation, is a non-profit corporation organized in Maine to carry on Reich's work. The petitioner Silvert is a licensed physician and natural scientist who has employed the principles of Orgonomy in the treatment of patients and worked with Reich in recent years in the development of experiments to establish the universal scope of Orgonomy.

The Injunction Claimed to have been Violated.

On February 10, 1954, claiming to act in the capacity of agents of the Federal Food and Drug Administration, a group of officials of that department filed and caused to be served a complaint for injunction under Section 302 (a) of the Food, Drug & Cosmetic Act (52 Stat. 1043, 21 U.S.C. 332 (a)).

As the District Judge saw it,

> "The complaint alleged in general that the said defendants were manufacturing and introducing into interstate commerce certain devices referred to by them as orgone energy accumulators, and were representing in their labelling that such devices were therapeutic agents which were beneficial in the cure, mitigation, treatment, and prevention of innumerable diseases and conditions, including such serious and chronic ailments as cancer, anemia, arteriosclerosis, brain tumors, diabetes, gastric ulcers, Buerger's Disease, and leukemia. It was further alleged that such devices were not effective in the treatment of such conditions and that therefore, they were misbranded within the meaning of 21 U.S.C. 352 (a); it was also alleged that they were adulterated within the meaning of 21 U.S.C. 351 (c) in that their strength differed from, and their quality fell below, that which they were purported and represented to possess." (17 F.R.D. 96)

The "representations" which the complaint contained were purportedly encompassed within the various books, articles and other written material therein mentioned. The prosecution has also stated in releases to newspapers that experiments were conducted which proved the "representations" to be false.

On February 25, 1954, Reich, not represented by counsel, wrote a letter to the District Judge. He said that his work was basic natural research. He made the point that

> "Scientific matters cannot possibly be decided upon in court."

> * * * * *

> "Inquiry in the realm of Basic Natural Law is outside the judicial domain of this, or any other kind of social administration anywhere on this globe, in any land, nation or region."

> * * * * *

"On the basis of these considerations, I submit that the case against Orgonomy be taken out of court completely." (Petitioners' Rec. App. Vol. I, 2nd Part, pp. 18 to 21)

Judge Clifford, presiding at the District Court, overlooked or disregarded Reich's plea to dismiss the complaint. He declared the defendants in default. The agents of the Administration then made it appear to the court

"* * * that the defendant, (sic), unless enjoined therefrom, will continue to introduce or cause to be introduced or deliver or cause to be delivered into interstate commerce orgone energy accumulators, devices within the meaning of the Federal Food, Drug and Cosmetic Act, 21 U.S.C. 301 et seq. which are misbranded and adulterated, and in violation of 21 U.S.C. 331 (a) and (k); and the Court having been fully advised in the premises; * * *." (Petitioners' Rec. App. Vol. IV, page 67a)

The petitioners have charged from the beginning and presently claim that the court was not "fully advised" but received fraudulent advice.

The petitioners charge that evidence was suppressed, falsified and even manufactured. Statements were taken out of context; words and sentences were omitted, and meanings were thus ascribed to literature which were false, corrupt and designed to lead the District Judge to believe that he was being "fully advised", when, in truth, the administration of justice was being perverted by the agents of the Food and Drug Administration to their own ends.

As a result of the fraudulent advice received by the District Court, it entered an injunction which ordered the defendants to return accumulators, to destroy them, to destroy books, to withhold other books, and it prevented the defendants from giving out any information concerning orgone energy accumulators or their use. It required further that the affirmative acts of the defendants be done under the supervision of representatives of the Food and Drug Administration.

The first charge of contempt is based upon these decretal paragraphs which go far beyond the complaint. The second is also defective in that there was no proof that what was shipped was either misbranded or adulterated.

The Contempt Proceedings

The information charging the petitioners with contempt was filed by their former attorney who is now the United States Attorney for the District of Maine (Petitioners' Rec. App. Vol. II, p. 236 et seq). It was purportedly laid under §302 (b) of the Food, Drug and Cosmetic

Act (284 U.S.C. Section 332 (b)), and charged that Reich and the Foundation failed to comply with the injunction and that the three petitioners acted in concert to violate the injunction (Petitioners' Rec. App. Vol. IV, p. 96a et seq.).

Immediately the Foundation moved to dismiss for lack of jurisdiction (Petitioners' Rec. App. Vol. IV, p. 89 (a)). Then, on October 10, 1955, motions were made and argued on behalf of all of the petitioners to dismiss the information and vacate the decree of injunction for suppression and falsification of evidence (Vol. IV, pp. 94a, 110a).

In order further to prove the fraud and suppression which appellants charge permeated the entire case from its inception, on November 4, 1955, the appellant Reich argued his motion to show "illegal misrepresentations in Court of pertinent facts" (Petitioners' Rec. App. Vol. IV, 126a). The motion was denied on that day, despite the argument of Reich that he sought to proceed "with enumeration of the misrepresentations of pertinent facts" (Petitioners' Rec. App. Vol. IV, 139a). He was prevented from so doing by the Court, although at that time none of the appellants were represented by counsel (Petitioners' Rec. App. Vol. IV, 130a).

Thereafter on November 17, 1955, the appellant Reich sought to further his claim of fraud and suppression of evidence by seeking to inspect material subpoenaed from the Food & Drug Administration, including reports on experiments, but that motion was denied as well. The prosecution opposed the motion and successfully sought the quashing of the subpoena (Petitioners' Rec. App. Vol. IV, 156a).

No testimony was permitted to be taken and no hearings were held on any of the motions which were all denied.

Again, at the trial itself, the Court prevented the development of such evidence by the petitioners when it ruled at virtually the outset of the trial:

"I am not interested in anything that took place prior to the issuance of the injunction." (Petitioners' Rec. App. Vol. II, p. 7)

When the witness Berman was asked what kind of effect the accumulator had upon him the court struck his answer that it had a good effect (Petitioners' Rec. App. Vol. II, p. 45). Later, when the witness Bowker was asked whether the accumulator worked, the court ruled:

"We are not interested in that." (Petitioners' Rec. App. Vol. II, p. 66)

The petitioners urge that the denial of hearings on their motion to dismiss and the rulings of the Court below deprived them of the opportunity to show that the entire decree was the result of a fraud and conspiracy, and that they were thus deprived of substantial rights and convicted thereby without due process of law.

ARGUMENT

THERE CAN BE NO CONTEMPT OF AN ORDER PROCURED BY THE FRAUD OF PUBLIC OFFICIALS PERPETRATED UPON A COURT OF THE UNITED STATES OF AMERICA.

Where public officials betray their sacred trust and obtain judgments by the perpetration of fraud upon courts of the United States of America, such judgments are and must be a nullity.

On November 5, 1956, the very day this cause was argued before the Court of Appeals, this Court handed down its opinion in *Mesarosh v. United States of America* (—U.S.—, No. 20, October Term, 1956). Chief Justice Warren there stated:

> "Mazzei, by his testimony, has poisoned the water in this reservoir, and the reservoir cannot be cleansed without first draining it of all impurities. This is a federal criminal case, and this Court has supervisory jurisdiction over the proceedings of the federal courts. If it has any duty to perform in this regard, it is to see that the waters of justice are not polluted. Pollution having taken place here, the condition should be remedied at the earliest opportunity.
>
> " 'The untainted administration of justice is certainly one of the most cherished aspects of our institutions. Its observance is one of our proudest boasts. This Court is charged with supervisory functions in relation to proceedings in the federal courts. See *McNabb v. United States,* 318 U.S. 332. Therefore, fastidious regard for the honor of the administration of justice requires the Court to make certain that the doing of justice be made so manifest that only irrational or perverse claims of its disregard can be asserted.' *Communist Party v. Subversive Activities Control Board,* 351 U.S. 115, 124
>
> "The government of a strong and free nation does not need convictions based upon such testimony. It cannot afford to abide with them."

The *Mesarosh* case was the most recent expression of this court in a long series of decisions commencing with *Mooney v. Holohan,* 294 U.S. 103, in which it has been consistently reaffirmed that judgments and sentences which rest upon a violation of fundamental constitutional rights because of fraud or suppression of evidence are subject to collateral attack.

Even more importantly, the petitioners charge and were prevented from proving that the injunction in this case was obtained through a willfully malicious and oppressive plan or scheme, motivated by ill will against petitioners on the part of persons who used the color of their official status to betray their positions and to defraud the Courts.

Both of the lower Courts have proceeded upon the assumption that the motives of the agents of the Food and Drug Administration, no matter how evil or depraved, were immaterial. This was and is error, for a public official is responsible for the evil results of his evil acts evilly motivated.

The rules governing public officials were declared by this Court in *Wilkes v. Dinsman,* 48 U.S. 89, 129, 130, 7 How. 89, where Justice Woodbury said:

> "Hence, while an officer acts within the limits of that discretion, the same law which gives it to him will protect him in the exercise of it. But for acts beyond his jurisdiction, or attended by circumstances of excessive severity, arising from ill-will, a depraved disposition, or vindictive feeling, he can claim no exemption, and should be allowed none under color of his office, however elevated or however humble his victim.
>
> "For the justification rests here on a rule of law entirely different, though well settled, and is, that the acts of a public officer on public matters, within his jurisdiction, and where he has a discretion, are to be presumed legal, till shown by others to be unjustifiable. (*Gidley v. Palmerston,* 7 Moo. 111; *Vanderheyden v. Young,* Jolins (N.Y.) 150; 6 Har. & J (Md) 329; *Martin v. Mott* 12 Wheat. 31)
>
> "This, too, is not on the principle that innocence and doing right are to be presumed, till the contrary is shown. (1 Greenl. §§ 35–37) But that the officer, being intrusted with a discretion for public purposes, is not to be punished for the exercise of it, unless it is first proved against him, either that he exercised the power confided in cases without his jurisdiction, or in a manner not confided to him, as with malice, cruelty or wilful oppression, or, in the words of Lord Mansfield, in *Wall v. McNamara,* that he exercised it as 'if the heart is wrong' (2 Carr & p. 158, note.) In short, it is not enough to show he committed an error in judgment, but it must have been a malicious and willful error. *Harmon v. Tappenden* et al., 1 East, 562, 565, n.

The original cause, having been an action for an injunction, required an application to the court for the entry of a default judgment. Such a default could not have been entered by the clerk by reason of Federal Rule of Civil Procedure (55 (b) (2)).

The requirement for application to the court arises from the rule that whether or not equitable relief will be granted in any case is always a matter for the sound judicial discretion of the court to which application is made (*Petroleum Exploration Co. v. Public Service Commission of Kentucky,* 304 U.S. 209, *DiGiovanni v. Camden Ins. Assn.,* 296 U.S. 64, 70).

The District Judge recognized these requirements when he said in the decree he signed that the court had been "fully advised". The petitioners contended that the advice which the court received was false and deliberately misleading.

They were prepared to show that the prosecution knew that the allegations of the complaint were sham and that if there were independent proof presented to the District Judge, such proof was manufactured by the prosecution. In none of the literature which has been proscribed by the injunction does there appear any of the so-called false claims of adulteration and misbranding.

Such fraud on the part of the prosecution renders null and void the very decree the petitioners were found guilty of violating, and they have been erroneously denied the opportunity to prove their charges.

In *United States v. Ragen,* 86 F. Supp. 382 (D.C. Ill.), District Judge Igoe held:

> "A prosecutor is supposed to be an impartial representative of public justice. * * * A society cannot suppress lawlessness by an accused through the means of lawlessness of the prosecution. A society cannot inspire respect for the law by witholding its protection from those accused of crimes. It was and is the prosecuting attorney's duty to assist in giving a fair trial to a defendant. Read v. United States, 8 Cir., 42 Fed. 636; Berger v. United States, 295 U.S. 78, 55 S. Ct. 629, 79 L.Ed. 1314. A prosecutor must, to be fair, not only use the evidence against the criminal, but must not willingly ignore that which is in an accused's favor. It is repugnant to the concept of due process that a prosecutor introduce everything in his favor and ignore anything which may excuse the accused for the crime which he is charged."

> * * * * *

> "Corruption is an act of an official or fiduciary person who wrongfully acts contrary to duty and to the rights of others. State v. Shipmen, 202 N.C. 518, 163 S.E. 657, 669. Its effect vitiates the basic integrity and purity negativing that which is vital to the due course of justice."

The Court of Appeals read the record and recognized that petitioners had proof that a fraud had been perpetrated upon the District Court by agents of the Food and Drug Administration, but held that the petitioners were powerless to show that fraud at their trial.

It is respectfully submitted that the holding of the Court of Appeals arose from a misapprehension of the basic principles involved. The lower court proceeded on the assumption that any document called an injunction, temporary or permanent, must be obeyed as long as it is in force and effect, (App. page 6), and cited, in support of that proposition, *Howat v. Kansas,* 258 U.S. 181; *United States v. United Mine Workers of America,* 330 U.S. 258.

In none of these cited cases was the injunction obtained by federal officials who betrayed their own offices and at the same time betrayed a court of the United States.

Howat v. Kansas, 258 U.S. 181, dealt with the violation of an order made pursuant to an unconstitutional statute prior to the declaration of its unconstitutionality. The *United Mine Workers* case dealt with a temporary injunction which had been issued to maintain the *status quo.* The order and decision in that case proceeded on the assumption that the District Court unquestionably had the power to issue a restraining order for the purpose of preserving existing conditions pending a decision upon its own jurisdiction.

The petitioners have never questioned the power of a court to maintain the *status quo.* What is questioned is the validity of an order obtained by public officials who betray their own trust and also defraud the courts.

The Court of Appeals cited *Hazel-Atlas Glass Co. v. Hartford-Empire Co.,* 322 U.S. 238, in support of the suggestion that there were limited remedies and procedures for relief from an injunction obtained by fraud. The *Hazel-Atlas Glass Co.* case dealt with private litigation between private parties, and even there Justice Black, writing for a majority of this Court, suggested that the people of the United States had an interest in the litigation because it involved a patent and thereby authorized an unusual procedure. He said (page 246):

"Surely it cannot be that preservation of the integrity of the judicial process must always wait upon the diligence of litigants. The public welfare demands that the agencies of public justice be not so impotent, that they must always be mute and helpless victims of deception and fraud."

Even in the *United Mine Workers* case, 330 U.S. 258, to which the Court of Appeals referred in support of its proposition, Mr. Justice Frankfurter stated (page 312):

"In a democracy, power implies responsibility. The greater the power that defies law, the less tolerant can this court be of defiance."

There is no position of responsibility or power which requires more intolerance of this Court than the position of public official of the United States of America. While it may be true that in litigation between private contenders our courts might require a more formalistic approach upon the part of a defrauded litigant, there can be and there is no justification for that requirement where the fraud has been perpetrated upon a court by persons acting under the cloak of the majesty of the United States of America.

The Court of Appeals failed to draw the important distinction that exists between erroneous orders and void orders. In the cases which that learned court cited in support of its position that any injunction must be obeyed, the attack upon the injunction was that it should not have been granted. In the case at bar, the attack is that the order was entirely void. Although it was called to the attention of the Court of Appeals, it overlooked the overwhelming weight of judicial authority to the effect that a person charged with contempt may always show in his defense that an order is void. (*Ex parte Rowland* (1882) 104 US 604, 26 L ed 861; *Ex parte Fisk* (1884) 113 US 713, 28 L ed 1117, 5 S Ct 724; *Re Ayers* (1887) 123 US 443, 31 L ed 216, 8 S Ct 164; *Re Sawyer* (1888) 124 US 200, 31 L ed 402, 8 S Ct 482; *Ex parte Buskirk* (1896, CA 4th) 72 F 14; *Exparte Robinson* (1906, CA 9th) 144 F 835; *Lewis v. Peck* (1907, CA 7th Ill) 154 F 273, cert den 207 US 593, 52 L ed 355, 28 S Ct 258; *Brougham v. Oceanic Steam Navigation Co.* (1913, CA 2d NY) 205 F 857; *Abbott v. Eastern Massachusetts Street R.Co.* (1927, CA 1st Mass) 19 F2d 463; *Beauchamp v. United States* (1935, CA 9th Cal) 76 F2d 663; *Russell v. United States* (1936, CA 8th Minn) 86 F2d 389; *Graham v. United States* (1938, CA 9th Cal) 99 F2d 746; *Western Fruit Growers, Inc. v. Gotfried* (1943, CA 9th Cal) 136 F2d 98; *United States v. De Parcq* (1947, CA 7th Ill) 164 Fzd 124; *Pueblo Trading Co. v. El Camino Irrig. Dist.* (1948, CA 9th Cal) 169 F2d 212, cert den 335 US 911, 93 L ed 444, 69 S Ct 482; *United States ex rel. White v. Walsh* (1949, CA 7th Ill) 174 F2d 49; *Evans v. Pack* (1878, CC Mich) 2 Flipp 267, F Cas No. 4566; *United States v. Debs* (1894, CC ILL) 64 F 724; *Foot v. Buchanan* (1902, CC Miss) 113 F 156; *American Lighting Co. v. Public Service Corp.* (1904, CC NY) 134 F 129; *United States v. Atchison, T. & S. F. R. Co.* (1905, CC Mo) 142 F 176; *Brotherhood of R. & S. S. Clerks v. Texas & N. O. R. Co.* (1928, DC Tex) 24 F 2d 426, mod on reh 25 F2d 876, affd (CA 5th) 33 F2d 13, which is affd 281 US 548, 74 L ed 1034, 50 S Ct 427).

The rule of *Howat v. Kansas* and the *United Workers* cases (*supra*) should not be applied under any circumstances to the case at bar. For whatever may be contended as having been the rationale in those cases must yield to concern for confidence in the purity of justice and the integrity of public officials. As Justice Frankfurter pointed out in *Helvering v. Hallock,* 309 U.S. 106, 119, 60 S. Ct. 444, 451:

> "We recognize that *stare decisis* embodies an important social policy. It represents an element of continuity in law, and is rooted in the psychologic need to satisfy reasonable expectations. But *stare decisis* is a principle of policy and not a mechanical formula of adherence to

the latest decision, however recent and questionable, when such adherence involves collision with a prior doctrine more embracing in its scope, intrinsically sounder, and verified by experience."

The suppression of evidence and fraud on the part of the prosecution must not be given judicial approval by a slavish adherence to the procedural argument that the petitioners did not appear to contest the entry of the decree. Such an argument might be made by a private litigant, but certainly cannot be set up by public officials. In *United States v. Saunders,* 124 F. 124 (8th Cir.), Circuit Judge Sanborn stated at page 126:

> "Whatever public officials are empowered to do for the benefit of private citizens, the law makes it their duty to perform whenever public interest or individual rights call for the performance of that duty. Supervisors v. United States, 4 Wall 435, 446, 18 L. Ed. 419; City of Little Rock v. United States, 103 Fed. 418, 424."

The public officials who prosecuted the action for a civil injunction were required not to impose upon the court by suppression of evidence and bad faith.

This rule of adhering to fair dealing and lack of fraud on the part of public officials has been applied mainly in criminal cases. But we have been able to find no rule which prevents prosecuting officials from committing fraud in criminal cases but permits them to defraud a District Court in the prosecution of a civil cause. Quite the contrary is true, especially in a proceeding which interferes, as this one does, with the pursuit of their profession by physicians.

> "A person's business, profession or occupation is at the same time 'property' within the meaning of the constitutional provision as to due process of law, and is also included in the right to liberty and the pursuit of happiness (Butcher's Union Slaughterhouse Co. v. Crescent City Stock Landing Co., 4 S. Ct. 652)." (People v. Love, 298 Ill. 304, 310)

The petitioners in the case at bar and the defendants in the main action had the absolute right to rely on their respect for American institutions and their knowledge that the prosecutors could not honestly prove the allegations of the complaint. They had the absolute right to rely on the cloak of purity which surrounds public officials and the presumption they will perform their duty honestly.

When that cloak has been used to defraud a court for the purpose of making it seem it has jurisdiction in a case where none exists, the court should set the entire proceeding aside under Federal Rule of Criminal Procedure 12.

The District Court had the power, under 21 U.S.C. § 332, to enjoin only such activity as fell within the prohibitions of 21 U.S.C. § 331, except paragraphs (e), (f) and (h)—(j). If the allegations were not true and there was no falsity, adulteration or misbranding on the part of the petitioners, the court had no power to enter the decree. Therefore, when it was apprised of petitioners' charges, the District Court should have ordered testimony to determine whether "* * * they (the jurisdictional allegations) were evidently made 'for the purpose of creating a case' cognizable by the Circuit Court, when none in fact existed" (Chief Justice Waite in *Robinson v. Anderson,* 121 U.S. 522, 527).

And even if the petitioners had not raised the issue of fraud and suppression of evidence in the lower court, since it goes to the heart of the jurisdiction of the court, it is so basic to the administration of justice that it must be noticed by the court at any time during the pendency of the proceeding (Rule 12 (b) (2), F.R.C.P.).

CONCLUSION

Concern for the administration of justice requires that public officials charged with that administration refrain from perverting justice to their private and individual purposes. In this case such a perversion occurred and the result of the judgments below is that those perversions have received judicial sanction by the sacrifice of reality to form. The dignity of the courts of the United States of America cannot be served when decrees, obtained by the fraud of public officials, are enforced by contempt proceedings. No citizen of the United States should be deprived of his liberty as the result of the connivance and fraud of public officials.

THE WRIT OF CERTIORARI SHOULD BE
ISSUED AND THE JUDGMENTS BELOW
REVERSED

APPENDIX 8

An Analysis of the U.S. Food and Drug Administration's Scientific Evidence Against Wilhelm Reich *

Part One: The Biomedical Evidence

By RICHARD A. BLASBAND, M.D. †

In 1954, the United States Food and Drug Administration, through court action, enjoined Wilhelm Reich and the Wilhelm Reich Foundation from transporting across state lines orgone energy accumulators or any literature describing accumulators or any other so-called orgone energy device. In addition, all accumulators were to be dismantled, descriptive literature burned, and all of Reich's books containing the word "orgone" were to be withheld from distribution unless all references to orgone were deleted (1).

This was a most significant achievement for the forces of the emotional plague in its American campaign against Reich, a campaign that began formally and publicly with a smear article by Mildred Brady in *Harpers Magazine* in 1947 and ended with Reich's tragic death in Lewiston Penitentiary in 1957. In February, 1954, prior to the injunction decree, the government served Reich with a summons and complaint that charged him with delivering misbranded and adulterated devices into interstate commerce in violation of the Federal Food, Drug, and Cosmetic Act. The accumulator was alleged to be misbranded in that Reich's literature falsely represented it as an outstanding therapeutic agent, beneficial for use in all diseases, particularly in the cure, mitigation, treatment, and prevention of such diseases as cancer, diabetes, anemia, etc. In addition, the complaint alleged that orgone energy is "non-existent." [1] Rather than argue against the complaint as a defen-

---

* From *Journal of Orgonomy*, Vol. 6, No. 2, November 1972. Reprinted by permission of the author. In this article Dr. Blasband examines the biomedical tests upon which the FDA hoped to prove its contention that the orgone accumulator was a fradulent device.

† Medical Orgonomist. Diplomate in Psychiatry, American Board of Psychiatry and Neurology. Fellow, American College of Orgonomy. [This and the following footnotes are in the original. Ed.]

1. A more detailed and exceptionally lucid account of the legal proceedings may be found in David Blasband's article "United States of America v. Wilhelm Reich," *Journal of Orgonomy*, Vol. I, Nos. 1 & 2, 1967, and Vol. II, No. 1, 1968.

dant in court, Reich wrote a "Response" to the court wherein he maintained that matters of basic natural science cannot be decided in courts (1). Later in February, much of the complaint was restated by the government in Request for Admission. Reich's failure to deny was construed by the court as an admission of the facts set forth.

Before proceeding legally, it was incumbent upon the FDA to disprove Reich's claims about the existence of orgone energy and its physical manifestations and physiological effects in health and disease. Various hospitals, clinics, private medical practitioners, and research establishments were granted funds, supplied with accumulators, orgone blankets, shooters,[2] and Reich's literature in order to run a series of tests on normal and pathological states in mice and humans. In addition, a survey and critique of the physical aspects of orgone energy were made by an FDA physicist.

The biomedical tests focused on the treatment of cancer but also included investigation of normal physiological effects, the Reich Blood Test, anemia, genital infections, ulcerations and burns of the skin, and diabetes. All of these tests, excepting that on diabetes, which is too fragmentary and complicated, are reviewed below with critical commentary.

Normal Physiological Functions

FDA Test 1

a. The investigator, a professor of physical medicine at the Mayo Foundation, reviewed the literature on the medical effects of the orgone energy accumulator (ORAC) including the effects of excitation when sitting in it, namely sensations of "soft glow," "prickling," "heat," and signs of reddening of the skin and elevation of body temperature; and overcharge producing nausea and pressure in the head. That exposure to orgone-radiating bion cultures [3] presumably results in conjunctivitis, inflammation, and tanning was also mentioned.

Twelve human subjects were then tested for the effects of the ORAC on blood pressure, respiratory rate, temperature, and pulse rate. The subjects sat in the ORAC for thirty minutes daily, six days a week for three consecutive weeks.

Results: According to the data obtained, in practically every sitting there was some change noted during and after using the ORAC. For

2. Small accumulators with metal cables leading to iron funnels for localized treatment.
3. Bion cultures are growth of energy vesicles, primary biological OR energy units, on nutrient media. Orgone energy was first discovered in the bion cultures.

example, the following results were noted on one subject during three days of testing:

June 2, 1952	Before	During	After
B.P.	160/100	160/100	150/90
Pulse	68	78	80
Temp.	98.4	98.2	98.2
Resp.	17	17	17
June 3			
B.P.	154/74	142/74	140/76
Pulse	80	78	80
Temp.	98.4	98.6	98.6
Resp.	18	17	18
June 4			
B.P.	140/74	138/72	134/72
Pulse	80	84	80
Temp.	98.4	98.2	98.0
Resp.	18	18	17

On June 5, 6, and 7, the subject's temperature went up 0.2 degrees F. while sitting in the ORAC, and, on the 6th and 7th, another 0.2 degrees after leaving the ORAC.

Another test on normal human subjects involved the measure of the amplitude of the pulse of a finger. This test is an indication of the quality of circulation.

Results:

In ORAC

Subject	Beginning	12.5 min.	25 min.	immediately afterward
1.	10.7	10.8	16.7	15.3
2.	12.2	10.3	9.3	13.2
3.	8.9	9.3	10.6	7.0
4.	12.2	17.0	13.8	16.4 (millimeters)

FDA Conclusion: "In no instance throughout all of these studies were we able to confirm the claims for subjective and objective changes made in the literature. If a patient perspired or if the circulation was slightly increased it was only in an amount which could be expected in any person who sat in the closed box on a hot day. None of the spectacular local changes or systemic changes described in the literature were found to exist insofar as our checking of these claims was concerned."

Comment: A review of the literature reveals that no "spectacular" changes were claimed by Reich with regard to the above-tested parameters. Reich does say that temperature will rise from 0.5 to 1.5 degrees F. while using the ORAC in the case of unarmored subjects (2). The 0.4 degree change noted in some of these tests is close. The basic effect of the ORAC is a gentle vagotonic expansion. Paradoxical results due to clamping down against the expansion will be found in armored subjects. Results may be understood only from a functional framework.

The investigator agrees that certain changes did indeed occur but proceeds to explain them away as being due to a "cloesd box on a hot day." First, the ORAC is open sufficiently in front to provide for circulation of air. I personally have never felt one to be "closed" or "stuffy" except where DOR was high or from accidental overcharge. The walls are always cool to touch. Most important, however, is the fact that one could not validly reach the investigator's conclusion unless the results were compared to suitable controls, *i.e.,* the same subjects sitting in an identical metal-less enclosure on the same day. This fault in experimental design invalidates the entire test.

Cancer

Reich's Findings on Cancer

In 1948, in his book *The Cancer Biopathy* (3), Reich reports his findings regarding the etiology and treatment of cancer. In brief, he found that the cancer process as a premortal putrefaction secondary to characterological resignation, sexual stasis, and organismic "shrinking" due to energy loss. The cells lack a normal charge and lose their integrity and cohesive strength. They then break down into more primitive functioning energetic units, bions. Bions, in turn, may reorganize into protozoa, the cancer cell per se, or disintegrate into various forms of rot bacteria and a virusoid type of carcinogenic particle Reich called the "T-body."

Observation of blood in various clinical conditions, including cancer, led Reich to the development of a blood test. This included determination of rate of red blood cell disintegration into bions in physiological saline, estimation of the cohesive quality of the blood under autoclavation, and culture for bacteria and T-body growth. Integration of the results of all three tests permitted an estimate of the orgone energy level of the organism and diagnosis of the cancer biopathy—a condition that exists months or years before actual tumor formation.

The discovery of the biological orgone energy in cultures of radiating sand bions led Reich to attempt the treatment of cancer in mice. The softening effects on tumors was striking. Discovery of the ORAC permitted a simpler method of treatment. Mice with spontaneously-developing tumors were placed in a mousesized ORAC for one-half hour each day. The over-all life span of the treated mice was found to be two and one-half times greater than that of an untreated control group. There were about thirty mice in each group. Reich found that use of the ORAC slows cancer progression by increasing the OR charge of the red blood cells. The charged cells then destroy the T-bacilli and protozoal cancer cells without the organism's needing to give up its own charge. In this way, the cachexia and anemia, which always accompany cancer, are prevented or, if already present, are alleviated or eliminated. A serious complication, however, results from the need to eliminate the tumor breakdown products. This often leads to severe renal and liver impairment and sometimes directly to death.

After the success with mice, Reich accepted human patients for treatment. It was understood that no patients were to be accepted for treatment unless their personal physician had agreed that the case was hopeless and that the orgone therapy of cancer was still in an experimental stage. No promise of cure was made, and no fee charged.

Reich reports that 13 cases of hospital-diagnosed, X-ray-treated cancer and 2 cases that he had diagnosed were treated with orgone therapy. All were in the advanced stages of the disease. All experienced some relief from pain and decrease in tumor size. Breast tumors disappeared in all cases. In 3 cases, there was no prolongation of life; in 6 cases, life was prolonged by five to twelve months, and, in 6 cases, the shrinking process was stopped. The following cases were reported in some detail:

1. A 57-year-old widow with tumors of the cranium and bone of the arm received daily treatment with the ORAC for eight weeks. The cranial tumors became smaller and softer; the tumor material was eliminated via nose bleeds. X-rays confirmed the tumor shrinkage. After two months of treatment, the patient developed aversion to the ORAC because she could not tolerate her increasing sexual sensations. She died shortly thereafter.

2. A 33-year-old woman suffered from severe weight loss, intestinal hemorrhages, and excruciating pains in the rectum. A colostomy had been previously performed for cancer of the colon. She received treatment with the ORAC for ten weeks, during which her blood tests and hemoglobin level improved, pain decreased, and her appetite improved, but she failed to gain weight. Destroyed tumor cells were found in the intestinal discharge. She terminated treatment because of her severe neurosis and died about nine months later.

3. A 42-year-old woman developed tumors below both knees two

months after radical excision of the left breast for cancer. She complained of pulling pains in the arms and neck, headaches, chronic constipation, and severe pains in the legs. She received treatment with the ORAC for eight months. Four days after begining treatment, she was able to walk better and the numbness in arms and legs disappeared. Two days later, her family physician found the tumors to be smaller and advised continuation of treatment. X-rays at the end of two months of treatment showed far-reaching disappearance of shadows in her bones and complete disappearance of the tumors of the knees. One year after terminating treatment, she was still well.

4. A 45-year-old man had been diagnosed as having inoperable carcinoma of the esophagus with almost complete obstruction. He was unable to take solid food, and took liquids only with difficulty. He received treatment with the ORAC for twelve weeks. During this time, choking sensations disappeared, energy level improved, he became able to swallow soft foods without difficulty, gained five pounds, and showed improvement in his blood picture. He was still alive and working eighteen months after terminating orgone therapy.

Four cases are reported briefly, describing problems of elimination of tumor material. One patient died of suffocation due to swelling of the throat in her attempts to eliminate a softened brain tumor; another died of cardiac decompensation following kidney failure in eliminating a stomach tumor; a third died of kidney complications following softening of ovarian tumors; and a boy of five died of enlargement and degeneration of the liver in the course of eliminating an adrenal tumor.

In summary, then, it is clear that, despite some serious problems in eliminating tumor material, Reich found that high concentrations of OR exerted a distinctly beneficial, life-positive effect on the cancer process. Also, despite the elimination of tumors in several cases, "cures" could not be claimed because of the remaining characterological and biopathic structure, which is the core problem in the disease.

FDA Test 2, on Cancer

a. *Cancer Mice:* The Jackson Laboratory in Bar Harbor, Maine, was given a grant to study the effect of mouse-sized accumulators on mice with leukemia and mammary adenocarcinoma. Monocytoid leukemia cells were injected into 200 "BAF 1" mice, half of which were treated with the ORAC for 30 minutes daily. Mammary adenocarcinoma cells were injected into 100 "DBA 1" mice, half of which were treated 30 minutes daily in the ORAC.

Results: There were no noted differences between the control groups and the treated groups in rate of death, final age at death, weight gain, or malignancy of the autopsied tissue.

Comment: This test is so different from Reich's mouse experiments that it cannot be considered a valid test of his claims. The Jackson Laboratory used transplanted tumor cells instead of letting the tumors develop spontaneously. Spontaneous tumors grow more slowly and permit a natural development of defensive reactions. According to one authority, transplanted tumors are, in effect, grafts and not new growths generated by any kind of "cancer agent" (4). We would therefore expect any life-positive effects of the ORAC to show up far more readily with the spontaneous tumor than the transplant. Further, the energetic state in leukemia is quite different from that of other forms of cancer and must be treated as a separate problem.

Of greatest importance is the fact that the treatment rooms at the Jackson Laboratory were located only 100 feet from two X-ray machines which were used at least several times a week. I was studying at the Jackson Laboratory at the time and conveyed this information to Reich. He replied, informing me that the oranur effect produced by the irritation of OR by X-radiation would produce spurious results.[4] When the investigator in charge of the experiment was informed of this fact, he admitted to not having read any of the literature where the oranur problem is discussed. He said he wished to remain "completely objective."

b. *Brief treatment of genital cancer in humans:* Nineteen women with malignant tumors of the ovaries, uterus, or cervix were treated with the ORAC or OR blanket for fifteen minutes daily for one to seventeen days, depending upon the case. Most of the women were about 45 years old, most had received prior treatment with X-ray, and a few had received radium, also. In practically every case, the cancer tumor was massive or widespread throughout the abdomen and pelvis. The average duration of treatment was four or five days, though several were treated for only two or three days. Seven patients died while in the course of orgone therapy.

FDA Conclusion: "In no instance was there any evidence to suggest that this form of treatment is efficacious in the management of patients with carcinoma."

Comment: This test was run at Johns Hopkins Hospital. I have always found large city hospitals to be either energetically "dead" or overcharged from oranur. They are one of the worst places to test the effects of orgone energy. The laboratory must have been testing for "miracles" if they thought they would see any significant results from the ORAC with such brief treatment in such an extensive disease.

4. Studies carried out by the Oranur Research Laboratory show a significantly shorter life span in cancer mice treated by the ORAC in an oranur environment.

c. *Various Other Forms of Malignancy in Humans:* Eleven terminal or near-terminal patients were treated with the ORAC or OR blanket at Holy Ghost Hospital in Boston. Six of the patients were in their seventies or eighties and several were senile, blind, or deaf. Included were four cases of carcinoma of the breast, five cases of gastrointestinal carcinoma, a case of carcinoma of the prostate, and a case of carcinoma of the cervix. Practically all had received prior surgery, X-ray treatment, or homone therapy. The ORAC or OR blanket was used for ten to thirty minutes daily for five days up to sixty days.

FDA Conclusion: Except for one case where it was noted that the patient felt a "pleasant warmth," the effects of the ORAC and blanket on pain, tumor size and consistency, and clinical course were deemed "not noticeable."

Comment: Here again, this is a large city hospital, and it is therefore a poor place to test the effects of orgone energy's life-positive qualities. Despite this, there were some interesting reactions recorded in the case protocols which were apparently ignored in the test conclusions. Length of treatment was apparently determined by "how much the patient could tolerate." We are not told, however, what criteria were utilized in determining this tolerance. The patient who felt the "pleasant warmth" stopped using the blanket because of "lack of interest" in the experiment. This sounds very much like an aversion reaction because of intolerable sensations. This 78-year-old patient with metastases from a primary breast tumor lived for another six months after thirty days of treatment with the blanket. In all cases, the duration of daily treatment seems short, though this well may have been due to limits of tolerance to OR.

All of the cases are poorly described, especially with respect to the criteria utilized in estimating the effects of the ORAC or OR blanket. Six of the patients were apparently too decrepit to give an accurate appraisal of subjective changes. In most of the cases, no mention is made of changes in clinical course or tumor size or consistency following use of the OR devices. Where mention is made, it is fragmentary and inadequate.

The Reich Blood Test

Reich found that the rate and form of disintegration of red blood cells into bionous vesicles was one indication of the degree of orgonotic vitality of the organism as a whole (3). The RBCs of a healthy person with reasonably high orgonotic charge will appear at a magnification of 300 power under the microscope to be oval and taut, with deep blue frames, well-defined membranes, and strong energy fields. Disintegration usually begins at 3 or 4 minutes, when large blue bions will form.

At the end of the test period, 20 minutes, some cells will still be intact.[5] In cases of shrinking biopathy, with or without tumor formation, the RBCs will often appear misshapen, the frames a pale blue, the membranes poorly defined, and the fields weak. Disintegration proceeds rapidly into small bions or spikes of T-bacilli and is often complete within 2 to 10 minutes.

FDA Test 3

The government test consisted of examining the rate of disintegration of RBCs in two groups of subjects, those "believed to be healthy," all employees of the Nassau Hospital in Mineola, N.Y., and those with a known diagnosis of malignancy of various organs. There were fifteen subjects in each group. The blood was examined in physiological saline solution and Ringer's solution. The per cent of "crenation" [6] of the red cells was recorded at 5, 20, and 30 minutes.

FDA Results and Conclusions: No statistical analysis or conclusions are reported. Our own analysis reveals, however, a striking difference between the RBC disintegration rate in the two groups. This is summarized below:

Percentage of Breakdown in Physiological Saline

	50–100% at 5 minutes	*80–100% at 20 minutes*
Proven cancer	10 out of 15	9 out of 15
Normals	4 out of 15	6 out of 15

Comment: The above results are impressive confirmation of Reich's findings. There are two and one-half times as many cancer patients as "normals" with 50% disintegration within five minutes. Among the "normals," we find that three out of the four with rapid disintegration rates were hospital personnel dealing directly with patients, and they most likely had ample exposure to the debilitating effects of X-radiation. One of these was a radiologist, another a supervisor in obstetrics and gynecology. Except for one nurse located in central supply, all "normals" with slow disintegration rate were in nonmedical positions —accountants, researchers, etc. A follow-up today of the four suspect cases might well reveal actual tumor formation.

In lieu of concluding that Reich's test can indeed diagnose cancer, the government investigator offers a number of objections designed to

5. Since atmospheric nuclear bomb tests in the 1950s, red cell disintegration takes far longer in general because of the overcharge caused by atmospheric oranur.

6. Crenation is a shrinking of the red cell due to changes in salt concentration. Lacking orientation in orgonotic phenomena, this is the closest the investigator could come to an adequate description of bion formation.

explain away the positive findings. These include the question of covering the preparation between observations, the use of Ringer's solution, the inconstancy of RBC disintegration from day to day, and false positive results. Of these, only the last two are of any possible significance.

The investigator found that weekly tests of the same individual revealed marked changes in percent of "crenation" ranging from 5 to 100% at 5 minutes and comparable changes at 30 minutes. This inconstancy, the author says, ". . . no doubt results from crenation being a phenomenon which occurs in red cells which have been removed from their normal environment to an environment of physiological saline solution or Ringer's solution, neither of which are capable in many cases of maintaining the normal red cell shape."

We, too, have noted variations in rate of disintegration. This does not, however, invalidate Reich's test. OR levels do vary from day to day and week to week. However, when repeated testing is done, the general energy level is reflected in the disintegration rate that most often appears. In the test for constancy just described, on the third and fourth weeks, the rate was 60% and 100% respectively, but on the first, second, fifth, and sixth weeks, it was 5% at five minutes. If the Reich autoclavation and culture tests also indicated a high energy level, we would feel confident in assuming the 5% figure to more accurately reflect the general energy picture. In any case, when in doubt, repeated tests can be run. As to the author's "explanation," we would want to know *why* these solutions are in some cases capable of maintaining RBC shape while in other instances they are not. It is far more likely that the inconstancy has something to do with the living cells, which are always changing, rather than the solutions, which are precisely mixed to maintain normal salt concentration and osmolarity.

In regard to the false positive results, the investigator cites two cases in which, he maintains, a diagnosis of malignancy would have been made on the basis of the Reich test, but none was found. What was found was a benign breast tumor in one case and gastritis in another. To an orgonomist, these are not false positive results. If supported by the other two parts of the blood test, these results would indicate decreasing orgonotic vitality. Indeed, the patients in question were suffering from severe disturbance in energy metabolism; the tumor and gastritis were the overt symptomatic evidence. The relationship between benign and malignant lesions and gastritis and cancer of the stomach is well known to medical science (5).

The investigator also offers the following opinions: about bions—"usually called crenation"; about T-bacilli—"many correspond to . . .

myelin forms, chylomicrons, and 'blood dust' " and their ". . . breaking off [from the RBC] is a familiar observation"; decrease in pulsatory
activity in orgonotically weak blood—". . . is again a familiar general-
ization that crenated cells do not show the flicker phenomenon to any
appreciable extent"; and "The orgone energy field . . . does not correspond to anything which is seen with the microscope. . . ."

Reich never maintained that many of the things he described were
not "familiar." His point was not their familiarity but their *significance*.
Crenation is a mechanical process signifying only the concentration of
the salt of the artifical medium. Bions and T-bacilli are indications of
inner bioenergetic charge. It is of no significance to a classical mechanistic physician that RBC pulsation decreases in cancer. To an orgonomist, this phenomenon is the very essence of the cancer process. The
investigator's blindness to this essentially different way of seeing things
is literally borne out in his complete inability to see the orgone energy
field around the red cells.

We note with interest that "blood dust" exists; the hematologist's
"air germ," we presume.

Anemias

In the orgone therapy of cancer, Reich noted improvement in the
charge of the blood with regular use of the ORAC. Concomitantly,
blood hemoglobin levels also improved. Reich states that the effect of
ORAC on blood is one of the "best established" findings and that
anemias were eliminated within three to six weeks (3: p. 283).

FDA Test 4

Twelve cases of anemia were treated with the ORAC at the New
England Baptist Hospital. Ten were cases of acquired hemolytic anemia,
myelophthisic, or iron deficiency anemia secondary to underlying cancer. There was one case of pernicious anemia and one of unknown
origin. All patients received the ORAC treatment simultaneously with
blood transfusion, ACTH, penicillin, and other drugs. Routine red cell
count, hemoglobin, and hematocrit tests measured patient progress.
Treatments with the ORAC usually lasted for one hour each day. The
average length of treatment was ten days to two weeks, although there
were a few who were treated for thirty days.

Results: "A careful analysis of the results of this series of experiments reveals no case in which the 'orgone energy accumulator' was of
clear-cut benefit to the patient. In several of the cases, the patient continued to fail in spite of the 'orgone energy accumulator' and other conventional treatments. In some, the expected benefit was derived from

the usual form of treatment, but did not appear to be enhanced by the use of the 'orgone energy accumulator.' "

Comment: In some respects this test was better-conceived than the clinical cancer tests. The author certified that no X-ray equipment was located in that part of the hospital where treatment took place, and the length of individual treatments and total duration of treatment seem satisfactory. Again, however, there is still the problem of the energy state of the large hospital. In addition, there is a serious flaw in experimental design—the simultaneous use of other forms of treatment. Granted, there is an "expectable" clinical change with the use of various medications, and, in some clinical studies, it is possible to say whether a change was remarkably better or worse than expected. But in an experimental testing situation, one must control for all possible variables in order to definitively conclude that a single agent had produced a change. The failure to do this invalidates this test for any conclusion beyond the vague statement given that the cases *"did not appear"* to be enhanced by the ORAC. Another uncontrolled variable is the possible antithetical effect of various drugs on OR. It is known for example that penicillin has a life-positive and sulfa drugs a life-negative effect on the entire organism. The effects of other medications, especially in combination with high concentrations of OR, are completely unknown.

There was again an "aversion reaction" to the use of the ORAC. A 68-year-old man with anemia of two and one-half years duration refused to enter the ORAC after nine treatments.

Minor Genital Disorders

FDA Test 5

a. Six cases of cervical infections were treated by the FDA investigators with the orgone shooter. Though it is not stated, presumably a test tube filled with steel wool was attached to the end of the shooter cable and then inserted into the vagina for treatment. Reich found that bacteria in the vagina will be immobilized after only one minute of irradiation with the shooter (2: p. 36). Patients in this test received irradiation for one to four minutes: Cultures from the cervix were taken before and after treatment.

FDA Conclusion: In all cases, the conclusion was that "Orgone energy did not affect the bacterial flora of this patient."

Comment: Reich did not claim that OR would kill all bacteria, which is what would be necessary for there to be complete lack of organisms on a culture. Tests for *immobilization* of bacteria, which Reich did claim, were not done. Therefore, the test is not a valid test of Reich's findings. Interestingly enough, despite the tester's disclaimer, there were indeed definite changes in the bacterial flora. In most cases, prior to treatment the cultures grew non-hemolytic staphylococcus aureus, gram-negative rods, and alpha streptococcus. In two of these, after treatment there was no growth of alpha streptococcus and in one case no growth of streptococcus and staphylococcus.

b. Twelve patients with a protozoal infection of the vagina, trichomonas vaginalis, were treated with the OR shooter for one to five minutes weekly for one to four weeks, depending upon the case. Before and after treatment, the vaginal discharge was examined microscopically in a hanging drop preparation and in a dried smear.

Result and FDA Conclusion: Four patients described a "warm sensation" while being treated. In all cases, protozoa were seen before and after treatment in the hanging drop preparation. In two cases, no protozoa were found on the dried smear following the third treatment and before and after the fourth treatment. The conclusion in all cases was, "Orgone energy did not affect trichomonas vaginalis in this case."

Comment: Reich described the "immobilization" of trichomonas when they were brought into proximity with the highly charged sand bions (SAPA bions) (3: p. 250). We are not told in the clinical protocol whether the protozoa seen in the hanging drop preparation were living or dead, moving or immobile. One cannot say, therefore, whether this aspect of the test was a valid replication of Reich's studies. The absence of protozoa in the two cases may indicate a decrease in their number because of the OR treatment.

This change is not commented upon by the tester, nor does he find the "warm sensation" at all remarkable. His negative conclusion obviously does not take all the facts into account.

Superficial Wounds and Burns

Reich reported the healing of two cases of chronic, intractable, varicose ulcers after several weeks of treatment with the OR shooter (3: p. 287). Burns were found to heal rapidly with little pain or blistering (3: p. 285).

FDA Test 6

Case a: The patient complained of anesthesia of the great toe of the right foot, of four weeks' duration. There was a 3 to 4 cm. ulceration at the base of the proximal phalanx. A three inch funnel attached to an OR shooter was held two to five inches from the ulcer. The patient stated that he felt a "breeze" at the outset of treatment and, at the end of ten minutes, the toe felt "warm." Bacterial cultures before and after treatment revealed no change. There is no further comment on the clinical course.

Case b: A young man, paralyzed from the waist down following an automobile accident, was having considerable trouble with draining decubitus ulcers over the hips. Two months of antibiotic treatment had been of little help. The right wound was treated for twenty minutes with a six-inch funnel held nine inches from the skin. The left hip remained untreated. The examining physician makes no further report on the patient except to state that, "the patient says that the wound on right side is draining less than the wound on the left and is healing faster."

Case c: A 38-year-old man was admitted to the Maine General Hospital in Portland, with first, second, and third degree burns of the face, neck, and both arms, following an explosion of illuminating gas. A large funnel attached to the OR shooter was used over the area of the right hand and forearm. Five hours later, blisters began to appear over the burned surfaces of the body including the treated area. The case protocol does not mention a comparison between treated and untreated areas.

Case d: The patient was admitted to the accident ward with burns of the face, ears, nose, neck, dorsum of fingers and hands, and volar surface of the wrists, following an explosion of a stove. The six-inch funnel attached to the OR shooter was placed about four or five inches from the right side of the neck for twenty minutes. Within five minutes of beginning treatment, the patient said that the neck felt better and that it was less painful than the face and hands. Fifteen minutes after conclusion of treatment, the neck still felt better than face and hands. The next day, there was no evidence of blistering of the neck, but there was some blistering of the face, forehead, right ear, and the dorsum of the right hand. The neck continued to heal nicely, while crusting, blistering, and pustule formation continued in the other burned areas.

FDA Conclusion: No conclusions are stated in the case protocols.

Comment: These are, in general, poorly studied and reported cases, especially with respect to follow-up after treatment. Subjective and objective effects of orgone energy are obvious in three of the cases. The apparent failure in case c—the patient burned by exploding illuminating gas—remains unexplainable, though, as mentioned above, no comparison between treated and untreated areas was mentioned. The relatively DOR-free area of Portland, Maine, compared to Boston and Baltimore may have been a significant factor in permitting the life-positive effects of OR to be manifested.

DISCUSSION

Certainly one could not have expected the investigating scientists and physicians to conduct a functional inquiry into the biomedical effects of orgone energy. Functional thinking, as Reich once put it, is something one has to "get into the blood." It takes years of work with orgone energy and the investigation of life with respect to its orgone-energetic qualities before one can get this organic "feel" for it. For those steeped in mechanistic tradition all of their professional lives, functionalism is an attitude, I believe, that is impossible to achieve, especially without characterological restructuring.

What one could have expected, however, is objectivity, fairness, and neutrality. Except in a few instances, this, too, was missing. The tests were so poorly designed in the main, one can only conclude that the principal attitude of most of the investigators was one of contempt, thinly veiled by scientific objectivity. One doesn't read Reich's literature because one wishes to remain "completely objective." Another uses senile, deaf, and blind patients in a study where subjective response is important.

If we take a purely mechanistic orientation, we find that there are two conclusions that may be drawn from the tests. When mice with transplanted mammary carcinoma and mice with transplanted leukemia are treated with the ORAC in the vicinity of X-radiation, there will be no change in life span or tumor characteristics. And, when near-terminal or tumor-ridden cancer patients are briefly treated with OR accumulators or blankets in large city hospitals, there is no apparent change in life span or tumor characteristics. For reasons given earlier, however, these are not appropriate tests of Reich's claims and are therefore invalid as evidence against him. All the other tests are flawed in experimental design or actually demonstrate a life-positive effect from the ORAC or OR shooter, so no negative conclusion is permissable.

Reich's not appearing in court was certainly correct for the reasons he gave, but there is little doubt that, if he had chosen to appear, the FDA would have been hard put to disprove his work on the basis of this evidence.

References

1. Blasband, D.: "The United States of America v. Wilhelm Reich," *Journnal of Orgonomy,* 5:56–129, 1967.
2. *The Orgone Energy Accumulator.* Rangeley, Me.: Orgone Institute Press, 1951.
3. Reich, W.: *The Discovery of the Orgone, Vol. II: The Cancer Biopathy.* New York: Orgone Institute Press, 1948.
4. Blasband, R.: "Cancer Research: A Comment on the Literature," *Orgonomic Medicine,* 2:75–81, 1956.

APPENDIX 9

An Analysis of the United States Food and Drug Administration's Scientific Evidence Against Wilhelm Reich *

Part Three: Physical Evidence

by C. Fredrick Rosenblum
July 1973

The first set of actual tests to be considered consists of three experiments done by a Dr. Little at Bowdoin College. The entire report consists of a single typewritten page, containing one paragraph for each experiment. It is so extremely condensed that little is available except results; this is poor scientific practice, since the tests can neither be repeated exactly nor analyzed for technique. We will consider each test briefly below:

(1) The first test is an attempt to detect "heat waves" in or near (it is not clear) an accumulator by detecting changes in the index of refraction of the air by the "knife edge" test. Results were entirely negative. There is no supporting description of the set-up, which must include whether or not fluorescent lights, x-rays, etc. were present, as well as the weather—in other words the conditions under which the accumulator was used. It is not even clear, from the scanty description, if the apparatus could detect heat waves if they were present in the magnitude likely to result if the accumulator were working.

(2) The second test consists of an attempt to show differences in the rate of electroscopic discharge within and without an accumulator. The report states:

> "Identical quantitative measurements were obtained both inside and outside the orgone accumulator . . . Results were exactly what would have been expected . . ."

Again, there is no supporting description of the set-up or the experimental conditions. We can only conclude that, on the basis of orgone physics, the orgone tension inside and outside the accumulator must

---

* From *Journal of Orgonomy,* November 1973. Reprinted by permission of the author. Fredrick Rosenblum, an orgonomic physicist, examines the physical tests upon which the FDA was prepared to prove in court that no energy such as orgone existed.

have been the same. It is most interesting that identical discharge rates were "exactly what would have been expected;" we will come back to this later.

(3) The third test was an attempt to reproduce the temperature difference. It reads in part:

">. . . Simultaneous measurements of the temperature within the small "shooter" box and a copper lined box of the same size picked up at random about the laboratory were made . . . Identical and reproducible vertical temperature gradients were found in each . . ."

It is hard to conceive of a sloppier experiment. Absolutely no attempt was made to match the control; it is extremely unlikely that a box "picked up at random" would be balanced thermodynamically with the accumulator, and there are no supporting measurements to demonstrate balance. There is not even the indication that they were aware this was necessary. Worse, from the description the control itself would constitute a one-fold accumulator. Finally, there is no graphical data, no indication of the period of time involved, and no description of the weather, laboratory conditions, etc. From all standpoints this is totally invalid test; a minimum requirement in reproducing someone's experiment is to demonstrate that one is aware of all the parameters the originator feels are important, and take them into account, even if they are not well understood at the time.

The main body of experimental evidence is contained in a brief entitled "Investigations on the Orgone Energy Accumulator" and represents experiments done at MIT under Dr. Kurt Lion. It begins as follows:

"I do not argue at all with Dr. Reich's theories, beliefs, or his physical hypotheses. I do not intend to discuss whether his science is right or wrong . . . I also do not claim that I understand his theory, but I do claim that I know how to measure temperature."

The paper also ends with a similar statement. It is extraordinary to note that most of the brief consists in doing *exactly* what Dr. Lion said he would not do; namely, engage in theoretical discussions of Reich's theories, beliefs, and physical theories! There are also several descriptions of classical theories of physics, such as the ionization mechanism in the geiger tube or in electroscopic discharge, presented as fact. This is done not to give a fair comparison of classical theory and orgone physics; but rather to bias the discussion, with no mention of numerous experiments designed exactly to test these theories.

Each of the five basic experiments will be presented in sequence below. The first five pages are devoted to a detailed discussion and analysis of the theory of how the accumulator works. Dr. Lion has already stated that he does not understand the theory, and in these pages he proves it. Consider:

> "It is hard to understand how such an accumulator is expected to work. If the outer plastic layer *absorbs* the incident atmospheric or cosmic Orgone Energy, then one should expect that this incident energy is wholly or at least partly *absorbed* before it comes in contact with the metal, and that, therefore nothing or at least not much can enter the metal, let alone the inside of the "Accumulator." This effect is even enhanced by the effect of the iron sheet which "repels" or "reflects" that amount of Orgone Energy that is transmitted through the absorber and sends this radiation back into the absorber."

He concludes as follows:

> "We may summarize our results obtained so far by stating that we were unable to understand how "Orgone Energy" can be collected or accumulated or concentrated in the Orgone Energy Accumulator. We are unable to understand it even in terms of the inventor's own explanation . . ."

Dr. Lion has already stated he does not intend to address Reich's physical hypotheses, and that he does not understand the theory, but cannot resist analyzing theory anyway. It is hard to know why Dr. Lion has so much difficulty, when a clear and concise description is readily available from a few lines in the *Cancer Biopathy:*

> "The metal walls reflect the energy and the heat to the *outside* as well as to the inside. So, in order to provide an insulation against the surrounding air, we cover the metal box with organic material such as cotton . . .
> *The outside of the apparatus consists of organic material, inside of metallic material.* Since the former absorbs the energy while the latter reflects it, there is an *accumulation* of energy. The organic covering takes up the energy from the atmosphere and transmits it to the metal on its inside. The metal radiates the energy to the outside into the cotton and to the inside into the space of the accumulator. The movement of energy toward the inside is free, while toward the outside it is being stopped." (2)

It is not reasonable to expect Dr. Lion to comprehend orgone physics on a functional level; it is reasonable to expect an accurate understanding of a simple description.

Temperature Measurements

This is the title of the first section containing actual experiments. It begins with more theoretical discussion, including a remarkable conclusion that orgone should continuously enter the box, converting into heat until "temperatures of thousands of degrees would be obtained." This is ridiculous; a high school text will tell you that a dynamic equilibrium would soon be established, with heat flowing to the outside, to prevent such a buildup. Such a statement would never survive presentation to any reputable scientific journal.

There are several pages of discussion of the difficulty in making meaningful measurements, since the environmental temperature is fluctuating, with an accurate description of the lagging effect. It is concluded that one could either place the accumulator and control in a constant temperature environment, or make a great number of measurements and average them, to overcome this problem. Both approaches were used; however, no attempt was made to thermodynamically balance the accumulator and control, and the inbalance is clearly evident in their graphs, which show frequent crossing. There is further no description of the laboratory, fluorescent lighting, weather, etc. The first experimental results, carried out over two weeks, are as follows:

accumulator average: 20.18° C
control average   : 20.27
air temp. average   : 20.06

They conclude: "There is no indication of an effect of orgone energy."

The result from this experiment certainly does not support this conclusion. If the accumulator were not functioning, a meaningful average of the three temperatures should be equal within the limits of experimental error (hundredths of a degree); clearly they are not. It means at least that the averaging technique is invalid (i.e., insufficient data). It may also mean the presence of drafts, some orgone function present, etc. *In any case the temperature differences need to be explained.* The experiment is meaningless because the control is invalid; to be valid, it must show an average temperature equal to the air within the limits of precision of measurement. The large difference between control and air temperature (0.21° C) makes it impossible to evaluate the functioning of the accumulator, since this difference is larger than To-Tair. (0.12° C).

The results of the second test, also carried out over a two week period, are given below:

local temperature: 24.80° C
control   : 24.77
accumulator   : 24.58

In this case the control is much more reliable, since it differs from the air temperature by only 0.03° C. Yet this section is concluded:

"If anything, then the Orgone Accumulator shows the lowest average temperature as compared with the room outside the accumulator or with the control box."

Incredible! Dr. Lion accepts the fact that a pattern exists, but the meaning of his finding totally escapes him: that *any* average temperature of the accumulator which is different from the air, whether positive or negative (in this case 0.22° C) is a significant departure from the main body of modern physics. It can only be concluded that Dr. Lion is either blindly committed to a negative conclusion on the accumulator, regardless of the data, or that he does not understand the basic physical principles underlying the experiment.

Electroscopic Observations

Unfortunately, one does not find any observations in the sense of experiments in this section; it is *entirely* theoretical. The main thrust is that a slower discharge rate in a metal box is expected on theoretical grounds, due to shielding from ionizing radiation, and therefore Reich's observations in the accumulator are meaningless as evidence for orgone energy.

This section begins with a discussion of electroscope functioning:

"Now, there is one statement I have to make that may sound superfluous, but it is necessary, namely that: an *electroscope* measures *electricity,* or, more accurately, it measures electric charge."

It goes on to a discussion of discharge mechanisms, positive and negative ions, humidity, cosmic rays, etc. There follows several quotations from the Cancer Biopathy, in which Dr. Lion endeavors to show that Reich was confused, did not know what he was talking about, and that electroscope discharge is an electrical process and no connection between this purely electrical process and orgone energy is shown. Reich's own candid and puzzled statements about an energy which has electroscopic effects but is not electromagnetic are used against him. In short: electroscopic discharge is an electrical process, can only measure electrical phenomena, and should discharge slower in a metal box anyway. This is the entire substance of this section.

Such an approach, of course, does not stand up to the most basic principles of scientific methodology. Since the electroscope is *defined* to respond only to electrical energy at the beginning, other possible interpretations are precluded; yet the theory of ionization was precisely what the experiment challenged. One cannot analyze new theories by asserting old dogma.

This brings us to the second criticism: this section completely ignores a number of other experimental findings, which not only require explanation, but are entirely relevant to any discussion of the relationship between orgone energy and electroscopic observations (about which Dr. Lion is puzzled). These include the charging of rubber gloves in the accumulator, the charging of a celluloid disc in the sun, the correlation of the discharge rate with the weather and especially with To-T. It further does not mention the fact that Reich was aware of the objection of less ion contact with the electroscope in the box, and tested it, by circulating the air with a fan (theoretically increasing contact with ions in the air) but with no measureable effect on the discharge rate.

Third, no responsible scientific evaluation of an *experimental* phenomena can exist without further *experiments*. It is clear, of course, that Dr. Lion would have simply asserted the classical theory even if he had done the discharge rate and found a slowing, but it is ludicrous to discuss the theoretical implications of an experiment which was not even performed. This is a most basic investigative principle, and it is only by rigorously adhering to such principles that progress is made. We may recall that at Bowdoin College (to their credit) the discharge rate within and without the accumulator was actually tested; not only did they find the rates to be identical, but that this was "exactly what would have been expected." It would be hard to find a more dramatic refutation of Dr. Lion's methodological approach. Evidently these two physicists cannot draw the same conclusion from the same classical theory. And that is exactly why experiments are necessary.

Finally, we may mention in passing (although this experimental evidence may not have been available to the FDA) that the discharge rate *near* (but not in) an accumulator was found to be signifigantly slower than one far removed from an accumulator. Obviously this test removes the objection about shielding, and poses even more difficulty for the classical physicist.

Geiger Muller Counter Reactions

This section begins:

> "We come now to a new possibility of proving the existence of Orgone Energy, the Geiger Muller counter reactions . . ."

Already, this approach is a methodological error, from the standpoint of "proof": demonstrating orgone functions with GM counters requires the presence of functioning accumulators to charge them. Yet the author goes on to say:

> "This may indeed sound encouraging, especially after we had not found how alleged Orgone Energy could be collected in the Orgone Energy Accumulator, after not finding the temperature difference To-T

which the inventor claimed as convincing proof for the existence of Orgone Energy . . ."

If the investigator does not have a functioning accumulator, how can the tubes be charged? This is indeed the hard way round for "proof," since any accumulator which could charge GM tubes would also show a measureable To-T.* Reich himself did not consider the findings in the GM tubes to be satisfactory proof of orgone functions, which is why he went on to construct the vacor tubes, to deal with the objection of ionization. The GM reactions represented, historically, a further extension of knowledge about orgone energy, rather than an attempt at further proof. The present experiment simply assumes that the accumulators were functioning at all times and under all experimental conditions; such an assumption is simply not in accord with numerous other findings (such as variation with the weather).

Dr. Lion continues in the text by outlining the classical theory of GM functioning as an ionization process, and the normal use of GM counters. Then he states:

"I do not know whether the discoverer of the Orgone Energy used his counters under *abnormal circumstances,* nor do I want to explain his findings of abnormally high counting rate."

He then spends the next few pages implying that Reich's GM tubes or the counter was used improperly, or was damaged, or defective:

"If I were to continue experiments with a counter which was completely dead, even in the vicinity of an X-ray source, I would be extremely doubtful as to the validity of such experiments . . . Although the author is fully aware of the possibility of a defective counter that is "completely dead," and that, several days later, gives him 6,000 to 10,000 counts per minute, or that gives him an electric shock when he touches the handle, and although serious damage of such a counter is a more than likely possibility, he draws the conclusion that the counter was now soaked with Orgone Energy . . ."

Again:

". . . that otherwise the number of counts can go up considerably, or can go down, that a Geiger counter when overloaded can be temporarily or permanently damaged so that the readings taken with such a counter do not have *any physical meaning.*"

---

* Theoretically, it might be possible for an accumulator to have a charging function in the presence of zero To-T, although there is no experimental evidence to support this. The point is that To-T is the most reliable parameter yet found to establish that an accumulator is indeed functioning.

Obviously, the meaning is clear: any GM counter which does not behave in the prescribed fashion is damaged. This *really* begs the question, because it was precisely the abnormal functioning which led to a new discovery. Fortunately this kind of thinking did not prevent experiments from being done.

In the tests, three tubes were used. The first was left uncharged, as a control. Another was used to make readings in a "shooter" immediately, and after 39 days of charging. The last was used to test a large accumulator in a hospital, immediately and after 30 days of charging. The results were consistent: in all cases a 15–20% decrease in counting rate was observed when tubes were in the accumulators, before and after charging.

This experiment clearly demonstrates the inability of the mechanistically-trained physicist to comprehend functional experiments. There is no realization that the experiment cannot be repeated mechanically. Actually, Reich's experiment was not repeated at all; he mentions he felt the presence of an orgone room, operating over a long period of time with a high local energy concentration, was necessary for the effect to occur. Testing was done with single accumulators, without the presence of an orgone room, in an environment and atmosphere which is not described (he obviously does not realize that this is not only important but crucial). No "dead" period is described, which Reich felt was an indication that changing was taking place. Further, any location with high voltage, fluorescent lighting, or x-ray machines (this automatically disqualifies the hospital test) invalidates the experiment. These factors are not mentioned. Finally, no comment whatsoever is made on the results of the vacor tube experiments. In summary, results of any geiger counter testing cannot be compared with Reich's findings until the conditions under which they are carried out approximate those existing in Reich's laboratory.

Quivering Waves

This section begins with a quotation from Reich, reading in part:

> "Wavelike quivering and flickering of the atmosphere."

There follows a discussion of heat, and Reich's inconsistent statements about it, and Reich's claim that he could visualize the flickering with an orgonoscope. An attempt was made to visualize the flickering—not in the atmosphere, nor with an orgonoscope—but in an accumulator, by attaching a piece of paper with straight lines to the inside and illuminating it with an electric bulb:

> "However, of four observers, not one has been able to see any quivering or flickering waves within the Orgone Energy Accumulator."

The control consisted of a hot plate which clearly showed quivering above it when the heater was turned on.

First, the experiment requires a functioning accumulator in a reasonably clean environment, with observers who are characterologically free enough to see orgone movement if it were present. Second, no atmospheric tests—such as the West to East flow, or flickering between the stars—were made, nor were there any observations in an orgone room. Third, in the Cancer Biopathy (3) Reich describes how the observations are made: that it requires the eyes to be dark-adapted for at least one half hour, that an orgonoscope with celluloid disc and magnifying lens was used to objectify the experience, and that a dim green bulb whose intensity was varied was placed in the accumulator to increase visibility of the phenomena. He further describes the use of the orgonoscope in the daytime, and the care and patience necessary to visualize the flickering. None of this is mentioned in the present observation. The nature of the "electric bulb" is not specified, but was probably an ordinary white bulb, in which case all possible visual observations would be totally washed out. Again, we may state that the experiment was not carried out under conditions which even begin to resemble those used by Reich.

The "Objective Visibility" of Orgone Energy

This final section represents attempts by Dr. Lion to obtain effects on photographic film from the orgone energy. It begins with several pages of description of observations in the orgone room (which are mentioned but not actually repeated). There follows the argument that if the orgone can be seen, it must have sufficient magnitude as to register on photographic emulsions. In the experiment, a strip of sensitive photographic paper (with a control strip in another container) was placed in an accumulator for 90 hours and developed—with no evidence of exposure. The conclusion:

> "We can only draw one conclusion from these experiments: The light that Dr. Reich claims to have seen did not exist outside of his eyes."

In the Cancer Biopathy (4) Reich does describe successful experiments involving photographic plates, although under different conditions: he mentions that all plates in a room with a number of bion cultures consistently showed fogging. Here it would have been more meaningful to repeat Reich's experiment with bion cultures; it is specifically mentioned that the visual phenomena were less intense without the cultures. We can only conclude that the orgone concentration present was not of sufficient intensity to cause a photographic effect. It is most interesting that another published experiment, which is quite easy (technically) to perform, is neither mentioned nor attempted: that of the x-ray of the field of a pair of hands.

Conclusion

This material, then, is the entire substance of the FDA's scientific case on physical grounds against the orgone energy accumulator. As such, it is a sad commentary on the level to which the quality of a scientific inquiry can fall; obviously the experiments are far below normal scientific standards, or those of any major journal. We may briefly summarize the salient features: highly biased viewpoint, both in the FDA itself and among the actual testors; sloppy experiments; misinterpretations and distorted readings of simple text; contradictions in their own theoretical conclusions; and even meaningful results, which are ignored.

What can we say about the investigation in general terms, from a larger standpoint? Obviously orgone physics poses special problems for the mechanistically-trained scientist, who is simply not prepared to deal with functional phenomena. Yet it may still be asserted that or-gonotic phenomena *can* be rationally evaluated by classical science, with the present model of scientific inquiry. The principle is simple: attempts to reproduce new findings must be carried out under conditions as similar as possible to the original situation. This does not require the investigator to accept or even fully understand the nature of a new theory; it only requires an ability to grasp what the originator describes and believes is important, and to repeat it, even if it appears nonsensical. In this the FDA experiments show their most glaring deficiency. It simply cannot be stated that the conditions under which the tests were carried out, in most cases, even vaguely resembled the original environment. And until this is realized, and taken into account, it cannot be said that Reich's work has undergone a fair scientific evaluation.

References

1. C. Fredrick Rosenblum, *An Analysis of the United States Food and Drug Administration's Scientific Evidence Against Wilhelm Reich, Part Two: Physical Concepts,* the Journal of Orgonomy, Volume 6, Number 2, Nov. 1972.
2. Wilhelm Reich, *The Cancer Biopathy* (New York: Orgone Institute Press, 1948), pp. 99–100.
3. *Ibid.,* pp. 89–94.
4. *Ibid.,* p. 73.

APPENDIX 10

Plans and Instructions for the Accumulator *

Construction of a three-fold
ORGONE ENERGY ACCUMULATOR

I. *Construction of a three-fold orgone energy accumulator*
  1. General information
     a. The accumulator is made in six panels which are to be screwed together. All panels except the bottom are constructed in the same manner, and differ only in dimensions. Each panel consists of an inner surface of iron and an outer non-metallic surface which enclose a braced wood frame and alternate layers of glass wool and steel wool.
     b. The materials specified may, if necessary, be replaced by other materials: celotex, plastic or other wall board may be used in place of the upson board; felt cotton batts, rock wool, etc. may replace the glass wool; steel wool, held by wire mesh may replace the inner sheet iron. If substitutions are made, some adjustments in dimensions of the frames may be necessary.
     c. Consult the accompanying drawings and tables for dimensions, construction details, etc.
  2. Construct the frames.
     a. Cut the 1¼″ x 1¼″ pine to the specified lengths. Mitre the corners and join with corrugated fasteners. Brace each frame with a 3″ piece of pine placed in the center of the frame. Join with corrugated fasteners.
     b. Construct the bottom frame with ¾″ x 1¼″ pine. No bracing is necessary.
  3. Attach the outer surface.
     a. Cut upson board to fit inside the rabbets of each frame. Fasten in place with small nails.
     b. Cut two pieces of ¼″ plywood the same size as the bottom frame. Screw one piece of plywood to frame using flat head wood screws.

* Plans and Instructions for the accumulator were issued by the Wilhelm Reich Foundation on request. Their ready availability emphasizes that the Foundation was less interested in profit than in providing accumulators for as many people as possible. Later models used metal (non-aluminum) screening and polyethylene instead of steel wool and glass wool.

4. Place the glass wool and steel wool in the panels.
   a. Place a layer of glass wool about ¼″ thick upon the inner surface of the upson board and inside one of the frames. Avoid lumps and holes. Do not compress the glass wool.
   b. Next place a layer of steel wool upon the glass wool. Steel wool pads when unrolled are the correct thickness. Make the layer as uniform as possible; leave the steel wool "fluffy".
   c. In a similar manner place the remaining alternate layers of glass wool and steel wool in position.
   d. Place the glass wool and steel wool in the other panels.
   e. Bottom panel has different number of layers. (See drawing)
5. Attach the inner surfaces.
   a. Cut the sheet iron slightly smaller than the frames. Round the corners and file the edges where necessary. Punch holes through the iron and nail to the frames with small nails.
   b. For the bottom panel, screw the remaining piece of ¼″ plywood to the frame. Then attach sheet iron over this.
6. Attach side supports to bottom panel.
   a. Cut two pieces of 1″ x 3″ pine stock 24″ long.
   b. Screw them onto the outer surface of the panel, across the front and back.
   c. The supports should project 1¼″ from each side of the bottom panel.
   d. Attach a slider to the under surface of each projection.
7. Assemble the accumulator
   a. Place one side in position on the projections from the bottom panel. Drill two screw holes through frame of side panel into bottom frame. Screw through side panel into bottom panel using 2½″ wood screws.
   b. Place the back in position. Drill and screw through side into back.
   c. Place the other side in position. Drill and screw through side into back and bottom.
   d. Place top in position. (It will project over front of side panels.) Drill and screw through top into both sides and back.
   e. Screw three hinges to the door frame. Place the door in position and screw through the hinges into side frame.
   f. Screw the hooks into the door, the eyes into side frame; one set on the outside, one set inside. The inside hook will screw into the brace of the door frame.
8. Coat the outer surface of the accumulator with shellac.

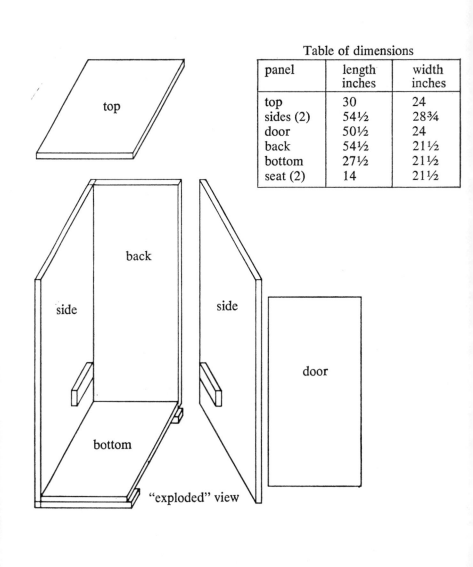

Table of dimensions

panel	length inches	width inches
top	30	24
sides (2)	54½	28¾
door	50½	24
back	54½	21½
bottom	27½	21½
seat (2)	14	21½

top

back

side

side

door

bottom

"exploded" view

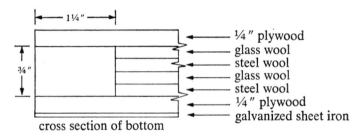

1¼"

¾"

¼" plywood
glass wool
steel wool
glass wool
steel wool
¼" plywood
galvanized sheet iron

cross section of bottom

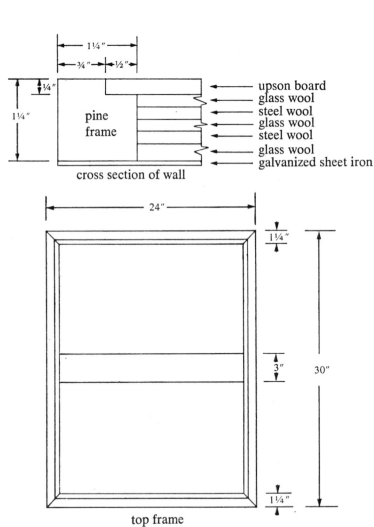

1¼"

¾" ½"

¼"

1¼"

pine
frame

upson board
glass wool
steel wool
glass wool
steel wool
glass wool
galvanized sheet iron

cross section of wall

24"

1¼"

3"

30"

1¼"

top frame

Materials list

ITEM	APPROXIMATE QUANTITY
Upson board	55 square feet
Galvanized sheet iron	60 square feet
Glass wool (bats)	14 square feet
Steel wool	5 pounds
¼″ plywood	10 square feet
* 1¼″ x 1¼″ pine	100 lineal feet
¾″ x 3″ pine	12 lineal feet
Corrugated fasteners	5 dozen
Flat head screws	4 dozen
Round head screws, 2½″	18
Hinges	3
Hook and eye	2
Gliders	4
Nails	

* Must be rabbetted ¼″ by ½″

HOW TO USE THE ORGONE ACCUMULATOR

The orgone accumulator is a collapsible cabinet which is made in six pieces that are easily assembled by means of screws. The orgone energy is collected by a certain arrangement of organic and metallic material. "One layer" actually consists of two layers, one of organic matter on the outside, the other of metallic matter on the inside. Organic matter absorbs and holds, while metal attracts and reflects orgone energy quickly. It is, therefore, obvious that by layering the accumulator always with organic matter toward the outside and metallic toward the inside, a direction is given to the orgone energy directed from the outside toward the inside.

The beneficial use of the accumulator is accomplished by *daily, regular* sittings within the radiating enclosure. Ventilation of the enclosed space is secured through openings above and beneath the door. The atmospheric orgone energy does not "seep" through openings, but penetrates the solid walls. In relation to the accumulator, the organism is the stronger energy system. Accordingly a potential is created from the outside toward the inside by the enclosed body. The energy fields of the two systems make contact and after some time, dependent on the bio-energetic strength of the organism within, both the living organism and the energy field of the accumulator begin to "luminate" i.e. they become excited and, making contact, drive each other to higher levels of excitation. This fact becomes perceptible to the user of the accumulator through feelings of prickling, warmth, relaxation, reddening of the face, and objectively, through increased body temperature.

There is no mechanical rule as to HOW LONG one should sit in the accumulator. One should continue with the orgonotic irradiation as long as one feels comfortable and "glowing." The sensitive person will, after a while have "had enough." This manifests itself in the feeling of "nothing happening any longer." It is explained by the fact that, in a truly self-regulatory manner, the organism will absorb only as much orgone energy as it requires. After a certain level has been reached, the sensations become unpleasant. Pressure in the head, slight nausea, ill feelings all over, and dizziness are the most common signs indicating that OVER-IRRADIATION has begun. If such is the case, one simply leaves the accumulator and takes some fresh air and the symptoms of overcharge quickly vanish.

Under no circumstances should one sit in the accumulator for hours. This can cause serious damage. In a three fold accumulator one session should not be longer than 30 minutes at a time. It is better, if necessary, to use the accumulator several times a day at shorter intervals than to prolong one sitting unnecessarily.

The size of the accumulator should fit the size of the person who uses it. The inner metal walls should not be further away from the body surface than 2 to 4 inches. A small child in a large size accumulator would not attract enough energy. The average adult size will be suitable for most people.

It is not necessary to undress completely in the accumulator since orgone energy penetrates everything. However one should not wear too heavy or woolen clothes since this will prevent quick contact and excitation.

The accumulator may be set up in any room. The room should be aired thoroughly every day.

Never attach *exposed* electric wires to the metallic portion of the accumulator since it is possible to receive a shock. A small reading light may be attached to the inside.

The accumulator may be cleaned by wiping the metal surfaces with a damp cloth. Do not let it get wet. Water absorbs and holds the orgone energy and thus prevents the creation of an orgonotic potential inside the accumulator. When the humidity exceeds 80%, the atmospheric orgone tension is reduced and the accumulator may function poorly, therefore longer sessions may be needed.

The Orgone Energy Shooter: The shooter is built according to the same principle as the big accumulator. This accumulated energy within the shooter is now directed through flexible iron hollow cables (BX cable) from which the inner wires have been removed, toward the local region to be irradiated. On small areas it suffices to keep the outer end of the BX cable at the surface at a distance of about one eighth of an inch. On larger areas a funnel should be inserted, corresponding in size approximately to the afflicted area to be irradiated. The mechanism of the irradiation effect consists in that the particular local area draws energy from the shooter box through the BX cable. The latter should be insulated with tape or plastic, organic material on the outside, in order to form in itself a radiating structure with metal inside and organic material outside. One should not irradiate for more than *2 to 10 minutes at a time*. The irradiation may be repeated at frequent intervals if necessary.

The Chestboard: The chestboard is a rectangular board which serves the purpose of bringing the orgone energy field of the door of the large accumulator closer to the body. To use it one should rest the board upright about 3 inches from the body upon one's knees, the metal surface facing the organism. Remove after a few minutes, or as soon as local sensation of heat is experienced.

The Seatbox: The seatbox is built into the newer (1950) models for the purpose of further orgone energy concentration, from which orgone energy for local irradiation may be derived via an insulated cable. This seat is composed of two boards which should be placed with their metallic surface towards the inside. The orgonomic potential of the space thus created may be enhanced by loosely stuffing the seatbox with ordinary steel wool (3 to 5 lbs.).

The following areas should be irradiated daily while sitting inside the large accumulator by means of the seatbox or shooter, for a few minutes each:

a. eyes with lids closed, not more than 1 minute each,
b. root of nose,
c. mastoid bone,
d. mouth and throat,
e. heart region,
f. upper abdomen (over solar plexus).

Stop irradiation immediately if burning or discomfort is felt.

INDEX

Explanatory Note: The entry for Wilhelm Reich is subdivided as follows: (1) Childhood and youth, (2) Domestic and personal affairs, (3) His work and ideas in Europe, (4) His work and ideas in the U.S., (5) Actions and opinions relating to FDA investigations, (6) Actions and opinions relating to his legal trouble, (7) General.

375